Also by the Author

Special Agent in the Pacific, WWII:
Counter-Intelligence—Military,
Political and Economic.
New York: Rivercross. 1995.

Managing with Scarce Resources (Editor)
San Francisco: Jossey-Bass. 1993.

Cost Containment for Higher Education:
Strategies for Public Policy and
Institutional Administration.
Westport, Connecticut and London:
Praeger. 1991.

Econometrica (Managing Editor)
1948-1953

PHILOSOPHY OF A CONCERNED ACADEMIC:

Within and Beyond the Ivory Tower

William Brand Simpson

University Editions, Inc.   Huntington, West Virginia iv

Library of Congress Catalog Card number: 94-90749
ISBN: 1-56002-534-4

First published in 1995

University Editions, Inc.   59 Oak Lane, Spring Valley
                                 Huntington, WV 25704

The paper used in this publication meets the minimum requirements
of the American National Standard for Information Sciences—
Permanence of Paper for Printed Library Materials, ANSI Z 39.48
- 1984.

To Ruth Decker Simpson, my colleague

in the preparation of the manuscript

TABLE OF CONTENTS

viii

TABLE OF CONTENTS

PHILOSOPHY OF A CONCERNED ACADEMIC

PREFACE

To a considerable extent we allow circumstances to determine the course of our lives and that of society, and we need to regain the initiative. The main thrust of this book is the significance for the individual of developing a sense of mission, in particular a personal philosophy consisting of criteria for selecting among options as to the use of one's life.

The book has particular relevance for college-age youth and the faculty and administrators of colleges and universities. It offers a very human account of an individual who analyzed situations as a concerned academic and sought results as a practicing activist. The account draws in part upon the author's experience in academic and governmental positions, nationally and internationally, and working with many who became Nobel Prize winners.

The book includes discussion of the process by which an individual makes decisions and takes charge, and of the satisfaction to be gained from empowering oneself and others with the capacity for intelligent choice and leadership, within a boundary of concern that is expanded considerably beyond the individual.

The autobiographical reflections and writings herein are the product of as wide a variety of experiences as an individual could hope to encounter, including some an individual would hope to avoid, from the perspective of one whose concern has been to empower others at local, national and international levels.

1

A Master Loyalty

I was in a reflective mood in 1953 and 1954, traveling around the world for more than a year, interviewing along the way, and thinking about what would contribute to more peaceful relations among nations, in particular, changes in education. That sabbatical followed upon intensive counter-intelligence and war crimes work in World War II and an intensive postwar period of professional activity.

Again I am in a reflective mood, which is not surprising since I am now on emeritus status, and officially at least, retired. My thoughts of a professional nature have been partially set forth in scholarly publications, but some of the larger issues with which I have long been concerned have not yet been adequately addressed.

Take, for instance, the matter of the extent to which one should take charge of his or her own life. The premise, of course, is that this is at all possible. To a great extent, our tomorrows unfold from our yesterdays. Each of us is constrained in what we can do, whether by iron bars, energy level, monetary resources, obligations to others, the extent of our education and skills, our aptitudes, or our preconceptions, or some combination of these and other factors. Perhaps more than by anything else, we are constrained by our mental attitudes. Although our situation be bounded on all sides by constraints, there will remain some opportunities open, however small in scale and unlikely in prospect, which we could explore and act upon if we but had the will to do so.

I have said to college students, who on the whole are an advantaged group, that individuals tend to be overly impressed by the attractiveness of conforming—even in following others in flaunting convention. They should bring to bear their own skills, knowledge, and perspectives to gain insight into possibilities which may not be apparent to others, nor to themselves without some initiative. But the course of least-effort is to be accepting of circumstances, and willing to play out life according to the events that befall one.

Even without any initiative on our part, we grow, behave, learn, change, have an affect and are affected. Even without seeking to serve any particular purpose, we inform our senses, develop skills, act and are acted upon, and experience positive or negative reinforcement. We develop concepts as to what we value (positively or negatively) and expectations as to the payoff in terms of such values as a consequence of actions.

As I have expressed it on other occasions, an objective or goal is formed through awareness of a benefit that would be foregone, or a cost that would be incurred, were such a focus to effort not provided. That awareness depends upon what is regarded as fact, the significance attached thereto on the basis of value orientation, the boundaries within which there is acceptance of responsibility, and the alternatives conceived.

Initiatives arise from awareness of a problem, by which is meant here a discrepancy between a situation as it is and a situation that is preferred. Although at first we may not be aware that we are doing so, what is preferred is successively redefined in the process of solving a problem as the costs involved become apparent. This is as it should be. A goal should be pursued as long as the expected additional benefit is greater than the expected additional cost. The preferred situation is then expected to yield a total benefit that exceeds total cost by the most that is possible.

On the one hand, we feel the pull toward achieving a preferred state, possibly a materialistic goal; on the other hand, there is concern with the qualitative aspects of the path to that goal, i.e., the sacrifices and benefits to be experienced by reason of the means selected. Depending on the individual, different importance is attached to the attainment of goals and to the implications of the means employed. Not entirely separate from that, different importance is attached to long-term considerations and to short-term considerations.

For some individuals, the motivating influence of long-term goals is diminished by the pursuit of more immediate gratification. Whatever is in short supply relative to immediate desire becomes a transient goal—whether it be food and water, sex, drugs, money, sleep, a sense of security, or whatever—and long-term goals are deferred, if reached at all. When that need is sufficiently met, our energies are redirected to achieve what is next most demanding of attention.

For some, the way of proceeding through life, particularly the effect upon others of the means selected, is more important than the attainment of materialistic goals.

For most individuals there is neither abandonment of short-term desires nor complete self-denying deferral to others. Rather there is a feeling that we may pay the piper for too much play today, an awareness of standards that should be observed in our relations with others, and a sense of apprehension as we make compromises along the way. We grope for what is best to do, and drift rather than make steady progress toward long-term objectives.

What is needed is what I refer to as a "master loyalty" which gives a sense of purpose—mission, if you will—to one's life.

For those finding this in religion, it is a one-time taking charge of one's life in order to place it in the service of, and to some extent, at the direction of, a body of doctrine accepted by faith.

A different type of master loyalty is a personal philosophy, by which I mean a set of criteria by which you judge what purposes you seek to further. It is not fixation on a specific goal, but adoption of criteria which can be drawn upon to guide your choices among alternative courses of action that open up as a result of the conjunction of your personal behavior and events of the world. It is not incompatible with faith, but draws more on our reasoning abilities. You remain in charge of your life within the constraints mentioned earlier, but as you change, and as circumstances change, you can make new appraisals to guide your behavior.

Having a "master loyalty" is no assurance that you are on the side of the angels. The phrase could refer as readily to a focus on what most individuals would consider self-serving and even sordid, as it could to what most would consider selfless and even noble. What it conveys is that you are guided by a strong sense of purpose, and accordingly take charge of your life in such manner as will contribute to the realization of that purpose.

An individual could be motivated to take charge and retain charge through some combination of expecting satisfaction from the role per se and expecting satisfaction from the goal accomplished. Such motivation presupposes that the individual has confidence in his or her abilities. That is a matter to which we now turn.

2

Developing Self-Confidence

I have thought at intervals over the years as to how I came to formulate my own philosophy of life. My recollection of my parents' influence was that it was strongly supportive of my schoolwork (setting aside quiet time for study, bartering for a good dictionary in the midst of the Great Depression, helping with French, etc.), but there was no pressure that I should excel or continue my education beyond what was customary at that time. I recall no body of precepts, simply the presumption that one would do one's best and be forthright in dealing with others.

My father, John Alexander Simpson, left school early so he could enter his father's business in Greenock, Scotland. In accordance with primogeniture, he was displaced by his father's first son upon his father's death, and left for America in 1910. He came west to Portland, Oregon, at the confluence of the Willamette and Columbia Rivers, an area reminiscent of the River Clyde of his homeland. It was difficult then, as it is today, for an immigrant to become established. In the early years he sold goods along the street from a horse and cart, operated an elevator, sold automobiles, and then worked in a shoe repair shop before opening a retail store of his own for British leather goods.

My mother, Janet Christie Brand, attended private Kilblain Academy in Greenock, and then studied for an extension certificate in music from the University of London. She came to this country in 1914 to marry her fiance from Greenock. She tended to remain apart, abiding by British social conventions that were not part of the American scene.

I could not accept the idea of pride being based on social class, and at an early age I translated this into the view that self-confidence and assurance should be based on what one could accomplish.

Inflammatory rheumatism and a leg fracture that was not properly set interfered with my earliest schooling, which was at Sunnyside School in Portland. However, I caught up and when the family moved I attended Alameda School there.

Receiving recognition of one's ability can be an important source of encouragement. I still remember from grade school my satisfaction upon receiving from a teacher a document compiled for the George Washington Bicentennial, and from another teacher a blue ribbon for artistic design. In later years, with roles reversed, I appreciated the importance of giving recognition to students during my own teaching career.

I remember writing short notes for the *Alameda Spokesman*, representing my classmates on board the historic battleship Old Ironsides on its visit to the west coast in 1933, and giving a talk at grade school graduation ceremonies.

The Class Will in the *Alameda Spokesman* opened with the lines, "Bill Simpson, being of Scottish descent, Shall will no one a trait or cent." The Class Horoscope said I was known by my "wit." The Class Prophecy included the lines, "And working hard as one of their crew, Bill Simpson works as few men do." The Class Ambitions included the paragraph, "When dependable Bill Simpson becomes director of a high class railroad there will be fewer railroad wrecks caused by careless managers." They were on the wrong track, however, as to my career and philanthropy.

Being given responsibility early in life is conducive to one's thinking things out. The best way to learn is to be required to teach. At Grant High School a mathematics teacher asked me to teach a trigonometry course for occasional weeks to my classmates. This I did, with some relish and yet trepidation. That was in 1936-37. Another teacher referred students to me who had questions on their schoolwork or personal affairs for help during school hours. I also branched out and offered an after-school counseling service based in my home. A teacher would bring a problem student, sometimes accompanied by a parent, and while my mother served tea to the adults I talked to the student in the other room. I tried to find out what made the students tick, interpreted their studies as the means toward objectives they already had, and encouraged them in their studies. I was able to motivate such students, who had sometimes been failing, into being superior students academically. I also encouraged them to take an active part in a variety of extracurricular activities. If a parent had come, I would suggest that the student be allowed to pursue activities in a balanced manner without being pushed.

It was my experience that it was possible for me to be active on a broad front and at the same time turn in a good performance in high school studies. I played golf frequently on various of Portland's many courses, played tennis and badminton, attended dances, was president of two clubs, collected stamps and autographs of statesmen and pioneer pilots, annually went aboard each Navy ship attending Portland's Fleet Week, dabbled in city planning as a hobby (which plans turned out to be close to what later was adopted), raised tropical fish, read whatever I could find of Zane Grey's westerns and Conan Doyle's Sherlock Holmes, and worked off excess energy by landscaping our grounds. The exercise of initiative, the efforts at being creative, the development of leadership qualities, and the change of pace offered by physical activity were all important.

I sensed at the time the importance of students receiving peer guidance on academic problems and on other matters as well. In my senior year in high school I interested several school clubs in making it a form of school service, and I returned after graduation to give a talk in the auditorium on that topic, and provided a written report and proposal. This led to some funding from a foundation, but I do not recall the details.

While I was encouraging my classmates, my teachers were encouraging me by their receptiveness to my work and by a series of awards for scholarship. A teacher submitted an assignment I had prepared which was awarded second place in the Oregon Life Underwriters Association letter-writing contest. I also participated by invitation in a city-wide forum on "Saving and Spending: The Problem of Under-Consumption," and in an off-campus economics debate. On another occasion a newspaper carried a photograph of me shaking hands at an awards banquet with a student from another high school with the same first and last names who had also won scholarship awards.

At high school graduation ceremonies in 1938 the principal lightened things up by assuring the audience, after asking me to come forward for one award after another, that all had been earned. One award was the Euclidian Cup for excellence in mathematics, another was the Fletcher Memorial Scholarship applicable toward college, referred to as "the highest honor of the graduating class" in a letter from the principal and in the newspaper. In writing my thanks to the high school faculty, I indicated that it was my intent to combine my interest in mathematics with work in statistics and economics. I learned afterward that they were amused by this plan, since there had as yet been little done along such lines. Ten years later, a period that included college and the interruption caused by World War II, I administered an international professional society that combined mathematics, statistics and economics, served as managing editor and then co-editor of an international journal of econometrics, and was administrator of a research organization that worked in those fields.

The relevance of the foregoing to developing my own personal philosophy is as follows: I found over the years that I had a talent for seeing things in context and for evaluating alternatives; a talent not only for analysis, but also for organization and leadership. Everyone has, or should work toward developing, some special talent. It is a scarce resource, and should be used accordingly. Thus, I came to apply as one of the criteria for myself that I should choose those options that would make the best possible use of the talent I could contribute. Making such a decision requires that an individual be contemplative as to the significance of events, and as to what alternatively could have been possible. While the views of others should be valued, an individual should have self-confidence in searching out for himself or herself the values to apply in evaluating alternative courses of action.

I have reasoned that I should do my share in assisting with activities that meet an immediate social need, but since such activities yield early gratification they tend to attract participants, and accordingly my contribution should be monetary, if possible, rather than the direct use of my time and energy.

My personal efforts, therefore, to the extent that I had the choice, have been focused instead on activities that were not likely to be undertaken by others, or if undertaken, were unlikely to produce results I would regard as satisfactory.

I will describe the criteria arrived at in the chapters that follow, and provide illustrations from my own life. I should add at the outset that the personal philosophy I developed is not an easy one to follow, and perhaps should be followed in moderation. In retrospect, while many things turned out well, I realize that some decisions I took were not the best. These I identify so that others may exercise caution should they be faced with similar decisions.

3

Hard Times—Active Times

Gaining self-confidence from having successfully carried through various projects was, for myself, an important factor in becoming a self-directed person. But can that experience be generalized to others?

Family life then tended to be more stable than it is now, and the young took more guidance from their parents than now appears to be the case. The automobile, with the independence it conferred, was available only to a few. Cigarettes, alcohol and sex also had a more limited and discreet role in student life than at present. Drugs were not in evidence at all. Gangs did not have to be contended with.

The changes that have occurred, including the introduction of television, have created diversions from investing effort in other activities.

Also limiting the applicability of my experience to others is that during my grade school and high school years I was supported financially by my parents. It was only after high school that I had to focus on earning money. For the many young people of today in high school who can give time to study only after many hours at a job, or looking for a job, my exhortation to be active on a broad front will scarcely be appropriate.

I did, however, grow up during the worst depression our country has known. Part of the time my father was unemployed. We had little money. The limitations on what one can do and the opportunities afforded will be different now. Nevertheless, one's self-confidence will be built now as it was then by accepting, even seeking, challenges, and from success in what is accomplished.

Brian Cowan, a nephew of my wife, asked me for a personal account of those years for an assignment in college, and I reproduce below the first part of my response.

February 16, 1990

Dear Brian,

We received your letter of February 5th, and I hope you have received my brief acknowledgment. Grading examinations, lecture preparation and work on a book manuscript have delayed my fuller reply, but I have been thinking about it. It has stirred many memories.

You sound very enthusiastic about your project, and I am interested too. I will help as much as I can through providing my recollections of the Depression and WWII period. However, this will only partly shed light on what it was like at Reed during the time that the United States was at war, since I graduated from Reed in May 1942, shortly after Pearl Harbor on December 7, 1941, and entered war service from Columbia University as a volunteer in the spring of 1943, upon completing requirements for the Master's degree. I turned down a variety of government appointments for the duration of the war since I felt I should share more directly the wartime experience which would be central to my generation.

I graduated from Grant High School in Portland in January 1938, planning to augment the $100 Fletcher Scholarship which the high school gave me by working until entering Reed in the fall. I canvassed every conceivable employment opportunity throughout the Portland metropolitan area, from the menial to positions of considerable responsibility. The country still had not emerged from the Depression, and no job was obtained. So I hand-printed cards which offered landscape-gardening services, and in the evenings I went door to door to schedule work. For 35¢ an hour I carted wood from the street to the basement, hauled sawdust, removed cement driveways, and of course cut lawns and trimmed hedges. Money was scarce. I remember two occasions when the lady of the house asked me to work fast since company was coming, then refused to pay for the fractional hour portion of the time worked.

Portland was hard hit by the Depression. In October 1929 our family was just moving to a new subdivision near the recently opened Grant High School. We had discarded part of our furniture because we expected to start fresh at the new location. I remember that the last trip from the old house was by city bus, with my mother carrying a birdcage with a yellow canary called Dicky. The Wall Street crash occurred just at that time. The canary had a perch to sit on, but for quite some time we settled for apple boxes. We were quite fortunate in comparison with many others. There was a colony of cardboard shacks under the overpasses at Sullivan's Gulch—it was called Hooverville. Equality in America became "Both the rich and the poor have the right to sleep under bridges." I can remember seeing men in heavy winter overcoats standing in line in the cold several abreast for block after block along West Burnside, waiting for food at a soup kitchen. In those years women were seldom in the work force, and they were scarcely to be seen in the food lines.

People were often generous to those seeking handouts during the Depression, but there was also less commendable behavior. Our neighborhood grocer would let customers run up large food bills on credit, then took control of their homes. My Dad had a store for British footwear at the corner of Park and Washington Streets in downtown Portland. His store had a British heraldic seal over the doorway, fine paneling and mirrors, and the first fluorescent lighting that Portland had seen. It was featured in the newspapers. The British Consul would send Britishers who were without funds but who needed shoes, and he outfitted them. When the Depression deepened, several of his well-to-do customers ran up large bills for expensive riding boots, etc., and then declared personal bankruptcy, retaining their homes and all that they had bought, but without having to pay. Although there were scarcely any customers by then, my Dad kept in his employ two sales clerks since they would otherwise have been unemployed. One later moved to Seattle only to return one night, via an unlocked freight elevator, to empty the store of much of its stock. My Dad refused to declare bankruptcy and instead borrowed money that my mother had inherited from her family in Scotland to pay for the stock. He gave up the store after the robbery and took employment with one of the chain stores which were a new phenomenon in Portland. He again went into business since his credit was good, but the store failed because of the competition from the new chain stores, and he went back to working for others.

In those years there was no insurance for bank accounts

and when the banks failed, that was that. I recall that I had a very small school thrift account in the Hibernia Bank, which closed its doors . . .

We used to listen to FDR's Fireside Chats on the radio. At first we had a crystal set and earphones, but others could also hear when we put the earphones in an aluminum pan to magnify the sound. About the time of the crash we had just acquired a Kolster radio. Roosevelt championed the role of government as broader than just keeping law and order. I remember hearing his famous speech in which he said we have nothing to fear but fear itself. He was accused of taking America down the road of socialism, yet today even conservatives would be reluctant to discard many of the programs he introduced. His programs did much to alleviate suffering, but they did not in themselves pull the U.S. economy out of the long Depression. It was WWII that did that: first the war that the Allies were fighting with the aid of our Lend-Lease, then the war effort following the Japanese assault on Pearl Harbor.

Portland was a popular port-of-call for the U.S. Fleet, and possibly still is. In the 1930's there was an Annual Fleet Week during which time there were many ships alongside the seawall in the downtown area. Each year I would go aboard each of the ships and talk to members of the ship's company. One year I was still aboard when that particular ship took its departure. It had to make a stop further down the river to let me disembark. The low mineral content of the Portland water apparently helped in the elimination of crustaceans on the ships' hulls. The annual visit led to a very good relationship between the Navy and the Portland community.

Portland was caught up in the activities of the war. Swan Island in the Willamette River became the site of one of Henry Kaiser's West Coast Shipyards where Liberty Ships were built, and also the U.S.S. La Porte on which I traveled to New Guinea (APA 151, amphibious personnel attack). To recruit enough labor for the shipyards, trains were loaded in New York with men literally pulled off the streets. In Portland, special bus lines extending throughout the city brought workers to the yards and returned them home. Women were recruited, including our neighbor across the street who informed my mother, while I was in the Philippines, that she wished the war would never end.

I entered Reed in the fall of 1938, just fifty years before you did, Brian. I worked hard at my studies and enjoyed them and the association provided with the faculty and the students. I remember that for one unit of special topics credit in mathematics I studied the original French Encyclopedia articles in that language on the mathematical economics of oligopoly theory. I wondered at times if I would do well enough at Reed. At that time, and perhaps now also, Reed did not give grades in the first two years, only a total at the end of that time which took account of both the breadth and quality of the students' work. I was surprised to learn that I had tied for the highest score for the two years.

My scholarships and earnings helped pay tuition but would not cover dormitory expenses, so I commuted daily. I spent long hours at Reed, often into the late evening, studying at the library and working. I served as chairman of the Student Committee on Educational Policy, and as chairman of the Student Library Committee, tutored in mathematics, handled discussion sessions of an economics course when Ackerman retired, and supervised the statistics lab. The college yearbooks for those years showed pictures of me in these various roles. I also provided some editorials for the college newspaper. I attended many of the dances and participated in Canyon Day and other events, and one year was a substitute on the college badminton team. I remember being on a tug-of-war team that pulled and was pulled back and forth through the muddy lake. For various periods I worked at the college library in the late afternoon, did mechanical drawing for the physics department, and repainted the walls in the basement of Eliot Hall. On Sundays and holidays I was in charge of the Business and Technical Department of the Portland Central Library. In the summers I worked variously on campus as strawboss in the cherry orchard behind the lake where some dormitories now stand, used a blowtorch on plaster in the stairwells of the old dorms during renovation, and poured cement sidewalks for what was then the new Student Union Building.

I enclose an amusing clipping from the *Oregon Journal*, November 19th, 1941, of an exchange between myself and the college president, Dr. Dexter Keezer, that reveals the Reed view of sports as an activity strictly for exercise. The item was also used on the "Richfield Reporter" news program which originated nightly from San Diego.

In March 1939, the Nazis marched into Czechoslovakia. I was on campus when I heard a news flash on the radio. I went to the college office and arranged for a radio to be available in the Chapel. Dramatic descriptions were heard of the events that were a prelude to the European phase of World War II. We had the sense of history in the making then, as we have had recently with events in China, Russia, Central Europe and South Africa.

I enclose a copy of the front matter for a compilation I made of the records of the Student Educational Policies Committee (SEPC) for the first six years of its operation, from 1936 to 1942. The idea for such a Committee was President Keezer's, and I believe that it was both useful for the College and important in the education of the participants. I served on the Committee for two years, including two terms as chairman.

I worked with two faculty members (F.L. Griffin and Monty Griffith) in developing a questionnaire for students to use in evaluating faculty, and spoke to a meeting of the faculty regarding it, following which it gained their approval. As I recall, there were at the time only two other institutions on the West Coast providing for student evaluations of faculty. I also directed a College Time Survey, with endorsement of both Student and Faculty Educational Policy Committees. I subsequently supervised a Reed Master's thesis based on my report of the Survey.

On December 10, 1941, following the attack on Pearl Harbor, I agendized with the SEPC a proposal for a Reed Defense Council, and subsequently worked to secure its implementation. I enclose a clipping from the college newspaper in that regard. Portland was very apprehensive as to a possible air raid by Japanese planes, and the city maintained a blackout at night, enforced by block wardens. Powerful searchlights traced the movement of aircraft until identified. The basement corridor of Eliot Hall was designated as an air raid shelter and tape was placed on the glass of the display cabinets lining the corridors to prevent flying glass. I coordinated various groups and assisted in liaison with comparable activities of the Portland city government.

A Wartime Curriculum Committee was formed in January

1942 consisting of several faculty members together with my self representing SEPC. I remember only one of the matters dealt with, namely, the introduction of what I believe was the first regular summer session at Reed. I drew up the plans and curriculum, initialed the report W.B.S., and distributed copies at a meeting of the group. Those present read the document carefully, and then voted to recommend it to the full faculty. About that time Professor William Blair Stewart (also W.B.S.) entered, and received congratulations on the report. The others had adopted it, thinking it had originated with Blair Stewart.

Blair Stewart (Professor of Statistics) and Frank L. Griffin (Professor of Mathematics) were co-advisors on my thesis, which dealt with mathematical statistics, and which I pursued along lines of my own design. I recall that the two of them, and Knowlton (Professor of Physics), who among others attended the defense of my thesis, which drew on several fields, exclaimed that only then did they fully understand what I had undertaken to accomplish.

Dexter M. Keezer, President of Reed, Paul Eliehle, Professor of Industrial Relations at UCLA, and Dean Wayne Morse of the University of Oregon Law School (later U.S. Senator Morse) served on a Labor Mediation Panel for the Twin Districts Dispute in the Northwest lumber industry. This was under the auspices of the National Defense Mediation Board. It was essential that the dispute be settled rapidly because of its effect on the war effort. Apparently a stalemate had been reached, and Dr. Keezer asked me to conduct a study of wage and benefit provisions and prepare recommendations. Accordingly, I brought together a three-shift office staff borrowed from local federal agencies. I carried out my assignment in the fall of 1941 and submitted the last report the first week of January, 1942.

. . . .

I add some detail and some recollections about Reed College not included in the above letter.

Writing essays was an integral part of a Reed education. The papers I wrote included:

Homer and Virgil—A Comparison of Impressions
Currency Regulation in the Roman Empire
Greek Economics from the Capitalistic Viewpoint

The Theory of Political Economy in the 17th and 18th
   Centuries
The Glory of War: A Satire Invoking Miguel de Cervantes
An Historical Survey of Interest Theory
Theoretical Criteria for Investment Decisions
The Theory of Value
Changing Attitudes Towards the Application of Mathematics
   to Economics
Economic Planning in a Democracy
The Corporate Entrepreneur
Private Property and Capitalist Democracy
A Problem in Monetary Expansion (a mathematical-economics
   discussion with statistical appendices)

Some commentaries on the Honor System that I wrote as an assignment were submitted by the professor, Barry Cerf, to the college newspaper and appeared as editorials. They were the subject of a special assembly called by the president.

Reed requires that students pass qualifying examinations at the end of their junior year for entrance into senior status. Another significant requirement is the writing of an original thesis during the senior year, which is thereafter defended before a faculty panel, as mentioned in the above letter. The title of my thesis was "The Z Distribution and Its Extension to Non-Normal Universes."

I referred to the College Time Survey in the letter to Brian. In that connection I designed, promoted and directed a statistical study of the distribution of students' time between academic and extracurricular activities and the relationship between course credit and time spent in preparation. I supervised the work of a staff of 12 part-time workers over a period of several months, analyzed the results in line with statistical sampling theory, and prepared a comprehensive report to the college community containing recommendations bearing upon educational policy.

During my senior year at Reed I became active at the request of students in the removal of two college deans. The dean of men was alleged to have repeatedly violated the confidence of student advisees by using recognizable details of their personal predicaments in classroom discussion. There were also allegations of improprieties in the awarding of contracts within the dean's purview which were being investigated by the faculty. The dean of women was insisting on a dress code which was destined for non-observance by the independently minded individuals making up the student body. The president of the college telephoned me at my home one evening and asked that I consider curtailing further effort in the matter. I indicated that I had given the matter much thought and had concluded I should see the matter to its conclusion. It was an awkward decision since I was working with the president in my capacity as chairman of the Student Educational Policy Committee, and, moreover, serving at his request as a consultant to the National Defense Mediation Board.

Within a few weeks, I cannot remember more precisely, I was called in late afternoon to the president's house, which at that time was on campus. The chairman of the Faculty Educational Policy Committee, which had also taken a position on these matters, was just taking his leave as I arrived. The president of the college, Dr. Keezer, informed me that he was leaving to take a position in Washington, D.C. as deputy administrator of the Office of Price Administration, an important contribution in view of the war. The two deans that he had appointed would also leave. He said that while he was not exactly ecstatic over the direction of my energy in the matter of the deans, he felt that I had acted properly. He suggested since I was about to graduate that I accompany him to Washington as an assistant. I had other plans, however.

I was elected to the Reed Chapter of Phi Beta Kappa, a national honorary scholastic society. Fraternities were not permitted at Reed, since exclusive societies were inconsistent with the freedom of association and openness of relationships that were part of the attractiveness of the Reed environment. Initially there was reluctance to establish a Reed Chapter of PBK. This opposition was overcome by adopting the policy of postponing election of members until graduation. I remember a walk across campus with Dr. Frank Loxley Griffin, head of the mathematics department, formerly chairman of the Faculty Educational Policy Committee, and subsequently acting president of the College. He told me of his satisfaction in nominating me for membership.

In later years, at an institution at which I was teaching, I opposed the institution's applying for a PBK Chapter. This was because, tied to that decision, a foreign language requirement would have been added to make the application attractive. The decision to require a foreign language, I argued, should be decided on its educational merit.

Reed College, at the time I attended, had just completed its first quarter century. It still retained many of those who had been the founding faculty, and who had turned aside offers from other institutions because of their enthusiasm for and dedication to the educational endeavors of the relatively new college.

Students, faculty, staff and administrators were all regarded as responsible colleagues, both in academic activities and in working together as part of the college community. In the words of an early Reed faculty member, they were "Comrades in the Quest." Classes were moderate in size. Discussion sections were small, stimulated and guided by probing, insightful questions by a faculty member, and alive with spirited discussion by all present.

Those admitted to Reed, largely by self-selection, were on the whole intellectually bright, interested in working with others, active socially, concerned with the larger community, and willing to take leadership roles. They would compare favorably with the best students at leading universities.

The contribution of a college experience is the acquisition of knowledge, the development of skills, and an appreciation of values. At Reed, a student does not select a major field until after a broad exposure to the liberal arts and sciences. In my case the skills developed through the curriculum were primarily techniques for reasoning and decision. These involve language, logic, statistics, mathematics, economics and econometrics. Courses in the humanities and social sciences contributed to my sensitivity to and appreciation of different value systems, as did my other activities at Reed and subsequent experience in the war and extensive travel.

Contemporaneous with the formal college experience is the process of finding out more about oneself, one's capacities and limitations, and a sense as to the types of activity likely to provide satisfaction. In part this discovery is simply the result of growing up, but the process is facilitated when, as at Reed, a student is treated from the beginning as a responsible adult. Reality testing is recognized as an important form of learning, including with that the acceptance of responsibility for consequences.

Since writing the foregoing I have read *A New Case for the Liberal Arts*, by David Winter et al. which in reporting on a study of the effects of different types of higher education institutions states: "From the evidence . . . we see that while the beneficial effects of liberal arts education are partly personal (for example, increased maturity of adaptation leading to greater life satisfaction), they are also very much social (for example, increased leadership motive pattern scores leading to involvement in voluntary organizations and more effective leadership and management).'' (p. 183)

I was impressed at the time with the opportunities for interaction provided by a relatively small institution such as Reed and I decided at the time that I left Reed that if larger enrollment were needed, I would favor a coalition of small colleges, such as the Claremont Colleges. As it happened, in later years I completed a further degree at Claremont and strengthened my belief in the association of small units as the way to proceed.

3.1

The Glory of War:
A Satire Invoking
Miguel de Cervantes

(1939)

It is over three hundred years since Miguel de Cervantes started Don Quixote and Sancho Panza on their famous journeys, and yet that famous pair is not forgotten, for they have marched down the years of history to the present day as full of life, vigor, and humor as the day they started. It has been said that by means of these two characters Cervantes smiled the chivalry of knighthood away. If Cervantes had also been able to live through the ages so as to be present today, it is likely that he would direct his satire against a conception of patriotism which provokes wars. He would have good reason for such an action, for over three hundred years ago he answered a youthful impulse to prove his heroism, and after insisting upon and receiving a dangerous post, he was seriously wounded by the enemy Turks. With body wounds and a hand maimed for life, he returned to civilian duties with no other recompense than poverty. Today Cervantes would find his native Spain prostrate under the toll taken by a war which used Spain as the practice battlefield of Europe. With these circumstances it is not difficult to imagine that Cervantes' modern *Don Quixote* would not greatly differ from the following:

The place: Any country.

The time: After a long peace, and before a long war.

Don Jose was the pride of the countryside. No one excelled him in knowledge of the exploits of Hannibal, Caesar, or other famous warriors. He knew what kind of cannon Napoleon used when he showed that cannonballs could destroy men as well as walls. He knew the number of troops under Wellington, and even the terrain of the battlefield of Waterloo. He was the proud possessor of the military uniforms of several nations and owned what he claimed was the very saber that the Kaiser had used in his ''saber rattling.'' Don Jose was well liked by his fellow citizens. He had organized a marching unit which he claimed was being trained to meet civic emergencies, although some were prone to say that it was an excuse for dressing up in a uniform and parading before the admiring eyes of the populace. Don Jose was a commanding figure in uniform, tall, broad-shouldered, and handsome; and when he appeared mounted upon a prancing white charger on public occasions, his dashing military figure captivated the hearts of the feminine element of the population and aroused the male element to silent envy.

He spent his spare time reading about the glories of war, the heroism of soldiers, and the prestige of warriors. He developed a fanatical attitude towards the preservation of the sacred honor of his country from any insult or indignity.

It so happened that one day he read some propaganda issued by a minor faction in the adjoining country which he deemed an insult to his native land. His patriotism was aroused, and he immediately issued a summons for his organization to assemble in full force. He put on his most brilliant uniform, glittering with his medal for first place in the shooting gallery at the local fair, and mounting his horse he took his position at the head of his men, who had by this time assembled. With flags flying, the small body of men marched to the civic square to the flourish of drums and bugles. The populace was aroused by the sound of marching feet, beating drums, and blaring bugles and gathered to discover the cause of the demonstration. The music stopped, and a hush fell over the expectant group as the commanding figure of Don Jose moved forward to address them. His indignation had grown to such an extent that he delivered a ringing harangue to the citizens urging them to seize arms and follow him in order to avenge the insult to their country. The appeal ran through the listening crowd like an electric shock as he played upon the taut nerves of the once peaceful citizens. In a mad hysteria the men seized whatever weapons they could find, and with hasty farewells to their families, left to join their comrades.

Among these men was Don Jose's neighbor, Sancho, who like the rest of the peace loving citizens abhorred war but was susceptible to stirring marshall airs, the waving of flags, the beating of drums, and the flourish of bugles. Everyone of them in a rational moment would have considered himself mad to set out upon such an adventure, but the sight of a dazzling uniform, the ingrained desire for personal glory, and a false conception of patriotism were more than a match for rational thinking.

As Sancho took his place alongside Don Jose at the head of the cavalcade, the contrast between the two became quite evident. Sancho did not gracefully ride a white charger as did Don Jose. Instead he bumped along on a farm horse trying to the best of his ability to imitate the erect military bearing of Don Jose. The latter bore a shining rifle which he claimed had once belonged to an Italian prince. Sancho's weapon did not have a colorful history such as Don Jose claimed for his. All that Sancho could remember of its past was that his father had once used it to scare away the tax collector. The differences in weapons was a marked characteristic of all those who answered to the drum and bugle. With Don Jose in the lead, the cavalcade marched out of the city following a modern Pied Piper of Hamelin, for like the hero and his suite in that legend of old they marched out never to return, drawn by the magnetism of their leader.

It was not long after the flags were out of sight, and the last echoes of the drums and bugles had died away that the people felt the sudden impact of their plight. There was no longer any patriotic shout to compensate for the loss of fathers, husbands, sons and brothers.

War developed out of that border incident, war which took a savage toll of all that lay in its path. As the turmoil of destruction subsided, two figures appeared in the little city which had suffered such losses. Hopes rose and fell in the hearts of the anxious citizens as each sought in vain to recognize in the strangers some lost friend or relative. Hope gave way to scorn, and scorn to ridicule as they recognized the strangers as Don Jose and Sancho. Don Jose looked older and more wearied than when he had set out to war, but he still wore his brilliant uniform and carried his gun and flags, while his faithful Sancho had charge of his drum and bugle. The post-war populace could not understand how it had once forsaken peace to follow this quixotic individual who had no more to offer than the vain glory of military renown. They had discovered that the gilt of military glory wears off or tarnishes long before its price is fully paid. To them, the simple-minded Sancho represented a state of mind to which they would never again fall victim.

The sad part, however, is that no sooner are the ravages of war dimmed by the passage of a few years than the populace suffers the pangs of strife all over again. Whether Cervantes were living to write that story today or not, the scenes would be re-enacted in every decade. At best, Cervantes could have laughed out of existence some of the romantic and chivalrous notions about war, and forced those considering war to face the actual horror and ghastliness which war occasions.

4

Government Service, Graduate School and the War

December 1941 through May 1943, the early period of U.S. involvement in World War II, was a transition period for me. I completed the work for the National Defense Mediation Board mentioned earlier, graduated from college, was on a federal assignment in Portland for the summer, and then volunteered for military service on completing a master's degree in New York, reporting for duty upon graduation.

The three-month summer appointment was with the Oregon and California Revested Lands Administration of the General Land Office of the U.S. Department of the Interior. Alternating sections of timbered land granted by the government many years earlier to the railroads had reverted to the government and had been placed in a sustained-yield forest management program. I surveyed the methods and problems of forest management for the purpose of working out improvements through the application of modern statistical methods. I devised charts for the comparative rating of supervisors by subordinates, improved a slide-rule method for determining the economic justification for blister-rust control in the sugar pine industry, provided recommendations on sample size and computational procedures for mill studies of lumber recovery, and prepared a report on the use of alignment charts in the analysis of logging costs. The last-mentioned report was necessary because I found that an approach used by the agency that had brought it considerable praise from its headquarters in Washington was seriously deficient. It was shown that charts published by the O. and C. Administration for use in estimating logging cost had been based not on relationships among significant variables, as should have been the case, but had been constructed on an ad hoc basis to give the answers for a limited set of values that were known to be correct for a past period. The charts had been "tested" using the same data that had been used in their construction. Another aspect of my work was that in providing a general mathematical solution for certain repetitive problems, one section of the agency's staff became redundant. I also learned about forest management, without, however, being able to recognize one tree from another.

I had already submitted applications for graduate school prior to the time of Pearl Harbor. Letters of recommendation written in support of my applications apparently were laudatory, since I garnered the following offers: teaching assistant in economics at Stanford University; teaching assistant in mathematical-statistics at the University of California, Berkeley; junior fellowship at Princeton University; scholarship in economics at the University of Chicago; tutorial fellowship in mathematics at Northwestern University; fellowship in economics in the Graduate School of Arts and Sciences at Harvard University; and a graduate resident scholarship in economics at Columbia University in New York. I accepted the last-mentioned offer, with it being agreed that my work would be in mathematical-economics and mathematical-statistics with a group headed by Professor Harold Hotelling.

I chose Columbia University since it had the strongest faculty in mathematical-economics and mathematical-statistics, individuals who were major original contributors in those fields. In addition to Hotelling, there were Abraham Wald, Jacob Wolfowitz, Theodore Anderson, and Oscar Lange. There were also well-established faculty in the separate fields of economics, statistics, and mathematics. Milton Friedman, whom I was to meet later in Chicago and Cambridge, was there in his pre-Ph.D. days doing classified research, and we met occasionally. There were ties between Columbia University and the National Bureau of Economic Research.

Wald, who was of Hungarian origin, was almost unintelligible on Mondays, after a weekend of speaking his native language at home. He kept his presentations abstract, and has been acclaimed as the father of various fields such as decision theory.

Oscar Lange was a visiting professor, having taken departure from the University of Chicago because, I learned later, of a conflict there involving methodology and ideology. He was particularly strong in the area of market imperfections, and oligopoly theory in particular. He was a good teacher and had an engaging personality. With one leg slightly shorter than the other, he hobbled around campus with an entourage of students hanging on his every word. Later he became vice president of his native Poland.

In one of my seminar courses I was the only participant not holding a teaching position at Columbia or elsewhere. One of my classes was in a large law court with Professor Hotelling holding forth from the well in the front. I remember one incident in which he rhetorically asked the class a question, to confirm a point he had made. I stood up and disagreed. He asked me to explain on the blackboard and also to cite authority in support of my position. I turned from using the blackboard and replied that he himself was the source of the mathematical proof, in a journal article that he had written which was more recent than the notes from which he was lecturing.

I wrote a thesis at Columbia for the Master of Arts Degree for the Faculty of Political Science, Philosophy and Pure Science entitled ''The Validity of Fisher's Z Test of Significance for Small Samples from Non-Normal Univariate Populations.'' My thesis, mathematical in nature, was conceived and completed, as at Reed, without assistance from the faculty.

The Navy had a Midshipman's School at Columbia at that time because of the war, so graduate resident scholars such as myself were housed in Sarasota Hall, a university apartment at the north edge of campus. Some meals were provided at the Lion's Den in John Jay Hall at the south end of campus. I did not realize that only half of my meal credit could be used during each semester, and suddenly found that credit was cut off until the new semester. I had difficulty subsisting. I would sit down at the Lion's Den, eat the rolls automatically provided, and order a bowl of soup, which as I recall was only ten or fifteen cents. Then on the way back to my lodging I occasionally bought a sack of oranges as well as a whole apple pie, which I found to be the least expensive form of subsistence. I lost so much weight that I could start moving before my clothes had to move to catch up.

Partly because of the Navy having taken over various buildings and partly because it was an urban campus, Columbia had little student life after regular class hours. Much of the student body spilled out of the subway along Broadway in the morning and were swallowed up by the subway in the late afternoon. I joined nearby

International House and attended activities there as a non-resident member, and ate occasionally at the rectory of Union Theological Seminary. I became treasurer of the Graduate Economics Club and chairman of the executive committee of the Graduate Social Science Club.

At times it was possible to obtain inexpensive balcony tickets, and I attended little theater plays off Broadway, or at the Cherry Lane Theater in Greenwich Village, as well as concerts in Carnegie Hall. Professor Hotelling and his wife invited me and other students for occasional Sundays to their home in a wooded section of Mountain Lakes, New Jersey. I took their attractive daughter to a dinner dance on New Year's Eve honoring Nicholas Murray Butler, President of the University. I did not pursue the relationship because I thought her far too young, perhaps eighteen! I also dated a girl from Barnard College across Broadway from the main Columbia University campus.

I had long jaunts that winter in Riverside Park along the Hudson River in the bitter cold, usually ending with a meal at a downtown Automat. I walked great distances in New York, using the subway to get to a new point to start my walk, and returning by subway or train. One itinerary was across George Washington Bridge to New Jersey and along the Palisades. I explored Manhattan from The Cloisters at the north to Battery Park at the south, and then Staten Island and the harbor by ferry.

Meanwhile the war was continuing. I had taken a Civil Service examination before the war started in which I ranked high. Offers, which I declined, came from the Chief of Ordinance of the War Department, the Office of Price Administration, and other agencies, all "vitally connected with the war program" for "the duration of the war and six months thereafter." I did not return the forms sent me by the Manpower Commission seeking to include me in the Roster of Scientific and Skilled Personnel which was for the purpose of enabling the government to show local Selective Service Boards why an individual should not be inducted. I applied to the Navy Midshipman School and then to the Army for a commission but did not meet eyesight requirements. In the spring of 1943 the Navy Department offered those on Columbia University scholarships who were members of Phi Beta Kappa the opportunity to take Japanese language training in Colorado for the duration of the war with service being required thereafter in Japan. Of the men I knew who were eligible, only a Mormon student, in addition to myself, declined the offer.

I wrote the Selective Service Board in Portland to say that I had about completed my degree at Columbia, and volunteered for active service. I said I would enter from New York, and even provided a stamped reply envelope to expedite the proceedings. I attended graduation ceremonies on campus on June 1, resigned a fellowship at Columbia that had already been awarded me for doctoral study, and reported for induction in downtown Manhattan. I memorized the eye chart, which removed that obstacle, and was accepted as a private in the U.S. Army.

I reported to a reception center at Camp Upton in Long Island, avoided Orderly Room assignments, and instead toughened up and acquired a tan by digging ditches for a sewage disposal plant. Then on to more uplifting experiences at Camp Custer, Battle Creek, Michigan. This was memorable mainly for meeting a girl at the U.S.O., Marg, a very fine person, whom I saw at every opportunity thereafter for canoeing in the Battle Creek River, long walks and dancing at a local club. After basic training I was stockpiled at Camp Crowder in Missouri, guarding German prisoners of war. I took leave whenever I could, and hitchhiked over much of the surrounding states. One time I slept on the morgue table of a local police station, and other times I slept in the luggage rack of the bus I was riding. On Christmas Eve I slept under the Christmas tree in the lobby of a St. Louis hotel.

We pulled an incredible amount of guard duty during the first few months (85 to 110 hours a week) which eventually tapered off to about 65 hours or more in a week. The monotony was broken by an attempted mass escape by German prisoners, an attempted bombing of a guard tower, a race riot, two successful escapes, and a three-day manhunt in the countryside. One night while patrolling a railroad line there was a rustling in the underbrush and no reply to ''Who goes there?'' As a result of my trigger-happy companion's fast action there was one less cow in that area.

As nominated spokesman for the men of the guard company, I rose at a meeting with the camp commander and delivered a scathing criticism of camp operations together with some constructive suggestions as to a method of guarding prisoners that would significantly reduce manpower requirements. The camp commander congratulated me for having said what I did, and thanked me for my suggestions, which he approved. Some of the men lined up outside the mess hall door to shake my hand and thank me. I was transferred shortly thereafter back to Fort Custer, along with several others, but the changes at Camp Crowder did go into effect.

At Fort Custer I learned that a Military Government School was located there. I was denied attendance since the class had already started. I requested permission to see a superior officer, but my attendance was again denied. So I talked to the fort commander who approved my request. Training was rigorous. Aside from classes (which assumed assignment to the European theater), I remember encountering obstacle course training again and all that went with it. I crawled across the muddy field under live machine gun fire until I clanked my helmet against metal. I found myself positioned under the barrel of a machine gun, which fortunately had stopped firing. I had a good score for shooting moving targets and for hitting targets after dropping to my knee and shooting behind my back. I graduated at the top of the Military Government class with a combined score for all activities of 94.9 out of a possible 100.

The next move was to Camp Beale at Marysville, California. I reproduce below an account from a letter written to my folks at that time.

> In the last two weeks I have traveled over 1000 miles and spent little more than a day in camp. We were called out at midnight for fire fighting and convoyed into the Mendocino National Forest in northwestern California. We arrived at base camp (elevation about 6500 ft.) about ten a.m., ate a combination breakfast and lunch, and then set off for the fire line. The hike into the fire was only about three miles, but it was over rough terrain. We climbed up and down over one ridge after another, losing some 2000 feet in elevation. Much of the way was almost vertical, requiring carefully selected footholds. We reached the fire about 3 p.m. We widened the fire break and set a backfire towards the main blaze. Then the wind whipped up and the fire raced down on us, a 40 or 45 foot high wall of flame. We tried to widen the gap until the last minute—until the fire was some 15 yards away and very hot—and then we beat a hasty retreat. It jumped the break and went out of control, so we had to move out for the time being.
>
> In the days that followed, a new fire line was built, the fire was brought under control, and mopping up (chopping down smoking trees, etc.) and patrolling were completed. Another

two battalions worked the night shift while we worked the daylight hours. The forest rangers pressed into service all available able-bodied men in the area, including lumber mill workers, hunters, etc. and recruited conscientious objectors and drifters off the streets of Sacramento. Also some convicts.

With the fire under control, we were about to return to Camp Beale when word came of a new blaze 20 miles away. So after coming off the fire line we entrucked for the new fire. The roads are full of hairpin turns so it was morning before we got there. The place was lit up by the fire, which was on the crest of a wooded ridge. It was a beautiful sight, destructive though it was. We made camp at Bevan's Flat and had a few hours of sleep before setting out again. This time trucks took us part way, and aside from our having to ford streams, the going was much easier, few places being steeper than 50°. A bulldozer was brought in to build the fire break, mowing down trees as though they were stalks of wheat.

It was a rough, dirty, and uncomfortable assignment. Few if any of us shaved for want of daylight, water and energy, so we were quite a picture. Without waiting to clean up upon returning, I put in for a three-day pass.

I shipped out of Camp Stoneman in California for the Pacific theater of the war, and served in New Guinea, Dutch East Indies, Luzon, Okinawa, and Japan. I was recruited in New Guinea as a special agent for the Army Counter-Intelligence Corps (within days of what I learned later was the minimum eligibility age), and was a member of the first CIC teams to enter the two metropolitan areas, Manila and Tokyo. This was a period of intense activity which I have written about in *Special Agent in the Pacific*. In Manila, in addition to breaking up espionage rings left behind by the Japanese, I handled collaboration cases, and conducted an inquiry into atrocities committed against Indian nationals. The latter part of my stay there I was in charge of the Economic Section of the Manila Counter-Intelligence Office. In Japan I checked on the security of the occupation forces, released individuals imprisoned for political beliefs, worked to make the thought control police inoperative, and kept informed of political activities. I also investigated war crimes committed against Chinese nationals brought into Japan as forced labor (both civilian and military personnel), and prepared a report on the situation in Hiroshima and Nagasaki.

Although *Special Agent in the Pacific* is mainly an account, written contemporaneously during the war, of my counter-intelligence and war crimes investigative work, I have added commentary as to the ''surprise attack'' aspect of Pearl Harbor, the reasonableness of expectations held as to Filipino political and economic non-collaboration, and whether it was necessary for the United States to use atomic bombs against Japanese cities.

5

Post-War Graduate Study and Return to Japan

On return to the States I declined an opportunity to continue intelligence work since I intended to complete work for a doctorate and enter university teaching. I received a letter from Mrs. Hotelling that her husband had moved from Columbia to the University of North Carolina at Chapel Hill, and it was suggested that I join the group he was assembling there. Columbia University also renewed the doctoral fellowship awarded prior to my entering war service. However, my thought was that I should take the doctorate in economics, since my earlier degrees had concentrated on mathematics and statistics, and I had Harvard University particularly in mind. I find a statement of that conclusion in a letter I wrote in July 1943.

I was expecting to apply at several institutions, and wrote from Japan in January 1946 to ask a family member to assemble the needed application forms, and to indicate that I would be applying. It was May by the time I returned home. I had been hospitalized in Japan about March for jaundice and pneumonia, the first contracted from Chinese prisoners of war and the latter from exposure and chill after my jeep went into a snow-covered river. I also stayed longer to permit new arrivals to become informed as to the network of contacts I had developed for intelligence purposes. I discovered on my return that only one university had been contacted, and that was the University of Chicago. Enrollments were overflowing everywhere with the end of the war and the GI Bill. I had been awarded a fellowship in economics at Harvard University in an earlier year, so with the hope that it would be reissued I contacted Harvard myself, but a telegram came back that all fellowships had already been awarded.

Attending the University of Chicago was not entirely out of the question. I had admired the work in quantitative economics of Henry Schultz, by then deceased, and in fact I later edited a diary for part of his life, and I was attracted by the writing of Henry C. Simons, also of Chicago, author of *A Positive Program for Laissez Faire*. So I arranged for an interview, and it was with Lloyd Mints, a faculty member with whom in later years I shared many breakfast conversations in the University Commons. Henry Simons, I learned, had become despondent, and had plummeted to his death past the window of the office I subsequently had at the University. I did not learn until later of the dissatisfaction shared by Simons and by Oscar Lange with changes underway in the Department of Economics at Chicago.

I decided to give Chicago a try, relying on the GI Bill for financing, and presented myself for classes in the fall of 1946. I discovered that Milton Friedman had just been added to the faculty, teaching a required course for which I had taught the discussion sections at Reed. The enrollment was large, and Friedman screened me out in favor of those who had stayed at Chicago throughout the war, but I remonstrated and stayed. I found that he taught economics as of the turn of the century based on Alfred Marshall's *Principles*, and that by my using models reflecting the more recent work in oligopoly theory by Oscar Lange and in monopolistic competition theory by Edward Chamberlin of Harvard and by Joan Robinson of Cambridge University, my work was considered as simply wrong. [Indeed it seemed incongruous that Milton Friedman, at a dinner at the Palmer House in 1991 for civic leaders and alumni on the occasion of the 100th Anniversary of the founding of the University of Chicago, took as his theme the importance of respect for diversity of viewpoint and innovation.]

A skit by junior staff in 1951 conveyed very well the core of the Chicago view of economics. They performed ''Member of the Faculty'' to the tune of ''When I Was a Lad'' from Gilbert and Sullivan's operetta ''H.M.S. Pinafore.'' The author of the lyrics was unidentified.

> When I was a lad I served a term
> Under the tutelage of A.F. Burns.
> I read my Marshall completely through
> From beginning to the end and then backwards too.
> I read my Marshall so carefully
> that now I'm professor at the U of C.

Since all products do compete
From automobiles to babies sweet,
The very existence of monopoly
I explain away as sophistry.
This sophistry is so good for me
        that now I'm teaching at the U of C.
Of laissez-faire I am the champ.
Outstanding member of the liberal camp.
With social zeal I've never burned,
With feasibility I'm unconcerned.
With social zeal I've never burned,
        with feasibility I'm unconcerned.

Aaron Director, Friedman's brother-in-law, arrived at the University of Chicago about the same time, becoming head of a new Law and Economics program in the School of Law, which gave effect in that additional arena to the Chicago viewpoint that self-interest should be exalted as the organizing principle of society through unregulated markets, since this would maximize total economic wealth, it not being a matter for concern should that increase the existing inequality in the distribution of that wealth.

Frank H. Knight, who had taught Friedman, was on the faculty at Chicago at the time I was there, and I attended his lectures on the history of economic thought and read various books and journal articles which he had written. I found much of value in his philosophical writings, and appreciated his refreshing emphasis on the fundamental aspects of the economic problem, but I did not arrive at the same conclusion as he as to reliance on an unregulated marketplace.

I did find a course in price theory that was in touch with reality: "Monopoly Elements, Prices and Public Policy," given by a young assistant professor, William H. Nicholls. It dealt with the shortcomings of existing law with respect to the public control of business and with possible alternatives to existing public policy. He made evident the need for criteria which are adequate in practice for distinguishing between those monopoly elements in industry which are socially permissible and those which are socially undesirable. Perhaps needless to say, Nicholls found it desirable to continue his career at a different university.

I took work on labor management relations under Professor Frederick Harbison who later moved to Princeton. The power-center technique which he used in analyzing the union movement was helpful, but he had no use for the mathematical models I introduced, somewhat similar to ones used by John Dunlop of Harvard. I took a course on human relations in industry with William Foote White which I found rewarding for its attention to the effects of frequency of interaction. A course with Gale Johnson was also quite rewarding.

I was beginning to settle in at the University in spite of the lack of receptiveness to my viewpoint. I rationalized that subsequently I would be more able to articulate my views than I would be were I among individuals with whom I agreed. However, I was never fully convinced by that rationalization.

After resigning the Columbia fellowship, I applied to the national Social Science Research Council and was awarded a fellowship for a twenty-one month period. The financing was welcome. I was purchasing books, and the decision procedure was to subtract the cost of the possible book purchase from my savings account, divide the remainder by the number of days left in the month, and see if that was enough to live on. I tended to resolve close calls in favor of books, so food costs had to be cut.

I had a pleasant one-room ground-floor apartment with a fireplace and a garden entrance. It was situated across from the University Field House and only a block from Mitchell Tower, the chimes of which I enjoyed hearing. Some doctoral candidates who had been on campus during the war came there for sessions in which I helped them, and myself, review economics and statistical theory.

I usually ate supper with a number of other veterans at the University Commons adjoining Mitchell Tower. We shared a long table and dubbed ourselves the "Six O'Clock Supper Club." We were a bit older than most students and perhaps more serious-minded about our studies. It helped our morale to get together. We had to compete against many who had been at the University throughout the war. There I met Marianne, an Army nurse who had served in Europe, and we started going together.

I became acquainted with Professor Paul H. Douglas, a crusader for social policy whom I much admired. He had just become president of the American Economic Association. He had served in Okinawa, as I had. He had been wounded in the arm, and waved that arm as he lectured. I enrolled in a course, "The Theory of Wages," taught by Douglas, and commented on it as follows in a quarterly report to the Social Science Research Council:

Contrary to its title, the course was oriented around the

Douglas-Cobb production function and consisted largely of repeated demonstrations that the use of the function gave consistent results in repeated applications. As a result of delivering numerous critical comments, I was invited [by Professor Douglas] to present an opposing viewpoint. This I have done in a series of lectures, seminars and discussions during the latter part of March and continuing by special arrangements into the current quarter. My principal criticism was the absence of logical rigor. There was no clear statement in the lectures, or in any of the published research upon which the lectures were based, as to what assumptions were being made of an economic or statistical nature, or as to precisely what was being subjected to investigation. Proper appreciation was not displayed as to the distinction between proving a hypothesis and merely showing that in a particular case it can not be rejected. In addition, conclusions drawn from the empirical findings were announced unaccompanied by the appropriate qualifications, and they were improperly interpreted and used as a basis for discussion of public policy. This latter arose from Professor Douglas' practice of applying to the individual firm results obtained from the study of aggregates without due regard for the problems encountered in the process of aggregation.

In view of the above, I devoted the first two lectures, together with subsequent discussion periods, to presenting a survey of the course materials, the lectures, and the published research of Professor Douglas, the emphasis being upon the orderly introduction of assumptions. The objective was . . . to determine the minimum qualifications necessary in order to make the production function a meaningful concept. In particular I rejected the approach which treated the Douglas-Cobb production function as a natural law, and emphasized instead the value of the production function as a technique of analysis. I was also concerned with the lack of attention paid to the economic significance of the various assumptions. No clear distinctions had been made between phenomena of a technological nature and those arising from the introduction of the price mechanism, nor between the different meanings of economic terms applied variously to the individual firm, the industry, or the whole economy. I therefore attempted to satisfy this deficiency by covering in the subsequent lectures the economics of the individual firm and the position of the firm in the industry. The treatment was semi-mathematical in approach . . . The lectures were well received and are said to have contributed toward the success of the course.

What was at issue in the foregoing was not critical to the political activity in which Douglas was engaged. I shared with Douglas his interest in social legislation and civil rights. In his memoirs *In the Fullness of Time* (1971, p. 127) he wrote, regarding the post-war Department of Economics at Chicago:

> I was disconcerted to find that the economic and political conservatives had acquired an almost complete dominance over my department and taught that market decisions were always right and profit values the supreme ones. The doctrine of non-interference with the market meant, in practice, clear the track for big business. Inequalities of bargaining power, knowledge, and income were brushed aside, and the realities of monopoly, quasi monopoly, and imperfect competition were treated as either immaterial or nonexistent . . . Furthermore, since market demand was based on the distribution of income . . . it reflected all the injustices of modern society.

I was there during the same period and fully concur in his comments.

Douglas felt stifled by the lack of intellectual diversity and by the closed mind attitude of the dominant faculty members. He resigned from the University. In 1948 he was elected U.S. Senator for Illinois, and then became chairman of the Joint Economic Committee of the Congress, and was regarded as presidential timber until a regrettable emotional outburst on the Senate floor.

A course which I took on the theory of income and employment taught by Professor Jacob Marschak deserves special mention for the excellence of its content and presentation. My earlier training in macro economics could aptly be called "depression economics" for the forces considered and the horizons admitted were those of a society just emerging from a depression. This contrasted with the new concerns which revolve about questions of controlling inflationary forces, of full employment, rising prices, and the large amount of liquid funds in the hands of the public.

Since many years have passed since I took the courses at Chicago it is best that I quote excerpts from quarterly reports I submitted to the Social Science Research Council as a fellow of that organization.

Marschak gave a convincing demonstration of the power and clarity which is attained through the use of behavior equations and macro-economic models, techniques identifiable with the Cowles Commission for Research in Economics. The usefulness of this method, if only from the pedagogical viewpoint, would seem to be indicated by the apparent facility with which the subject matter of the course was understood by an exceptionally large class having relatively little previous mathematical preparation.

At the invitation of Professor Marschak I presented an original paper on a mathematical and diagrammatic technique for considering the various possible alternative government fiscal policies and the effects which each might have upon the level of national income and employment, corresponding to various situations with respect to net private investment and the propensity to consume. The response to the paper was one of considerable interest and enthusiasm, and Professor Marschak integrated the technique into several of his succeeding lectures.

Marschak invited me to attend seminars conducted by the Cowles Commission for Research in Economics. The Cowles Commission was an independent research corporation concerned with applications of logical, mathematical and statistical methods of analysis. It had its offices in the Social Science Research Building at the University of Chicago across the hall from the Department of Economics. There were many of these seminars, featuring distinguished visitors from countries throughout the world. Shortly thereafter I was asked to also attend staff meetings of the Commission and encouraged to comment on preliminary presentations of research that was in progress.

After beginning classes in the fall of 1947 I was summoned by the Department of the Army to return to Tokyo to testify as a war crimes witness regarding Japanese atrocities. This was an outgrowth of an investigation I had conducted in late 1945 of a forced labor camp in northern Japan where more than 400 of 981 Chinese military personnel and civilians died within a fifteen-month period. Assurance was granted, although reluctantly, that I would be permitted to return in time to resume my University activities in January 1948. My status was that of an expert consultant to the Secretary of the Army attached to the Legal Section of the Supreme Commander of Allied Powers. Over 40,000 Chinese had been forcibly brought from China to be used as prison labor in Japan. The handling of the war crimes cases with which I was involved was expected to set precedents for the handling of other cases involving the use of forced labor.

I prepared the list of specifications under each indictment for each war crimes defendant, outlined the questions that should be asked by the prosecutor, served as a witness to identify my investigative report and the exhibits that pertained to it, and was cross-examined by the battery of defense attorneys and by the individual judges of the War Crimes Tribunal. During a recess in the trial, I returned to the labor camp in the snow of northern Japan and obtained additional evidence used in the trial.

An abridged copy of my 1945 investigative report and an account of my war crimes assignment in 1947 are included in the separate volume I referred to earlier, *Special Agent in the Pacific*. (The investigative work that I did on war crimes gained national prominence in Japan in recent years, as I will explain further in Chapter 19.)

While in the Tokyo area in late 1947 I carried out various other activities. Those of an academic nature I included in a January 8, 1948 report to the Social Science Research Council of New York, as a fellow of that organization. By arrangement with Dr. Stuart A. Rice, Assistant Director of Statistical Standards, Bureau of the Budget, Executive Office of the President, I conducted interviews evaluating the effects of a U.S. statistical training mission in Japan the previous year. One of the interviews was with Ryokichi Minobi, Chief of the Executive Office of the Statistics Committee of the Prime Minister's Office. His committee sought to centralize and standardize government statistics, make statistics reliable, and educate the Japanese to prepare statistics properly and to understand them. A basic difficulty was Japanese distrust of published government statistics. Statistics were used by the Japanese government more to lend support to policies already decided upon than to aid in the selection of the correct policy. During the war this took the form of using statistics to prove to the people that a Japanese victory was inevitable if not imminent. During the Occupation it took the form of using statistics to present to the people and to the Supreme Commander of Allied Powers (SCAP) the picture which the Japanese government would like presented. The public was not able to check the official version against other sources of data, for all privately-prepared statistical data were suppressed by the government during the war, and the agencies which prepared private statistical series had passed out of existence.

I also met with various Japanese intellectuals at their homes or at their universities and made inquiries as to the conditions under which research was conducted. Not only were physical facilities a source of hardship, but the financial provision, in view of inflation, was scarcely enough to sustain life. Professors were hence forced to supplement their university salaries by doing outside work, with the consequence that little time was left for research. Many of those I met had previously experienced the scholarly life in the United States and Europe. I brought together those Japanese econometricians who were in the Tokyo area for a meeting, and provided them with books and journal articles to be used as a circulating collection which would bring them up to date on developments in Keynesian macroeconomics, econometrics, and the theory of games from which they had been cut off due to the war. Letters that subsequently came back to the University of Chicago and were shown to me expressed great appreciation for this new opening up of Japan. In later years various Japanese university personnel who were visiting the Chicago area were routed to me by the U.S. government. Their main interests were econometrics, baseball games, and ice cream. Two of the professors had attended the 1947 meeting, Professor Isamu Yamada and Professor Ichiro Nakayama. Professor Yamada returned several times thereafter at seven year intervals to visit me in Chicago, San Francisco and Los Angeles.

I also contacted Mr. Paul Henshaw and Dr. Bowen Dees of the Fundamental Research Branch of the Scientific and Technical Division of the Economic and Scientific Section of SCAP. The latter contact was to encourage the preparation of an article on people's attitudes in Japan toward atomic energy. I also revisited the head of the Korean Government in Exile whose release I had obtained in 1945 from Akita Prefecture Penitentiary.

I returned in January 1948 to further graduate work at the University of Chicago. I was shaping an interdisciplinary doctoral dissertation, but it was as yet not sufficiently defined. I was interested in economic theory as a general theory of choice, the effects of organizational structure upon decisions reached, a comparison of the flow of information through administrative systems and through neural nets, and somewhat separately, the validity of short-cut methods of thinking.

I received notice that I had been awarded a University fellowship at Chicago for the academic year starting in Fall 1948. As it turned out, I was to be on the staff of the University of Chicago prior to that and accordingly released the award for someone else.

5.1

On Returning from a War:
An Essay on Moral Values,
Liberal Ethics and Education

(1947)

You cannot go through the experience of war in which you are forced to violate concepts of what is decent and right without beginning to question what had been accepted, and experiencing dissatisfaction and restlessness. You resent the ease with which people fall into thinking of war as an alternative preferable to a searching scrutiny and revision of the social techniques whereby individuals and groups act together as a unit to mutual advantage.

However, it is easy to fall into the ways of those one criticizes. A few weeks of dry clothing, of tolerable temperatures, of dairy products and running water, of sanitary facilities and cleanliness, and of conventional ''good solid people'' of soothing platitudes and sing-song small talk, and one gets ''back to normal,'' to the humdrum existence of self-imposed horizons, and to that complacency which places prime reliance upon our ability to ''muddle through.''

Yet some who experienced the unnaturalness of war will balk at the one-sidedness of the adjustment expected of them. They may be too impressed by the role played by chance, circumstance and personality in human affairs to place much reliance upon there being ''right answers.'' They may tend to be cynical and think that the best education to prepare youth for the experience of living would be that which taught just how rotten people can be and how best to get along in such a world.

Few observers are so callous as not to recognize that there are many changes which would improve the lot of man. Whether or not an individual takes an active and deliberate part in bringing such changes about is largely an individual decision. The nature and limitations of such action, the requirements of orderly progress, and the role of liberal ethics and education are the concern of the essay that follows.

Man by nature is a rational as well as a romantic being, yet of all things on which he economizes, he is the most economical of thought. Granted his power to recognize problems and the need for arriving at decisions, we must note that these decisions are generally arrived at within the narrowest horizons that include the basis for a decision. The obvious and the superficial successfully compete with the less obvious and the fundamental, while habit and faith rank high in the list of thought-saving techniques in decision-making.

Man revels in complacency. New ideas and old ideas presented from a fresh viewpoint which challenge accepted beliefs intrude upon his complacency. He attempts to resolve contradictions so that the ideas can be assigned places in his accepted pattern of thought. If this process of assimilation fails, and if an idea cannot be rejected upon logical grounds, his peace of mind is shattered; he is assailed with doubts which necessitate a reorientation of accepted beliefs in a new pattern reconcilable with the newly acquired ideas.

There is often a failure to view issues in their proper perspective and to grasp the full variety and nature of the alternatives. The alternatives consist not merely of different end results, but include in addition, different means, active or passive, by which each such end may be sought.

Beyond the question of awareness of alternatives lies that of the more or less conscious act of evaluating such alternatives as are recognized. It would be agreed by most that choice among alternatives is essentially subjective, and that the alternative selected is that to which one is most favorably disposed or least unfavorably inclined (depending on one's point of origin in the subjective pleasure-pain continuum) on the basis of a more or less critical weighing of the various relevant considerations. The process of evaluation, in this context, is essentially the problem of deciding what weights should be given to the different considerations. It is here that disagreement arises. Some would maintain that the weights or values to be identified with the different considerations are inherent in them; they are objective facts, and the subjective element enters only in that the considerations are but partially recognized. They would hold that certain alternatives are, as a consequence, inherently bad or inherently correct, and would make their decisions accordingly. But there are difficulties here even if the matter of inherent value is not questioned, for moral-ethical considerations are not the only factors to be taken into account, and even if they were, there would not be a simple choice between opposites, but rather a choice between ''goods'' varying in degree and perhaps even defying ordinal comparison.

Passing over various intermediate positions, we reach the view that the weights attached to the different considerations relevant to a decision as between alternatives are themselves products of various factors: the intensity with which a consideration is present, the probability of its presence, and its relative importance, in this last the socially validated values being alloyed with the personal motivations of desire or contemplated pleasure.

Values, moral-ethics included, are a product of the environment of which they are simultaneously a part. The causality does not run in only one direction, for it is a process of mutual determination. That it may seem otherwise is because as social consensuses their influence over individual action is more perceptible than the influence which the aggregate of such actions has upon changing those values. Values are of a multidimensional nature; it is not enough to state a value without attaching at least the space and time dimensions. Morals, we must observe, are in part a matter of geography. Ethics vary with the social order. Law is simply a social technique.

Our penchant for elevating socially validated values to the plane of ideals tends to place a moralistic premium upon conformity by the individual to social norms, and thus introduces that stability and continuity into the social processes without which organized society could not exist. But in order that stability not be achieved at the expense of progress, we must submit our ideals to reinterpretation in the light of experience. Ideals, clearly, can be no more final and absolute than the values upon which they are based, and the latter from the nature of their origin must always be regarded as subject to change.

An explanation of the world as it is must take account of the role played by chance, circumstance and personality in shaping the course of events. To an increasing extent the dominant circumstance is the distribution of power over means. The use of power in the attainment of the good life signified a change away from a life of self-denial and obedience, and toward a life in which it is considered the individual's right and duty to get ahead and look after his own interests.

The choice of particular ends and particular means to achieve them cannot be entirely divorced from what is given as the distribution of power. Government is an organization by which individuals act as a unit to mutual advantage. It is a social technique for formalizing a particular pattern or distribution of power over means, thereby maintaining stability and order. Since it is the presumption of liberal ethics that an individual is the best judge of his or her own ends and of the means to attain them, it must follow that that pattern of power is best which reserves to the individual the maximum freedom in decision-making and action that is consonant with stability in the social order.

This constitutes a strong argument against all forms of arbitrary action on the part of a social aggregate. Yet where completely uninhibited power lies with the individual, the pressure for conformity with socially validated values is no longer present, and personal motivation looms large as the sole determinant of choice in the selection of alternatives in decision-making. Observation of individual conduct does not provide grounds for the optimistic belief that actions based entirely on personal motivation will invariably be in accord with the general welfare of the aggregate, nor the welfare of other individuals composing it. A social organization, moreover, cannot long remain intact where similarity of such a highly volatile factor as personality is the only basis for expecting individuals to act similarly within certain classes of situations. These considerations suggest that again the choice is not one between simple opposites— between freedom and coercion—but rather involves a combining of these techniques so as to insure that maximization of freedom within the social aggregate which is consistent with the maintenance of the social unit. Thus the coercive forces of authority and custom will find a proper place alongside freedom of association. But it is preferable to err in the direction of abuse of freedom rather than the abuse of power.

The direction in which a free society evolves, as well as the nature of its socially validated values at a given moment, will depend greatly upon the intellectual capacity of the individuals composing that society. Here one must recall the difficulties in decision-making noted at the outset of this essay—those leading to lack of awareness of the variety and real nature of the alternatives and of the considerations relevant to a judgment on or between alternatives.

The larger question is to what extent an individual should be deliberately conscious of a role in shaping his or her own destiny. Should an individual be passive to surrounding circumstances, or seek to change them? Should conformity be the criterion of action, or personal drive? These are questions which face every individual; yet few consciously answer. In part it is settled without the necessity of deliberate choice. An individual is the bearer of a culture, has a conscience, reserves certain areas for exercise of faith, while certain other responses come almost automatically from habit or from unconscious analogy with experience. Yet there remains a considerable area for action based on conscious and rational choice, and within that area one has need for a personal philosophy of life.

To what extent will the individual try to order his or her own life, the life of others, and of society in general? An individual may envisage, perhaps on quite rational grounds, that certain sweeping changes in society will bring about a ''better'' life, and attempt to override existing social arrangements to achieve that goal. Such changes, however beneficial they might be, are not likely to be enduring when they are imposed on society by arbitrary action rather than arising from the voluntary decision of individuals to act as a unit in making such changes. Society rightly tends to regard such extreme deviation from social norms as being inconsistent with orderly progress in their redefinition, and would effectively discourage such actions when it has the power. Short of such extremes, however, society provides considerable latitude for individual action, partly through tolerance, partly through indifference, and partly through a genuine regard for the freedom of the individual. The specific form of permissible activity which is most potent in determining the direction in which society evolves is that directed towards influencing decision-making, and hence other courses of action. It typically involves one or more of the communication arts, and while it may be dignified by the term ''discussion,'' it more generally deserves the designation ''persuasion,'' a subtle form of coercion. It raises the crucial question of intellectual capacity and training, and what should be the objectives of general education in and for a free society.

It is obvious that in modern society everyone should not seek to be equally informed on all matters. In a large and ever widening set of activities there is a need for specialists, and this need is properly being filled by preparation in technical and trade schools, and in the graduate schools of universities. But while it is apparent to most individuals that preparation for earning a livelihood is important, it appears to be less obvious that education should seek to implement two more fundamental objectives: preparation to enjoy life in its full meaning, and preparation to assume responsibility as an individual in society. It is such preparation that is sacrificed by undue emphasis upon specialization. Education is too often looked upon as solely an intellectual experience, and in its narrowest form, as a period in which the mind is made a veritable storehouse of facts and figures. But the primary purpose of the mind is not to impound the product of other people's thinking; rather it is to discern, to sift and analyze, to weigh and evaluate, and to come to its own decisions based on rational choice.

Education should prepare individuals to think for themselves. It should provide them with suitable techniques of analysis to aid their critical processes, and it should widen the areas within which reason operates by breaking down the barriers of unreasoned intolerance, prejudice and hate. It must go further than this, however, if the broad objectives of education are to be realized. Rational choice cannot be fully exercised when awareness of the variety and nature of the alternatives and of the relevant considerations is impaired by too narrow an intellectual experience or by lack of social experience. It is nothing new to say that in higher education the former deficiency is more likely to be repaired by a curriculum offering the liberal arts than by one stressing specialization. But it is the latter deficiency that must call forth the suggestion that college or university be regarded as not just so many books and lectures, examinations and credits, not, that is, as an ivory tower where reason reigns supreme, but rather as an experience in living, where reason must contend, as it does in real life, with emotional and other non-rational elements. College should be regarded as an experience in which the individual, regarded as a mature and responsible entity, learns to live as part of a self-governing community—learning to strike a proper balance between furthering his or her own life and participating in the community and giving it direction.

6

Facilitating a Research Environment

In the period following my return to the University of Chicago in January 1948 I began to acquire a number of responsibilities related to econometrics, a field in which I had been interested over the previous decade. These included associations with the Cowles Commission for Research in Economics, the Econometric Society, and the international quarterly journal, *Econometrica*, and through them, contacts with many individuals, professional associations and universities. I recognized opportunities for service that I would be fortunate to have were I older with more degrees and academic stature. I reserved time for my doctoral program, but gave priority for several years to my new responsibilities. The common element in my several roles was concern with economics, statistics, and mathematics, which in combination is referred to as econometrics. Acceptance of econometrics by the economics profession was far from secure at that time: there was not yet sufficient attention to the requisite preparation in graduate schools, there were few teaching or research positions available in the field, and practitioners found it difficult to obtain publication of their articles in economics journals when they used mathematics. My colleagues and I shared the view that the immediate years ahead were a critical period in which econometrics would gain acceptance or remain an obscure academic field.

The responsibility which I first undertook was that of the newly created post of assistant director of research of the Cowles Commission, effective May 1948. This appointment by the University of Chicago came at a time when Jacob Marschak (formerly of the University of Heidelberg, University of Oxford, and the New School for Social Research in New York) was stepping down after a successful five-year period as director of research. His predecessor, Theodore O. Yntema, had left to become research director of the Committee on Economic Development and subsequently vice president for finance of the Ford Motor Company. The incoming director of research, Tjalling C. Koopmans (whose academic preparation was in The Netherlands in mathematics and theoretical physics and then economics) wished to concentrate as much as possible on his own research.

A brief explanation of the Cowles Commission may be in order. It was founded in 1932 by Alfred Cowles of the Cowles publishing family as a not-for-profit research organization, with an initial advisory committee appointed by the Econometric Society composed of prominent individuals from Yale University, University of Oslo, the London School of Economics, the National Bureau for Economic Research, and the Federal Reserve Bank of New York. An historical account of the early years of the Commission in Colorado Springs and of the years of affiliation with the University of Chicago starting in 1939 has been set forth by Carl F. Christ in an opening section of *Economic Theory and Measurement: A Twenty Year Research Report, 1932-1952*, which was published in lieu of the usual annual report while I was administering the Commission.

The Commission moved to the University of Chicago and retained its status as a not-for-profit corporation as a result of negotiations between Alfred Cowles and Robert M. Hutchins, then president of the University. This affiliation continued the university's association with quantitative economics which had been started earlier by Henry Schultz and with the mathematical-economics interests of Oscar Lange, who had been at Chicago before I had courses from him at Columbia University.

While I was serving as assistant director of research and subsequently as acting director of research and then executive director of the Commission, I regarded my primary responsibility to be that of assuring a stimulating research environment. A prerequisite for that was financial support for the Commission, which I strengthened through negotiating various arrangements. Our contract with the RAND Corporation (a conduit for U.S. Air Force funds) for research on ''activity analysis'' (linear programming) was, I believe, the first between that organization and an overall research group, in contrast to consultant contracts with individuals. RAND was represented in the negotiations by Dr. Charles J. Hitch, head of the

Economics Division of the RAND Corporation and chairman if its research council, who subsequently became Assistant U.S. Secretary of Defense and then President of the University of California. I insisted successfully that the contract provide financial support for the entire research process, starting with the development of a stimulating research environment through to publication of monographs, since it was the intellectual environment which made it possible to attract the talent to which RAND would have access through the Commission. This feature was obtained also in a subsequent contract with the Logistics Branch of the Office of Naval Research, headed by Dr. Fred D. Rigby, for research on decision-making under uncertainty. (As I recall now in the 1990's, neither Rigby nor I was aware at the time that the other was a fellow graduate of Reed College.) The Commission also had financial arrangements with the Rockefeller Foundation through the initiative of Jacob Marschak, and with various sources of funds which were in addition to contributions by the Cowles family and the University. It also had contracts with Princeton University Press and John Wiley Publishers. An extension of the 1949-1951 RAND contract was negotiated for 1951-1953. Application was also made to the Ford Foundation, as will be mentioned later. Guests at the Commission were financed by various foundations.

About 1951 I was approached by the Department of the Army with an informal proposal that the Cowles Commission serve the Army somewhat as a prime contractor with respect to its behavioral science research needs. A building would be financed on the Midway Plaisance, adjoining other University buildings. The Commission would have offices on both coasts as well as in Chicago and Washington, D.C. and could select that portion of the research that it wished to conduct itself. While my initial reaction to the proposal was that it was worth exploring, I had some reservations as to whether the rate of organizational growth that would be required would make it unduly difficult to recruit qualified personnel. I explored this tentatively with several on the Commission and with Mr. Cowles. He revealed, somewhat belatedly I thought, that he did not believe that the federal government should finance research. (We already had arrangements with the Navy and with the Air Force through RAND.) Mr. Cowles also indicated concern that this would dilute the significance of the Cowles family contribution to the Commission. The matter was not further pursued.

I insisted in contract negotiations with RAND and ONR that the work of the Cowles Commission not be given security classification, since otherwise the Commission's research would be denied the benefit of the working relationships maintained with productive research workers at foreign institutions, and visitors and resident guests at the Commission would have to be screened for their past and present political convictions. The project leader for the research undertaken for the Office of Naval Research was cleared for access to classified documents, but any such documents had to be kept apart from the Commission's premises.

In spite of the Commission's research not being classified, I was visited by two agents from the Federal Bureau of Investigation who identified several members of our staff as being on their list of alleged subversives. After making reference to my former role in military intelligence, the agents asked for periodic reports on the activities of their suspects and my assistance in seeing that they were removed from their positions. I refused, and ushered them out, but as I will explain in a later chapter, this was not without consequences. One member of the Commission's staff, originally a resident member and then a consultant, subsequently went public as having been a Communist Party member, which however, did not daunt the conservative university then employing him, nor the Nobel Prize Committee in making its awards.

With a reasonably adequate level of research financing assured at least for the present, and with the security classification issue apparently put to rest, I was able to turn more attention to developing further the faculty of the Commission. Already there were joint appointments in the Commission and the Department of Economics for the two senior staff members. The development of the faculty as a deliberative body was, I believe, an important accomplishment of that period. I identified thirty-seven separate "contentions," as I called them, that underlay my recommendations to the executive committee, and circulated them for comment in March 1951. The full text is in the archival material mentioned later. Points not covered elsewhere in this chapter include the following:

- That a primary objective should continue to be the maintenance and strengthening of an intellectual environment conducive to progress along significant avenues of thought.
- That the Commission should maintain its present close relation to the University of Chicago in the pursuit of its

research activities, in the interest of maintaining academic freedom and high standards of scholarly inquiry.

- That a broad formulation of the research objective of the Commission should be included in the articles of incorporation and the bylaws, and that changes in such objective, as well as major decisions on academic affairs, should require approval by the faculty of the Commission.
- That organizational growth must be carefully planned in order that it be accomplished without detriment to the quality of existing research programs.
- That a major objective must be the development on a long-term basis of a nucleus of first-rate research personnel at salary levels that allow them to look forward to a durable association with the group.
- That particular attention must be paid to the balance between empirical and theoretical effort, and to the array of skills represented.
- That these and other considerations tend to place limitations upon the extent and type of growth which can be assimilated at any particular time, and that decisions on undertaking research commitments should be the subject of a recommendation by the research faculty.

As stated in the application to the Ford Foundation submitted September 17, 1951:

> The three years since 1948 have seen the emergence of a Cowles Commission faculty as a deliberative body, the strengthening of the administrative structure of the Commission, and an increase in the self-government of the Commission under an active executive committee consisting of officials of the Commission as well as of the University. The same three-year period witnessed an approximate doubling of the level of operations as the significance and potential usefulness of the Commission's work gained it further support.

Mr. Cowles was remarkable in the latitude extended to the Commission in the conduct of its affairs, and there was but one incident that I recall in which he departed from that desirable relationship. He telephoned me from his office in the Chicago Tribune Tower to convey a reflection on the extent to which the research and supporting staff was Jewish. I responded that I had never thought about classifying possible appointees on that basis; it had always been on their potential contribution to the Commission's work. I said that I believed that basically the latter consideration was what he was most interested in, and that I would continue on that assumption. The matter did not, to my knowledge, arise again.

Professor Clifford Hildreth, a Cowles Commission staff member who subsequently was at the University of Minnesota, wrote in a later year (November 1982) to ask that I undertake to explain the rather considerable productivity of the Cowles Commission, at least for the period during which I was associated with the organization. This I did in a letter which appears following the present chapter as Annex 6.1. I understand that a copy has been placed in the archives of Yale University. A publication by Hildreth (1986) discusses the scientific content of the Commission's work. See also the account in *Economic Theory and Measurement: A Twenty-Year Research Report* (1952), referred to earlier. An indication of the productivity referred to by Hildreth was that whereas when I joined the staff in 1948 the last monograph issued by the Commission had been in August 1945, in 1950-51 four monographs were published through Wiley and a special monograph, *Economic Aspects of Atomic Power*, was published by Princeton University Press. A volume of Marschak's lectures was published by Augustus Kelley. Moreover, reserves were established for five additional monographs that were underway.

An effective support staff was essential. The expenses were shared by the Cowles Commission and the Econometric Society in approximate proportion to the services provided, but there was a small subsidy given to the Society. To head the support group I appointed Miss Helen Docekal, a Northwestern University graduate with postgraduate study in Europe, as administrative secretary. The staff included a financial secretary, an editorial secretary, the head of the Computation Laboratory and a group of mathematical technicians, the librarian, the office supervisor, and their respective assistants. Morale was excellent and their productivity was extremely high.

The wage policy that I formulated for the support staff of the Commission, an independent corporate entity, provided for slightly higher starting salaries than offered generally by the University and this succeeded in attracting the best and the brightest among applicants. Members of the Department of Economics complained as to their inability to attract the applicants they would have preferred. I was amused that the chairman of the department, the faculty of which espoused settling allocation strictly through the marketplace, asked that the Commission agree to engage in restraint of competition by offering only what the department could offer. I declined to engage in an "invisible handshake" that would obstruct the operation of a free labor market. The solution, I suggested, was that the department members should seek their own outside financing, and not rely on the central government of the university.

Koopmans and I differed on the relative weight to be assigned to (1) achieving results for the specific research at hand, and (2) developing human resources that could solve that and other problems in the future. Both of us recognized each as on objective. He tended to give greater weight to the first objective, while I gave equal weight to both objectives. Koopmans' interest was in faculty who could provide services helpful in his personal area of research, and for such length of time as this was needed. I understood this to be in the tradition of the European institutes with which Koopmans presumably was familiar. My view was that appointees should be selected who had developed technical competency certainly, but who also possessed insight, creativity, and initiative, in short, individuals who demonstrated capacity for contributions beyond a specific current assignment. Our respective appraisals of prospective and present staff members accordingly were different. This also had implications for the contribution that a staff member could subsequently make to another institution.

I set forth a program for the development of human capital in a two-page proposal, "Present Needs and Future Prospects," which is appended as Annex 6.2 to this chapter. An abridged version was published in *Rational Decision-Making and Economic Behavior*, 19th Annual Report, 1950-51, of the Cowles Commission. An expanded version was the basis for an application to the Ford Foundation.

The foregoing difference in viewpoint meant that we each saw the role of the research director in a different light. According to my view, the size of organization should not be limited by the research a single individual could supervise. There could be several principal investigators, each working with motivated and relatively self-directed staff members. As I wrote to the executive committee on April 2, 1952, under such an arrangement the role of the research director would not be to closely supervise staff research (which would be the responsibility of the research leaders of particular projects), but rather to develop the optimum synthesis of productive workers, techniques of cooperation, and intellectual environment. A combination of staff members would provide a capability that could not be expected from a single individual. As it turned out, we put into practice somewhat of a hybrid of the foregoing, utilizing senior resident staff to lead two projects, and senior consultants who became resident for specific periods to lead other projects.

As I wrote at that time, the opportunities for growth which presented themselves to the Commission were a tribute to the reputation of the senior research staff. However, it required both persuasion [of Koopmans] to obtain acceptance of these opportunities and reassurance on several occasions to prevent these research efforts from being summarily curtailed if not dropped entirely.

The Cowles Commission found its reason for existence and distinctive character in the following convictions: First, research involving several disciplines and transcending traditional subject areas can be developed by the use of techniques of cooperation which fructify the creative activity of an individual. Second, the results of research should be widely disseminated as a basis for further advances. Third, these results should be evaluated in terms of their ultimate relevance to meeting the major problems of society.

Looked at from within a year-to-year horizon, the obstacles appeared formidable. The emphasis in research on long-run usefulness together with the technical proficiency required to understand the work of the Commission made it difficult initially to secure acceptance of econometric research by economists and social scientists generally.

Acceptance of the econometric approach was growing. However, I believed that there remained a critical period in which it was essential that an organization such as the Cowles Commission continue to provide leadership in the development of theory, the demonstration of useful application, and the preparation of individuals to conduct further econometric instruction and research. (Concern for the development of such human resources was first added to the formal statement of the Commission's objectives in the preface to the annual report which I prepared for 1950-1951 and remained there until 1955.) The long-term future of the Commission, however, was by no means assured. It was incorporated in Illinois with an inactive board of directors consisting of members of the Cowles family. In addition to other positions, I served as the corporate secretary and as its registered agent. But the Cowles family had close ties with Yale University. Alfred Cowles was a graduate of Yale, and Irving Fisher of Yale, the first president of the Econometric Society, was an old friend of his father and his uncle. It was not likely that endowment funds in support of the Commission would go to the University of Chicago.

The University was committed to tenure for two senior members of the Cowles Commission staff, but the Commission needed the type of financial backing that would permit it to offer long-term commitments to additional senior staff. It was a period of retrenchment at the University and there was no prospect of a long-term commitment by the University to the Commission as a research center beyond such staff as would assist the two faculty members in their areas of personal research. Koopmans did not see this to be a problem to the same extent that I did.

A further consideration was that appointments were not likely to be approved by the University unless the appointee also appeared attractive to the Department of Economics. Since the methodology of the Commission involved simultaneous equation models, and this was associated in the minds of many with an active domestic policy role for the federal government, which was anathema to the ascendant viewpoint in the department, the likelihood of University support through further joint appointments was diminished.

Melvin Reder, a professor in the School of Business of the University of Chicago at that time, wrote (1982, page 10) of the ''fairly intense struggle underway'' between adherents to the ''Chicago view'' in the Department of Economics and members of the Cowles Commission, which ''battle engendered a great deal of bitterness.'' He identified three facets of the struggle: research methodology, political ideology, and faculty appointments.

I prepared an analysis of the prospects of the Commission under various scenarios and discussed them with members of the executive committee. With the approval of that committee, I discussed the matter at meetings with Chancellor Lawrence Kimpton, who followed Robert Hutchins as head of the University.

Assessing the options—the status quo, or an institute within the Division of Social Sciences, or reorganization of the Cowles Corporation so as to have an active board of directors that would have the confidence of sources from whom funds need be raised—the last-mentioned emerged as the option for which I sought support.

I prepared amendments to the Articles of Incorporation of the Cowles Commission, a set of formal By-Laws, and Statutes for the governance of the Commission, for filing with the Secretary of State of Illinois. These were prepared through extensive consultation with all parties and attorneys. An executive committee discussion of the composition of the board of directors in June 1951 was particularly useful. I had suggested that some members be identified with relevant professional organizations in order to bring added critical insight as to the broad directions of endeavor and to command additional prestige for and confidence in the Cowles Commission. I added that Mr. Cowles had stressed the desirability of a balance between lay and professional representation on the board. Theodore Schultz, chairman of the Department of Economics, stated that he agreed in principle with the proposal. However, he expressed a strong preference for finding lay and academic personnel of quality and competence regardless of their organizational connections. The great difficulty, he added, was in obtaining persons of really creative thinking. Ralph Tyler, dean of the Division of Social Sciences, then raised the point that members of the board bearing a representative relationship to other organizations might not feel entirely free to use their intelligence in the interest of the Cowles Commission and not the groups they nominally represented. In view of the foregoing, I modified the proposal such that the elected members of the board would be members-at-large. The documents provided for integration of the executive committee into the formal corporate structure, for appointment of a committee on investments and a committee on development, for realignment of responsibilities among the principal officers, as well as provisions relating to research staff, faculty, academic advisory committees, and the supporting staff. The documents were approved informally by the executive committee at that June 1951 meeting.

The decisions taken were reported in the Ford Foundation application that September, as follows:

> The three-man board of trustees is to be replaced by an active board of directors which is to be gradually increased in size so as to have additional lay and professional representation. Eight of the directors are to be elected by the board from among persons not on the staff of the University of Chicago, in keeping with the larger community with respect to which the Commission performs a function. Directors are to be selected

so as to assure that great breadth of viewpoint and valuable critical insights are brought to bear upon the problems, plans and policies of the Commission, with particular reference to the broad directions of the endeavor and its long-term development.

The new By-Laws provided that: ''The Executive Director shall be the chief executive agent of the Commission, shall be responsible to the executive committee and to the board of directors, and shall advise them on matters related to the interests, aims and policies of the Commission.'' By action of the Executive Committee of the Commission I was designated as Executive Director for a three-year term beginning July 1, 1951, the maximum permitted by the new By-Laws, and this was subsequently ratified by the Commission's Board of Directors.

I thereafter prepared information on possible nominees for the new Board and suggested considerations by which they could be ranked, including the following:

Groups with which useful liaison would be effected
Familiarity with administrative and organizational problems
Absence of major conflicting loyalties
Willingness and ability to devote time and effort
Genuine appreciation of research as a scholarly activity
Ability to distinguish important and relevant problems
Overall appraisal as to potentiality for independent
  creative thought on problems likely to concern the board of
  directors
Source of increased public confidence in the Cowles
  Commission as a recipient of funds

Jacob Marschak, who much later became president of the American Economic Association, was kept informed throughout these developments. A quarter century later I had occasion to introduce Marschak as follows at an interdisciplinary seminar at another university:

If you go back 30 years from now, Jacob Marschak was in Chicago—at the University there—as director of a research group that drew staff from all parts of the world and was itself international in reputation. The place abounded in exciting ideas.

Marschak personally was very productive—a shower of working papers, review articles, a chapter here, a book there, and journal article after journal article.

He stimulated discussion, offered seminars, and brought out the best from all those who worked with him.

Ideas were drawn from everywhere—yet through the collaboration that took place within the research group—there emerged approaches which were distinctive of the group.

These contributions now belong to the profession—as members of the research group accepted appointments throughout the country, and had students who themselves now teach with that as part of their background.

In the best sense, Jacob Marschak then and now has been many things to many people: friend, gentleman, teacher, productive scholar, research catalyst, and an intellectual in the human sciences.

6.1

Reflections on Group Productivity

January 9, 1983

Professor Clifford Hildreth
Department of Economics
1035 Management and Economics
The University of Minnesota
271 19th Avenue South
Minneapolis, Minnesota 55455
Dear Cliff:

This is a further reply to your invitation of November 16, 1982 to contribute views on the work of the Cowles Commission during the Chicago period (1940-54) to assist in your preparation of a review article for the *Journal of Economic Literature*.

My response will be limited due to commitments I have recently undertaken for the University on an overload basis, as part of an emergency effort to inform the incoming Governor, who is faced with a huge state budget deficit, of the economic impact of higher education in California.

I will focus on organizational aspects of the Commission's productivity (related to the topic of the third paragraph of your letter), primarily for the years that I was associated with the Commission, with a look forward to effects on subsequent productivity.

In explaining the intellectual productivity of the Cowles Commission during the Chicago period, various factors, in my view, were important:

1.1   The most critical input must surely have been the conception of what could be accomplished by bringing together contributions from economic theory, mathematics, statistical theory, and empirical data in cooperative research endeavors. (As research went forward, organization theory, information theory, and policy analysis were included.)

To appreciate the importance of this, one must recall that in the early years of the Cowles Commission, the value of interrelating the several disciplines had yet to gain any considerable acceptance.

1.2   Along with this must be placed the design of an intellectual environment that would attract and stimulate the best minds in these several disciplines.

As phrased in a memorandum I sent to the Executive Committee of the Commission in March 1951 (Contention 11), ''a primary objective should continue to be the maintenance and strengthening of an intellectual environment conducive to progress along significant avenues of thought.''

The environment provided by the Commission was important to the productivity of its members. As to possible improvement therein, see the enclosed paper, ''About the Problem of Improving the Social Pressure Field in a Group of Research Workers, Such as the Cowles Commission, Working on Related Problems,'' by Leo Törnquist.

1.3   Communication among staff members having different disciplinary backgrounds was facilitated by the common acceptance among those appointed to the research staff of logical and mathematical means for stating the nature of problems and their approach thereto.

1.4   The role played by the use of informal Discussion Papers, circulated at early stages of a research effort, should be especially noted.

1.5   Important too was that the research body assembled did not view itself as a self-contained system. Research of the group was given impetus from concepts from related disciplines and from the larger academic, governmental, and corporate community, work in progress benefited from comment by others in this country and abroad, and research products were disseminated broadly.

The specific techniques included consultant relationships, staff meetings open by invitation, formal seminars, facilities for visiting scholars, participation in cooperative research projects with other institutions, the relationship to the Econometric Society, and participation in professional meetings, as well as the Discussion Paper series, Cowles Commission Papers, Special Papers, the Monograph series, and association with the journal *Econometrica*. The extent of activity in these several areas increased significantly in the post-war Chicago period.

An example of collaborative arrangements, in this instance with Carnegie Institute of Technology, is described in an enclosure.

The research efforts of the Commission benefited from the Cowles Commission becoming an international center for econometric research.

1.6 Related to the above was the policy that the Commission's research not become subject to security classification, since this would impede the exchange of research findings, add requirements to be met by existing staff members, and possibly inhibit extending facilities to visiting scholars. (A project leader, if necessary, could be cleared for security purposes so as to have access to classified information, but security arrangements were not to extend to the Commission's programs.)

1.7 Important enabling factors were the seed money provided by the Cowles family and the Rockefeller Foundation, and the incorporation of the Commission as a separate entity (first in Colorado, and subseqently in Illinois), the latter being important for providing independence in the taking of initiatives and for administrative flexibility. The receptiveness of Cowles to the insight mentioned in 1.1 was particularly fortuitous.

1.8 Beginning in 1948, the conduct of research was furthered by officers of the Commission participating with University officers in an Executive Committee for the Commission, and through research staff members becoming recognized as the *faculty* of the Commission, with a deliberative role in academic matters.

To explain the effect of the work of that period upon *subsequent* intellectual productivity, the following can be mentioned:

2.1 The basic abstract character of much of the Commission's research, the broad perspectives provided for viewing subject matter to which it could be applied, and the methodology developed, all contributed to the seminal nature of the Commission's output.

2.2   Instead of having organizations such as RAND or ONR relate directly to individual research staff members through consultant arrangements, contracts were negotiated between the Commission and those agencies for support of the Commission's programs having relevance to that research. In the case of the RAND negotiation, this included support for the ''whole product'' of the Commission's activity, including resources for the commercial publication of research results to widen dissemination. Reserves were established, out of overhead reimbursements from various projects, for a series of monographs planned for the future.

2.3   Sponsors for contract research gave support because the Commission's research would fit into objectives of their program, and accordingly had a natural interest in drawing upon this research as a basis for other intellectual activity of a basic or applied nature that the agency subsequently supported.

2.4   The Commission contributed not only to the body of cocepts and the state of the art, but also to the development of human capital.

This occurred both through the growth opportunities that the research activities provided younger Cowles Commission faculty and visiting scholars and through the teaching activity of Commission members holding joint appointment in the Department of Economics.

As but one example of this, the contributions of Jacob Marschak can be mentioned. Pertinent to this are my enclosed notes for introducing him to an interdisciplinary seminar in 1975. Also enclosed is a letter subsequently received from him having reference to that.

The effect upon developments in Japan might also be mentioned. In the course of visiting Japanese intellectuals in 1947, I arranged meetings of Japanese econometricians and started a small circulating collection of Cowles Commission materials and other research materials from which they had been cut off during the war. A volume is forthcoming in Japan honoring the work of one of those who drew upon research of the

Commission in mathematical economics, econometrics and linear programming, namely, Professor Isamu Yamada, now emeritus.

2.5   The Commission influenced the curricular offerings available in universities elsewhere through demonstrating the value of preparation in mathematics and statistics for those engaged in the social sciences.

This was furthered as individuals associated with the Commission returned to or took university positions throughout the United States and abroad or established organizations offering econometric services which attracted public notice. Students and colleagues of these individuals have, in turn, further spread acquaintance with ideas advanced by the Cowles research group.

There were also *proposals* formulated for further encouraging subsequent intellectual productivity:

3.1   See the enclosed draft which I prepared on ''Present Needs and Future Prospects,'' an abridged version of which was used in the Cowles Commission Report for 1950-51.

See also the four-point proposal for developing human resources set forth on pages 17-23 of the 1951 application to the Ford Foundation, a copy of which is enclosed.

This emphasis and the proposals for implementation draw upon matters that concerned me in work with the Econometric Society.

I turn now to other matters that were of special concern to those guiding the Commission, particularly in the period 1948-52.

In the move from Colorado to Chicago, the Cowles Commission remained an independent research organization, with separate incorporation, but additionally it was affiliated in academic matters with the University of Chicago as a component of the Division of Social Sciences. The arrangement between Mr. Cowles and Chancellor Hutchins was never fully committed to paper, and upon Hutchins being succeeded by Kimpton, the University gave thought to bringing the Commission organizationally into the University structure as a committee or institute. This had implications for the independence of initiative and the administrative flexibility which were cited in 1.7 above as advantages of having a separate corporate form. It also had implications for the objectives served.

While the University would have continued its commitment to certain faculty holding joint appointment and tenure with a University department, one change was that there would have been no financial *commitment* to there being a center furthering the conception set forth in 1.1. In particular, it was unlikely that the human capital objectives set forth in 3.1 would be pursued on as broad a basis.

It was *possible* that a committee or institute of the University would continue in that manner, but it was a time of retrenchment at the University, and the most *probable* outcome was that the University's budgeting would be sufficient only for such supportive research staff as would facilitate the individual research of the senior members holding joint appointment.

Moreover, Mr. Cowles' ties to Yale University made it unlikely that endowment funds in support of the program would go to the University of Chicago.

There were also developments within the Department of Economics at Chicago (described by Melvin Reder in the recent article, "Chicago Economics: Permanence and Change," *Journal of Economic Literature*, March 1982), in which there came to be ascendancy of a particular orientation.

The latter two considerations had made it appear desirable, as early as 1948, to consider what would be entailed in assuring the continuance of the Cowles Commission as an independent research center. The nature of the Commission's opportunities as a center for logical and mathematical approaches to the social sciences, conceiving of economics as a general theory of choice, suggested that its role should be viewed in long-run terms and in a broader context than as the program of a single university.

In March 1951 I prepared and circulated to the Executive Committee of the Cowles Commission a statement of 37 Contentions relating to the future growth and decision-making processes of the Commission, with comments requested. There are points therein pertinent to this letter beyond those mentioned, so the enclosure may be of interest.

The proposals contained in that document took a position with respect to various difficulties, including the following:

A.   To attract senior individuals of the desired caliber, and to hold existing staff of demonstrated attainment, required an ability to assure continuity of appointment, and in some cases the tenure that sought-for individuals could obtain elsewhere, but the financial commitments involved therein were difficult to obtain from the University, even apart from periods of retrenchment, and even apart from whether or not the appointee would seem attractive to the Department of Economics. Financing from outside the University that could be the basis for such commitments was difficult to obtain for a family-held corporate entity.

Mr. Cowles agreed with the view that the Board of the Commission should be expanded as to lay representation, and that academic representation should be added. Substantial agreement within the Executive Committee of the Commission was reached on June 29, 1951, and names were submitted subsequently for consideration. (Xerox reductions are enclosed showing the information and criteria used in assessing individuals considered for purposes of lay or professional representation.)

Progress on organizational matters was reported in the 19th and 20th Annual Reports of the Commission. Articles of Amendment to the Articles of Incorporation of the Commission were developed, and were made part of the application to the Ford Foundation, submitted in September 1951. One director was subsequently added, but further steps were affected by the move to Yale University.

B.   A problem of concern, particularly to those serving as Director of Research and as Executive Director, respectively, was the view taken of the position of Research Director. This could be said to depend on a view of the objectives of the organization itself.

The tendency present in one view was to stress the importance of the Research Director's individual research interest. The organization is then valued primarily as a facilitator of that individual's research program. Personnel are added who can contribute to that area of research, and would tend not to be added were close supervision of the individuals' work expected to unduly burden the Research Director. I understood this to be the view of the University and the Department of Economics, which understandably was protective of the opportunity of its faculty to undertake research. To an adherent of this view, bringing the Cowles Commission within the University as an activity of the Research Director's own academic department would not necessarily be viewed as disadvantageous.

The view held by myself, first as Assistant Director of Research, then as Acting Research Director, and subsequently as

Executive Director, was that the responsibility of a Director of Research, as such, were the full potentiality of the Commission to be realized, was not that of supervising closely the work of all those appointed (for that would both inhibit that individual's own research, and also set a limit on what could be undertaken by the organization), but rather it was to encourage the development of a synthesis of productive workers, techniques of cooperation, and an environment conducive to creativity.

As set forth in Contentions 17 through 20 in the 1951 document enclosed: Both to safeguard a major portion of the research director's time for his own research, and to facilitate the decision-making process, the research director should avail himself of advisory committees and of project leaders. Such project leaders should be permitted that degree of independence of action which will encourage them to carry the major burden of providing initiative, stimulation, and direction to the project. (These) arrangements are particularly essential if the Commission is to enter upon additional areas where its research techniques can make significant contributions. Organizational growth must be carefully planned in order that it be accomplished without detriment to the quality of existing research programs.

Contention 15: Participation in the research group involves obligations as well as benefits, and great care should be taken in arranging the decision-making process so that from the individual's viewpoint the latter outweigh the former, this being particularly crucial where agreement to a cooperative or consultative relationship is being considered. (Also crucial in protecting the intellectual contribution of the research director.)

Contention 23: These and other considerations tend to place limitations upon the extent and type of growth which can be assimilated at any particular time, and decisions on undertaking research commitments should be the subject of a recommendation by the research faculty.

The difference in view did not pose a problem when the RAND contract, for instance, was being considered, since the research interest of the incoming Research Director was in that area. The matter did arise in considering various other possibilities for expanding the work of the Commission. The holders of each view tended to accommodate the other when appropriate under the circumstances, and productivity in the Commission as well served. However, in one case the different views could not be reconciled.

This is as much of a response as I can undertake at present in view of other commitments. I would be pleased, however, to clarify anything on request, and would welcome the chance to comment on a draft of the article to such extent as you would find that useful.

I authorize inclusion of this letter, and of the materials identified in the attached list of enclosures, in the Cowles Commission Archives, as suggested by your letter. The Törnquist enclosure is not on the list since you may want to consult him in the matter first.

I wish you well on your project. It is good of you to undertake it. Best regards.

Sincerely,
William B. Simpson
Professor of Economics

WBS:rs
List of Enclosures
Enclosures

6.2

Present Needs and Future Prospects

Of major concern to the Cowles Commission is the problem of building up the human as well as the financial resources which must be drawn upon if the research effort of the group is to keep pace with the potential usefulness of econometric research.

In the short-run the limitation is only financial, namely that the Commission needs additional long-term support which can form the basis for the commitments involved in adding major staff members from the existing pool of research workers.

In the long-run the problem is one of developing additional human resources which can be utilized for research and teaching in this and related areas. This requires the removal of limitations of ability and of interest, and the removal of barriers to the international exchange of information within the profession.

The Cowles Commission is seeking support to attack this long-range problem on four points: (a) A program of fellowships would be inaugurated by the Commission providing carefully guided fellowships of sufficient duration to permit study, travel, and training at other institutions as well as at the Commission and University of Chicago in general preparation for engaging in econometric research. (b) A series of conferences would be arranged at the Commission at intervals of about 18 months, each organized around a topic of interest to the Commission and to the profession in general. In each case a senior research worker would be added to the staff of the Commission for an extended period, the first part of which would be spent in advance of the conference doing research in the field and arranging for participation and expository papers, and the balance of the time being devoted to subsequent research and to carrying the conference materials through to publication. (c) The existing publication program of the Commission would be expanded to facilitate the dissemination of econometric research findings and expository work on techniques in particular, including selected non-staff material which might not otherwise reach publication because of its specialized nature. (d) The fourth part of the plan is to establish a study program aimed at recommendations for the improvement of communication within the profession. The various aspects of the program would be undertaken either by consultants of the Commission or through contracts with appropriate organizations. Although already undertaken, the intra-society study committee on the mathematical preparation for social scientists is illustrative of the type of activity contemplated. Another example would be an international survey of the facilities devoted to quantitative economics, proposed by the Econometric Society as a preliminary step toward coordination of research and the creation of experienced research workers.

Apart from the needs and prospects mentioned above is the long-run objective of securing an endowment which would assure to the Commission a permanent source of income. There is also a pressing need for additional space, both for the rapidly growing research and supporting staffs, and for the interested group of advanced students and research fellows which is attracted to the Commission from throughout the world.

7

Facilitating Scientific Communication

The environment for research at the Cowles Commission for Research in Economics was in various respects an open society. The research staff gained insight from researchers at universities throughout the world as well as from themselves, combined their talent with that of individuals in other fields, disseminated tentative results, took criticisms thus obtained into account, and published the resulting product. The Cowles Commission attracted scholars internationally as visitors or longer term guests, used consultants from several countries, provided a forum for guests through its seminars, distributed drafts of research papers widely for discussion, as well as reprints of journal articles, and published a series of scientific monographs.

As an example of comments furnished a staff member, in this case Tjalling Koopmans, I have included as Annex 7.1 to this chapter a critique I wrote in November 1948 after being furnished drafts of a paper by Rutledge Vining and a reply by Koopmans on methodological issues in quantitative economics. Their papers subsequently appeared, after revision on the basis of comments, in the *Review of Economics and Statistics*, May 1949. [The short-fall of the Cowles Commission approach with respect to hypothesis-seeking on which I commented in 1948 (Annex 7.1) has been highlighted recently in an article by Heckman (1992, pp. 883-84).]

Communication has been furthered by the Econometric Society through its journal *Econometrica*, through regular scientific meetings in various countries, and through various special affiliations and programs.

Concurrent with my responsibilities at the Cowles Commission, I was elected secretary of the Econometric Society in September 1948, and as such became a member of the Council of the Society. I was reelected in subsequent years.

Alfred Cowles, who had been instrumental in the founding of the journal, continued as treasurer of the society and business manager of the journal. I facilitated the execution of his duties with the aid of a newly-designated financial secretary, a position shared with the Cowles Commission. In addition to duties as secretary of the society, I accepted the responsibility for budgeting, personnel, contract negotiations with the printer of the journal, and arrangement of an independent audit for the society and its journal. A prominent econometrician in each of several foreign countries served as the recipient and transmitter of membership dues.

Separately from the foregoing I became managing editor of *Econometrica* in 1948, starting with preparation of the January 1949 issue. Professor Ragnar Frisch of the University of Oslo, who subsequently was awarded a Nobel Prize in Economics, continued as editor. In June 1951 the Council of the Econometric Society voted to designate me as co-editor, with Frisch continuing as editor.

The significance of the journal may be judged from the following quotation from the 1990 *Joint Register of Members of the Royal Economic Society and the Econometric Society:* "*Econometrica* is one of the most important and prestigious economic journals published in the world. *Econometrica* was recently ranked second in the world among the fifty journals most cited by the core economics journals."

The several positions that I held with the Cowles Commission and the Econometric Society fitted very well with my personal philosophy that I should so use my finite energies as to be a catalyst for others in achieving shared objectives. I thus achieved a multiplied effect upon matters about which I was concerned. I regarded the meetings and other programs of the Society and its journal as channels through which much could be accomplished.

An effective support staff was essential, and I have referred to that in the preceding chapter.

My view of editing a journal was more broad than that of selecting from among articles submitted those to be put into print. When I could detect the need for further research I would express interest in securing a manuscript on new work in the identified field.

In the latter part of my editorship I undertook to make more evident that *Econometrica* would consider research in interdisciplinary fields. For instance, in June 1951 I wrote to Frisch as follows:

> In addition to articles of empirical content, there are other types of articles I would like to see appear more often in *Econometrica*, and which would probably require some solicitation if they are to be made available. One such type is the interdisciplinary survey article which brings the reader of *Econometrica* up to date on developments which are in other fields but nevertheless of potentially great significance to econometric work. Such articles would be expository in style, but of prescribed length, would utilize mathematical presentation where appropriate, and would emphasize the cross-threads with economics. References to the relevant literature, especially of empirical content, would be encouraged. I would like in particular to seek such an article from such as Paul Lazarsfeld of Columbia on latent attribute analysis and the making of social-psychological models; from such as Anatol Rapoport on the work of the Rashevsky group on the mathematical theory of socio-economic relations; from such as Bavelas of Massachusetts Institute of Technology on the work at his institution and at Ann Arbor and elsewhere on the general nature of group relations; from such as Max Woodbury of Princeton on cybernetics and the mathematical theory of communication; and from another on recent work in the provision of a formal theory of administration and organization. It would by my hope that one such survey article could be included in each of next year's issues, the twentieth year of publication of *Econometrica*.

The provision of critical services for manuscripts (whether eventually published or not) was, to my mind, an important function of a professional society. Manuscripts selected for refereeing were generally examined by more than one individual, selected on the basis of the aspects of the paper that should bear scrutiny. I frequently requested revisions and the resulting manuscript was again refereed. Occasionally when I saw the possibility of a productive collaboration, I explored having the referees work directly with the author. In all cases I made it clear that the decision on publication was contingent on the quality of the revised paper. Where possible, manuscripts that were not accepted were returned with constructive suggestions to improve the possibility of their acceptance by an alternative journal.

When an author's methodology lagged behind that which would be most productive, I commissioned a colleague to draft a revision that was then submitted to the author for possible adoption, with credit to the colleague. In retrospect, this practice was probably too venturesome, if not intrusive, and even when it resulted in often-cited articles, I fear that the authors had less than kindly thoughts as to my intervention.

Papers that were strictly within the field of mathematical statistics were not accepted since alternative publication channels were available. The following are excerpts from letters that I wrote in 1949 in turning back some manuscripts on mathematical statistics:

> The basic editorial policy of *Econometrica* consists of publishing those original papers that are significant directly or indirectly as contributions toward the development of econmetrics. Within the framework of this policy there has been a gradual evolvement of selective criteria for coping with the recent considerable increase in the volume of papers submitted.

> Stress has been placed, in selecting papers for publication, upon the main object for which the Society and its journal were created, namely, the promotion of studies that aim at a unification of the theoretical-quantitative and the empirical-quantitative approach to economic problems. This includes mathematical-economic theory, because without mathematical formulation of hypotheses, their empirical testing is often impossible. This does not mean that *Econometrica* will not publish original and significant papers on mathematical statistics, but greater weight in selection will be given to papers which are explicitly related to the objectives of the Journal and its readership.

> Two considerations are kept in mind: (1) That *Econometrica* publish that selection of articles which will furnish its readers with a balance between different topics, approaches, etc. which best promotes the interests of the Econometric Society and its membership. This would not preclude the occasional publication of an article which invades neighboring fields, the purpose being that of inspiring readers with new associations of ideas. (2) That *Econometrica* recognize that it performs a function to the social sciences in general by publishing high-caliber papers in its field which, because of the

employment of mathematical methods, would not be accepted for publication by other journals.

As to the frequently encountered and valid criticism that there were not enough articles in *Econometrica* that combined theory and statistics, I wrote as follows in 1951:

> I believe you know that I am quite in agreement with you. It is not an editorial prejudice against empirical papers, merely the lack of significant contributions taking that form. As I recall, my letters seeking papers on macroeconomic topics (written to quite a number of persons who might be aware of such material) also contained a reference to the journal's keen desire for such work. On numerous other occasions I and others have sought papers of an econometric nature, but the progress is slow. In the meantime the solution can only be, not the rejection of articles on mathematical economics, but further steps to encourage individuals to give the journal a chance at papers which combine economic theory and statistics. I am hopeful that the empirical papers to appear in the October, January and April issues will suggest to others that the journal is interested in such material. I am considering inserting an editorial note in the January issue requesting further submissions. Should other concrete steps along these lines occur to you, please do not hesitate to make them known to me.

A different type of criticism related to the geographic origin of authors. In response to such criticism I made the following reply in March 1952 to a French economist:

> Your reference to the desirability of maintaining *Econometrica* as an international review prompted me to review recent issues of the journal from this viewpoint. In addition I looked at those issues which are in preparation.
>
> I find that of the seven issues from April 1951 through October 1952, there has been or will be an article by a French author in each issue except that of January 1952. I note also that there are major articles by authors from the following countries: Norway, England, Switzerland, Japan, Israel, Canada, and The Netherlands, in addition to France. There is a possibility that one article will be published by a German author. In addition, among the foreign-born American authors the following countries are represented: Austria, Hungary, Russia and The Netherlands. Reports published on meetings in Italy, Japan

and India and to be published on meetings in Belgium, Japan and India contain abstracts from a great number of further countries.

In addition it should be noted the editor, co-editor, and associate editors are drawn from various countries.

It was the practice of the journal to publish manuscripts in either English or French. A member of the society in South America recommended in the latter part of 1952 that a brief resume in Spanish accompany each article. This would be of assistance to readers of the journal who had some difficulty with the English or French languages but would be willing to work through an article once they had learned that its contents were of interest to them. I proposed a modification of this to take account of the possible difficulties in meeting publication schedules. I proposed that the journal include a short Spanish-language description of the articles which had appeared in the preceding issue. Permission would be granted Spanish language publications to reproduce this information. I believed that this would increase the accessibility of econometric work to the Spanish speaking countries and significantly broaden the influence of the journal and its international character. I arranged for translation of a seminal article by Abraham Wald from German into English which was published in October 1951. A translation of an article by Daniel Bernoulli which had appeared first in Latin in 1738 and then in German in 1896 was commissioned in 1951; it was published in the January 1954 issue of the journal.

To assist in my work on *Econometrica* I appointed extremely competent editorial secretaries, shared with the Cowles Commission. Miss Emilie Rashevsky served first in that post, followed by Mrs. Jane Novick and Mrs. Ruth Skinner. I retained responsibility for encouragement of submission of manuscripts, selection of referees, evaluation of their comments, recommendations for revision, planning of balanced contents for each issue, interpretation of editorial policy, recommending new policy as needed, and so forth.

Professor Frisch was increasingly withdrawing from an active role, so in mid-1950 he directed that papers from European authors henceforth be sent directly to the editorial office in Chicago. He retained a veto on approval of manuscripts, but the exercise of initiative and of judgment had for the most part shifted from Oslo to Chicago.

The existing group of associate editors of *Econometrica* had been passive for some time, so after approval from the Council and from Frisch, I arranged in early 1951 for a new enlarged group of associate editors from various countries. Each appointment was for a short time and would be renewed only if the individual remained active. Individuals were selected from among those likely to know of manuscripts suitable for publication in the journal, aware of and with access to competent referees for manuscripts assigned them, and competent to handle refereeing diplomatically. They were not permitted to foreclose the possibility that I or Frisch might not accept a manuscript or might call for more revision.

I desired that *Econometrica* be open to publishing an article on its own merits irrespective of whether the author was a prestigious researcher or a virtual unknown. When manuscripts by prestigious authors were not accepted, pressure was occasionally put upon me to reconsider, sometimes through other individuals enlisted by the author.

A problem that frequently had to be faced was that of securing reduction of articles to publishable size. In one troublesome case in early 1952, a prominent French author submitted a 75-page single-spaced manuscript and insisted that it should be published without change. This was not possible financially, but the question remained as to whether some portion of it could be published. The manuscript was assigned to an associate editor who obtained a detailed evaluation of the entire manuscript from one referee and appraisals of particular sections of the manuscript by three other referees. The conclusion of each was strongly adverse to publication. Separately I obtained the confidential views of three Europeans. Of these eight individuals, six later were awarded the Nobel Prize in Economics. In writing the author I toned down the harsh comments of referees. The author attempted through various channels to have the decision overruled. Portions of the article, in revised and abbreviated form, were later accepted for publication in different issues of the journal after I had withdrawn from *Econometrica*. The second of such articles was accompanied by a disclaimer by the editor that indicated the author had to accept responsibility for the paper.

In another case a manuscript of 38 pages from an author in Egypt was reduced to four double-spaced pages through revisions encouraged by an associate editor. The manuscript finally appeared as a one-page note, quite in keeping with its contribution.

I developed and received approval from the Council for a policy whereby printed pages beyond sixteen in number could be published if warranted by the importance of their content, were they financed by a page charge borne by the author.

Jacob Marschak passed on to me from European contacts the request that European manuscripts be given a less thorough refereeing and be accepted at a lower level of contribution than other manuscripts. This was proposed in order that more European articles could be published in the journal.

Along the same lines, Frisch consulted me in 1952 on a French proposal that originated from the author of the rejected 75-page manuscript. It included provisions such as the following: That there be a French editorial secretary who for each French-language manuscript would poll the French-speaking fellows of the Society as to whether the manuscript should be accepted. Manuscripts would be judged primarily in terms of the literature known to French-speaking Fellows. Manuscripts were not to be subject to requests for revision when this would be resented, and so forth. I replied that an editor would find it extremely difficult to reject a paper that had been favorably recommended by the Fellows, and editorial judgment would be surrendered to an intellectual cartel in the French-speaking countries. I further responded that for there to be independence of editorial judgment the impact of the French speaking Fellows on the editorial process should be as individuals, in order that a bloc of opinion not be formed against which a decision could be taken only with difficulty. I also indicated that a copy of the manuscript should go through the usual refereeing process in order to secure an independent appraisal in terms of research in this country and internationally, with the concession that the latter appraisal need not be decisive in the publication decision. There already was an associate editor from France through whom this could be arranged. What was at issue, aside from pride, and that was no small matter, was an attempt by disconcerted authors to institutionalize the existing insularity of their research. What was needed was a facilitation of international scientific communication, not the erection of barriers to professional criticism.

Research methods that had gained acceptance in the United States, or even more broadly in English-speaking countries, were not in all cases part of the approach used by already-established researchers in other countries. As I look back on this now, I can see that one could have argued for a phasing-in as to what was expected, leading to a convergence of standards. But neither I nor those proposing the lesser standards gave thought, as I recall, to the dynamics of the situation. This particular request, which was denied, was blatantly for special privilege.

At the time that I took the various positions with the Econometric Society, the established reaction to the poor state of financing the journal was to limit the number of pages of *Econometrica*. Dwindling support had been leading to reduction in the size of the journal, which in turn diminished support. I put into effect an alternative approach, in which pages were added that were set aside for features that would attract financial support from additional readers. That approach, together with expanded membership recruitment and expanded Society activities, made possible a doubling of the number of journal pages and a doubling of membership in the Society within a four year period. Professor F. Divisia contributed an article in French which charted the growth of the Econometric Society. It appeared in the January 1953 issue of the journal.

An abstract in small print was added following the title of each article. An introduction or a summary was required at the beginning of each article. Authors had to abandon the argument that ''the topic is too complicated to be described in words.'' A verbal exposition was required alongside mathematics to allow the reader to readily gain the central contribution of the presentation without investing the effort to follow the mathematical development. Survey articles were commissioned. A book review editor, Professor Gerhard Tintner, was appointed, and a book review section became a regular feature for a twenty-three year period thereafter. Frontispiece portraits of econometricians were added. A supplement to the journal was prepared by Kirk Fox in 1952 which contained a twenty-year analytical subject guide and author index to *Econometrica*. All articles, abstracts, discussions, book reviews, and miscellaneous items contained in the journal were thoroughly indexed to make the material readily accessible to research workers in econometrics and related fields.

The other position which provided opportunity for me to facilitate scientific communication was that of secretary of the Econometric Society. In that role I gave attention to increasing the effectiveness of meetings which customarily were held annually, one in Europe and one in the United States, and to adding meetings available to individuals in other parts of the world.

The meeting in The Netherlands in September 1948 was the first European meeting held since World War II. In 1949 the meeting was in France, with opportunities for attendance also at the meetings of the International Statistical Institute at Berne, Switzerland, and the Income and Wealth Conference at Cambridge, England. The meeting was in Italy in 1950, in Belgium in 1951, and in England in 1952.

It was the custom of the Econometric Society to hold an annual American meeting in conjunction with the American Economic Association and related social science organizations in a major U.S. or Canadian city, usually between the year-end holidays.

I initiated the addition of an annual summer meeting, starting in 1948, in conjunction with the American Mathematical Society, Mathematical Association of America, and Institute of Mathematical Statistics, usually on a college or university campus. Emphasis was upon papers of a mathematical and technical nature. The Society also began to meet an intervals with the International Congress of Mathematicians, starting in 1950 at the Congress at Harvard University.

In 1950 I established the practice of holding a regional meeting of the Society each year on the West Coast. This was usually in conjunction with regional meetings of the mathematics and mathematical-statistics associations. Participation by the Western Economic Association was encouraged.

As mentioned in an earlier chapter, I convened a group of members of the Econometric Society in Tokyo, and provided for the circulation of materials bearing on econometric advances during the war, at the time of my return there in late 1947, and established various lasting contacts. Formal annual meetings of the Econometric Society started in Japan in 1950. In 1952 the Japanese members of the Econometric Society, through arrangement with the Science Council of Japan, sent an official delegate to the Chicago meetings.

The increased level of activity of the Society and initiatives from members in India led to annual meetings of the Society in that country. A preliminary planning meeting was held in India in 1950. In 1951 and 1952 there were two meetings there in each year, one in conjunction with statistical associations and one with the Indian Economic Conference.

In September 1952 I wrote to Professor Paul Samuelson of the Massachusetts Institute of Technology, then president of the Econometric Society, regarding proposed meetings in Central and South

America:

> For the last few years I have been quite interested in increasing the participation of the Latin Americas in the affairs of the Society. Recently I sought the reaction of members of the Society in Central and South America and in the Caribbean countries to the beginning of meetings at points accessible to them. Encouraged by the response, I contacted the Inter American Statistical Institute on the matter of possible cooperative sponsorship of such meetings should they be formally proposed by our organization. The IASI has indicated its receptiveness to coordination between meetings of the Econometric Society and the Institute in Santiago, Chile in November 1953, concurrent with the first meeting of the departments of economics of Latin American universities.
>
> The great distances involved make any large gathering at some single central point quite out of the question at this early stage of the development of econometrics in Latin America. However, I believe it is not too soon to encourage, on a very modest scale, small groups to gather for a day or two of sessions at several points where members are concentrated and which are accessible to others now or potentially interested. From such first steps can be expected the gradual development of meetings as we know them in this country. I have in mind that for 1953 the Society could encourage such sessions to be locally organized in Mexico City, Rio de Janeiro, and Santiago, the last one being concurrent with the other meetings mentioned above. Letters would be written here on your behalf.

In setting up meetings in various parts of the world, I arranged, in consultation with others, for individuals to chair the program and local arrangements committees. In the case of meetings in the United States that were to be held in hotels, I visited the cities selected and entered into agreements for the use of meetings space, usually some years in advance. I served on various of the program committees and attended the meetings. In addition to sessions planned by topic, there were sessions for contributed papers.

I increased the use of discussants who had an advance opportunity to study the papers. They were called upon prior to open discussion. This permitted a more penetrating discussion than would otherwise have been possible. A summary of each discussion was added to the reports published of the meetings.

One of the meetings of the Econometric Society that was particularly memorable for me was the 1949 Boulder, Colorado meeting, the second of the newly initiated summer meetings held jointly with the mathematical associations. One session with which I was particularly concerned as Secretary of the Society and member of the program committee was a joint session with the other organizations that was devoted to a symposium on the mathematical training of social scientists. I invited Frank L. Griffin, my major professor in mathematics at Reed College, to be a panel member, since he had been a member of the 1930 Social Science Research Council committee on the collegiate mathematics needed in the social sciences. The report of that committee was published in *Econometrica* in 1932. I also asked Harold Hotelling of Columbia University and Jacob Marschak, the latter to be chairman of the session. Marschak added others to the panel. A report of the symposium appears in *Econometrica*, April 1950. At the conclusion of the symposium, a motion by George Kuznets of the University of California, Berkeley, called for a committee to conduct a study in close contact with various national bodies. Following that I obtained endorsement of the study proposal by officers of related organizations (17 organizations, as I recall), and in consultation with them put together the original committee. I declined Marschak's suggestion that I serve as chairperson, and instead wrote William Madow, Department of Mathematics, University of Illinois, who accepted that role.

Some indication of the questions facing that committee can be found from the following letter I wrote to Madow:

I have now had an opportunity to study your recent memorandum outlining the organization and program of the study committee of which you are chairman, and my comments are indicated below.

The effort which went into organizing and holding the Boulder symposium out of which the resolution to create the committee arose was directed toward the long-run improvement of college and graduate curricula necessary to provide adequate mathematical training for social scientists. It was recognized that there was considerable range in the need for mathematical training among students of social science subjects, according to the roles which these students ultimately plan to assume, these roles varying from those who draw upon the existing body of knowledge for teaching or other applications to those who seek to extend that body of knowledge through research and perhaps even attempt some integration of thought between social and physical scientists.

The differing needs of students [should be] taken into account not in terms of number of years of expected education but in terms of the function or role which the students intend to perform.

Referring again to the objectives for which the present study committee was constituted, I must express some concern about the change in objective which seems to be indicated by the new title you have suggested giving to the committee. It was recognized that part of the need for mathematical training arose from the mathematical prerequisites for a knowledge of the statistical techniques found to be of value in the social sciences. It was not contemplated as serving the purpose of the committee, however, for it to recommend that extent of mathematical training which would be required to train those who would be statisticians first, and social scientists only second. The mathematical training of those who would develop statistics is clearly different matter from that of those who would apply or develop the social sciences.

I recommend strongly, therefore, that the title of the committee be either ''Committee on the Mathematical Training of Social Scientists'' or, if the added explicitness is desired, ''Committee on the Mathematical and Statistical Training of Social Scientists.''

I wonder if the organizational structure you have indicated is not too ambitious and perhaps unwieldy. There is, for instance, the practical question as to whether or not anything closely approximating the proposed representativeness of the sub-committee can be obtained without an amount of effort which would seriously delay the beginning of actual study of the problem. Is it, for instance, necessary that a certain number not have had mathematical training, or is it sufficient that (whether trained mathematically or not) the individuals possess reputations in their respective fields which would make their constituency receptive to their recommendations, not as a mathematician speaking in favor of mathematics, but as an economist, for instance, giving his considered views on a matter on which he is competent to speak?

One final point, although thought need not be given to it until much later, I would recommend that a fourth item be added to the program of the committee, namely, the study of possible ways and means whereby the recommendations of the study committee can be implemented.

The support given the committee by the Social Science Research Council and the good works following therefrom are chronicled elsewhere.

Gerhard Tintner accepted responsibility in 1951 for a project consisting of the collation of definitions of econometrics and preparation of encyclopedia and dictionary entries. His report was published in *Econometrica*, January 1953.

In April 1952 I circulated to about fifty individuals a memorandum on two proposals for extending the activities of the Econometric Society into areas where I believed it could be of considerable service to the profession.

The first proposal was that the officers of the Econometric Society be authorized to arrange for procedures whereby unpublished provisional materials of interest to members could be reproduced and given limited distribution on the basis that all initial costs were borne by the originator of the material or his institution and the costs of filling subsequent requests were borne by the recipients.

The response was almost evenly divided. However, certain considerations put forward by Professors Hotelling and Leontief as well as by Samuelson, convinced me that the Society should not enter that activity without further study. The considerations related to (a) the screening of materials to lighten the burden on readers (both the screening exercised by authors in selecting material for circulation and that of editors in selecting material for publication); (b) leaving the author as sole judge of the distribution of preliminary materials; (c) the avoidance of priority fights which might result from the circulation of material ''in the shadow zone between publication and non-publication''; and (d) avoidance of centralization which reduces inter-research group communication.

The second proposal was that the officers of the Econometric Society be authorized to arrange for a publication channel intermediate between journal and book publication, to be known by some title such as ''Occasional Papers of the Econometric Society,'' for materials critically selected by its editors as being of interest to members of the Society (articles too long for *Econometrica*, econometric doctoral dissertations, translations, etc.) for which the author or his institution is willing to participate in meeting publication costs.

The replies were predominantly in support of the proposal, and it was approved. I comment here only on the objections that were raised.

One objection related to the editorial burden of providing critical review of both the formal correctness and scientific importance of contributions before they would be accepted as Occasional Papers.

A related objection was that it would be difficult for the editors to refuse the publication of material as Occasional Papers since the authors would meet all or part of the cost of publication. This was not so much a question of diplomacy and of the employment of impartial procedures, as it was of whether or not the exercise of impartiality and insistence on standards would enjoy continued support should material be declined from those of established reputation. The caliber of the material in question, not the prestige of the individual, should determine acceptance. As I wrote to the president of the Econometric Society at that time, it was an open question as to whether the Society had attained the political maturity needed to assure that support. I had in mind the pressure that was occasionally brought to bear upon an editor in connection with not publishing a manuscript, and the lapses of those who should have supported the independence of the editorial function.

The Society's intention to sponsor a series of special publications was announced to readers in October 1954.

At the time I was withdrawing from my Econometric Society responsibilities, I was making arrangements for the publication of a Japanese translation of Trygve Haavelmo's "The Probability Approach in Econometrics," which had appeared in *Econometrica*, July 1944. It was in preparation by Isamu Yamada of Hitotsubashi University, Tokyo. Royalties from the sale of the edition were to be used for the purchase of econometric materials for presentation to libraries in Japan.

The Econometric Society was a component of the Allied Social Science Associations and had a relationship to the American Academy for the Advancement of Science which resulted in joint meetings being held with sections of the two organizations. I maintained a close working relationship with the officers of the various related organizations.

Starting in 1949, I served, together with Jan Tinbergen of The Netherlands, as representative of the Econometric Society to the International Statistical Institute. Usually this was more a formalism than a matter of practical consequence, but it did provide for communication. A commentary on a provisional report of the International Statistical Institute to UNESCO on the future of statistical education was prepared by Harold Hotelling at my request and was submitted to the ISI.

The Econometric Society also provided consultant services to the Economic and Social Council of the United Nations in 1949.

The Econometric Society cooperated informally with the Training Center for Economic and Financial Statistics which was being established in Santiago, Chile, by the Inter American Statistical Institute and Pan American Union as part of the technical assistance program of the United Nations. A consultative panel was appointed by the Society to assist in designing a set of courses appropriate to the objectives of the Center's program.

Upon invitation in 1951, the Econometric Society established a representative relationship with the Division of Mathematics of the National Research Council, under the auspices of the National Academy of Sciences of the United States. John von Neumann of Princeton University was the designated representative.

In February 1951, after approval from the Council, I attempted but without success, to obtain UNESCO support for an international survey of research groups, centers of instruction, professional organizations, and serial publications related to the quantitative approach in economics. What did emerge after some exchanges of correspondence was agreement that the Econometric Society would prepare a report on the teaching of econometrics to be incorporated into UNESCO's general report on the teaching of economics. A stipend was authorized by UNESCO, and I obtained agreement from Professor Gerhard Tintner to undertake the study. Countries included within the report were Egypt, France, India, Mexico, Poland, Sweden, and the United Kingdom and the United States. The report was transmitted to UNESCO in May 1952. It was published in *Econometrica* in January 1954, and was included by UNESCO as part of a series on the university teaching of the social sciences.

Members of the Society were encouraged to identify possible candidates for membership for whom their name could be used in a letter of invitation to join. This proved to be a successful approach.

Much to my surprise I found that the popularity of the Society in South America had already become such that enterprising members were selling their endorsement of others for membership. They added appropriate initials after their names to indicate the honor that they believed membership conferred. The mercantile aspects of this membership effort had to be discouraged.

An emeritus membership status was approved by the Council in 1951 and an institutional non-voting membership was approved the following year.

The costs of carrying a large inventory of back volumes of the journal were reduced by offering libraries complete sets to date at an attractive price. These libraries were then a source of new subscriptions. By 1952, the journal was being mailed to over 2700 individuals and libraries in 72 different countries. A geographical index of members and subscribers was added as a feature of *Econometrica* starting in 1949.

I gained much from the presentations that I heard at the many sessions of professional meetings I attended. I also valued the friendships that I developed among members of the profession.

Econometricians are people first and social scientists secondarily. They have their own frailties and shortcomings. I mention four cases among individuals who have received the highest professional recognition for their academic contributions: (1) When I pointed out a mistake in a mathematical proof, an author asked me to edit out a few lines so that it would not be noticed. (2) An author who learned of a way to improve his paper from a presentation at a meeting incorporated it into his own paper without attribution. (3) A professor accepted appointments from three or possibly four universities as of the coming September intending to play off one against the other at the last moment.

The fourth example affected the course of my own life. It happened early in 1952. I was working in the evening in my university office when the research director for the Cowles Commission came in, emotionally distraught. There was an uncontrolled outpouring of problems in his personal life, including his sense of personal inadequacy, which I would have preferred not to hear. This was in spite of his immense professional capability in his own field of research. (See, for instance, the appreciation of Koopmans' work in Malinvaud (1972).) He then recounted in detail, with evident satisfaction, how he had worked against me on various matters on which he had expressed no reservations. I thought that we were working together quite well.

I had developed, in consultation with the faculty of the Commission and the chairman of the Department of Economics, an offer to an earlier full-time staff member of the Commission who was currently a consultant, of a joint appointment at the University in the Commission and the Department of Economics. Koopmans revealed that, unknown to others at the time, he had independently contacted the potential appointee (a one-time Communist Party member and future Nobel Prize winner) and intentionally influenced him to decline the offer.

Whether or not Koopmans had given in to pressure from the Federal Bureau of Investigation because of my refusal to engineer the departure of staff members in whom the Bureau had an interest (see preceding chapter), I can only speculate.

I was greatly surprised and shaken by these revelations. Koopmans had benefited considerably from my work for years, although we had different views as to the role of a research director, as described in the previous chapter. Only recently the University had extended my contract for several years with considerable improvement in salary, a supplement for a pension plan, and one-fourth of my time to be set aside for my own research. One factor explaining Koopmans' behavior may have been his opposition to the growth of the Commission. Another factor may have been his discomfiture with the hostility shown him by Friedman and his supporters at Chicago. Since I was a proponent of the Commission continuing at Chicago, though even more independently organized than before, I was viewed by Koopmans as an obstacle to the Commission being moved to Yale University.

Several at the University, as well as myself, attempted to work out a reconciliation without success. It became difficult for us to work together. I could see no alternative but to leave a position which I had come to regard as fulfilling and worthwhile and suitable to my abilities and interests. I reluctantly took a paid leave of absence from the University and the Cowles Commission starting several months later, with my resignation as Executive Director to become effective a year from the following September, that is, in September 1953.

Although others argued against it, I decided to withdraw also from my positions with the Econometric Society and *Econometrica*. Accordingly, I indicated to the Council of the Econometric Society in

May 1952 that I wished to resign as Secretary effective October 1952 following the completion of four terms in that position, but would continue as Co-Editor of *Econometrica* until March 1953. In the interim I assisted in the transition. Robert Strotz of Northwestern University was named to be the next managing editor. He took over the incoming manuscripts for *Econometrica* and I completed work on those already under consideration. The January 1953 issue and the *Twenty Year Author and Analytical Subject Index for Econometrica* were completed before I left Chicago. The offices of the Econometric Society were transferred first to Yale University and then to Northwestern University. Strotz, incidentally, some years later became president of Northwestern University.

The Cowles Commission gave up its announced move towards a publicly responsible active board of directors for which I had been the principal proponent. Shortly thereafter, the Cowles Commission ended its independent corporate status and its academic affiliation with the University of Chicago and was transformed into the Cowles Foundation for Research in Economics, an activity of the Department of Economics at Yale University. Five members of the Commission made the move to Yale, Koopmans having led the way by accepting a visiting professorship at Yale in 1954. Alfred Cowles and members of his family provided Yale University with endowment funds for the activities of the Cowles Foundation.

So ended the period at Chicago which Professor Isamu Yamada of Tokyo, a frequent visitor to the United States, described as the "golden years of the Cowles Commission and econometrics." A commendation of my efforts was added by the staff to the page proofs of the *Twenty-Year Research Report of the Cowles Commission for Research in Economics*. In addition, the following appeared in the April 1953 issue of *Econometrica*:

> The Society wishes to express its appreciation for the devoted services of William B. Simpson, who resigned recently as secretary of the Society and as co-editor of *Econometrica*.
> Largely as a result of his vigorous efforts the Society and the Journal have both doubled in size during the past four years.
> That this rapid growth in the Journal was brought about without deterioration of publication standards is a tribute to Mr.
> Simpson's editorial diligence and persistence of purpose. Other evidences of his ardent interest in the development of econometrics are to be found in the increase in Society meetings through-

out the world, greater participation by the Society in co-operative arrangements with other professional groups, completion of the twenty year author index and analytical subject guide to *Econometrica*, and the expansion of Society finances. Mr. Simpson's contributions toward the achievement of Society objectives and the energy with which he pursued them will long be remembered.

Letters of appreciation were received from many individuals, including R.G.D. Allen (London School of Economics and Political Science), Alfred Cowles, F. Divisia (Ecole Polytechnique Laboratoire D'Econométrie), Ragnar Frisch (University of Oslo), Wassily Leontief (Harvard University), Paul Samuelson (Massachusetts Institute of Technology), Jan Tinbergen (Netherlands School of Economics), and Herman Wold (University of Upsala).

It was a period in which I worked with individuals of great accomplishment. Of those on the Cowles Commission staff or its Executive Committee, ten had by 1991 received the Nobel Prize in Economics. Of those serving with me in editing *Econometrica*, an additional five became Nobel Laureates. There was occasional contact with four more who received that honor.

Fundamental approaches which shaped econometrics were being developed at the Cowles Commission, approaches which have been carried by former staff members to universities throughout the world. Some of these ideas, as they relate to model building and to mathematical programming, have been described by me in the course of writing *Cost Containment for Higher Education: Strategies for Public Policy and Institutional Administration* (1991).

A significant aspect of this period was that the combined efforts of the Cowles Commission, the Econometric Society, and its journal *Econometrica* contributed to econometrics progressing from the endangered discipline list to acceptance in the social science profession. Additional journals have since appeared to publish the increasing flow of econometric materials. The Cowles Commission (Foundation), the Econometric Society, and *Econometrica* have all continued in subsequent years to contribute to economic theory, measurement, and application, and to empower others to work upon the human problems that are still with us.

7.1

Some Issues in Methodology

(1948)

In these comments on Koopmans' reply to Vining I stress not the broad areas in which I find myself in agreement with the draft manuscripts in question, but rather the misgivings to which they give rise.

The manuscripts by Vining and Koopmans appear to share faults common to most discussions generated by controversy. Each writer focuses his attention on that portion of the range of problems for which his own methodology is the more appropriate, with the effect of placing such emphasis upon the propriety of his own methodology as to suggest that no room exists for that of the other contributor. Since there are impressive truths to be gleaned from both articles, understanding would be advanced if more recognition were given to the complementary rather than competing aspects of the respective arguments.

Much of the value of Vining's paper lies in his discussion of the nature and importance of "hypothesis-seeking." Yet Koopmans gives this brief mention, expressing an inability to see any difference in kind between the problems of hypothesis-seeking and the problems discussed in the theory of estimation or in the Neyman-Pearson theory of hypothesis testing. It is surely possible to distinguish between the activity of choosing the direction of investigation and the activity of the investigation itself. If so, is it not reasonable to suppose that the most appropriate techniques for one activity differ from those appropriate for the other? Although any such line of demarcation must indeed be conceptual, it should serve to separate, at least for purposes of discussion, the problem of so approaching materials and ideas as to allow that unrestricted and free roving of the intelligence which is necessary for the gaining of new insights and suggesting of fresh hypotheses, from the problem of so fashioning these same materials and ideas against a background of accepted hypotheses as to allow the extraction of the maximum amount of information. Realism would seem to demand that a difference in kind be recognized as existing between these two problems.

Vining, in springing to the "defense of empiricism as a fundamental part of scientific procedure," is really talking abut the first of these problems. In doing so, he performs both a service and a disservice for the empirical approach; the former by speaking forth on its behalf, the latter by doing so in terms of a particular piece of research on business cycles (by Mitchell and Burns) which many would regard as having progressed beyond hypothesis-seeking and into the stage where the employment of statistical procedures against a formal theoretical structure would be more fruitful.

Vining moreover somewhat confuses Koopmans' advocacy of using a theoretical structure (e.g., measurement not without theory) with an unstated advocacy of the mathematical (or rather symbolic) form of expression, and in doing so holds forth unnecessarily against the mathematical approach.

Whether or not social usefulness is a relevant criterion for economic research was discussed controversially rather than cooperatively by Koopmans and Vining largely because each addressed himself to a different problem. Koopmans, I assume, would not deny that the exploratory, sometimes introspective, search which points out new approaches to economic problems should not be restricted by a research criterion of (immediate, apparent) social usefulness, while Vining, I feel sure, would agree that when a set of hypotheses has been decided upon, the criterion of social usefulness is relevant to economic model construction.

Vining's general position with respect to measurement with theory takes the following form when applied to behavior questions in particular:

(a)   that to rely upon a theoretical structure based upon the motivations of the individual economizing agent in his conscious problem-solving state of mind is unduly restrictive and puts a straight jacket upon economic research, there being possibly more fruitful alternative approaches;

(b)   that "the aggregate has an existence apart from its constituent particles and behavior characteristics of its own not deducible from the behavior characteristics of the particles;''

(c)   that the behavioristic relations and technological restrictions currently employed are perhaps not the most fundamental autonomous relations and may not possess the degree of invariance ascribed to them, being, as Veblen pointed out, ''functions of an institutional variable that is of a highly complex and wholly unstable character.'' Supplementing what Koopmans has to say in regard to these points, I would offer the following comments:

There is little question but that the individual agent is an appropriate unit of analysis, but the danger lies in thinking too narrowly of his actions as being rational economic behavior. The rationality of individual action is itself open to question. Thinking is in large measure a crisis activity, and a wide range of responses come almost automatically from habit, or from unconscious analogy with experience. Thus, the exigencies of the present are met by actions based in large part upon ex-ante data . . . This is partly a matter of non-rational behavior and partly a mater of imperfect information . . . Beyond the question of awareness of alternatives lies that of the more or less conscious deciding what weights should be given to the different considerations . . .

Economics has so far only imperfectly integrated such conceptions into its treatment of human behavior. The maximizing, economizing, mini-max motivations, and so forth which are ascribed to individual action in its economic aspects inadequately cope with the problems involved. The dynamics of investment decisions remain largely unexplored and investment is treated as an autonomous influence. The analysis of the equilibrium of the consumer starts with an indifference map which is presumed to already reflect the interplay of the considerations (other than opportunity) entering into choice. What is essentially a dynamic process of interaction between an individual and other individuals and the social structure is replaced by a static picture. Aside from such recognition as is given to complementary commodities, consumption decisions are largely treated moreover as though they were taken independently, whereas perhaps a majority of purchases are made as part of a consumption pattern to which the individual has been committed by circumstance or by an earlier choice. The treatment of entreprenurial decisions is perhaps in no better state. Far too little has been done in investigating the development and role of expectations. Here one must not overlook the curious phenomenon that in economics changes in the current state of knowledge of the subject matter actually change the field of inquiry. The question of the reversibility of economic relations is also one deserving further thought. Any study of the behavior relations under-lying a supply curve for labor should, for instance, take into account the fact that the threshold values for entering and leaving pecuniary employment are different, because of the changes which take place in the individual's pattern of social interaction.

The social scientist who seeks to express the uniformities of action which exist between different individuals in terms of funda-mental behavioristic relations has no easy task. From the viewpoint of the economist, moreover, it is not enough that the existence of psychological propensities be established, since these propensities may find a subtle expression through actions other than those directly affecting the market.

One of the main problems confronting the economist is that of taking into account the effects on the economic mechanism of the politico-sociological-psychological influences regarded generally as non-economic. The general tendency seems to have been to either classify the influences as being relatively invariant or to account for the influences by random terms introduced into the structural equa-tions. There has, perhaps, been more interest shown in specifying the nature of the joint probability distribution of the random variables appearing in the model, than there has been in isolating as separate variables more and more of the unexplained variation . . . To this extent there may be a conflict between efforts to obtain information efficiently, and efforts to construct an explicitly complete theoretical model. It also, undoubtedly, has been due in part to the need for keeping economic models within manageable size. But unless one places extremely great emphasis upon the role of chance, circum-stance, and personality upon human affairs, it is hard to justify relegating almost all ''non-economic'' influences into catch-all ran-dom terms. In particular, it would seem to become increasingly difficult to justify the hypothesis of normality for their joint distribu-tion.

We turn finally to Koopmans' denial of Vining's claim (see b above) that an aggregate can have ''behavior characteristics of its own not deducible from the behavior characteristics of the par-ticles.'' Koopmans counters Vining by maintaining that whatever happens must be worked out by the actions of individuals and is deducible from their behavior characteristics. This calls for some qualification. Vining, for instance, has pointed out that there are ''social organisms that are distinctly more than simple algebraic aggregates of consciously economizing individuals.'' An aggregate may be regarded both as an initiating force and as a conditioning force. The informal aggregate known as a mob initiates actions commonly attributable to mob psychology, not to the behavior characteristics of an individual considered by himself. Formal aggregates such as governments initiate action which again is not deducible from the behavior characteristics of an individual. This independent existence of an aggregate capable of initiating action is in fact reflected in economic models by appropriate exogenous variables and by the inclusion of institutional or technological restrictions.

The role of the aggregate as a conditioning force is really more the matter at issue. But while the (conditioning) influence upon individual action of an aggregate (via the existence of social consensuses) is more perceptible than the influence which the individual has in changing the socially validated values, it is nevertheless an influence which is worked out through the medium of the individual.

The solution would seem to be not a denial of the importance to be attached to a study of the aggregate itself, but a recognition that for many problems the influence of the aggregate is sufficiently invariant as to enable one to regard it as the background against which the behavior characteristics of the individual are to be analyzed. Just how fundamental and invariant are the behavior relations so attained may be better judged in the light of the above remarks.

8

Evolvement of a Philosophy

In my opening chapter I wrote about taking charge of one's life and about the role of a master loyalty that gives one's life a sense of purpose. I focused on a particular type of master loyalty—a personal philosophy—which allows an individual to remain in charge of his or her life within the constraints that are operative. It consists of criteria by which to judge what purposes to further. As you live and learn, and your personal behavior conjoins with events of the world, you make new appraisals to guide your behavior.

Much of learning is informal, unstructured, and without focused purpose. Even so, there is a process of obtaining information, forming views, and arriving at conclusions which are tested against reality.

We develop concepts as to what we value (positively or negatively), and expectations as to the payoff in terms of such values if we follow one or another course of action.

The facts that we take into account depend on the existing boundary of our concern (or put another way, the horizon within which we acknowledge to ourselves a sense of responsibility). What we regard as facts depends also upon our perceptiveness and sensitivity to elapsed and possible events within that boundary, which is interrelated with the distinctions we can categorize through the conceptual richness of our language.

For purposes of our discussion, we can separate conceptually the following stages of inquiry, however informally they may be conducted:

(1) Formulation of an hypothesis from given information.
(2) Reasoning as to the implications of this hypothesis.
(3) Comparison of those implications with perceived reality.

(4) Enlargement of our information as a basis for a possible alternative or modified hypothesis, which leads again to stage (1). Stages (2) and (3) comprise hypothesis-testing, Stages (4) and (1) comprise hypothesis-seeking.

For many individuals, what I have identified as "hypothesis-testing" takes the form of experiencing consequences. More deliberative individuals will consider consequences in advance. For some this may be by excluding from their concern possible effects on many contemporaries as well as individuals in the future, applying unexamined values, and employing other short-cut methods of thinking in order to arrive at conclusions with the least effort that will restore a sense of complacency.

Part of a personal philosophy will be a subjective criterion for selecting, for instance, among alternative career choices and life styles. You may, for example, depending upon whether you are venturesome or cautious, seek to maximize expected satisfaction or minimize expected regret.

In *Hamlet* (Act I, Scene 3), Shakespeare has expressed the following thought which is usually taken for granted:

This above all: To thine own self be true.

And it must follow, as the night the day,

Thou canst not then be false to any man.

Were this assertion entirely valid, virtue would automatically be assured. A hedonistic bottom-line personal philosophy and a completely unregulated market system could then be justified. However, there are arguments to the contrary that should be persuasive.

One is that when you use others as instruments of your own purposes, being concerned only with the effects upon yourself, there will without doubt still be effects upon others, not all of which will be true to their best interests. Also, there are costs that will come back upon you as a boomerang. As John Donne has expressed it (*Devotions*, XVII, 1624):

No man is an island, entire of itself; . . .

never send to know for whom the bell tolls;

it tolls for thee.

The extent to which the personal pursuit of satisfaction is identifiable with serving others will depend, among other considerations such as your values, skills, knowledge, on the boundary of your concern, that is, upon how inclusive is the group for which the advancement of its welfare would bring you satisfaction. It depends upon the extent to which you are influenced by possible positive or negative effects that projected actions would have upon others in the present or future. My conception of being moral consists of taking the indirect and subsequent effects of one's actions into account in one's decisions. In this sense there is a moral dimension to be considered in selecting the purposes to be served.

Decisions reached from a narrow viewpoint leave one smaller in spirit for being self-centered. One foregoes the enhanced level of feeling experienced by being appreciative of the complex of human relationships from which one cannot be fully separate. As expressed in "A Creed" by Edwin Markham, Poet Laureate for Oregon (*Lincoln and Other Poems*, 1901):

> There is a destiny that makes us brothers:
>   None goes his way alone:
> All that we send into the lives of others
>   Comes back into our own.

Related to this is the advantage of gaining access to knowledge and to diverse capacities and perspectives which are better coordinated with you than aligned against you. Or to quote Markham again, this time his poem "Outwitted" (*Shoes of Happiness & Other Poems*, 1915):

> He drew a circle that shut me out—
> Heretic, rebel, a thing to flout.
> But Love and I had the wit to win:
> We drew a circle that took him in!

Participation within academe follows from recognizing the contribution of a shared governance approach to guiding institutions of higher education. It is the empowerment of a highly qualified body of individuals in the furtherance of shared objectives. Within business, it follows from recognizing the importance of interrelating with a corporation's multiple constituencies: stock and bondholders, governing board, corporate bureaucracy, labor force, customers, and the general public. What it means in the relations of sovereign nations will be considered in the following chapter and especially in the annexes thereto.

It has already been mentioned that a personal philosophy, since it consists not of fixation on particular objectives but of criteria for selecting purposes to serve, allows flexibility to adjust to outside influences upon one's life. In addition, one's personal philosophy, i.e., set of decision criteria, should evolve with personal growth, particularly growth in analytic skills, appreciative capacities, knowledge, and as stressed in an earlier chapter, confidence in one's own abilities. At first one takes much on authority, but with increased confidence in one's knowledge and skills, one will defer less to others and rely more upon one's own judgment. You begin to consider the extent to which the differences you have with others reflect differences in information available or in value orientation. Hopefully, you apply improved analytic skills to testing your hypotheses and an openness to enlarging the boundary of your concern, modifying as necessary your hypotheses.

As one values his or her talents more, and recognizes that they may be relatively scarce, it makes sense to seek that they be used efficiently. Thus I learned techniques for accomplishing objectives (serving as a catalyst, inspiring others, coopting, delegating, instructing, giving credit to others, etc.). Empowering others conserved my resources when I was fully engaged.

Efficiency addresses the ratio of measured output to measured input. It does not address the question as to whether efforts are in the best direction. There may be several combinations of purposes served that are efficient, but only one that is optimum from the standpoint of one's set of values. To find the optimum use of your talents may require casting your net more broadly as to what you take into account, searching for new hypotheses and courses of action. In contrast to the deductive analysis used in the reasoning to conclusions that is required for testing hypotheses, the search for modified or alternative hypotheses is an inductive process. I have commented upon this contrast in the essay on methodological issues (Annex 7.1) which precedes this chapter.

Since the values served and the boundaries of concern are largely individual matters, a philosophy of life that leads one to efficient use of one's talents and to purposes that are optimal in terms of one's values does not guarantee that the direction of effort will serve society. Assisting others to be effective is an act of optimism. It is undertaken in the belief that as more and more individuals derive satisfaction within broad boundaries of concern, the self-motivated actions of individuals will enhance rather than diminish the sense of community essential for a society.

An individual taking charge of his or her life, guided by initial proclivities and a personal philosophy, could focus on serving purposes in any of many areas of activity: business, public service, professional work, the arts, environmental concerns, and so forth. In the case of academe, as I said in a journal article (1985), individual faculty come into academic life for a variety of reasons: love of ideas or interest in a particular field, liking for the activity involved in teaching or research, interest in the effects that may be produced, or some combination of these.

My own choice of an academic life was because I looked upon it as providing opportunities for making fundamental contributions: research in analytic methods that could further understanding, and teaching that empowered the young. I was also interested in working with people and with organizing activities that would accomplish shared objectives. My satisfaction tended to be drawn less from the nature of the activity itself, which on occasion brought adverse reactions when one stood on principle, than from the effects that I could assist in bringing about.

I viewed theory then, and still do, as an eminently practical approach to having an effect upon human affairs. When our objective is to be aware of and act with respect to things as they are, and not with respect to things as they appear to be or should be (a moral valuation), then it is apparent that we must not let the superficial aspects of a situation obscure fundamental relationships. This calls for a recognition of the dominant forces at work, an understanding of the relationships which tend to exist among them, and an ability to apply this information to a particular situation in the light of the circumstances peculiar to it.

Theory provides an abstract statement of relationships while certain variables are regarded as unchanged in value. It is without content, but can have relevance to a particular situation once it is interpreted in terms of specific referents, with the conclusions adjusted to take into account the extent to which conditions that have been taken as given are not satisfied.

My upper division and graduate studies and my research and employment had until then related to a great extent to analytical techniques and hypothesis-testing. Alongside, I had made a concerted effort to understand the context within which applications would be made and what could be considered as alternative public policies. While I would not recommend that one should seek it out, the experience of the Great Depression was an important element in my background. Subsequently I volunteered to enter military service in World War II since I anticipated that my subsequent work would have a bearing upon many individuals, and I believed that I could better understand what was appropriate if I shared what undoubtedly was the major experience of many of my generation. For somewhat the same reason, but also because I believed I could be effective, I volunteered for overseas service, and then for the first combat counter- intelligence units to enter Manila and subsequently Japan.

My professional activities since that war—facilitating a research environment, and facilitating scientific communication, as well as attention to the early preparation of individuals for analytic work—were of the type that empowered others to be effective, with far-reaching consequences, along lines of accomplishment from which I drew satisfaction. This was in line with the personal philosophy I expressed in the preceding chapter that I should use my finite energies to be a catalyst for others in achieving shared objectives.

It was particularly satisfying that I could strengthen support for econometric research work, the Econometric Society, and its journal *Econometrica* during a critical period in which the outcome of each was yet by no means assured.

The events described at the close of the previous chapter, however, seemed to call for a period of detachment from customary pursuits. I was deeply hurt by the deliberate damage done to my career by a close associate who had benefited considerably from my contributions. I turned to considering, in a world context, hypotheses that might be useful in giving effect to a vow taken on an Okinawan hillside.

9

In Search of Hypotheses

With administrative responsibilities related to econometrics set aside, I turned my attention to a matter that had concerned me for some years. On Okinawa during WWII I lost many comrades when a plane crashed in attempting to land on an airship darkened due to an alert for approaching Japanese aircraft. This and earlier events in the war led me to decide while in Okinawa that I would work toward averting future clashes which cut down so many individuals in the prime of life on both sides. What little I could do would have to be in areas in which I hopefully had something to contribute.

Before I enlisted in the war, my research for the bachelor's degree in mathematics and the master's degree in mathematical-statistics had been on the improvement of hypothesis testing. More specifically, both theses were concerned with determining the extent to which statistical tests of significance retained usefulness when normality assumptions underlying them were not satisfied. My initial doctoral research after the war was concerned with the extent of validity of shortcut methods of thinking by an individual (of which the use of significance tests is a special case), and with what could be carried over to the study of decision-taking in an organization from a study of information flows and reactions in the neural system. Moreover in econometrics, once a theoretical model had been formulated, possibly a stochastic simultaneous equation model that hypothesized an explanation for phenomena, there was the numerical specification of the parameters, followed by testing the hypothesis by comparing with reality the values predicted by the model.

In brief, my emphasis to date in mathematical-statistics and econometrics had been on the deductive processes involved in testing initially-stated hypotheses. As to economics, what particularly interested me were those aspects which could be generalized into a theory of choice that was general in the sense that the alternatives need not have a monetary dimension.

In the period ahead, my concern was focused upon searching for a sustainable hypothesis as to a strategy that would lessen resort to war. This was a shift in emphasis from deduction to induction, yet I did not stray far from deductive logic since the hypothesis with which I began was that research and education designed to increase the ability of individuals for intelligent choice, if undertaken in countries throughout the world, would contribute to peaceful international relations.

Such education would need to be made available not only to those who are relatively undereducated in the United States and abroad, but also, and especially, in view of their likely role in policy, to those who already had experienced full access to what existing educational opportunities could offer.

My focus would be on improving the prospect that individuals would be capable of intelligent choice. I understood that decisions are reached in various manners by informal groups (oligopolies, teams, lynch mobs, etc.) and that policies adopted by formal organizations reflect decision processes that require more explanation than simply aggregating individual behavior, but these areas of inquiry were at least conceptually separable. They were, moreover, being addressed by research conducted by the Cowles Commission under a contract I had negotiated with the Office of Naval Research. I viewed this as contributing to diminishing the likelihood of war.

I recognized also that the benefits to be obtained from increasing the ability of individuals to make intelligent choices were determined in part by the individual's initial body of knowledge, and by the access the individual had to new information and to stimuli that would lead the individual to reconsider what was known. Both the initial conditions as to knowledge and access to information are a function of the social institutions and political arrangements of one's country. To improve upon such matters was at least conceptually separable from working toward individuals having improved command of the techniques for intelligent choice.

But what is initially known and the access one has to further information depend not only on institutional arrangements, they depend at least as much on the individual's personal horizon, or boundary of concern, within which space and time dimensions an individual perceives and internalizes what transpires. That horizon is determined by the scope of an individual's interests, by the provision within an individual's vocabulary for conceptualizing distinctions, by the sensitivity of the individual to stimuli, by the individual's sense of identification with or empathy with others, and perhaps by some sense of responsibility. Interrelated with the foregoing, in part as cause and in part as effect, are the individual's values, sense of purpose, and erection of goals.

While these considerations determine the data to which an individual would apply such techniques for choice as he or she might possess, the hope would be that education (including provision for improved grasp of the techniques of choice) would in turn broaden an individual's horizon or boundary of concern such that a sense of satisfaction could be achieved by an individual through furtherance of the wellbeing of others, the horizon being progressively extended.

An essential ingredient is that the individual understand the knowledge he or she possesses and the information to which there is access. This is closely related to but not entirely dependent upon the reasoning techniques that an individual can bring to bear. Understanding requires reference to a body of relationships which is taken, at least tentatively, as correct. If new information does not fit into a particular hypothesis, a reasoned modification of the hypothesis is one option to pursue.

To broaden my own horizons, and to reflect on tentative hypotheses against the background of different cultures and environments, I undertook a fourteen-month trip around the world, interviewing princes and paupers and many inbetween, encountering conflict in many places, and giving thought throughout as to how such conflicts could be minimized in the future.

The challenge I set for myself was both an intellectual adventure as well as something of a physical marathon. Could I, in the face of conflicts the world over, interpret present cultures against the background of their past, penetrate the patchwork of improvisations, and identify for attention possible effort of a long-run nature that could be significant for peaceful relations among nations.

I visited heads of colleges and universities, ministers of education, information and cultural affairs officers, communication media staffs, and political figures. Naturally the viewpoints of frequenters of nightclubs, casinos, race tracks, and the bullring also had to be obtained—to get a balanced set of ideas. I used non-directive approaches in my interviewing so that the responses were not, as a matter of courtesy, shaped to fit preconceptions on my part. I even operated a pneumatic drill for a shift underground in a coal mine in Wales to establish rapport before interviewing miners on socialist policies. In New Delhi I provided a representative of the Ford Foundation with suggestions as to how to facilitate the interpenetration of ideas among different cultures. In various Colombo countries I put forward a recommendation for the formation of an institute for advanced study at some central point such as Brisbane. I describe these two matters more fully in Annexes 9.1 and 9.3, respectively.

The trip served additional purposes: I followed up on work I had done earlier in Manila as head of the economic division of the counter-intelligence office, and visited there my wartime friends, Antonio and Leonie Jalijali and their family, and Florencio and Esperanza Jaime; gathered extensive material on cultural and propaganda exchanges between Hongkong and the Chinese Communist mainland from interviews with British and American officials to be used by a friend for a Master's thesis in the interdisciplinary Committee on Communication at the University of Chicago; examined the original manuscripts of Walras and Pareto, pioneers in mathematical economics, at the Academy in Lausanne, Switzerland; met with professional friends such as Professor Edmond Malinvaud, Institut National de la Statistique et des Etudes Economiques, in Paris, and Sir John R. Hicks, a Nobel Laureate, All Souls College, Oxford University; relived old times with Paul Katona, an Hungarian wartime friend of the New Guinea and Philippine period, who at the time of my visit was the Voice of Hungary for the British Broadcasting Corporation in London; brought tidings from the President of Reed College to various Reed alumni throughout my trip; and visited relatives in Australia, Scotland and England. The trip also served as a diversion after seven strenuous years since the war and partially satisfied my interest in other peoples and countries.

I traveled first toward Asia, my third trip there, and then followed the western tide of empire. Over one hundred points, on five continents, were included in my itinerary. Travel was mainly by air as far as western Europe, after which the method of travel varied from place to place. I returned to the United States on the Cunard liner H.M.S. Queen Elizabeth. I made specific reservations for a few sections of the trip, but left the schedule as open as possible. No accommodations were booked in advance except for places like

Indonesia where they were required before a visa would be issued. While this permitted great flexibility, it also meant that as darkness approached, I had to scout around for a place to spend the night. I traveled light, carrying everything in a small attaché case so I was able to move about readily without having to return to any point to pick up luggage. I used the drip-dry clothing which had recently become available. My travel case was intentionally inexpensive and battered so as to deter theft. I confined my acquisitive tendencies to small items such as carvings which I packaged at intervals and sent back to the United States.

At several places on my trip I was preceded by a few weeks by Adlai Stevenson and his entourage, and his autographed photograph was on the desk of several of the officials I interviewed. I learned too that a staff member of Senator Joe McCarthy, at the opposite end of the political spectrum to Stevenson, had also visited several of the officials.

At that time, about forty years ago, there seemed to be no challenge that I could leave unmet. What was the tallest tower, I climbed. What was the deepest catacomb or Egyptian tomb, I descended. I made a point of swimming in every sea and ocean I encountered, however hot or however cold, and nearly drowned off Old Faleron in Greece. The farthest south on the trip was the southern coast of Tasmania; the farthest north was Scandinavia. The hottest was Agra, India, site of the Taj Mahal, where the train not only arrived behind schedule, but was the preceding day's train. Agra, I was convinced, is an abbreviation for aggravation.

There were also incidents that were amusing. While I was house guest of the U.S. Chief of the Economic Mission in Bangkok, my host invited a prince of the royal family of Thailand (formerly Siam) and his bride to visit. At a late moment he discovered that I had not brought along a tuxedo. He decided that the next best thing was that he and I should wear native garb, shapeless pajamas and T-shirts. The Prince arrived resplendent with top hat and tails, the Princess wore a long evening dress. The contrast was striking, but it did not dampen the evening's activities. The Prince had been educated in the United States, where among other things he learned to play the saxophone. With his help, an audience was subsequently arranged with Prince Dhani, the last Minister of Education before introduction of the constitutional monarchy. A lengthy session with him yielded insight into the relationship between Buddhist doctrine and education in that country. Incidentally, my host's home was guarded by soldiers with machine guns slung on their shoulders. Tanks rolled up next door to protect the Prime Minister's residence from a possible coup d'etat.

Bangkok was a city of temples, heavy traffic and dust, female enticement, and considerable inefficiency. I noted, for instance, that while the main post office had separate mail slots accessible facing the street for various classes of mail and different destinations, inside the building all the mail chutes poured into a single receptacle.

Traveling among islands in Indonesia which were under the control of rival armies involved several customs searches of both person and luggage. At one point an official noted the silica gel used to protect my film from the high humidity. The crystals had taken on a beautiful purple hue, and the unsophisticated official mistook them for precious stones being smuggled. I poured some into his pocket, and he waved me through.

In Djakarta I was aghast at what appeared to have been a blood bath on the steps of the cobwebbed post office, only to be reassured that it was juice ejaculated by natives chewing betel nut.

Istanbul, formerly Constantinople, is a city adjoining and pierced by bodies of water: the Bosphorus which divides the European and Asia Minor portions of the city, the Golden Horn which divides the old Stanboul sector from the modern sector, the Sea of Marmara, and the Black Sea. To the south, the Dardenelles, scene of the battle of Gallipoli of World War I, connects the sea of Marmara with the Aegean Sea. I took several excursions by water, one of them up the Bosphorus to the Black Sea. By a strange quirk of circumstances I was landed at a port in Asia Minor, the last before the Black Sea, where military security considerations precluded tourists. The local sheriff decided I should sit at the end of the dock, sealed off from town by a gate until the next ship. But I wrote a protest in French which held out for a stroll through town and a seat in a beer garden. A Turkish naval officer appeared who had been in the States. Over the protests of the sheriff my request was fulfilled, with the sheriff trailing behind. Two hours later I sailed for ports where my presence was not disputed.

In Rome I attempted to assemble packing materials for dispatching some fragile objects, but the materials I needed were nowhere in evidence, and I did not speak Italian. I explained in a bookstore-stationers shop as best I could what I wanted, and everybody was helpful in bringing out boxes, wrapping paper, straw, etc. Soon the place was in a shambles with wrapping materials spread over the display counters, and everybody trying to help, including the proprietor, the cashier, at least one customer, and three salesgirls. I tried unsuccessfully to recapture the initiative, but with little success. Finally I drew a cartoon of a long automobile with me at the wheel and all the salespeople at the back as "back-seat-drivers." They thought it uproariously funny, and soon were engaged in drawing cartoons also. So I managed to retrieve the stuff and pack it the way I wanted.

On a more serious note, I visited the Acropolis and other fine ruins of noble Greece. Even sat for some hours at the Parthenon thinking over some of my work, hoping that by some process of osmosis I would benefit from the philosophical heritage of that site. I tried that again along Philosophers' Way bordering the River Neckar in Heidelberg.

I worked at my writing in a variety of settings, among them the majestic Grand Pacific Hotel in Suva, Fiji, a humble retreat at the southernmost point in Tasmania, the Raffles Hotel in Singapore, a picturesque open-air accommodation in Bali, a houseboat in Kashmir, a mountain top in Cyprus, an elegant small hotel across from St. Stephens Cathedral in Vienna which was under the care of the Ministry of Monuments, a hotel balcony overlooking the Plaza in Lisbon, a Left Bank garret across from Notre Dame Cathedral in Paris, and finally, the reading room of the British Museum which was near my lodgings in the Bloomsbury section of London.

The Left Bank garret was recommended to me as an inexpensive lodging when I inquired at the Paris airport on arrival in the early hours of the morning. I slept late, and was surprised to find the breakfast table was still so busy, all others being scantily-clad, bosomly females of the Toulouse-Lautrec variety. I had received the off-shift room rate at a Parisian brothel.

I enjoyed companionship where I could find it. Sometimes paths would cross again. An attractive American girl with whom I explored the ancient part of Jerusalem turned up again in Vienna, and we waltzed in a chandeliered ballroom to a string quartet playing the romantic "Blue Danube"—the only dancers on the floor, due to my penchant for eating early by European standards. My travels paralleled those of a young Australian woman in Pompeii, Sorrento and Capri, and her companionship added to the occasion. In New Zealand

I met two vivacious Australian girls on a world tour going in the opposite direction to mine, but we met again in London, visiting together various places in southern England, and were good friends and correspondents subsequently. I met a Lapland girl in Copenhagen who claimed descent from King Robert the Bruce of Scotland—he had been a refugee in her homeland—and she showed me some of the highlights of Scandinavia and saw me off at the airport to Scotland. I saw much of Scotland, England, Ireland and Wales, especially the well-known universities, and many not so well known, and visited many relatives, but I spent the most time in London working on academic matters.

I stayed at a lodging on Gower Street across from the University of London and attended various activities on campus. I often ate at a nearby college cafeteria and learned from discussions with Nigerian students who shared the dinner table of the damage that missionaries had perpetrated upon Africa, drawing on the Bible to enforce discipline and conformity among the tribes, then changing their interpretation when some contrary construction better fitted their convenience.

My Gower Street lodging turned out to be operated by a lesbian. On returning from Trafalgar Square on New Year's Eve, I found a party there in progress with a full complement from the gay community.

While in London I saw on television the spectacle of Senator Joe McCarthy browbeating witnesses.

The London fog became extremely heavy compared to other years, and drew attention even in the U.S. media. It was called a "killer fog," and there were daily death statistics; several people died on nearby Tottenham Court Road. The mantle of heavy fog restricted the movement of air through my room and fumes from the gas heater caused me to have extremely bad headaches. At least that is what I eventually took as the explanation for them. However, I visited University Hospital just up Gower Street and X-rays were taken. I looked at the prints hanging on a wire for drying and the interpretation by the radiologist—something about a possible brain tumor that would require invasive techniques in order to be sure. I removed the material from the wire and quietly left the hospital.

The foregoing influenced me to return to the United States probably earlier than otherwise. The ocean voyage on the Queen Elizabeth was relaxing and the shipboard company was very pleasant, but I was pleased to eventually see the Statue of Liberty. By that time I qualified for the category referred to at the base of the statue, where it said something like ''Give me your tired, your poor.''

Liz, my friend from the Committee on Communication at the University of Chicago, was aware of my health concerns and met me part way to Chicago at Oberlin, where I stopped off to see Dr. Blair Stewart, formerly of Reed, who had become dean of faculty at Oberlin College. Subsequently he was to become president of the Associated Colleges of the Mid-West.

In Chicago I was happy to see Marianne again, the former Army nurse who had been a close friend for many years and with whom I shared many memories. She headed up an experiment with the use of a recovery room at the University of Chicago Hospital. We have kept in touch over the many years since then.

I was back in Chicago after a trip of fourteen months, but it was not for long, and I soon went on to the West Coast.

What emerged from my trip were some observations and hypotheses set forth in the writings which accompany this chapter. The first three—''World Leadership—Long-Term View,'' ''Assisting Other Nations,'' and ''Moving Toward Intelligent Choice''—were completed while I was a guest at the University of London in 1954. The fourth consists of excerpts from letters I wrote in Kashmir and Cairo about my travels.

9.1

World Leadership—A Long-Term View

Under the heading, "We Look at America," the following editorial comment appeared in the *Dublin Evening Herald*: "The mental attitude of hustle and go-getting has one drawback from the long-term point of view . . . People who are always in a rush do not take time to think. One slight criticism that can be made of the Americans is that they have the know-how technically but make few contributions to thought." The full glare of world leadership into which the United States has emerged following World War II is startling in its abruptness, and it is sobering in the realization of the responsibilities that such leadership carries. Americans do have the aptitude for "getting things done." But it is also important that we achieve a sense of perspective and of direction—that we give searching thought to identifying ultimate objectives and the efforts most basic to attaining them. And it is there that we are being most properly criticized.

For more than a year now I have been traveling around the world—visiting over forty countries on five continents, starting from the United States by way of the Pacific. The itinerary included, for instance, primitive Polynesia and Melanesia in the Pacific, as well as British-colonized New Zealand and Australia; the cultures of the far Orient as well as the Philippines, Singapore, Hongkong and Portuguese Macau; the jungle-encircled ruins represented by temples in Bali and Ankor Wat in Cambodia; Vietnam and Thailand; the various parts of what had been British India; Middle Eastern places such as Babylon, Baghdad, Damascus, Beirut, Baalbek, Jericho, Jerusalem, Cairo, Karnak and Thebes on the Upper Nile; then to Cyprus, Turkey in Asia and in Europe, and the Balkans, Greece, Italy, throughout Western Europe and on to Scandinavia and Britain. Soon I will return by way of the Atlantic.

I spoke with people in many walks of life—foreign aid officials; cultural affairs, public relations, and information service officers; local government personnel; educational leaders, faculty and students; editors and journalists; the lay-minded and the theologian; professional men and woman, artisans, shopkeepers, laborers in factory, farm and mine; even some princes and some paupers— sometimes expressing my own beliefs, but mainly questioning, listening, learning, and trying to understand the impressions gathered from this trip and two earlier periods in Asia. I heard plausible arguments on both sides of many questions. I saw tremendous energies poured into implementing the conflicting conclusions on which men of good will have acted. There is a cliché about the world growing smaller; a corollary to this is that whether we like it or not, an international morality must emerge—an inter-social consciousness adequate to the now broader range of man's activities. There is a groping for it, of course, that is going on. But can we arrive at a way of living together which is not simply a product of circumstance and a rationalization of the distribution of power? And can we do this in a manner which does not violate the fundamental values held by others?

Political differences in the world are being dealt with at many levels. General humanitarian aims are set forth in United Nations declarations and United States policy statements; regional organizations are being developed which through the interrelated allocation of authorities are presumed to lessen the possibility of aggression among its members; and nations are being equipped for self-defense and to take their position in the alignment against the Soviet bloc. We recognize the important role of leaders who strive to develop their economies, and the difficulty of their task in view of the pressure of expectations of their people; supporting them with economic aid and technical assistance, and encouraging the needed inflow of capital for industrialization. And we hope that with rising levels of material well-being, aided by programs of mass education and encouraged by informational activities as to democracy, freedom of choice, etc., the people of these lands will gain added appreciation of the freedoms which would be lost under communism.

Nevertheless, I have felt misgivings grow as I lived with these problems on my journey. Foremost is uncertainty as to whether the

United States has given sufficient thought to a modus vivendi looking beyond security to the establishment of the confidence basic to an unthreatening coexistence of such different arrangements of political and economic life as are represented by the communist and non-communist worlds. The United Nations is relevant in this connection, but its role has been weakened to the extent the United States has initiated and pursued international programs independently of it, and by the lack of arrangements through which unfavored governments seeking recognition might come within its framework.

Averting a clash with the Soviet earns for the free world the opportunity to solve underlying problems in a more orderly fashion. One may question, however, whether we are in fact acting with the needed dispatch and scale of effort. Technical assistance, encouragement of outside private capital, and emphasis on "trade not aid" are all valuable, both as to approach and in lightening the burden of sponsoring nations, but will have to be vigorously pursued to be of decisive magnitude. Even in a country advancing well with our aid, economic development is likely to be a political issue, and further and possibly more rapid advance may be sought. There is need for realizing the capital resources required for rehabilitating Korea and Indo China, for developing Asia and Africa, for giving support to wavering economies in Europe, and for countering social and political unrest in South America. I doubt that the American taxpayer has a realistic conception of the demands this may place upon our economy, or that our security depends, in part, upon resolving the economic problems of our adherents.

That part of our security which rests upon the maintenance of bases in Asia, Africa, and Europe is subject to possible weakening as governments, to avoid apparent dependence upon the United States and to secure maximum benefits from the world situation, become increasingly receptive to Soviet offers of trade and economic concessions tied to lesser commitments to the free world. To maintain a system of satellites of our own would require forbearance on our part if coercion is to be avoided. The hopes of the free world are pinned on nationalistic forces within the Soviet and its satellites, which itself can create new problems.

I have wondered whether we are sufficiently aware of difficulties facing attempts to explain America's role to the world. Our incantations on democracy, freedom of choice, the dignity of the individual, etc., for instance, lose much of their force alongside the incongruity of our backing, although on different and defensible grounds, leaders who are anything but symbols of political liberalism. Due partly to approach and partly to scale of resources, our information program, moreover, does not have sufficient access to the average citizen. It has to struggle just to offset misconceptions as to America and, more importantly, the resentment that is currently prevalent. Admittedly the harshness of the criticisms made against us reflects in part such factors as the loss of national confidence experienced by the French, the painful adjustments of Britain, politically and economically, to a lesser role in world affairs, the reluctance of nations more concerned with regional issues (as the Arab League is with Israel and Suez) than with the free world scrimmage with communism, and so forth. It is important to bear in mind that there are bases for these resentments in our own attitudes and actions, and that until at least mitigated, they remain formidable obstacles to the effectiveness of our information program and to confidence in our leadership.

For over an hour I listened and gave answer to a prominent Indian scientist in Calcutta venting his displeasure with the United States. It was an outpouring of assertions regarding American and Soviet policy and indictments of American motivation based upon limited experiences in the United States, on hearsay, "admissions" in our press, and Soviet propaganda. Subsequently on the plane I took note of those of his assertions I remembered. Examples: That Russia is and has been desirous of having communism and capitalism coexist peacefully in respective spheres of influence, but U.S. militarism has prevented this. That American action in Korea being outside the United Nations framework in its first days was analogous to the Japanese attack on Pearl Harbor. That political and economic imperialism motivate American intervention in Asia. That there is an initial proclivity on the part of the American people to side with the entrenched interests in a foreign country rather than with a popular movement, and to employ the hydrogen bomb rather than peaceful techniques. And there were the inevitable references to American racial intolerance, McCarthyism, and mounting juvenile delinquency. Various of the allegations had been heard earlier on my trip and were to be heard further on, and new ones were encountered as I entered the Middle East and Europe. To get at the basic sources of the antagonism requires partly that we understand better those with whom we deal; also that we understand ourselves better. There has probably been no greater opportunity than now to ''see ourselves as others see us.''

''But Sammy owns the ball.'' That, to paraphrase a recent critic of the United States, summarized a reason often given in Europe for heeding American's signals and playing by our rules in the contest with the Soviets. It is not the wisdom of our youthful nation, but Uncle Sam's dollars which earn us the leading role.

More serious is the attitude that the United States poses a threat to world peace by the very policies we advocate to safeguard it—that American policy that started with a police action and widened to the task of building security for the free world offers only the prospect of a stalemate between two power blocs, the leadership of each having at command the means to plunge the world into atomic destruction. Our continued shift in emphasis from economic aid to the more immediate effectiveness of military assistance, reflecting an appraisal of the timetable of communist intentions and the need to quickly arrive at a position of strength from which to negotiate, together with our concern that the exploration of alternatives not undermine adherence to the global strategy of containing communism or endanger negotiations for Western European unity, has led to a characterization of American policy as too rigid and as mistaking a military policy for a foreign policy. This emphasis on military agreements, our position with respect to trade with the Soviet bloc, our nonrecognition of Red China, our emphasis on moral righteousness (one critic: ''The United States is a self-appointed deputy God in international affairs'') were all repeatedly cited as creating dangerous cleavages. Nor has our recent concentration on atomic weapons and air power, and references to countering Soviet aggression at points of our own selection, been reassuring to free world critics of America, being no answer to rigidity of response and possibly creating a ''shadow zone'' of incidents of insufficient provocation for atomic retaliation. The alternative implied by critics, but never spelled out in full, seems to be a more fluid approach that avoids pronouncing hard and fast lines of difference, relies on compromise and the reduction of tension through guarantees and increased contacts, and concentrates on orderly arrival at a basis for live and let live. As I interpret the Indian viewpoint, such should have been the approach from the outset. Others apparently consider that it should have been adopted once readiness to engage in police action had been demonstrated, and some minimal security was achieved from which to negotiate. Definitely over-simplified, this nevertheless points up how many Europeans and Asians see the problem of American foreign policy and explains their adopted role as mediators between "the errant extremists," namely, the Soviets and the United States.

Observers note that early constructive "initiatives" of American foreign policy—among them the policy reversals which set aside the "hard peace" for Germany and Japan, the formulation of the Marshall Plan for Europe, the accelerated attention paid to underdeveloped areas, as well as the pressure for Atlantic and European community—came not as the implementation of humanitarian aims, but as ad hoc responses to the communist threat, and were defended domestically in terms of "enlightened self-interest." A common element of need on the part of ourselves and other nations of the free world is a different thing from a community of interest in which the welfare of each is regarded with equal concern. There is apprehension, fed by curtailments of economic aid and possible reduction in ground forces, that when our immediate interests can be adequately served by narrower commitments, we will withdraw as we have before from the responsibilities of world leadership. This not only gives rise to a feeling of "being used," it encourages as well a "hedging" against the day when that withdrawal comes about and the various nations have to live with present day enemies at their doorsteps.

"Why," I have heard asked, "is it that, is spite of America's well advertised generosity in world affairs, its role is still the subject of resentment and some suspicion?" When neutrality from the Soviet-Free World struggle was to be lost by acceptance of aid, this could be understood. Indonesia rebelled at the military implications of the mutual security program and accepted only the less partisan technical assistance; Burma even threw off the latter. Marshall Plan countries, however, added little to their commitments, yet in Italy and France I sensed a strong reaction against American aid. In India and in England I found resentment against America at its strongest outside the communist world. In West Germany, on the other hand, little resentment was noted, the explanation offered by a German official being their feeling of having outdone all others in making effective use of U.S. aid, as evidenced by the marvel of reconstruction they have brought about, and by the stability of their government. It is possible that we have been slow in understanding the psychology of a recipient. We are having to learn that gratitude is not a stable basis on which we can build our relationship with other nations. There is a sense of obligation which accompanies gratitude which needs to be worked off through reciprocal acts, or it will be offset by rationalizations which in turn may give rise to resentments. We should, I believe, reconsider the notion that we can make decisions first in terms of our most apparent interest and then make lump-sum payments to other nations through a variety of agencies to bring about needed adjustments.

In a multitude of ways, critical Asians and Europeans manage to convey that they regard the American as a peculiarly uncomplicated soul, his impatience a sign of immaturity, and his perpetually disappointed optimism as to expecting things to actually work efficiently as evidence of naivity. Many are convinced that no standard of living could be worth the pace and competitiveness of our way of life—that we are too occupied with seeking success to be able to enjoy it.

There was warfare, active or at stalemate, riots and disturbances in a surprising number of places that I visited. And I saw much of the daily struggle of people to survive and maintain self-respect, in countless cities from squalid Bangkok to the picturesque but impoverished Alfama section of Lisbon. As one wanders midst quaint, narrow streets in worker neighborhoods, one senses how slowly and sparsely the material aspects of existence which we take for granted have filtered down to the great body of the people, and how limited is the range of their enjoyment and their access to information. There is war, not as a struggle between nations, but as a daily struggle against hunger, disease and degradation of spirit. Yet the strongest impression which I carried away was not of conflict and struggle, but of the sense of composure for which individuals strove, and often attained—particularly in Asia, perhaps to a lesser extent in Europe, and assuredly to a lesser extent in America.

Nowhere did I find people with as great a capacity for being happy, in spite of poverty or misfortune, as among the Thais of Siam and Cambodia. They seemed little concerned about the objective of an activity; wait, and the goal would ultimately be revealed to them. And if things did not work out well, as understandably was often the case, we would hear "Maipen rai" ("Oh, never mind!"). In part a by-product of centralism, this reluctance to erect goals and unwillingness to stake one's happiness on particular outcomes, also has roots in the Buddhist teaching that the determinate is inevitably contingent and transitory, and that the individual should find his happiness and composure in becoming attuned to the certain and ever continuing boundlessness of the nature that is all about him, and of which he is a part.

Other Eastern philosophies also adjust the expectations and demands of the individual to a realistic appraisal of what, on the whole, is likely to be the lot of the average man, and thus provide him with a sense of detachment from the troubles of life which enable them to be borne with philosophic calm. There is a side to our Western culture, perhaps most represented in America, which appears to reflect quite the reverse. There is more of an activistic spirit, an optimism about shaping environment to meet our needs, a readiness and ability to plan activities over a period which may encompass an investment in temporary disadvantages in return for deferred but enhanced satisfactions, a resultant concern about goals, a tendency to rationalize the elusiveness of such ultimate goals as composure and happiness by elevating as symbols of success the instrumental material things of life and even the accepted activities through which they are acquired. Behind this lie such factors as the development of Western scientific thought, the impulse of secular activity given by Protestantism, the individualistic nature of our political heritage, the impact of utilitarian hedonism, and the promising and rewarding opportunities of the open frontier. Lost somewhere along the way was the capacity for the fullest of aesthetic experience and a sense of personal tranquility for the individual.

There is a feeling abroad that when differences are found, an American acts on the presumption that it is the American way of life which provides the measure, and that the others have fallen short. In sensitive Asia, the feeling is stronger and applies to Western people in general. The attitudes revealed in our policies and in actual relations with other peoples are made subject to this criticism. It is as though we believed that if others had more information, more preparation for intelligent choice, and divine guidance, they would see the universal merit of our activist way of life, our style of democracy, our free enterprise economy, and our particular theistic religion. An obstacle in itself to mutual understanding, this is a source of resentment that impairs the receptivity of others to our ideas.

Many with misgivings as to the exclusive righteousness of our position in international affairs find their fears reinforced by what has been transpiring on the domestic American scene. In the minds of Asia and Europe, the idea of America as a place where man can speak his conscience without fear is being lost. This became apparent as in country after country I encountered concern over the phenomena associated with McCarthyism. It is not that we have sought to ferret out those endangering our form of government, but that the American people have tolerated procedures that have made vulnerable to character assassination those who depart from orthodoxy of viewpoint on certain topics within the purview of investigating committees. Few abroad understand the diversity of America; that most anything can be true, and also the opposite. The ideal being lost is one of the few which have correctly symbolized our way of life to the people of the world. The inept handling of this one matter has largely offset the benefits of our overseas information service, since the United States has demonstrated in the conduct of its own domestic affairs an insensitivity to the very point—that compatibility rather than conformity is required for stability—which appears to underlie much of the resentment against American leadership.

Leadership requires, in addition to a sense of direction, a technique for coping with difference. In this we may also be hampered in certain respects by the nature of our religious heritage. In theistic religions the emphasis on having enjoyed exclusive access to the fundamental truths engenders an attitude of tolerating difference until conversion to the faith is possible. While appropriate to the achievement of a uniform moral sense among those to whom the religion has predominant access, this attitude has divisive implications when applied to a social complex of competing theologies as well as non-theistic cultures, each with its own bailiwick. The essential core of religion I take to be faith in some concept of relation between man and his environment that lies beyond the bounds of science. The tendency has been to enlarge that core to include rituals, institutions, and values that originally served to give concrete meaning and implementation in terms of the society in which people lived. Means habitually employed to achieve an end already regarded as good themselves became regarded as values, and inflexibility is introduced.

If one seeks out the criterion by means of which one value is balanced against another with which it is in competition in a given situation, and continues this procedure even to those values regarded as absolute, one comes, I believe, to a conception of the parent ''good,'' not as a quality that can be inherent in any action or thing, but as a relationship, in particular a relation of harmony in context.

We are, it is true, moving in the direction of political forms that encompass diversity on the basis of compatibility rather than seek adherence of the individual to a common morality. However, instead of recognition of the integrity of differences in values, there tends to be only a grudging acceptance of difference as a concession to expediency.

Recognition of the integrity of difference is particularly important when points of view differ as much, for instance, as between America and Asia. In America the aggressive tactics of communism on a world-wide front are regarded as an obvious danger. There is extreme skepticism about the much-vaunted superiority of the communist arrangement of economic life, and grave concern about the implications it has for the political and religious freedoms of the individual. In Asia there is not the economic and educational background to permit that awareness to be so comfortably maintained. There the struggle is against hunger and privation, and against ignorance; and in the areas that have known the anomalies of Western influence and Western indifference, there is a particular sensitivity to anything suggestive of exploitation and discriminatory treatment. There is little thinking through to the ultimate consequences involved in the alternatives. The choice between the orderly democratic processes for social and economic reform and for industrialization, and the communist promises of a better life through direct action that eliminates obstructions and erases contradictions, tends to be made in terms of immediate material and emotional appeal, considerably influenced by the communist explanation of a free enterprise economy as capitalist exploitation of the masses. The non-activist spirit of the East, in its various ramifications, has made easier the job of selling the communist solution. The free world, on the other hand, has had to concern itself with instilling in the people of Asia the attitudes needed to make our way of life seem desirable as well as the aptitudes for making it work.

With limited access to information or the opportunity to verify it, many Asians today believe that it was the power of Russia that won World War II, that the West has engaged in germ warfare and is responsible for atrocities, and that real personal freedom exists only within the Soviet family of nations.

There are those in Asia, including influential leaders, who do recognize the dangers inherent in communism, particularly the entanglement in control from Moscow, but they also cast a wary eye upon Western influence in general. Their countries seek rapid economic development, but not at the price of their taking over Western culture intact. As a former education minister in Thailand expressed it to me, they are seeking the ''middle way'' so that a more materialistic emphasis does not come at the expense of their aesthetic values and sense of composure.

The majority of those outside the Bamboo Curtain in Asia are probably not unalterably on either one side or the other of the ideological conflict. But in traveling through these vast areas, I gained the impression that they tend to share a common resentment against the Western democracies for what they consider to be interference in struggles of their own to improve their way of life. They see little reason for Western concern for what transpired in China, then in Korea and Indo-China, and for the guerrilla warfare still underway in the Philippines, Malaya, and until recently in Burma and Indonesia. The invitation extended to the United States was short and to the point: ''Get out of Asia.''

Limits on what can be accomplished in developing resistance to communism are set perhaps more by the religious-philosophical heritage of the people than by any other factor. In the Far East, for example, there seemed to be a tendency to introspection and contemplation of environment rather than to activity in public affairs, to have an acted-upon attitude of accepting outcomes, to be skeptical of social integration beyond the family level, and to look for solutions that required as little of the individual as possible. An appraisal of these or related attitudes on the part of the various peoples of Burma through Indonesia would, I believe, have warranted far more and earlier concern as to the susceptibility of that area to communism than the guarded optimism of our policymakers has seemed to indicate. Something the same might be said, among theistic religions, of the effect of Catholicism on Italy, and to a lesser extent upon France. Several factors appear to be operative, among them the non-participatory nature of doctrinal interpretation and Church government, the appeal to aesthetic and emotional more than to logical faculties, and the achievement of composure through an adjustment of expectation to realization that seems to emphasize more the acceptance of status than the development of potentialities. From these arise, I believe, a non-activist attitude toward responsibility relevant to understanding the political instability characteristic of Italy and of France, and the tendency of the people, particularly in

Italy, to be sympathetic to communism in spite of the doctrinal opposition of the Church and their own highly individualistic temperaments.

I noted a sharp contrast to France and Italy in the sense of discipline, the ability to work in groups, and the respect for authority which seemed to characterize the Germans. In a sense it was the reverse phenomenon to the Latin countries—greater ability to act as a group, but seemingly less attachment to individualism of viewpoint. It raised in my mind a question as to how to cultivate that component of each culture that is inadequately represented without loss of the stronger characteristic already present.

Conversations in Bonn, the capital of the Federal Republic of Germany, have been reassuring: Germans deeply regret their past "isms," they recognize the Russian menace, they know their place is with the Western powers, and they are uninhibited in their flattery of the America which gives them aid. Documentation of the seventeenth of June revolt in the Soviet sector was presented as evidence of the desire existing for democratic institutions. It was equally consistent with protest against restrictions on freedom and the lack of success of the authority over them, with the desire for a different, less restrictive, and more successful authority, with the need even for democratic institutions, but not necessarily of the desire for or readiness for them.

I recall the Liberty Bell in the tower of the Schoenbaum Rathaus, the West Berlin City Hall, and also the torchlight funeral of the West Berlin mayor, Ernest Reuter. Thousands came from both East and West Berlin to show respect for a leader of democracy. The coffin was pulled by black-shrouded, plumed horses, followed by a riderless horse, a steel-helmeted drum corps with muffled drums, and mile after mile of people carrying candles in a procession that seemed never to end. A display of tremendous emotional appeal by the common man for an heroic figure and a promising way of life.

There seemed to be an optimism about instilling democracy, possibly a reflection of Occupation policy, I do not know, which reminded me of our own efforts to sell democracy in "packaged" form to the Japanese. There, even a democratic constitution was prepared for them, and was given effect through respect of the Japanese people for the authority of the emperor. Leadership of the few in crystallizing support for particular political forms, and in establishing the structure suited thereto, can be expected. The forms and processes of democracy can, for that matter, even be imposed upon people accustomed to discipline. But democracy is more fundamentally a matter of attitudes than of actions, and while some of the requisite attitudes can be instilled in the populace (for their seeds are certainly present in all), the most limiting factors are surely the underlying philosophical conceptions of the people. In pre-war Germany these worked very much against the democratic view of society, but in Bonn the opinion was expressed that the psychological catharsis of the war and post-war debacles had done much to wipe clean the slate and prepare it for new impressions.

Two conversations, not necessarily representative of German thinking, stand out in my mind in this connection: one with a refugee intellectual in Berlin who had escaped from the Soviet sector, the second with a political journalist in Frankfurt. My Berlin acquaintance counted himself as a convert to democracy. More than that, he wanted to broaden support for democratic institutions and volunteered quite specific remarks on the subject. The essence of his proposal was that mass media could, through constant repetition and demonstration of the meaning of democracy, bring the attitude of the people ''into line'' with the requirements of a democratic state. In Hongkong I spoke with British, Chinese, and Americans active in matters of public relations, information services, the press, radio, rediffusion, etc. about Hongkong as both an initiator and target for propaganda—an area of particular interest as one of the few (Vienna and Berlin are others, and Trieste was once) that have relatively free access to both sides of the ideological controversy. It was instructive to learn of the rationalizations that led to particular modes of behavior and use of these various channels of mass media, and to contemplate the impact on the recipient populations. I have no doubt that the present techniques of influencing public opinion, let alone improved ones, can be useful, but unless the public as individuals already possess a certain command of facts, a genuine interest in and opportunity for free access to information, and a well developed ability to process the information which they obtain—conditions I would not concede to be often satisfied—the potentialities of the mass media are likely to be more nearly sufficient for doing harm than for doing good.

I mentioned a Frankfurt journalist. His proposal was of a related nature but somewhat broader. It ran as follows: Individualism and discipline are both needed for modern society, but not all are able to reach this understanding. There should therefore be in every society a special group of men who prepare problems in a way that the man in the street can understand; who explain and disseminate; and who create the desired atmosphere by their manner of conducting themselves and their enterprises. The group should be concerned with both representing the interests of the people and in leading them in finding their interests. "And," he added, "we will have the group anyway; best to recognize its good possibilities than to have it and not recognize them." I asked if he had in mind a balanced approach over the long run of developing "the group" for leadership *and* improving the basic competencies of the many as individuals. His answer was emphatic: We must work "for the coming of the group"; one should not rely on the people. And he ended the interview abruptly. Interpreted in the most sympathetic way as referring to an expanding strata of responsible citizens from which leaders and experts emerge, it has merit. But it is difficult to be content with emphasis on a special cadre of intellectual elite, however public spirited it may be.

Soviet signs, "You are now entering the democratic sector," erected at the approaches to East Berlin, reminded me of the remark of a Hong Kong official that the communists "have stolen all the best slogans and symbols. They are for peace—they use the dove, the olive branch . . ." I found Stalin Allee in the Soviet sector to offer a long stretch of handsome buildings, similar, well planned, decorated with red flags and party slogans—used as apartments for party members and for government operated stores. To the sides of this showpiece are the gaping ruins of the ordinary man's Berlin. Youth groups and workers were to be seen marching and chanting in unison behind red flags and Soviet officers. I looked at the citizens at their tasks, at their products in the shops, at the contemporary art and writing of the people, and found no evidence of individualistic expression or enterprise. And back in the Western zone, I watched the distribution of Eisenhower packets ("smear packets" according to signs in the Soviet sector) to long lines of East Berliners who had come for them at some risk and to whom the contrast between sectors was obvious.

Should superiority of the non-communist arrangements of economic affairs in providing material advantages be used as a symbol? Or should freedom, or something else? Just what is it that we stand for? Putting stress on material well-being has the disadvantage that already there is reluctance to follow in our footsteps for what is viewed by many as an over-emphasis on our part of the materialistic side of life. And disillusionment as to the effectiveness of a communist economy does not of itself assure the attitudes required for political liberalism. More decisive in the long run, however, is that though approaches differ, concern for the material well-being of the individual is a common bond of the communist and non-communist worlds. It could be the basis for economic cooperation, admittedly difficult to achieve so as not to endanger security, in the process of which each economic system could learn from the other and the techniques needed for working together on a wider range of matters might be developed. At present, emphasis on the economic superiority of the non-communist approach inclines our policy toward measures intensifying that contrast and stands in the way of such cooperation. And such comparisons discourage the Soviet from freer exchange of information and persons, a needed step in reducing international tensions.

Material well-being is not essential for composure, for that can be achieved at any above subsistence level of material well-being. Composure can even be endangered by too much emphasis on material things. Nor is material well-being an essential to happiness, which can be cultivated from the appreciation of simple things. It does, however, serve as an incentive and as an outlet for creative effort which draws forth certain of man's potentialities.

Should freedom of the individual be the main emphasis? Communism, however, does not so much deny freedom as a goal as it elevates such "freedoms from" as freedom from want, from exploitation, and from social and economic inequality above "freedom of" belief, of choice, and of action. The wild surging of ideas, the uncoordinated individual expression, inspired and full of feeling, which can characterize art as an instrument of the individual for winning power, is entirely lost in the coordinated "party line," non-deviationist sterile product that emerges once communism is in power.

But no man is completely free, and on occasion there is need to concede some of one freedom in return for more of another. The choice is not between simple opposites—freedom or the coercion implicit in control—for both techniques are required by society. It is the criteria for combining them which vary from one society to another. In much of the free world, in fact, economic freedoms have been abridged by socialism without loss of other freedoms of the individual. I recall listening to a debate on socialist measures in the

Parliament building in Wellington, New Zealand.

Freedom, moreover, is to be valued not for itself but as opportunity, and needs to be interpreted in terms of the benefits to be obtained by its exercise for it to be appreciated. The freedom in Oriental culture which seemed most prized was not to influence outcomes or acquire particular accouterments of living, but rather to contemplate and appreciate existence in its immediate or intuitively apparent aesthetic and emotionally satisfying, yet timeless aspects. Freedom is not the ultimate criterion. What you fall back upon in deciding on what freedom to yield is the value you rank higher. Freedom is valued as a means to satisfy the desire for a relation of harmony in context.

Definitions of increased freedom as being an increase in the number of alternatives available suggest the shortcomings of freedom as an ultimate goal. Maximum freedom would correspond to being faced with making choices from an infinite set of alternatives, and the uncertainty and indecision related thereto are the antithesis of happiness and composure.

I am convinced that where we wish to work with peoples of other lands, we must do so with and through their cultures, and not in opposition to them. If we want their friendship, we must help them achieve *their* goals. If we want to influence them and retain their friendship, we must show how our recommendations serve their underlying values, and as far as possible, are consistent with their instrumental values (those values derived as the result of the habitual employment of particular means).

I believe it essential that our approach neither reflect upon Eastern culture nor hold Asians dependent nor obligated to us, that its objectives be meaningful to the individual in terms of his everyday life, and that it provide for his growing awareness of his potentialities as an individual in the fullest sense. Were we to see our objective as being the furtherance for individuals of the fullest life possible consistent with peace of mind, I believe the response would be better than to objectives phrased in terms of democracy, material improvement, dignity of the individual, freedom, world peace, etc.

A definition of aim in terms of a process that preserves composure is a concept of progress not partisan to either the East or the West; each has much to learn from the other. Is not the way of achieving any goal the important thing? Is the real end really the means to any end?

Underlying factors such as the philosophical conceptions of a people, the initial command of facts, the extent of interest in and opportunity for access to information, as well as the ability to process the information obtained, must to a considerable extent be taken as already given in much of the effort forthcoming in time of crisis to meet real and present dangers. Yet they set limits on what can be accomplished, are ever resurgent as principal factors, and will remain as dominant considerations in such matters as future alignments of peoples reflecting racial or religious incitements. Russia, for example, may again be an ally of the West in a struggle which sees China and India, and possibly Japan, championing the dissatisfaction of Asia and Africa.

There is the problem of finding a way of living together that will stand the stresses and strains to which the fabric of society may yet be submitted. It should be the aim of leadership to resolve immediate difficulties in a manner which at least does not intensify broader and subsequent problems. This is not always possible through leadership that emerges only at time of crisis and solves its problems day by day. One might hope, as the present tension eases, that this nation will temper its natural desire to get on about its own affairs with an appreciation that our interest is best served by stability and welfare not just within our own boundaries but of the world as a whole, that this requires a continuing long term effort, and that our leadership can be most effective within multilateral efforts that not only preserve the psychological balance of our relations with other nations, but also develop the mutual confidence and sense of responsibility that come from participation in joint endeavors.

Attention must be particularly directed toward the type of effort which is short of quickly satisfying yield. One of the most difficult of tasks is to create a system of incentives that will assure sustained effort on matters having a payoff in the remote future. A crisis usually produces its own incentives in calling forth the effort needed to meet it, but not so for long- run evolutionary programs. Until we have developed more facility than we now possess in structuring such incentives, we are less masters of our fate than we might like to imagine. The main targets for our concerted efforts continue to be the product of circumstances that become crucial—war, depression, ideological controversy—rather than targets of our own choosing. We have surrendered initiative to the force of circumstances and have not yet retrieved it.

It is likely that we will see much compromise with circumstance and concessions to pragmatic attitudes. Having pitched our effort on the high plane of moral proctorship of the world, it is possible we will suffer a sense of disillusionment. Coupled with other forces moving us to retrenchment, it may result in a passion for withdrawal amounting to a policy of self-containment. Preparation in advance for a long-term role in world affairs that requires lesser deployment of resources would seem to recommend itself in terms of reasonable prudence. A suitable long-term policy embarked upon in supplement to short-term measures could both work toward an earlier mitigation of future problems, and through identifying our ultimate goals, strengthen confidence in our leadership.

Contact between peoples, even though greatly increased, would not of itself, I believe, bring about better relations on essential matters. Nor would it be enough if we did recognize the fine points of each other's cultures and respected their values. Beyond awareness and respect for each other's differences is the need for practical adjustments for the infusion of one culture by another and for their coexistence. Adjustments will be made in day-to-day operations and practical affairs because certain things ''work'' and are found useful. But I doubt if solutions on the most fundamental points will emerge in this manner. Compatibility, not uniformity, among nations would be furthered by long-term programs of cooperative intellectual endeavor on problems of common interest, characterized in their definition by a low specificity of culture content, so as not to exclude the dissenting parties. This is partly in order to have access to needed insight, reflecting the observation that in most cases each has much to learn from the other, and partly to facilitate eventual acceptance of what emerges.

I discussed in New Delhi with a representative of the Ford Foundation some thoughts along the following lines: I was impressed by the extent that revered scriptures—religious writings, epic poems, etc. which were part of a country's culture influenced the approach taken to solving problems. Yet such writings reflected ways of dealing with problems under circumstances that have since changed considerably. How is the infusion of ideas to be facilitated from other cultures that are not ''hung up'' on this or that manner of approach by reason of having a different cultural heritage? The exchange of students, faculty members and experts has been one approach, but it has encountered what has been termed the ''brain drain,'' because many do not return to their native lands. The basic elements of my suggestion were as follows: (1) Select a topic for a week-long conference that is a problem of concern to several countries that differ in cultural heritage. (2) Select as participants individuals who already have established lines of communication with their context and to which context they are going to return. Examples would be ministers of religion, editors, leaders of civic fraternal groups, labor officials, welfare officials, teachers, as well as those with professional and applied experience in the problem. The expectation is that these people are both firmly attached to indigenous values and dedicated to reaching solutions on practical problems for their own constituencies. (3) Make clear that there is no intention that the group itself would recommend, supervise, or carry through the solution of the problem. (4) Provide an opportunity for each participant to see the value of approaches used by others, and in what respects his or her own culture contains an obstacle to implementing that approach, an obstacle possibly traceable to an earlier social expediency. (5) Do not attempt any consensus report, or attempt to convert one individual to another's position; being reconciled even to individuals returning with hostile attitudes. (6) The presumption of this approach is that the series of discussions will act as a non-threatening catalyst that will facilitate change. In particular, it is expected that the individuals, with both a cultural background and a practical bent, will cut the cloth of their own culture to more nearly fit the problems of their times, especially with respect to inhibiting factors within their religion, philosophy, literature and arts, and that as opinion leaders they will be in a position to contribute to a change in public attitudes in regard to cultural obstacles to change.

What are the implications for the direction of effort of considering a relation of harmony in context as the parent good? Applied to the individual, it points to the ''good life'' as one providing composure with respect to environment. That it is human nature to seek that composure, in spite of physical disequilibrium within the individual, and psychic awareness of problems (discrepancies between existing and preferred situations), through rationalization, limiting horizons, and other attitudes toward life—through a narrow selfishness, in fact—is a basis for pessimism as to man's innate tendency for goodness. For sacrificed is not only the composure of those toward whom he thereby acts insensitively, but also his own harmony in the broader context with respect to which he has chosen to ignore the implications of his actions. With increased appreciation of personal freedom and individualism there is also an augmentation of the problems of achieving compatibility within society. The tendency for society to be concerned with an external morality, with authorities, and control makes sense in this connection. But it is to be noted that these social forms, in turn, take on a selfish aspect as problems broaden beyond the society they serve. Posed for us is the question of achieving a balance between the tendencies of individualism and social control, leading to composure for the individual and a relation of harmony in the broadest context.

We must be alert that man, in being shepherded in the social interest, does not lose his sense of autonomy and the impulse to make the most of his potentialities. Composure with respect to the environment for the individual can be found at most any extent of use of his capabilities. What we must explore is whether pressing for the fullest possible life for the individual consistent with his composure can contribute to a more peaceful world.

9.2

Assisting Other Nations

For an American traveling abroad, one of the strongest impressions is of the extent of U.S. activity throughout the world. The taxes paid and the congressional appropriations of which one reads are translated into such things as literacy campaigns and armaments in Vietnam, irrigation plans in the Middle East, freighters discharging military cargo in Istanbul, troops in occupation duty and in the NATO forces in Europe, and informational and cultural affairs activities throughout several continents. Impressive in itself, it produces an added impact when one realizes the extent of American influence already exerted through the foreign operations of its religous, commercial, professional, and philanthropic organizations, through the employment of American experts by foreign governments, and through American participation in the work of the United Nations and its specialized agencies. The United States has become not only the leading exporter of tourists, it has become as well the major exporter of capital and technical know-how. In all these ways and more, the United States has made the impulse and drive of its way of life known in the remotest corners of the globe. What is seen in the way of official activities is largely the outgrowth of a succession of programs, starting with U.S. participation in UNRRA after World War II, which broke with the isolationist self-containment policy that held sway following World War I and saw expression even at the close of the second world war in the abrupt cancellation of Lend Lease.

There is recognition that we are trying to buy allies with our aid program. Aid, as furnished under the mutual security program, involved a clear loss of neutrality in the Soviet-West struggle. In Indonesia there was quite a turmoil over this and only the less partisan technical-assistance program was acceptable. The economic and technical assistance under the latter program, though accepted, is often a source of apprehension in various countries, the suspicion being that foreign aid is more concerned with developing those aspects of a nation's economy that fit into the world scheme of things, than with such development as would put the country itself in the most favorable situation. Burma renounced its acceptance of U.S. assistance just shortly before my visit to Rangoon, and newspapers were still speculating editorially as to the reason. Front pages were filled with accounts of Chinese nationalist irregulars who were wreaking havoc on Northeast Burma and with play-by-play newsflashes on the progress of triangular Rangoon-Washington-Taipeh negotiations with Chiang Kai Shek on evacuation of his partisans. Tension was high and the prestige of the United States, as the presumed backer of Chiang, fell to new depths. But in Rangoon I met with Everett Hagen, advisor to the Central Bank of Burma, and other economic advisors, and found that a comprehensive program was still being pushed through contracts between the Burmese government and American private agencies.

What of other countries that are ambivalent in their attitude toward the United States? India, of course, seeks the role of the great neutral. As I write this, Pakistan appears to waver toward accepting American military aid, an action not likely to please India, for the geographically-split country of Pakistan is a neighbor on both its west and east borders.

I visited some twenty places in Arab lands stretching westward from ancient Babylon in Iraq to modern Beirut on the Mediterranean, and extending southward from the snowy cedars of Lebanon through the Holy Land to the scorching Valley of the Kings in Egypt. In that area the free world struggle against communism is almost pushed from view by the preoccupation of the Arab countries with controversies raging over the Israel question and British control of the Suez. My visit to Syria took place prior to the election of Syria's strong man as president. Acceptance of technical assistance from the United States would be difficult in view of the intense anti-Western feeling which existed. Syria would have no qualms about accepting American military aid, but that has been checked by the prospect that such armament would be deployed against Israel. Arab resentment against the United States, it need scarcely be added, springs from America's actions, actual and alleged, in support of Israel. In conversations with many it became apparent that the Arab believes the resentment to be reciprocated by us, and it is difficult to reassure them that American opinion is not strongly anti-Arab. Effective work was being done by the U.S. Information Service, but it would take much greater resources to remove the backlog of misunderstandings and prepare the public through education to be more discerning in the future.

Aside from Greece and Turkey, in which countries economic and military considerations were linked from the first, American policy appears to have evolved from narrowly conceived objectives through a period based on broad economic considerations into the present period which looks first to matters of military security. The first phase was that of the termination of Lend Lease through the Fulbright arrangements, and the early loans to France and Britain for reconstruction. The second phase started in early 1948 with the European Recovery Program that was inspired by the Marshall Plan. Economic recovery was the underlined objective, recovery which was expected to put Western Europe back on a free-market economy, externally as well as internally, and create an effective deterrent to encroachment by the communist ideology. The shift in emphasis to creating an armed barrier against communist aggression, a need made vitally obvious by the developments in Korea, found expression in the Atlantic and Pacific defense pacts, and in the bordering of the Soviet bloc by a ring of strategic bases in Asia, Africa, and Europe. The U.S. has taken the position that the communist threat of aggression must be countered by a continuing and coordinated effort on a global scale. It has not subscribed to the Indian view that there would have been no difficulty had only matters been allowed to run their course. The positive stand taken by the United Nations in Korea even yet seems desirable to the aggression-inviting wavering on the part of the West which preceded that action.

The variety of activities known in an all inclusive way as Point IV were first the responsibility of an Economic Cooperation Administration, then of two agencies: the Technical Cooperation Administration in the State Department, and the more autonomous Mutual Security Agency. Some reshuffling and sorting out took place to avoid both agencies operating in the same country. During the period reported upon here, there was some anticipation (with corresponding apprehensions on the part of personnel) of their being brought together again in a single Foreign Operations Administration. The foreign informational activities of the government were similarly in the process of the inevitable shake-up that occurs with a change of administration in Washington, a grouping together of the information offices of various agencies in a new agency that would be separate from the State Department. Many of the phenomena, both good and bad, noted in connection with the foreign aid and informational services were a by-product of these imminent changes. Some problems will be corrected or assume new forms. This would particularly be true of such matters as the coordination of aid programs within a country (especially difficult in MSA countries since officially it was for the inviting government to propose the forms of assistance); the coordination, particularly in terms of temporal horizon, of programs of countries closely related geographically and hence strategically; and the provision of suitable liaison with other agencies pursuing related tasks or objectives. New problems will naturally appear.

There is talk of providing experts rather than dollars, possibly through private agencies, and of having American private investment fill the gap as foreign aid is curtailed. But private capital is not likely to feel attracted to areas bordering on the Soviet bloc, or characterized by political or currency instability. Civil disorder or the possibility of expropriation are also deterrents, as in areas of emergent nationalism, fanaticism, or anti-Western feeling. Guarantees protecting private capital against loss, if made adequate to encourage large scale development, would be extremely vulnerable to domestic political criticism. And as U.S. title to assets increased in the various countries, pressures for official intervention to protect this property could be expected to materialize in event of difficulty. Political expediency domestically, but more than that, the feelings in the recipient countries, might shift the function of providing investment guarantees to an agency of the United Nations. And there is bound to be pressure for experts to be selected from other countries as well as the United States, for experts tend to channel investment in production equipment to their country of origin, and neither the aided countries nor America's industrial competitors wish to see a particular country grow more dependent upon the United States in this manner.

Another voice to be heard is that of the citizen of the aided countries. Point IV has captured the popular imagination. Those who are close to the soil, not just the officials, have spoken enthusiastically, almost fervently, of development plans or possibilities under Point IV. Expectations have been raised perhaps too high for what can be realized in the foreseeable future. It will not be easy to retrench on our aid program without incurring resentment that will strain such good will as has been developed.

Far from discussing a contraction of foreign aid, countries like India may well be in a position to bargain effectively for aid on a scale not yet even reached. It was pointed out to me in India that Pandit Nehru's Congress Party, next to which in adherents is the Communist Party, depended for continued support upon being able to show progress in dealing with the plight of the Indian masses, that the prevailing standard of living was too low to permit capital saving for industrialization through cutting back of consumption, that advances made by the Soviets under successive Five Year Plans showed that it soon would be in a position to supply India's capital needs, that India would need to look toward the Soviets for help if needed funds were not forthcoming from the United States, and finally, it would cost the American taxpayer only a certain number of dollars and cents per capita each year. Here again it is the military and diplomatic aspects, this time the importance of keeping India and its growing following outside of the Communist orbit, which gives the problem its particular twist.

It is possible that the United States will work more through the instrumentalities of the United Nations once the need to serve immediate objectives has passed. While the Marshall Plan stated openly that it aimed at erecting a bulwark against communism in the form of strengthened political and economic institutions in Western Europe, a rather free hand was given the European nations in drawing up the program and carrying it out in the pre-Korea period without commitments being exacted in return. But whatever the precise form of the aid programs of the future, the precedent has been set for cooperation between nations which in breadth of effort and in understanding is perhaps the best product of our day.

Can a program of economic aid and technical assistance obtain sustained results? Does the emphasis given the role of the expert provide an answer to a more orderly world?

One of the most important facts to grasp is that seldom is there any simple, direct approach to solving what is considered to be a problem in another society. Take the familiar case of the food resources-population ratio in India. A priori it might seem that if the food supply per capita needed to be increased, and the resources available for the task were extremely limited and fixed in amount, effort should be concentrated upon increasing crop yield and irrigated acreage and in gaining acceptance for birth control. Reduction in mortality rates through improved health and sanitary standards could come later; in the meantime the existing high mortality rate was an ally in keeping the population from even further outdistancing the food supply. This may seem brutal but logical. On closer examination it is seen to be neither. This was impressed upon me by an agricultural field worker who was faced with this very problem. We were on a plane trip over northern India and he pointed out what was being attempted in the areas we traversed. And what he said made sense when I walked through teeming villages of central India. Developments must go hand in hand. It is not that sanitary and health standards must be raised so that labor engaged in agriculture will be on its feet and effective. There is no shortage of man-hours even though individual laborers may be below full effectiveness. It is that a great inertia exists as to the adoption of improved agricultural methods. And to provide incentives through which such inertia is overcome, the agricultural worker must have an appreciation of the ways of living which are more readily opened up to him if he follows certain courses of action. The same applies to his gaining an insight into the desirability of limiting family size through birth control. But to instill such an appreciation requires a broad and varied approach of which even the improvement of health and sanitary conditions is but a single facet. Add to this that not all improvement is within the reach of individual effort. Non-polluted wells, local education, the purchase of special equipment, etc., require cooperation at the village level or higher. Measures aimed at irrigation and land reclamation or at improved roads and cooperative arrangements for marketing, for instance, require effort at least at regional levels. Add to this matters of import-export balance, and the inward flow of capital funds that are of national and international concern, and we are far and away from what seemed like a simple and direct avenue to correcting the food-population ratio.

With changes in detail we have the same thing in other countries: the simple approach has its complications, the broadened approach requires planning and coordination; and the investment of the advisory expert in a broad cumulative-effect program brings the exercise of influence which borders upon control. To initiate a program, to carry it out, to follow through so that results are not lost—all this requires skill, patience, and humility, as well as financial support—but unfortunately often it requires as well that there be intervention at various levels to assure the success of the undertaking. Monetary reform, institution of or improvement in budgeting procedure, attention to methods of public administration in the recipient countries are examples.

But control enters the picture in other ways as well. The implementation of policies originating under aid programs have at times involved a continuation of economic controls even when the program (as in the case of ERP) aimed at the achievement of free-market economies. Interference in matters of local politics can not always be avoided in spite of precautions. The Mutual Security Program provides that only such projects will be initiated within a country as are requested by the host government. To get a well-balanced program in countries facing decisions on development for the first time often involves the exercise of careful persuasion by members of the aid group, the cultivation of its contacts with members of that government, and a consideration as to how such parties are made to appear in the eyes of the people. This builds support for those already in office if they are found to be cooperative. There is also a natural reluctance on the part of the aid group to starting from scratch as would be the case if such officials were replaced by others. What aid personnel would regard as politically neutral conduct may in practice have the effect of strengthening the status quo at the price of a political fluidity which would have given better expression to the wishes of the people themselves.

Efforts to give all political groups equal identification with the aid program would not be received sympathetically by a government in power, nor is it certain that they would be undertaken by the aid officials with respect to such groups as would be unlikely to provide the stability and cooperation required for the program's success. These difficulties would be present even under the favorable assumption that the underwriters of the aid program had no axe of their own to grind. If solutions are sought internally without the participation of foreign assistance programs you are back to matters of economic planning, and the balancing of effectiveness through greater centralization of controls in economic matters against the resultant political implications for personal liberties. Control need not enter the picture to the extent indicated if the program is kept modest in scale and objectives, particularly if experts or teams are attached to local authorities and activity at the national level is minimized. But then effectiveness is of course also reduced. The unfortunate fact is that in many of the Asian countries, the relation of huge populations to resources is such that only large scale national programs can make visible headway and these tend to require outside participation, both factors reintroducing the phenomena of control.

Ask members of a foreign aid team what they have to contend with in assuring sustained results, and they are likely to come up with examples of two phenomena: the emphasis on short-term impact arising within the program and the difficulties of support within the recipient country.

The importance of short-term impact in the design of the aid program, whether longer term results are planned for or not, is elevated by several factors: the various military and strategic considerations mentioned earlier, extraneous to, but not necessarily in conflict with, the economic interests of the recipient country; the short periods over which funds are assured in advance; the fluctuation in the level of authorized program expenditure; and administratively related matters such as turnover in personnel, etc. In this the aid program is facing difficulties not uncommon with most enterprises.

The matter of securing local support is somewhat different. A major asset in accomplishing the job is to understand the viewpoint of those you seek to benefit—in this case through an awareness of and appreciation of the culture of the recipient country. This again seems a familiar matter, but its apparent sameness with what one encounters in less ambitious assignments may explain the almost universal tendency to overestimate the extent to which different peoples act with respect to the same values. Prior acquaintance with the country and its people, or at least a thorough orientation, would seem to be obvious and minimum essentials for personnel. It is not certain, however, that more than perfunctory attention is given to this in the midst of the many other problems attendant upon staffing an aid mission.

In the context of the present international crisis, the nature of the program targets and the short temporal horizon clearly bring pressure upon an expert to impose his own viewpoint in order to get the job done. Some things can be accomplished by direct imposition and not later revert. The abrupt westernization of Turkey by Mustafa Kemal (Ataturk) in the 1920's appears to be an example. But this is not generally the case. The Netherlands planning official who commented bitterly to me upon U.S. insistence on use of American procedures in various matters is not likely to continue their use when the pressure to do so is removed. You have to work through the value system of a people to develop the attitudes upon which sustained results will depend. Support has to be carefully cultivated starting from the already existent concepts of need.

When an aid program is assured of operating over a sufficiently long period, it can select techniques and plan their relative emphasis and impact over time so as to go a long way toward meeting such difficulties. Informational activities of the sponsoring agency can be directed at the average citizen and particularly to those who are in key positions to influence pubic opinion. Certain of the latter can be approached to play an active or advisory role in the local conduct of the aid program. Individuals strategically situated in the social structure from the viewpoint of influencing public opinion, or suitable for participation in the aid program, can be sponsored for survey or training trips abroad which will tend to give them the same background as that of the foreign aid mission. Facilities for training technicians can be encouraged in the recipient country. Technicians from countries encountering similar developmental problems can be made a part of the program's personnel. The ''opposite number'' system of pairing a local technician and a member of the mission is useful for gradual turning over of responsibilities. A sense of participation and identification with the work is encouraged through various sharing arrangements sought with local authorities, with an understanding as to local continuance of the project after a certain point, where possible. With few exceptions, however, these techniques are better suited for putting across the viewpoint of the mission's personnel than they are for apprising the latter of factors which might appropriately cause them to wish to change it.

In one Asian country, the aid administrator took delight in repeated comments as to just how little he needed anthropologists. This continued for some days even after I disclaimed any such identification. Perhaps he was right, but he could have made use of a staff member with some skill in planning. I discovered from conducting separate interviews with individual members of the economic mission staff that projects had been undertaken with little thought as to how the outcomes would be coordinated. Trucks would arrive prior to the completion of roads to their destination, modern farm equipment was due for delivery prior to any local expertise having been developed for their maintenance and repair, crops were introduced before essential changes in irrigation techniques had been learned, and so forth.

Foreign aid programs and the efforts to instill democracy, like the related activity of internal economic planning, all too often operate with objectives having only a tenuous relationship to the values held by the individuals making up the public. They employ the most efficient means suited to their respective purposes—means which generally involve a control aspect, whether it is in obtaining acceptance of a viewpoint, teaching a set of values, development of and reliance upon respect for authority, or other manipulation of the attitudes of a people. That in doing so they may place in jeopardy values which the individual holds to be more significant is the inevitable danger.

Regardless of how enlightened or benevolent a program may be in conception, in practice it tends to retain its basic characteristic of reflecting ''right answers'' determined by experts and control from the top rather than the working out of free choice.

9.3

Moving Toward Intelligent Choice

The importance of the decision habits of the individual has not gone unnoticed. Policy-makers, social scientists, professional people in various branches of medicine, public opinion experts, public relations personnel, educators, propagandists, experts in psychological warfare and its domestic variant, advertising, are just a few of those concerned. The nature of their interest varies naturally with their respective fields of endeavor. In part, an understanding is sought which will improve predictive ability, a useful adjunct of control in its various forms.

If the values held by individuals are to be made effective, there must be a shift of emphasis in the long run away from control and toward the working out of free choice. A prerequisite for this is improvement in the thinking techniques and ability of the layman. This applies to large masses of the world's population not yet having adequate access to education. But it also applies to those who have benefited from all that formal education has to offer, and this I have found less readily conceded.

I recall an interview with the president of one of the leading universities in the Philippines. He was confident that students acquire an adequate skill in reasoning within the present educational system. If there are some shortcomings in the finished product, well, there will always be leaders in society who will know how to do the thinking for them. Now that is a respectable point of view. But I do not share it.

A statue on the Midway Plaisance at the University of Chicago has an inscription which includes the phrase:

No, man passeth, time endureth.

The most exhaustible resource for an individual is the fleeting moment of life, but for society—and it is society which shapes education—time has an enduring quality. Perhaps in this may be found an explanation for the limited concern which society has for the urgency to a given individual of his or her having access to an educational system that is at its best.

The nature of the educational system certainly changes—witness the changing notion of what constitutes an educated person—but it would not be unfair to state that the educational system demonstrates more responsiveness to the viewpoint of special interest groups than to the community as a whole.

In structure, our educational system today is a hodgepodge of ''something old, something new, something borrowed, something blue.'' It is the result of the many diverse conceptions which society has of education: as a transmitter of cultural heritage, an instrument of political viewpoint, a market for textbooks, an employment for teachers, a place that takes care of the children for certain hours, a training needed to get ahead in the world, etc. We will focus in the comments that follow upon needed improvement in the ability of individuals to make intelligent choices.

A variety of shortcomings in decision-making were encountered in my travels: lack of recognition of the full range of alternatives, giving rise to the selection of what may be best for only a limited range of circumstances; ignoring considerations pertinent to the evaluation of a particular alternative; evaluation of alternatives with respect to the present rather than over the long run; inability to systematically handle matters involving probability or uncertainty in future periods; non-recognition of sins of omission, etc. There is also the tendency to assume that the values, thinking habits, and attitudes that yield satisfying guidance for the daily scene should be adequate for longer term quests. That which is intermediate and instrumental, moreover, comes through practice to be taken inflexibly as a goal in and of itself. Relative to what was needed in their respective roles— breadth of horizon in its many forms—seemed to be the scarcest intellectual resource among the many encountered at all levels. Matters are often examined within boundaries that are selected, if selected consciously at all, without regard to whether the interrela- tionships among the factors involved are sufficiently explainable within the sectors thus arbitrarily set forth. There is a lack of attention to the reliability of data. Is is often assumed that approximate methods of analysis will give at least approximate answers, and that additional refinements would simply assist in determining them more precisely, ignoring that improved techniques might actually reverse the conclusions to be drawn. Situations cannot be evaluated instantaneously in their totality, but it is not generally appreciated that with approximate methods the conclusions which emerge may be a function of the order of consideration as well as of the data. Both between individuals and between societies, it is often assumed that the other has the same values, or inferior values. Behind the lack of facility in techniques is confusion in the minds of many as to the elements that should enter into the decision process.

These may seem academic matters, but in their effects they translate into the standing armies with which Pakistan and India face each other in Kashmir, the bitterness between the Arab League and Israel, and the tension and drama in all parts of the world which finally command our attention when events have gone too far.

The inadequacies in man's ability to think intelligently are so prevalent, even among the educated and their leaders, in America as well as abroad, that they are taken for granted, if noticed at all. They become the basis for a defeatist attitude as to the extent to which the arbitrary element is needed in the relation of society to the individual—the arbitrary element which in its excesses impairs the opportunity of the individual to make effective those values which he holds. Those who object to the notion of more upward assertion of ideas rather than control usually put forward arguments reducible to questioning the competence of individuals to participate in decisions. While relevant to overnight redistribution of power, such criticism merely strengthens the proposal to increase that competence.

When you hear the shrill voice of a Pakistani girl praising Mao Tse Tung for bringing prosperity to China (''proved'' by China's gift of aid to India), and for bringing happiness to his people (''proved'' by the glowing reports of government-sponsored Chinese students), what do you regret? That our propaganda did not get there first? Or that she was not able to distinguish between proof and simply the nonrefutation that is demonstrated by consistency between observation and supposition. When basic competencies in sifting out what is true from what is false have not been developed, as was so often the case in Asia and Africa, it is small wonder that truth backed by reason makes less impact than an action that arouses the emotions. Perhaps by our aid program and varied informational activities we will win over Asian sentiment. But the skepticism given our documented refutation of the accusations by the Soviets that we engaged in germ warfare is not encouraging, nor the passing notice given the exposure of atrocities in Korea.

It is not possible to persuade people to decide on their every action consciously and deliberately in full awareness of ultimate goals. We are not going to have people engage in the meticulous process of scientific research in the course of their thinking, nor are we going to such extremes as to push faith and emotion out of human behavior. But it is the essence of my difference with the Philippine educator that there exists vast room for improvement, and that only when we embark on the long process of achieving it will we have moved away from reliance on a succession of patchwork remedies.

Limitations on the exercise of reason are of a varied nature. An individual may not have access to information, either in the sense of physical access or of adequate capacity for sensory perception. An individual, moreover, is the bearer of a culture; he has a conscience; he reserves certain areas for the exercise of his faith; while certain other responses come almost automatically from habit or from unconscious analogy with experience. Even when recourse is made to a deliberative process, there is the interplay of many factors, among which the emotions may play a significant role in determining the result.

Let us reflect upon the range of responses of an individual to cognitive awareness of a problem, wherein by a problem is meant a discrepancy between an existing condition and a preferred condition. We will assume this awareness is above the threshold at which preferences are invoked, although not necessarily effectuated. The individual has various options: (1) If the existing condition is that of others, the problem may be recognized by the individual as existing only in his or her discomfiture, and not with the other principals, who are not aware of a discrepancy. (2) If there are side effects upon the individual, the latter may be motivated to make others take action even though they do not share the concern. (3) If others share the same problem, the individual can leave it to large-group processes such as elections or certain types of market structure, or rely on the response being delegated to small-group processes such as a task force or committee. (4) If the individual views the discrepancy as strictly his or her own problem, there are the following options: rationalize a narrower boundary of concern in order to exclude the problem; attach greater weight to current sacrifices than the benefits that would be subsequent, tilting the balance against taking action; rely complacently on one's ability to "muddle through"; cloud awareness through the use of drugs; react on the basis of rules and regulations or internalized constraints; subordinate attention to the problem through assigning higher priority to other concerns; defer an action so that the outcome is determined by chance; adopt an option that "buys time" so that one can procrastinate; redefine the preferred state in terms of more attainable expectations in view of the costs involved; simplify the action called for by adopting shortcuts in reasoning that may or may not be justified; allocate resources to achieve the preferred condition, but only insofar as this affects one's interest; and so forth.

The phenomenon dealt with here has to do with solving the problem as defined in terms of an initial level of aspiration. Individuals adopt some combination of the foregoing options. One conception of behavior is that an individual makes choices among alternatives in such a way as to maximize his expected satisfaction from the resources at hand. A particular set of courses of action is followed only until, relative to the costs involved, the expected satisfaction yielded by one member of the set falls below that of one outside the set, whereupon a substitution is made. Indeed, the choices of a particular individual might seem illogical to an external observer because of differences in initial information on which choice is based, the derivation of satisfaction from different sources, inflexibilities as to substitutions within the set, etc. Difficulties also arise in connection with the measurement of satisfaction, the comparability within an individual of different kinds of satisfaction, and the comparability of indices of satisfaction of different individuals. But by concentrating on regularities of behavior appearing in the actions of a group of individuals, one can characterize the response to be expected from changes in resources or in costs, where the presumption seems warranted that the demonstrated acts of preference are motivated primarily by properties of the alternatives themselves. It has by no means been shown, however, that individuals do, in fact, attempt to maximize some aggregate of their various satisfactions, let alone that they do so by considering the satisfaction-cost relationships of the various possible alternatives.

Consistent with the foregoing, but by no means proved thereby, would be an explanation of human action as an attempt to restore physical equilibrium of forces within the body, and an explanation of thinking in terms of a search for psychic equilibrium, or composure, by a process which for brevity might be termed that of minimum effort. According to this view, an individual tends to act within a framework (plan, budget, routine, etc.) oriented towards the satiation of those needs which are most pressing, whether from their primacy for survival, or their continuity, intensity, reoccurrence, etc. Reasoning (conscious thinking distinguished from simply having thoughts) occurs when there is blocked action, and is of a problem-solving type directed at removing a discrepancy between an existing and a preferred situation.

The individual adds bits of information into his existing conception of things so as to enlarge his body of knowledge, seeking consistency within the given frame of reference if possible; otherwise admitting first some and then other parts of his framework to question in order to find a solution. Certain factors such as his accepted pattern of beliefs, his customary set of values, his horizon, etc., are reexamined only in the most major instances.

Reflective reasoning is seen to be very much of a crisis activity, occurring in the first instance from an obstructed intent, and assuming full scope only in the extreme circumstances under which an individual is willing to reexamine his plan in all of its aspects. Except in such crises, thinking consists of a groping about in various directions from the existent situation, in search of whatever will, without undue effort or disturbance of his present framework, yield an adequate solution. And aside from that exceptional case, there is no assurance that the solution settled upon will correspond to that obtained under the criterion of maximum expected satisfaction per unit cost, unless account is taken of the value an individual attaches to not disturbing his existent framework, and hence the high cost ascribed to approaches which would place more of it in question.

There is a second type of phenomena at the individual level: In contrast to the quest for personal equilibrium at the initial or reduced level of aspiration, there is a dynamic phenomenon whereby as a result of growth in an individual's confidence, resources and vision as to what could be possible, the level of accomplishment at which equilibrium is sought is raised.

At various points I refer to individuals in some Asian countries as typically relating to objects more in an appreciative than in a functional mode, that is appreciating an object for itself instead of valuing it as a means to some other end. Related to that impression, which may or may not be widely applicable, is the impression that people of the Orient, to the extent they are not influenced by Western attitudes, tend to be less goal-directed than individuals in the West. I viewed them as more concerned with the first of the two phenomena described above, the seeking of personal composure, while the Westerner was viewed as more concerned with the second, a dynamic whereby a continually higher level of satisfaction was sought, higher at least in terms of material well-being.

Without defending such a broad-brush characterization, I would comment now simply that to the extent individuals appreciate their existing context, they are assisted toward the goal of personal composure, while to the extent an individual views objects in terms of their possible use as means, an activist role in seeking satisfaction at newly defined levels, whether higher or merely different, is the more likely.

It would seem preferable that the choice as to way of life remain with the individual, yet this is influenced in various ways, for there is some truth to each of the following assertions: some religions incline individuals towards acceptance of their present condition and focus on a hereafter; the work ethic inclines individuals to work for work's sake; governments incline individuals to keep their behavior within certain bounds; and advertising, beyond bringing information, creates desires that are often unrealizable.

To be avoided is the frustration attendant upon the movement toward equilibrium being judged too slow, also from one's aspirations increasing beyond one's ability to cope with them. Happiness is related to the rate of fulfilling expectations as well as to the absolute levels attained.

Seeking composure within the framework of a given lifestyle versus deferring composure until a more inclusive lifestyle is attained are not the only alternatives.

Another way of life would be to seek as full a development of one's potential as is consistent with retaining personal composure, that is, as is consistent with keeping unsettling aspects of the process within bounds that the individual can handle.

Relaxation of tension relative to one's context through bringing realization and expectations into accord could be regarded as the underlying parent good sought by human behavior.

Understanding both the diversity and commonality of individual behavior is important in dealing with individual-group and intergroup behavior.

Horizons within which problems are solved will need to be broadened to include other peoples, other areas, and future times. Part of one's individuality requires an understanding of and bonding with others if one is to enjoy satisfaction and experience fullness. There must be concern in the adoption of a policy as to the indirect and subsequent effects upon others, referred to in the terminology of economics as the cost and benefit externalities of an action. There must be incentives operating, such as satisfactions to be gained from others achieving their goals, which in turn requires sensitivity and awareness beyond one's customary boundary of concern. There must be recognition that there are various ways to achieve personal composure and that the movement to more satisfying levels will be at a pace that reflects among other factors the extent to which appreciative versus functional modes of viewing objects are ingrained in an individual's outlook.

The process of civilizing man has been one in which society has sought the more easy solutions. It has used education (in its various religious and lay forms) not just to liberate man from ignorance, but also to control him through procedures resulting in leveling, uniformity, discipline, common philosophical outlook, perpetuation of the given distribution of power, etc.

The melting pot approach to diverse cultures has the limited applicability that when individuals of different backgrounds come under a particular governance, some minimal adherence to common practice is needed. Subject to that consideration, the richness of diverse cultural heritages should be protected. The educative process should promote within individuals reconciliation of the need for absolute values in achieving social integration and social stability with the advantages of a relativistic viewpoint in obtaining intercultural understanding.

The worthies of our day will speak for adhering to a moral course in our dealings with others, but it is important that we act in the spirit of our morality, not simply in terms of the specificity that reflects our own culture. Confucian philosophy seeks to bring forth a compassionate feeling within individuals toward other human beings and thus build a good relationship within the family, and by extension, outward to others. If there is any essence to morality it is the spirit of unselfishness, of being concerned with the effects of our actions on others. I am quite at odds with those who deplore this wider view on the ground that our culture's specific morality does the job, when it merely does it for ourselves. A society must teach its ethics, but if taught as derivations and in an increasingly broader horizon, progress will be in the desired direction.

However, even if compatibility rather than conformity is sought as a basis for achieving ongoing relationships among individuals, groups and nations, the tendency of individuals (and by extension, organizations) to seek the resolution of pressures by least-effort approaches makes common action to resolve problems difficult to achieve. Enlarging the horizon within which problems are solved, as mentioned, would contribute to peaceful relationships. So also would acceptance of the importance of the values held by individuals in the context of their particular culture. A Fiji Islander and a Viennese citizen differ, but each has a sensitivity to stimuli which for his culture is not in any sense wrong or inappropriate. Too often, when there is not indifference, there is tolerance in the sense of allowing someone else to be wrong. Beyond that, increasing the capacity of individuals for intelligent choice should lead to the resolution of problems in a more satisfactory manner than at present, whether through enabling one to recognize the wisdom of settling for and appreciating what is already at hand, or through facilitating the use of means for the attainment of more remote objectives.

It is apparent that if emphasis is to be shifted from control techniques to the working out of free choice (to maximize the potentiality of the individual, etc.) a broad approach is required to develop the layman's facility for intelligent choice. Certain skills in the communication arts, prior factual background, interest in and free access to information, and the ability to process information—all these are certainly needed.

Education at present claims a relatively small fraction of the resources of the aid programs of the United Nations and the United States, a larger share of the resources of missionary groups and private foundations. Assistance programs are concerned partly with the training of experts, partly with improving the competencies of the people as laymen. Both approaches are clearly needed unless it is expected to impose the ''right answers'' by coercive techniques.

European colonial policy left a gap in the educational preparation of the indigenous populations. It will take years simply to construct the physical plant needed for meeting the most basic educational needs. Experience in administering schools is acquired slowly in countries coming out from dependent status. In Vietnam, for example, it would be unrealistic to assume that the Ministry of Education would even have basic data as to existing schools, let alone be effective in administering them. Nor can students always go where there are schools, assuming family resources permitted travel, for with many governments, either from a desire to control the entrance of foreign cultures or the need to conserve foreign exchange, the movement of students is a matter for individual negotiation at the national level, and permission is not always granted.

I was impressed, however, with the competent attack presently being made upon the problem of mass illiteracy in Vietnam by the Mutual Security Mission's section on information and education. Imagination and resourcefulness were shown in the preparation of materials and in the provision of short courses in literacy for mixed groups wherever buildings were available.

Textbooks are a problem in underdeveloped countries. They are scarce, very scarce. In Baghdad I learned that a Dutch enterprise was negotiating with the government of Iraq to publish translations of selected European materials for students in that country. It would be too much to expect that the Soviet bloc has not realized the possibilities present in providing selective translations to textbook-starved countries.

There is the ever-present problem for teachers and research workers of making ends meet. In a survey of university facilities in Japan in 1947 I became very much aware of the wretched conditions into which the academic person had fallen as a result of the disruption of education by the war and by post-war inflation. And in Singapore the lucrative temptations of private tutoring make inroads on the availability of underpaid teaching staffs.

There are great difficulties in providing adequate teacher training. Equipment for classrooms and laboratories is inadequate. The quality of staff in higher education is also a matter of concern. An official of one Asian university quoted a colleague as saying, upon glancing around a staff meeting: ''And to think all these are faculty . . .''

One subject that came up frequently in private conversations, in Hawaii, the Anzac countries, Hong Kong, Singapore, and in Egypt, to mention but a few instances, was the depressing lack of stimulation from keen faculty colleagues. In many countries there is support for only one person in a field, in contrast to the departments in the United

States. Advanced degrees are seldom provided, with the result that contact with a mature group of students in one's own subject is lacking. This prompted me to raise the suggestion in several Colombo Plan countries that the several countries combine in support of an institute for advanced study at some point relatively central to them, such as Brisbane, so as to provide a stimulating meeting ground for those on leave from their own institutions, as well as superior facilities for graduate training.

A difficulty to overcome is that support for education or research from business or industry, directly or through national philanthropic foundations, is not something to be counted upon in most countries.

Education in many countries suffers from too much emphasis on substantive content, and too little on how to think. As I stressed in an earlier essay (Annex 5.1), the primary purpose of the mind is not to impound the product of other people's thinking, but to discern, to sift and analyze, to weigh and evaluate, and to come to its own decisions based on rational choice.

This viewpoint is reflected in a variety of educational approaches, though it is not clear that they really come to grips with the matters here discussed. Research is needed on two parts of the problem: techniques of thinking and the way to teach these techniques. The basic building blocks need to be explored that are required for thinking out choices between alternative courses of action under various assumptions as to the degree of information, the cost of collecting information to offset uncertainty, and the effort of thinking. And the principles for operating upon these ''building blocks'' have to be investigated with respect to determining which short-cut methods of analysis can be sensibly employed. This approach would have to build upon the existing mode of thinking, assumed here to be that described earlier as one of minimum effort. By improving the result to be obtained for a given expenditure of effort, thinking would be improved without need for depreciating the value an individual attaches to complacency. A considerable literature already exists relevant to such research but falls pitifully short of the needed insight. It is no easy task and will require many years, perhaps generations.

Only the barest suggestions are made here as to the second stage, that of finding ways to teach improved methods of thinking. In the form that recommendations on improved thinking emerge from the research stage they probably could be conveyed only in special courses, these being preceded by or interrelated with courses in tool subjects such as mathematics, philosophy, logic, etc. But our interest is not in specialists, or even in the already selective group represented by those having access to higher education. We are interested in upgrading the ability to think, all the way along the line, but the emphasis most needed is on finding forms which can be employed for the great body of the people. Moreover, the techniques must work when used by average teachers. In fact, the techniques must be sufficiently hardy to stand up even under some abuse in how they are used. From this it can be gathered that while a great deal of sophisticated thought must go into the two stages of research, what is called for is a product of utmost simplicity in conception. We are asking for a lot, and asking is something different from delivering, but to agree on that for which we must strive would itself be a step forward.

Were I to speculate as to the general nature of the solution, it would be: first, that improved thinking techniques would be conveyed, not by special courses, but by the way all courses are taught; second, that individuals would be made to feel themselves in the various decision roles referred to in a subject matter; third, that the ''building blocks'' of thinking would be emphasized so as to stand out from the multitude of contexts; and further, that historical decisions, descriptions of contemporary behavior, and training of a recommendatory nature be taught so as to bring out clearly the ''building blocks'' involved, and which principles of operating upon them were, are, or should be applied in the respective cases.

Teachers tend to be judged by their competence in transmitting to students the substantive content of a course. Years later, indeed perhaps just after completing a course, the student will have forgotten the great bulk of that substance. Justification for having been given the course will be in terms of certain residual benefits presumably accruing to the student in later life, such as having enhanced the individual's rational and appreciative capacities, as well as having developed understanding of the relationship individuals have with their context. But few courses are actually designed to maximize the probability that these hoped-for end-products are indeed produced, let along retained. There is need to dig deeper into the phenomena involved, taking advantage of recent research in communication and information theory, the study of organizational behavior, etc., all of which have profound implications for learning.

When significant progress has been made in both respects—the research on techniques of thinking and the way to teach those techniques—we truly will have improved the prospect for intelligent choice.

9.4

Letters from Kashmir and Cairo

(1953)

Kashmir

I am enjoying life in Kashmir. But first let me tell you of my time in India before reaching here. It is now eleven days since I came to India. I did not like the heat in Calcutta, and the swarms of beggars were a pathetic sight. I wished I had a canteen on my belt again—the water was bad for drinking and also most of the local concoctions, and in the dry heat I became unbearably thirsty.

Professor Mahalanobis sent a car to bring me to his Indian Statistical Institute in a suburb of Calcutta. It has over 600 employees in a number of buildings amidst gardens and pools. The press which printed the Calcutta supplement of *Econometrica* is also located there. I was shown many courtesies and had a long talk early in the afternoon with Mahalanobis. Later in the day I had tea with him and with two of his colleagues and the topic he introduced was U.S. foreign policy in Asia. He dragged in all sorts of "proof" of the U.S.'s evil intentions. Such of his charges as were more substantial I made a note of subsequently on the plane. I gave the group a statement of U.S. foreign policy, but the fact that an influential Indian official such as Mahalanobis entertains such notions is cause for thought.

I went to New Delhi by way of Patna, Benares, and Lucknow, but did not stop en route as originally planned because of the choking dust storms. The main impression during the flight was of how parched and baked was the land. River and canal beds were dry and dusty. Clouds of dust were so bad that initially there was doubt if the plane could land in New Delhi for lack of visibility. Disembarking was like walking into a blast furnace. 112° in the shade. So dusty that it was like night in early afternoon. I visited the Consulate for mail, Indian government buildings for a Kashmir permit, and airline offices to straighten out reservations, then left by train for Agra.

The crowded out-of-date train facilities were made worse by the heat and choking dust. I arrived about midnight in Agra to find it was 117° in the dark and furniture felt hot enough to burn one upon touching it. Sleep was impossible, but the next best thing was to make life as less uncomfortable as possible. The cold water was hot, but I soaked thick towels with water, then placed them over me in bed. A ceiling fan quickly started the water to evaporate into the dry room, and first the water turned cold, then I became cooler, and things seemed better. But in 20 minutes the water-laden towels were dry and crisp, and it was a constant routine all night to resoak the towels.

Early that morning I traveled by rickshaw to the Taj Mahal, then by horse car to the Red Fort in Agra. Both were impressive. I was surprised to find camels throughout the area. By 10 a.m. the temperature was 110° and I returned to the wet towels. The return trip to New Delhi was no better, for due to train delays it took from 3:45 p.m. to after midnight to make the trip. The temperature rose to 114°.

I stayed first in Delhi and then in New Delhi, and in the course of two days saw much of what was to be seen. Probably overdid things, like climbing 349 steps to the top of the only remaining ruins of the first of eight cities of Delhi, and back down the 349 steps, of necessity. The remnants of many earlier cities abound in fields that are almost desert.

Temperature was 113°, about the season's record high. The monsoon rains are due and that will end the long drought, the dust, and extreme heat. The pre-monsoon months are ones well spent out of India!

A hitch developed when I went to the airline in the morning, ready to depart for Kashmir. The airline employees had gone on strike, so I was tied up in Delhi, though I did get away a day later.

After the sequence of hot countries I have been through, Kashmir seems like heaven on earth. It is warm but not hot during the day, and cool in the evenings. I have not gone to a hotel, but for somewhat less cost I engaged the houseboat ''New Swift'' with its accompanying four servants. It is 80 feet long, has large well-furnished rooms (living room, dining room, galley, 2 bedrooms, 2 baths), and has been used by a series of notables such as William Bullitt and other ambassadors. To the rear is another craft carrying a family of 9 supported by the rent. The boat rent also provides partial livelihood to two other family groups. The houseboat is moored in a sylvan-like stream between the city of Srinagar and a series of nearby lakes.

To get around, I have taken on a full-time basis a 30 foot "shikara," the local name for a long, narrow, gondola-like craft similar to the canal boats of Venice. As I write you I am in the shikara on one of the small lakes. We are alongside a small floating garden, and turned so I am in the shade. I have two boatmen for the typical journey, but when we go upstream against heavy current, it is necessary to add a third man. Without the extra man, the cost is approximately a dollar a day. The shikara carries a sign, "Sunshine, happy, lovely, spring seats." I am lying on a red-patterned couch with a canopy over head, and bright yellow side curtains that can be adjusted for protection against the sun.

The scenery is beautiful—Kashmir probably rates as the Switzerland of Asia. The architecture seems patterned after Swiss chalets. On almost all sides I can see towering snow-capped ranges of mountains, part of the approaches to the Himalayas. Not so far over the horizon in one direction or another are Russia, China, Tibet, Nepal, Pakistan, Afganistan, and of course the rest of India.

Kashmir was the scene of bitter fighting between India and Pakistan about 1947, but it is quiet now a a result of a cease-fire line which divides Jammu-Kashmir province into Pakistan and India sectors. At the dinner table in a British club in Srinagar I found myself in the company of a Hindu, a Moslem, and quite appropriately, a member of the United Nations team of observers to keep the peace. The area is predominantly Moslem. Although Pakistan is Moslem and India more Hindu, many Moslems in Kashmir see a better economic future with India, and are pro-India.

The surface of the lake is calm, but shimmers in the sunlight as passing boats set ripples in motion. To my right, looming up over the lake, is an ancient fortress built on a hill by an early Mogul. Behind me a Hindu temple crowns another hill. In the foreground in all directions are green lake grasses, gracefully bending willows, and tall waving poplars. Close by I can see down into the water and enjoy the swaying underwater plants. The lake abounds with fish—at this place most are four inches or less in length, but fish of several pounds are nearby. The fish dart about in schools and are of beautiful hue in the sunlight. Tried plunking my feet into a group of fish and found they surrounded them, nibbling at my legs. Experimented with photographing the fish in this quaint activity.

Other craft go by, and I hear the local Kashmiri dialect above the splashing of oars. Another sound, one I would prefer to ignore, is that of one of the boatmen at the rear of this boat as he smokes a huge water bowl pipe. Sounds like a sink that needs Drano. Sometimes a small boat goes by with musicians playing music on flute and drum. Persistent water-borne merchants try to sell everything under the sun. There are the sellers of flowers; the confectioners; the giver of massages, turkish baths, and haircuts; the fruit peddler; the seller of film and postcards; also jewelers, merchants of papier-mache products, tailors, etc., etc., to mention but a few. Their persistence is very wearing on diplomacy.

I have been purposefully lazy here—a holiday away from the fast pace of the main itinerary. Have gone only where I could by boat—stretched out, getting a tan or sleeping or just watching the peaceful scene. Have learned something of Mohammedan philosophy, partly from the turbaned "skipper" of the houseboat who sometimes sits in the prow of the shikara. Also studied the Moral Rearmament (Oxford Group) position via a local convert who has supplied the literature. Had brief visits with a Scotch couple on holiday from New Delhi where they are with the World Health Organization of the United Nations. Tourists are few and far between, so the natural scene is not diluted.

My departure from Kashmir was delayed one day, and I played a round of golf at a very high altitude, with correspondingly high score. The plane has to traverse a narrow canyon, and clouds would have prevented the pilot from seeing whether the wing tips were clear of the canyon walls.

Cairo

Tomorrow's newspapers may say that war started today here in Egypt. I hope not, but while there are the hours of waiting, let me tell you the story. When you read this you will already know the outcome, but perhaps these impressions may nevertheless hold some interest.

I have been in Egypt nine days. If nothing interferes I will be on a British plane leaving early Wednesday morning for the security of Cyprus. I came here by plane from Jerusalem, retracing in reverse much the same route the Israelites took according to the Biblical account. Separately I will write as to what transpired between

Kashmir where I last wrote, and Jerusalem. Briefly, my itinerary included India, Pakistan, Iraq, Lebanon, Syria, and Jordan.

You could probably guess that I visited the great pyramids and Sphinx at Giza, rode around on a camel, and climbed the passages inside the largest pyramid as much as was permitted. I had intended to go up the Nile by boat, but as it developed I went by overnight sleeper train. The boats have not operated since the last world war. The waters backed up by the dam at Aswan now cover much that had been the attraction to Aswan. I stayed in a near-empty hotel at Luxor, bordering the Nile—few people were around because this is the hottest season. Saw the ruins at Karnak, the temple and excavations at Luxor, and crossed the Nile in an ancient sailboat to the Valley of Kings at Thebes to see the tombs of King Tut and others. The last evening there I took the same craft for a cruise on the Nile at sunset. A memorable experience.

Cairo next claimed my attention, and then the port city of Alexandria. The latter is refreshingly more modern, cleaner and cooler than Cairo. A lake and bays combine to give the city both excellent harbor dock areas and recreational promenades along the sea. The balcony of my room commanded an excellent view of the sweeping curve of the shoreline. I particularly enjoyed a swim at crowded but colorful Stanley Beach on the Mediterranean; the Egyptian army band concert on the promenade at sunset; and the festive, cosmopolitan night life along the water's edge with its mixture of smart night clubs, bohemian sidewalk cafes, hurdy-gurdies, and horse and buggy transports. Pompeii's pillar, the Roman catacombs, Farouk's royal gardens, and the Alexandria zoo were also of interest. Enlivening the scene almost everywhere in Alexandria are red flame trees of exceptional beauty.

Also enlivening the scene was a near riot in which I was cast as a chief performer. My co-star was a fanatical Egyptian soldier who attempted to seize my camera, and when I resisted, attempted to manhandle me to get his way. A group of shouting Egyptians joined in, and only the intervention on my side of an English-speaking Egyptian bystander saved the day. I insisted on the soldier going with me to a police station, and in the hour consumed thereafter he was reprimanded by the police and apologized. I was given a police escort out of the area.

From Alexandria I went to Port Said, by way of Benha and Ismailia. From Ismailia onward, the route borders the Suez canal, much different in appearance from what I expected because it is without steep banks or locks (as far as I could determine)—just a wet ditch in the desert, bordered by tall grass. One hears of camels being the ships of the desert, but it is really strange to find great ships looming up amid the vastness of scorching desert sands, and gliding along so effortlessly. I was also surprised to find no clearcut demarcation between the canal zone and the rest of Egypt. British troops are garrisoned at intervals along the canal, but guarding is actually done by fast moving convoys which seem to go most anyplace they please in Egyptian territory.

In Port Said itself, the harbor and canal areas are barricaded and well guarded. Three Egyptian soldiers about every 100 yards, with single guards at inbetween points. Guards also throughout the city. Sand bags and barbed wire are much in evidence. I walked around a great deal, also hired a car to take me into the center of the canal area, and in and around the British encampments. An Egyptian elected himself my guide part of the time. I found he was an ex-convict convicted of smuggling dope, and was a commander in the riots against the British. He had a very interesting viewpoint on the Suez difficulty, but it suffered from being based in part on faulty information.

The Egyptian guards prevent any supplies (food in particular) from reaching the British from Egyptian sources. Ships and an airlift reportedly are used to feed the surrounded British areas. The streets of Port Said were quiet and orderly but I suspect there are occasional exceptions. One thing I noticed was a gang of young British in civilian clothes, armed with clubs and out in the city, possibly looking for trouble. I talked to one of them, but the reception was not encouraging.

Things went smoothly for me while I was in the critical areas, but once I was back in the city streets, another incident developed. An Egyptian soldier became abusive along the lines of the Alexandria incident, but this time we drew only four or five for an audience, and after some blunt exchanges of viewpoint and some manhandling, we parted company. After that I rode a ferry across the harbor to Port Fouad, and then returned and went in the surf at a fine beach on the far side of town.

I spent the evening at the Casino Palace in Port Said. There is not the same promenade there was in Alexandria, and the Casino seemed to be the hub of night life. It borders the harbor and is separated from the beach only by an Egyptian army encampment. My room had a small balcony which permitted one to sample a broad panorama. The arrangement of the hotel itself was interesting. A huge glass-domed conservatory-like roof stretched over the dining room, dance hall, casino, etc., and terraces, and most of the rooms looked out on to this scene from above. My room was just out from under the conservatory so I saw activity in both directions. Below and to the left were banners, bright colored lights, and umbrella-covered tables, and excited crowds which moved first to the tempo of Viennese waltzes, and then to the stomping of folk dances. To the right, some 50 feet away, were the bobbing fishing boats in the foreground (an ancient-looking sailing craft nearby looked particularly white and ghostly in the pale light of the harbor) and behind them, anchored at some distance, were large freighters and some passenger ships looking like glittering floating palaces.

My evening was interrupted by a police investigation of the day's incident. Then about eleven I went down on the quay between the casino and the ships and mingled with the local people out strolling for the breeze. It is a faintly lighted promenade which runs out toward the sea, the small craft on one side and the anti-aircraft nests, etc., beyond the wire at the other side. Here you meet the organ grinder and tambourine artist, competing against the music of the casino in the background; here also the seller of corn cobs roasted over charcoal. In Port Said there is the same mixture of old Arab sections and modern structures and the same cosmopolitan aspects as in Alexandria, but the city is less sophisticated—as a carnival differs from a night club.

In the morning, when I should still have been sleeping, I boarded an express train for Cairo. My luggage was placed in the same compartment as that of a European couple—I came to learn that the husband was British (a staunch hold-out against evacuation) and his wife, Italian. Several more crowded in. These were Egyptians. Our conversation became more cautious.

Between Said and Ismailia I again saw the canal. Compared to the prior day it was extremely crowded. I found that for one long stretch the canal is double, separate channels for traffic each way. Again I could not help thinking how strange it was to see the huge ships amid the sand, the canal water not being readily visible.

The air in the compartment was somewhat tense. (It was also stale, dusty, and in short supply considering the number of occupants.) I learned that a British soldier had been killed and there was talk of reprisals. The occupants came and left, and more information became available. It was not known that the soldier was killed, he was missing for three days and the British had served an ultimatum on the Egyptian government. The Italian lady leaned over to say that the Egyptians were boasting they would cut the throats of every Britisher. Her husband became quiet. The wife tried to be friendly with a child in the compartment.

At Ismailia, the vital point on the canal and scene of the bloodshed in January, the train was invaded by hordes of people. Families sought refuge without as much as bothering with tickets. There was talk about it being the last train out of Ismailia. But we did not know yet what it was all about. It was then about 8 or 8:30 a.m.

Shortly thereafter Egyptian police went through the train examining passports. The British couple were obviously disturbed that their nationality thus became evident to those in the compartment.

I went directly to the hotel upon arrival in Cairo. There I was besieged by questions. I sent for an English language newspaper; learned from it that the British ultimatum had expired at 9 a.m. at Ismailia and that British troops had taken over the city. That was the meaning then of all the rumors. The Egyptian government had declared a state of emergency throughout the country, the cabinet was in emergency session, and President Neguib had refused audience to the British diplomatic representative. The government broadcasts spoke of immediate preparation for war, and of the need to draw blood to settle the situation.

In early afternoon I set out for a trip about the city. Much was the same as usual, the exception being that many stared at me and some retraced their steps to get a better look. On the whole people were friendly. Some may have wondered if I were the missing Britisher. Most of the Europeans stayed indoors. They had in mind the burning of Cairo in January. About 4 p.m. the news boys started shouting an ''extra.'' It was snapped up eagerly by people from all sides. It was in Arabic so I could only watch faces for their reaction to the news. I decided not to ask for a translation. I continued to the poorer part of town and then back. Finally took a taxi to Groppe's where Europeans hang out for sodas. Bought a French language afternoon paper (headlines in red and heavy black) and read it inside Groppe's where it was almost empty. There were more details and the situation seemed as though it might break into open conflict. I verified at the airline office that a seat was open to Beirut the next day should it be desirable to leave on short notice, then returned to the hotel.

I started this letter on the roof garden of the hotel where I had dinner. A few Egyptians were there plus one European couple—otherwise empty. But the string quartet played beautifully and it was pleasant to be able to look out on the stars and see the shimmering reflections on the Nile. A shooting star—perhaps a falling star would be a more apt description depending upon whether one thinks of the possible clash or the break-up of the British Empire.

I have finished this letter in my room. The last news was at 11 p.m. and there were no new developments. I will stop now and wait for morning.

Next day

Today things look as though the world will muddle through another crisis. The above will show how scraps of information are pieced together, and how tense a situation can become.

I registered my whereabouts early this morning with the American Embassy. Spent two hours with a political columnist, then an hour with an educational administrator, followed by lunch at the home of an ex-University of Chicago student of economics who is now with Point IV. I will add just this much for the present since the columnist is about due here for another session with me which will last through dinner. Have gained some good insights into the Egyptian situation through today's efforts.

10

Starting Over

My experiences throughout the world had brought me added perspective as well as occasion to think through many of my ideas, but now I was ready to get on with my life.

On returning to the United States in the spring of 1954 I planned to study the philosophy of education and related topics at Stanford University. I had visited the campus en route to Asia the prior year, and I applied while still in London. A stipend was awarded, and I attended the summer quarter.

The campus was beautiful and the weather delightful, especially after a winter of London fog, but I did not find the course offerings in the School of Education to be challenging. Moreover, I took issue with the instructor's insistence in a basic course that papers prepared as though they were to be presented to the educational community not concede any merit to opposing points of view in order that no comfort be given to those who might dissent. This was certainly not an attitude toward differences in viewpoint which I could support. I decided to convert my registration to audit status, and supplemented class attendance during that term with my own program of reading and research on the philosophy, sociology and psychology of education, areas in which Stanford in now a leader in research.

In the fall I moved to the University of California at Berkeley, took a tower room on the edge of campus with a view of the Campanile, and explored what academic arrangements could be made there. I discovered that due to the amount of graduate credit I had already earned, I would have to satisfy the foreign language requirements before being admitted to the doctoral program. French was no problem, but the University did not accept mathematics as a second language at that time. I had attempted to learn German en route to New Guinea, and also subsequently, without making headway. The chairman of the Department of Economics arranged that I could audit graduate classes throughout the University as a guest and have library privileges. I attended the equivalent of half-time over a two-year period, attending courses in the philosophy of science, philosophy of language, logic, industrial relations, labor economics, and history of economic thought. Berkeley did not have a separate program in education.

Alongside this I worked on two projects of my own: developing a symbolic language to explicate the common foundations of language, logic and mathematics, and developing a course I might subsequently teach, tentatively entitled "Inquiry and Reform," which dealt with the methodology of the social sciences and their application to policy. I found the Berkeley experience quite stimulating—top-flight faculty, research seminars, excellent library resources, articulate socially-conscious students, a neighborhood of bookstores, and a vibrant student life. There were tentative suggestions from several units of the University that I might take a position, but I wanted to keep my most productive hours of each day for my own research, and thought it better to limit myself to activities that could be subordinated to that work.

During this period I became active in the Institute of Social and Personal Relations (ISPR), a not-for-profit organization headquartered alongside Lake Merritt in nearby Oakland, which was in the process of formation. It applied the behavioral sciences to meet individual and organizational needs in the San Francisco Bay Area. Dr. Jack F. Little, a Ph.D. psychologist, formerly chief of the Clinical Psychology Department at Oakland Naval Hospital, was head of the Institute. I served as liaison with the Oakland Area Council of Community Services, and advised senior citizen groups in qualifying for federal financial assistance in constructing large-scale housing for the elderly. I assisted the Institute in developing and adopting articles of incorporation and by-laws and served on its board of directors, continuing in that role for some years after I left the San Francisco Bay Area. The Institute developed a staff of thirty-five professionals from a dozen fields who provided volunteer services on a part-time basis in several locations in northern California. Clients who would have difficulty in paying a fee to the Institute received a waiver in advance, but this was held confidential to the provider.

One matter clouded this itinerant-scholar phase of my life, and that was money. None of my activities had been selected as income-producing, and consistent with expectation, none did provide financial support. I set aside funds sufficient to help with my mother's expenses in Portland for a year or so, since her funds had been largely used up by my father's final medical expenses and repayment of a mortgage. I was attempting to do my research, design a course to teach, attend some courses, and work with the Institute with no breakfast, and only a 37¢ lunch and a 37¢ dinner, each consisting of a hotdog and roll with soup.

I took a series of jobs through a temporary-help employment agency. I had not needed to take the initiative to secure employment since the depression years before college. The employment I was able to obtain at this time paid so poorly that I walked between nearby cities to save bus fare. For a short period I drove a stationwagon for a title guarantee company that had branches in various East Bay cities, delivering and picking up legal papers. The circuit-rider schedule was so tight that I had to skirt the speed limit to keep on schedule, and after a close call at a school crossing, I turned in my car keys. Then a woman bookstore manager employed me to sell books at a convention, which went all right until she made a request for personal off-duty services. Overlapping that was a job for several weeks prior to Christmas in a partially flooded warehouse on the Oakland waterfront, spraying fir trees with white plastic foam. No mask was provided so I improvised with a handkerchief. I also delivered merchandise. Once it was to the lobby of a financial building on Montgomery Street in San Francisco, to accomplish which I had to drive along the sidewalk, scattering pedestrians. Another night I crossed the southern portion of San Francisco Bay on a narrow pontoon bridge during a strong wind which whipped the canvas covering off the truck. I had great difficulty retying the canvas without being blown into the bay. The job ended on Christmas Eve, and since there was a pile of unsold trees, I asked if I might have one, which request was denied.

The employment agency next placed me with an association of credit unions as a consultant. The manager took me to a businessmen's luncheon to show me off as a good catch. It was an interesting phenomenon—businessmen wearing funny paper hats and required to wear a cowbell if they were late. An auxiliary printing organization was to be incorporated to issue stock, but its financial affairs had first to be untangled. I prepared a comprehensive report detailing seventeen types of adjustment in the financial records that would avoid redoing the body of the reports. I also prepared a sampling-standard cost system for estimating printing jobs in advance and for judging efficiency. A change in office procedures was also recommended for the handling of income so that all steps from the receipt of funds through final accounting would no longer be the responsibility of one individual. There was a treasurer as well as the financial clerk, but they lived together. They were married, but not to each other.

It was during this period that an event occurred which I have pondered occasionally since that time. After being employed in a position I was called in and confronted by information from an unknown source: (1) In 1945, as a counter-intelligence agent in Japan I released known communists from the penitentiary. [Not noted was that it was General MacArthur's policy at that time, as the Supreme Commander of Allied Powers, that all political prisoners be released in order to encourage a multi-party system in Japan.] (2) In 1949, I refused to provide the Federal Bureau of Investigation (as mentioned in Chapter 6) with periodic reports on members of the Cowles Commission the FBI regarded as subversive. [Not noted was that I had insisted successfully that the Commission accept only projects that did not require a security clearance, in order to have access to the most capable individuals.] (3) In the 1950's, as Secretary of the Econometric Society, I accepted the membership application of a philosophy professor in Colorado who volunteered that he was a member of the Communist Party. [Not noted was that the constitution of the Econometric Society, an international organization, stated there was no political test for membership.] (4) Also in the 1950's, I appointed as one of several associate editors of *Econometrica* an individual who was a known Communist. [Not noted was that I assigned that highly qualified individual only technical articles for refereeing.] Ignored was that my personal philosophy and my writings had been supportive of a decentralized participatory type of organization. Even ISPR had stressed non-directive techniques. I knew of no single source from which such information could have been obtained. In that post-McCarthy period, the use of an accumulation of half-truths to point to an incorrect conclusion was not uncommon. With such interpretations placed on my actions available on short notice from an unknown source, and without my knowing in any instance whether I should protest or not, it made application for any substantial position seem hardly worth the effort.

In a meeting Jacob Marschak suggested we have in Chicago on my return to this country, he warned me this would happen, but I did not fully accept that until it actually did.

[Sigmund Diamond is writing mainly about campuses other than the University of Chicago in his 1992 publication, *Compromised Campus: The Collaboration of Universities with the Intelligence Community, 1945-1955*, but he describes the FBI practice at that time of obtaining the dismissal of university personnel (himself included) who did not cooperate with the FBI in reporting on their colleagues, and also the FBI practice of blacklisting them so as to make appointment elsewhere difficult, if not impossible, during this period of years. Diamond, on page 39, mentions an example at Harvard in which an individual was investigated ''because he was a consultant for the RAND Corporation,'' an organization with which I had much contact, as I have described in Chapter 6.]

I felt devastated by this development. My research projects suffered, and I gave thought to staking out a different life. But the pull of my ideas was too strong.

This problem resurfaced in an encounter with the right wing John Birch Society in the 1960's when I was teaching for the Peace Corps, and again in the early 1970's when on behalf of the American Economic Association I investigated charges that the chancellor of a system of higher education had engaged in political discrimination against a liberal anti-war activist.

The position which Liz had with the Committee on Communication at the University of Chicago was eliminated through a consolidation while I was still at Stanford, and she came out to work in the financial district of San Francisco. As mentioned earlier, I moved to Berkeley just before the fall term in 1954. I shifted to a place overlooking Lake Merritt next to ISPR about 1956, and then later to San Francisco. Liz and I generally met on weekends, either in the East Bay or San Francisco.

A chance remark that I made in Berkeley as to being interested in Asia led to my being introduced to Alan Watts, a well-known advocate of Zen Buddhism and Dean of the American Academy of Asian Studies in San Francisco. Watts, who was born in England, first was an Anglican Priest, then an Episcopalian Priest, and then departed from both faiths. He had written about a dozen books on comparative religion, had a radio program in several cities, taped television shows, and went on lecture circuits.

The Academy was located in a large mansion in Pacific Heights overlooking the entrance to San Francisco Bay. It served as a graduate school of the College of the Pacific in Stockton. The work of the Academy, as set forth in its catalog, was three-fold: intensive studies of the cultures of Asia, leading to the master's degree; a doctoral program consisting of research, translation, and special studies in the cultural relations of Asia and the West; and a separate program of public lectures and special conferences held at the Academy or in locations outside of San Francisco.

Watts, in addition to being Dean, was Professor of Comparative Philosophy. There were also professors of Indian Philosophy, Islamic and North African studies (Rom Landau, author of *Moroccan Drama*, published by the Academy), Chinese studies, the Arts of the Far East (Sabra Hasagawa), and Sanskript. Other staff members covered Indic Studies, Arabic, Chinese, Cantonese, Japanese, and so forth. The advisory board of the Academy, largely honorary, included ambassadors from the Philippines, Lebanon and Saudi Arabia; former prime ministers of Indonesia and Pakistan; the former minister of foreign affairs of Thailand; the president of the University of California and the president of Stanford University; and certain business leaders. The board of governors included additional heads of educational institutions, consul generals of India and Pakistan, and other prominent Bay Area individuals. The founder of the Academy had his office on Sansome Street in the financial district of San Francisco.

After speaking with Alan Watts and the founder, I was asked to give a series of fund-raising lectures on Southeast Asia on a four-month appointment. I prepared the lectures but then was asked to first address certain other matters. I was requested by the founder to provide recommendations on federal legislation concerning an Asian-African Development Corporation that was to be introduced in the U.S. Congress by Senator Jacob Javits of New York. This I did, and was told later that my recommendations had been put to good use. Then I was asked to repair relations between the Academy in San Francisco and the parent institution in Stockton, since administrative working relationships had become somewhat irregular. I explored the matter with staff members at the two locations and obtained agreement on needed changes in procedures. I also convened the first meeting of the faculty of the Academy as a decision-making and recommending body, and provided them with an outline of faculty rights and responsibilities along the lines advocated by the American Association of University Professors. It was interesting to observe such a set of celebrated individualists of so many different nationalities learning to work together.

A pressing matter was the low morale among members of the faculty. They were paid very little and they kept body and soul together by living at the Academy and eating what was provided. I sometimes ate there when there was to be a lecture at the Academy that evening. During such meals I usually sat next to Watts and discussed my research on the philosophy of language as well as methodological matters that concerned me. I was greatly surprised on several occasions when Watts in his evening lecture demonstrated total recall and made my discussion part of his presentation, with comment, however, as to its origin.

I had a series of discussions with President Burns of the College of the Pacific, with the presidents of various colleges and universities who were on the advisory board or the board of governors, and with the executive committee of the Academy which included the presidents of San Francisco State College and business leaders such as Claire Giannini Hoffman, a director of the Bank of America and daughter of its founder. I also consulted Sir Cyril Cane, retired British Consul for San Francisco, who was a member of the Friends of the Academy. Several of the influential members of the group deeply distrusted the founder and did not want to be identified with approaches being made for funds. This was in spite of the image which he projected of being a philanthropist, a pillar of the community, a professed friend of Mahatma Gandhi, a self-described successful financier, and a mover and shaker. He had been featured in 1951 in full page articles in *Time* and *Fortnight*. His attorney volunteered that I might get a bullet in my back if I probed into the founder's past. I did so, nevertheless, and encountered the allegation in various quarters that under his original name he had made millions in South America during the war selling to the Nazi-Fascist Axis, and was now using the appearance of being a spiritually inclined philanthropist as a facade. This was, as far as I was concerned, an unproved allegation, but when I heard him speak with disdain in unguarded moments of the Asian members of the faculty, I began to wonder. Also, on several separate occasions he expressed the view that it was acceptable behavior to leave whatever impression will serve your purposes, even if others misunderstood you and you know that they do, as long as the words you use do not constitute a lie.

I obtained photostats of pertinent records from the founder's attorney and his bookkeeper, both of whom were entirely cooperative. I also made inquiries of the Internal Revenue Service. What I pieced together was that the founder had indeed changed his name since his previous activity, that his ''donations'' to the Academy were in fact recallable advances, that title to the physical premises of the Academy and its furnishings, which the faculty thought to be the property of the Academy, were still controlled by the founder; and that certification of the tax exempt status of the Academy had expired more than four years ago. The reluctance of potential donors to make significant contributions to the Academy became understandable.

The founder's sole control of the institution gave the Academy a ''private'' character which made the raising of public support difficult. Those with whom I spoke on the governing board confirmed that in their view a minimum condition for the Academy to be able to attract funds was that the founder disassociate himself from personal control of the institution. A member of the Academy staff provided me with a psychological profile of the founder indicating the latter's inability to receive donations gracefully due to their diluting the significance of his own contribution. (The similarity of this to Mr. Cowles' reaction to the obtaining of additional financing for the Cowles Commission came to mind.)

I discussed my findings with Dean Watts and the faculty of the Academy, and observed their cultivated detachment and calmness evaporate in the heat of indignation. However, I proposed, and it was agreed, that if the founder would step down, the catalog and other publications of the Academy would carry his name as founder. I was encouraged to consult a leading San Francisco importer of Asian art who was a member of the board of governors to explore his willingness to serve as chairman of the board. He agreed, on conditions that were judged acceptable.

Communications were sent by the dean and faculty of the Academy to the president of the College of the Pacific setting forth the Academy's problems and prospects, including the request that I be invited to attend deliberations on the matter as consultant to the Academy. Watts was resigning as Dean, but indicated that he would be available to serve as Director of Studies. Intense evening meetings of alumni, faculty, and friends of the Academy were held at the Academy to discuss these matters. Those attending prepared and signed petitions that I be named Administrative Dean of the Academy. However, I regarded my proper role as confined to facilitating the organization of the Academy to enable it to continue. Moreover, I had experience with their spare meals, and I was not a devotee.

The negotiations with the College of the Pacific, the board of governors of the Academy, and the principals involved went through various stages, and were still underway and proceeding satisfactorily when I turned my attention elsewhere. Before I left, however, I gave attention to related needs of the Academy. I formulated a new set of by-laws for the Academy which brought the organizational arrangement up-to-date and which would explicitly prevent any of the income or assets of the Academy from reverting directly or indirectly to the benefit of trustees or officers, reverting instead to the College of the Pacific; recommended annual audits by an independent certified public accountant selected by the Board of Governors; drafted a new exemption application for submission to the Internal Revenue Service; prepared a draft letter which the Executive Committee could use in approaching corporations for financial support; and prepared two additional key documents. The first was a development plan for the Academy, and the second was a comprehensive consultant report of over fifty pages on the problems and prospects of the Academy.

I was extremely busy during this period and slept on a cot at the Academy when it was too late to return to my lodgings. Several of the faculty who had rooms in the Academy building assisted me by taking dictation, typing, and duplicating copies, for what I was doing meant a great deal to them. The Registrar cooked breakfast for me. I did not mention that I had been getting used to skipping that meal. The House Manager even insisted that I accept his favorite pipe.

The development plan set forth various objectives to be served, identified the type and possible sources of financing in each case, and presented suggestions as to the means to employ. I mention some of the approaches since they may have relevance for other institutions: A. Recruit graduate students nationally rather than exclusively from local institutions. B. Increase interest in Asian and North African studies through: (1) summer workshops for secondary school teachers on integrating pertinent material on philosophy and psychology into the curriculum, (2) joint appointments permitting offerings at undergraduate college campuses, (3) provision for undergraduates to attend graduate courses while under the administrative supervision of an undergraduate college, and (4) preparation of instructional aids to further the teaching of Asian and North African studies. C. Serve the business community through conference-workshop meetings on the mentality and outlook of their Asian and North African counterparts, with keynote speakers and staff drawn from the Academy and the business world. D. Increase public appreciation of the Academy's potential through: (1) invitational symposiums, (2) collaboration on courses given through educational television channels, and (3) provision of honorariums for lecturers in the public lecture series at the Academy. E. Encourage academic attention to East-West problems and the work of the Academy through: (1) summer workshops on East-West communication, invitational to academic and government workers in this field, (2) an annual award for the best article or book published during the year in the fields of philosophy or psychology relating to East-West communications, as selected by an international panel of recognized stature, (3) sustaining patron status for *Philosophy East and West*, a journal published at the University of Hawaii, and (4) continuation of the Asian Study monograph series. And finally, F. Dramatize the objectives served by the Academy through designating annually one or more individuals in Asia, North Africa or the West as a Fellow of the American Academy of Asian Studies, to be selected by an impartial panel, for significant contributions during the year to East-West understanding, an appointment carrying a money stipend.

The separate consultant report discussed these matters in greater detail and also included the following suggestion which tied in with work with which I was concerned at the Institute of Social and Personal Relations concurrently with my role at the Academy:

> The Academy needs to be interested in the community if the community is to show interest in the Academy. It is proposed that possible contributions of insights from Asian culture to the easing of Western problems at the local community level (senior citizens, juvenile delinquents, marital discord, mental hygiene, and so forth) be the topic for several well-planned one-day invitational symposia and conference-workshop sessions for groups of social, business, labor, professional and educational people, with a panel drawn from the Academy staff and from among those in the community academically or practically experienced in dealing with the problems . . .

The consultant report also contained tables as to enrollment and tuition, existing and proposed budgets, insurance and bonding, and actual and comparative salary data, as well as recommended policy on the receipt by faculty members of outside income.

Certain passages from the consultant report that should have continuing interest for other institutions faced with comparable situations are included as Annex 10.1 to this chapter. On a related topic is a paper on economically under-developed countries that was completed in 1961, included as Annex 10.2.

A member of the Academy staff spoke about my work to the president of Golden Gate College (subsequently Golden Gate University), which is located in San Francisco. The college provided opportunities for college education (both general and professional) to qualified men and women whose economic circumstances require that they be self-supporting while obtaining their education. I was invited to visit in December 1956 and accepted a position as consultant to the president on the design and implementation of a program of college self-study and evaluation.

The program was needed as preparation for a report to the Northwest Accrediting Association, but I was concerned that it be instituted as a continuing mechanism for appraisal and adjustment of the college's policies. Drafts for each of a variety of areas were prepared, discussed, and revised by working committees of those faculty and staff who were most closely involved. There was then discussion within successively larger contexts and revision as appropriate. I coordinated all aspects of the study, but gave particular attention to those portions of the report to the accreditation agency that were concerned with the review of institutional objectives, strengthening of faculty, and administration of the curriculum. Of particular concern was the heavy reliance upon part-time specialists drawn from the San Francisco business community. Procedures were established for obtaining the viewpoints of newly registered students as to admission procedures, of continuing students as to instructional performance, and of alumni as to the appropriateness of their education. The student council was encouraged to appoint a student committee on educational policy.

The evaluation study made evident the need for a permanent organization of the college faculty, and the Dean of the Law School prepared a draft proposal for establishment of an Academic Council. I presided at a series of general faculty meetings in the fall of 1957 at which the organization of the Council was discussed, and thereafter prepared various revisions based on conclusions arrived at in those meetings and on contributions from those who could not attend. Provision was made for representation of part-time faculty. The Council, in turn, was represented on the joint faculty-staff committee on educational and administrative policy. In writing this now, I note with interest the following passage from minutes of the November 4, 1957 meeting which I chaired. "Dean Kelly said he doubted the sincere enthusiasm of most of the members for a council at all, that most of them probably were present because they were expected to be, and that he, for one, had no interest in seeing a council formed." The minutes recorded a general burst of protest. In spite of this opposition from the Dean of the College, the Academic Council was formed in January 1958 and went into operation.

In general, there was a movement along several fronts for bringing college policies into conformity with guidelines of the American Association of University Professors (AAUP). I had been accepted for membership in that organization after being recommended by Reginald Arragon, Professor of History at Reed College. I was teaching courses in economics at Golden Gate in addition to my duties as consultant.

In late March of 1957 I met Ruth, who soon became my wife, serving drinks on Geary Street in San Francisco. She prefers to explain that she was serving tea on the Social Committee of the Unitarian Church there, and we were both attending that Sunday. I proposed within the first two weeks, and she accepted. I used the argument that I needed a reason to get my library out of storage, but there was mutual understanding that there was a more significant basis. Our marriage was in early June, upon my teaching being completed for the spring, and we took off for Big Sur.

At the time I met Ruth I was living in part of what had been the mansion of a former governor of California, Hiram Johnson. It was located on the side of Russian Hill, and was reached by a zigzag stairway from Green Street far below. There was a cable car line at the corner. The formal gardens at the back, then in ruins, but beautiful in the moonlight, looked upon Nob Hill. The cliff had crumbled to within two feet of where I was living and an enterprising individual was renting out space at a reasonable price. My living room (and only room) looked straight down upon Fisherman's Wharf. Another window framed Coit Tower, particularly impressive when illuminated at night. Although the place had served me well, Ruth persuaded me that we needed larger quarters, and particularly a place that would not slide into the Bay, so we found an apartment facing Golden Gate Park.

At the beginning of the fall semester of 1957 I added to my duties an appointment as Director of the Liberal Arts Program and Associate Dean of the College. I planned to stay only a brief time, not longer than mid-1958, and even that simply to implement various policies for which I hoped to secure faculty acceptance. But first there was the matter of developing among those teaching the arts and sciences courses, both full and part-time, the sense of being part of an entity, the Faculty of Arts and Sciences, which as a body would be actively concerned in the betterment of the general education program at the College. Many of the faculty could attend meetings only during the noon period because of other employments in business or at other campuses. There had never been a meeting of these faculty members previously. I arranged that they meet at regular intervals for a catered luncheon with chamber music in the background, followed by a business meeting at which I gave an update of developments and encouraged discussion of possible recommendations on policy alternatives.

Working groups were established in the following areas: Natural Sciences (determining program objectives), Library Program, Remedial English, Mathematics (to introduce elements of the calculus), remedial study practices, tutorial assistance, grading and attendance procedures, catalog revision, student cultural events, and a social committee to plan regular functions in which members of the Arts and Sciences faculty and their spouses could participate and become better acquainted. In the spring semester of 1958 I was able to provide a comprehensive memorandum on revision of the curriculum in the area of Communication Techniques. By then there were also changes agreed upon in the mathematics offering, a newly designed course Values for Living was taught, the offering in psychology was strengthened (drawing upon Dr. Little from ISPR), the first offering in anthropology had been added, and so forth.

About this time it became apparent that opposition to developments in the Arts and Sciences area was growing among a small group of full-time administrators at the college, including the dean of the college, who wished to assure that ample funds be earmarked for increases in their compensation. They explored with an alternative accredition agency, the Western College Association, the possibility of the college being accredited as a specialized institution without strengthening the liberal arts offerings, and possibly with even less emphasis on the arts and sciences than before I was invited to the college. It was quite a different view from that which I understood to prevail at the time of my appointment as director of the liberal arts program and at the time that meetings of the arts and sciences faculty had been initiated in the prior fall. The deemphasis on the arts and sciences would be permitted by Western. I do not think that I have used the word "disgusted" in my writing so far; in any event, the word seems appropriate in describing my feelings in regard to the behavior of those who actively sought out this reversal of the college's direction.

I turned my attention in the following several months to a further redesign of the curriculum and distribution requirements in order to retain the best features of the changes that had been made while at the same time containing the costs for arts and sciences within a smaller than original total.

A several volume history of the college completed in recent years manages to overlook entirely the developments described in the preceding pages, and mentions only a fund-raising effort. The institution is now known as Golden Gate University.

For a year or so I had been exploring with various organizations the feasibility of individuals combining the benefit of periods of living in San Francisco, most likely during the summer months, with their own mix of educational and cultural experiences for which they could be granted transferable academic credit. I envisaged an overall coordinating body which would prepare an academic transcript for those who completed various amounts of specified activity at one or more of a number of institutions, including the Music and Arts Institute of San Francisco, San Francisco Conservatory of Ballet and Theatre Arts, American Academy of Asian Studies, Schaiffer School of Design, Institute of Semantics, Golden Gate College, ISPR, World Affairs Council, etc. Promotional efforts would initially be funded by the Chamber of Commerce. The name I had in mind for this, the University of San Francisco, which at that time was not used by any other organization, was subsequently taken as the new name for St. Ignatius College. I did not complete that project, but perhaps someone else will feel there is merit in pursuing its possibilities.

10.1

On East-West Relations

The large measure of self-direction allowed academic faculties in educational matters is important for the American Academy of Asian Studies, for if it is to further the best in East-West relationship, it must not press the Asian contribution into rigid molds of Western thinking. At the same time the problem is rendered more difficult by what in Western eyes appears as a non-goal-seeking tendency present in East Asian philosophy.

What is said here does not mean that no goals should be set for the Academy, or that the faculty should be left entirely to its own devices. The recommendation is that the Board formulate its view of the Academy in extremely broad and flexible terms. One possible formulation is as a continuing educational experiment on East-West relations.

At present, the main emphasis of the Academy is on communication, and the philosophy, psychology, the arts, and languages of Asia are given prominence . . . It is a source of strength in that it is in those aspects of Asian culture that the need for understanding Asia is perhaps greatest, and that the contribution of Asia to our own way of life is most valuable . . . At the same time, this is a source of weakness for the Academy. Under the most favorable conditions, psychology, and the speculative, aesthetic, religious and valuational fields of philosophy are the most suspect parts of the humanities and sciences in the minds of the general public. These fields come in for abuse not only from the lay individual but also from philosophers and psychologists of a different bent. Furthermore, areas of inquiry such as meta-linguistics and cybernetics dealt with in the Academy's work are beyond the ken of the vast majority—whether of academic background or not. Compounding these difficulties in being fairly appraised by the public, the approach emphasized in some of the studies at the Academy maintains that Asian philosophy and psychology can not be adequately appreciated with the detachment of a clinical technician—some amount of experiential involvement is essential. This approach tends automatically to be interpreted by many as one of religious involvement in view of the popular conception of Asian philosophy as being inseparable from religion or theology. Further, there is an inevitable feedback of the content of these philosophies upon the attitudes adopted toward administration. The tendency to associate the Academy with the esoteric has arisen out of the interplay of these various factors in the Academy's situation . . .

It is recommended that efforts go forward not only to preserve and strengthen that program, but also to develop other approaches to and facets of Asian studies. Except for the case of Islamic and North African studies, in which the Academy is in a leading position even nationally, (and except for South Asian studies as noted below), it is not suggested that the Academy undertake to compete with heavily staffed universities in the offering of an area study approach. However, as a fairly immediate step the Academy might seek part-time lecturers who could cooperate in an integrated course covering historical, sociological, economic, political and geographic background of the Asian world; later on integrated courses for each major region; and then such specialized courses as demand would support.

South East Asia studies need to be given more than token attention in the curriculum. With several philosophical viewpoints represented in that region, an area study approach may offer the best opportunity for an integrated view.

In addition, the Academy should seek to be in a position to attract at intervals of several years individuals from East or West who could stimulate additional directions of inquiry. Thus one might seek a professor who could approach the problems of communication from standpoints complementary to those already given principal attention at the Academy, or who could build up alongside the work on communication a program of Asian Studies around such disciplines as human ecology, ethnology, sociology, history and philosophy of science, or historiography. Potential appointees could be screened through invitation as visiting professor for a summer session, or through participation in the public lecture program or a summer workshop.

It is suggested that weight be given to the candidate's suitability for taking a turn as director of graduate studies, a post which might well rotate at intervals of about three years so as to assure balanced growth of the curriculum.

The faculty is only gradually becoming accustomed to functioning as a body. With its diversity in national origin, culture, religion, as well as philosophical viewpoint, it is a laboratory in itself for the study of intercultural adjustment.

It is suggested further that in the selection of faculty, weight be attached to the individual being a truly human and accessible personality. Partly this suggestion stems from the belief that the Academy should aim at remaining a small and select graduate school with easy access of students to faculty. Also it stems from the belief that in the teaching-learning process there is something to be learned from the instructor as a whole personality. This is believed to be particularly the case in grasping the import of Asian culture.

The best composition of the faculty with respect to Asian and Western membership is not entirely clear. The difficulty any individual has in correctly interpreting his own culture has to be weighed against the tendency to interpret a culture different from one's own only in terms of the categories appropriate to one's own experience. This calls for continuing consideration, and no settled view has been reached.

What may a student expect from attending the Academy? As yet this had been left largely unanswered. There is need to follow up those who have graduated to get their a posteriori appraisals, and those who left before completing a degree to sense what they felt was lacking. In student recruitment and in counseling there is need for greater use of material on the vocational advantages of attending the Academy. In general terms one can speak of possible roles in public service, in teaching, and in business, but more definite information is needed. There is a shortage of teachers having a background in Asian studies at secondary school through to graduate levels, but need and career opportunities are not always the same thing.

The Academy certainly contributes to an understanding and respect for Asian culture. In this it has relevance to the survival of our own culture, both in easing the interpenetration of systems of action and in increasing our effectiveness when discord is not successfully avoided. Its contribution has relevance also to the competitive struggles in the world of business, and more generally to the problem of the

Westerner being effective in an alien society.

There is another aspect of the Academy's contribution which has yet to be mentioned. This is in enabling a student to benefit in a direct personal way from his insights into Asian philosophy and psychology so that he may live more effectively and fully in his own culture. This is as intangible as is the contribution made by a liberal arts education. It is no less important than a liberal education in its possibilities for influencing the intensity and breadth of one's life experiences. It compensates for the activist bias to Western thought, suggesting that changes in one's own attitude are as important as changes in the external environment.

As yet there has not been sufficient study of students at the Academy to be able to generalize as to the type attracted. Nor is it possible from the data on hand to state from how wide an area the Academy currently attracts its attendance. It has been said at times that the Academy tends to attract to its public lectures and its courses individuals who are at odds with religion, who either are dissatisfied with their analyst or cannot afford him, who are escapists from the materialistic emphasis of our culture or seek rationalizations of their own internal world. In general, the overt behavior observed did not suggest that the above was true, but this was not conclusive either way. Such conversations as were held with students revealed them to be serious-minded, and that most had a good grasp of what they wanted. They tended to have a heterogeneous preparation in accord with the interdisciplinary as well as the intercultural emphasis of the Academy. Beyond that it was not within the competence or opportunity of the consultant to judge.

From what has been said it is clear that the faculty needs within its numbers some who are particularly adept at interpreting Asia in terms of what it means for effective living in our own culture. For it to be otherwise, the Academy would have removed the ocean but not the mystery which separates Asia from us. What is transmitted is potent in possible consequences for an unsettled person. More than is usually the case for an educational institution, this invests the Academy with responsibilities relating to the conduct of the individual student and the need to think out the consequences of educational policies. It is suggested that in part, at least, appropriate safeguards rest in making evident whenever possible the affinities existing with Western religions, and as explained more fully subsequently, in relating the insights gained to practical problems of our own community.

The formal organization of the Academy seems eminently suitable for an institution of its particular kind, in providing considerable autonomy in operation while preserving a relationship to the College of the Pacific which gives ready access to a considerable reservoir of experience upon which the Academy may draw.

The picture suggested of the Academy then is something like this: the gradual development of a central core offering a truly comprehensive and integrated approach to Asian culture and its environment, combined with varied pioneering and experimental efforts which may provide an increment to the core or may be discarded. It is this growing edge which should constantly reinvigorate the teaching of the core and which may serve as a catalyst to educational efforts elsewhere. The Academy must always be prepared to face the possibility that it has paved the way for making part of its efforts only duplicative of offerings and approaches it has served to inspire in neighboring institutions. This combination of attempt at stable permanence yet participation in constant flux underlies the concept of the Academy being a continuing educational experiment. It forms a basis appropriate to the continued interest of major foundations, and suggests the long-run desirability of seeking the participation of Bay Area educational institutions in its support as a resource center for Asian studies.

In this enterprise it is the task of the administrator partly to plant the visions of others, partly to take direct actions, but even more to make possible, through working with all concerned, an environment in which incentives and satisfactions are such that the work continues within the broadly defined, predetermined framework established by the Board.

10.2

Opportunity Cost and Underdeveloped Areas

(1961)

The wayfarer,
Perceiving the pathway to truth,
Was struck with astonishment.
It was thickly grown with weeds.
"Ha," he said,
"I see that no one has passed here
"In a long time."

Later he saw that each weed
Was a singular knife.
"Well," he mumbled at last,
"Doubtless there are other roads."
—Stephen Crane (1899)

It is with some audacity that one suggests that the academic worker, the dedicated searcher for truth, has, along with the layman, been deterred from cutting to the heart of what concerns him. The apparent has for too many been the real. The readily-won reward has for too many been the measure of worth. The uncultivated paths of thought have been returned to weeds, each a knife to discourage entry.

The deterrents are not difficult to identify. A list, however short, would mention the short payout-period criterion used in selecting publication-yielding subjects for research. The desire to be practical, even in theory, works a disadvantage in the search for insights that would be isolated links in as yet unforged chains.

Gunnar Myrdal, in *An International Economy*, refers in various contexts to how explorations by social scientists are bounded unnecessarily by drawing value horizons too narrowly, by the power balance in society favoring social statics, by unwarranted optimism pressing in from our milieu, and by reluctance to ask awkward questions.

Economists from time to time have made efforts to cut through and behind the trappings and presumptions of this world and the money calculus to the ''real'' aspects of economics. Robinson Crusoe economics, Adam Smith's deer and beaver example, and the classical theory of the monetary veil illustrate what I have in mind. The concept of opportunity cost—cost in terms of the benefit foregone in the best alternative use of a resource—offers one cutting tool for clearing away the overlay that obscures what is basically involved.

Whose Problem Is It?

Is the concept of an opportunity cost being attached to foregoing change in a society meaningful when resources are allocated in accordance with tradition and custom without consideration of alternative uses? If alternatives are not considered, is there a sacrifice involved? What is needed for opportunity cost to exist is an *awareness* of alternative uses of a resource that make it scarce relative to the array of possible uses. A situation in which there is need for choice in the allocation of a scarce good between or among alternative uses is what we term ''an economic problem.'' Opportunity costs enter here, but how they are figured would depend on *whose* economic problem it is.

Before modern transport and communications it was possible to identify societies which were largely traditional in their ways of solving their economic problems rather than market-oriented, and which either through isolation, indifference, or plain common sense, had not yet been caught up in what we popularly call the rising tide of expectations. Such areas were then the concern of National Geographic caravans, missionaries, and colonists. Those intervening in such areas spoke in terms of the ''white man's burden.'' Others, drawing on relativistic views as to the nature of values and goals, could reply that those who disturbed such societies were solving not the problems of those who were indigenous to the area but their own problem of being disturbed by what seemed a cultural anachronism.

In recent years we have witnessed two associated changes which were not expected at the accelerated rate at which they have occurred. One is that lesser development countries of various types—politically mature or newly emergent, tradition or market-oriented, under or overpopulated, poorly or well endowed with resources—have tended to internalize the problem of development as a consequence of rapid changes of tastes, that is, they have tended to make it their own problem. The other change, which occurred within the economically advanced countries, has been elevation of the problem of underdevelopment to national concern. The effort to aid such areas is no longer a cross to be borne in unselfishness, nor simply the exercise of man's commercial instincts. It has become a matter of competition among developed nations vying for the allegiance of the lesser developed countries, including many left long neglected with the dual economies which became the hallmark of colonialism.

The Erection of Social Goals

Policy presumes an element of control and an element of preference. In the case of underdeveloped areas, the preference for different outcomes than experienced to date is proving strong enough for the attempt at control to be made. Social goals are being erected—change is sought, or the acceleration of change—and efforts to implement the attainment of these goals are being pursued.

Private domestic and private foreign investment initiatives for needed advances in the economic development of the lesser developed countries have been demonstrably inadequate. This has given rise to decisions being taken by central authorities, both domestic and foreign to the country, in the absence of an effective impersonal market mechanism. These decisions are of two broad types: One type has been concerned with structuring conditions for private investment that would encourage its volume and channel its direction. The other has been concerned with public investment to supplement (sometimes to supplant) investment from private sources.

A choice between policies which take such economic development as comes along, and policies which work actively toward guiding and accelerating that development, has been seen by the lesser developed countries and the more advanced countries alike as not properly judged only in terms of the expenditures involved. The essential element has been recognition of the opportunity cost of inaction, namely, the advantage foregone by not furthering economic development. Relative to such cost, expenditure for a development program has seemed less formidable.

Indeed, it has been the progressive acknowledgment of the cost of inaction by the effective government of a country that has led to additional specifications (in this case economic growth; at other steps, economic stability, economic freedom, economic efficiency, economic justice, and so forth) as to what shall constitute satisfactory performance by the economy. With the erection of such additional goals, it has become the role of government to provide a more structured framework for private business decisions, requiring as a consequence more specialized and precise instruments of policy than would otherwise be the case. The choice between balanced and unbalanced growth is partly to be interpreted in such terms.

The orthodox policy is balanced growth wherein balance is sought in the demand for products and in the supply of inputs. In contrast, in a policy of unbalanced growth dramatic situations of unfulfilled opportunities are created to induce more individual initiative. There is lesser subsequent government role than under a policy of balanced growth. Fewer specifications can be set, however, as to the extent or direction of growth that will result.

Are There Alternatives for the Longer Term?

Are we correct in being persuaded that there are alternatives to be evaluated and choices to be made by society with respect to its long-term developments? Does it make sense for society to weigh the opportunity cost of alternatives, or are the choices already foreclosed in important respects?

These questions may be too imperfectly conceived. Let us approach the matter in another way: Certain lines of thought circumscribe one's sense of what can be accomplished by each lesser-developed country by itself, by advanced countries with respect to them, or by international organizations. I refer here not to the difficulty which uncertainty introduces for policy-making (to which reference is made subsequently), nor to objections raised in terms of the outlays required or the impact on personal freedom, but rather to those lines of thought which make positive policy seem less effectual or even futile over the long run unless provision is made for a change away from the existing structural framework.

The Marxian historical dialectic falls in this loose grouping of viewpoints. So also, but without the same degree of inevitability, do several of the ''stages of economic growth'' type of theory, including that offered by W.W. Rostow as a non-communist manifesto. These viewpoints sketch out somewhat of a mold for what will happen, give or take some years, give or take some details, and give or take some degrees of inevitability.

Of normative rather than necessarily descriptive relevance for policy, but nevertheless also dulling the point of a positive social policy, has been the view that there exist natural and automatic adjustments which will take place in a laissez faire, free-market economy to restore proper order to economic affairs. The theory of international trade based on comparative advantage, however, failed to provide for major change in the position of a lesser developed country relative to the more economically advanced nations with respect to type of industry, skill level of labor force, and so forth. Failing in this respect, comparative advantage theory has invited an attitude accepting the favorable relative role of the advanced countries.

The Changing Context of Economic Development

Economics I take to be the study of institutions through which society organizes the decision-making involved in allocating among different employments those resources that are scarce relative to their possible uses. But what of the process whereby the goals of society are erected and institutions are developed to implement them? Does this lie outside of economics?

By an "institution" I mean here a pattern of behavior that is developed around the performance of some function, or attainment of some goal, so as to permit this accomplishment through those involved working together in specialized roles. Since the function can *itself* consist of influencing the erection or revision of a goal and the structuring, as through "rules" or through "authorities," of the behavior patterns through which the pursuit of such goals is to be conventionally channeled, *how* this function is performed, which is what is meant above in referring to the "process," may also, to the extent there is a theory of such change, be expressible in terms of institutions.

The relevance of this to the problem of underdeveloped areas lies in the key role that changes in behavior pattern play in the process of economic development and growth, and the essential need for an understanding of the institutions, in the sense of the term used here, through which such change comes about.

It should be noted that what is needed for any particular

situation, is both a theory of economic development and a theory of *under*development, provided that the development policy differs from previous policy in kind and not simply in degree. We should avoid seeking explanations in too simple terms for the relatively underdeveloped state of an economy. For instance, we may take account that investors and businessmen native to a lesser developed country are relatively few in number, and possibly somewhat un-skilled, but we need not attribute irrational economic behavior to them. That those in a position to aid domestic capital formation engage instead in conspicuous consumption or speculative ventures, or elect to invest their funds outside their own country, reflects the fact that what they have selected *are* the favorable alternatives from the standpoint of private satisfaction, and that the domestic economy offers inferior economic opportunities.

A model, mathematical or otherwise, constructed to reflect the theory of development on which policy is to be based, will contain what are variously called policy parameters or instrument variables, the selection of which will depend in part on why an area has in fact fallen behind others. A particular structure (set of numerical values which have been econometrically derived for the parameters) will be correctly specified only if the appropriate model has been employed, but the model (although itself dynamic in certain respects) presup-poses some institutional context or understood manner of change in context. Correspondingly, as will be further discussed in a subse-quent section, the investment criteria chosen in planning development will depend on the theory of underdevelopment assumed.

We are thus back to the question posed above—whether the process whereby the goals of society are erected and institutions are developed to implement them lies within economics or outside of economics. That in practice there are inducements to leave the matter to the care of others is suggested by Myrdal, as indicated in the opening paragraphs of this paper. There is, moreover, the admonition by Lionel Robbins that an economist, *qua* economist, should take the ends or goals to be served as given, and concentrate on illuminating the implications of alternative courses of action in terms of such goals.

This could be done for alternative value premises, and the appropriateness of particular policies could be evaluated in the light of such premises, but according to the view being discussed, the economist should stop short of expressing judgment on the alternative values or ends served.

This injunction, viewed most constructively, is against beclouding or confusing the function of explicating a course of action by (unstated) insertion of the economist's own values. It also reflects the useful contrast of a staff role for the economist with the line role of the policy maker, who merges the contributions from experts from different disciplines. Put differently, in a way which I understand should be attributed to Harold Laski, the expert should be *on tap*, rather than *on top*. Yet if followed literally, the admonition that economists should take ends as given has a static bias.

It is *not* being ethically neutral to set forth our alternatives rather thoroughly and repetitively over time in terms of given prevailing values, while abstaining from inquiry as to their moral basis, as to how they came into effect, and as to the process whereby new values and supporting behavior might replace them. It has been found quite possible, for instance, while maintaining that presumed ethical neutrality, to argue against economic planning as disturbing an automatically free enterprise system, while holding it to be somewhat less than professional to suggest, as has Karl Polanyi in *The Great Transformation*, that the market system is itself the product of planning.

Jacob Viner is said to have remarked that ''Economics is what economists do.'' Perhaps to be preferred would be that ''Economics is whatever the economist's specific professional tools give him particular competence to do.'' Economics, in a broader view, could be even said to provide a general theory of choice. Alternatively stated, economics could be regarded as the logic of choice, a description suggested by Charles Hitch.

However the economist's range of activity is delineated, the contributions made by cultural anthropologists, sociologists and those of related disciplines to this area make understandable the assertion attributed to Simon Kuznets that there can not be an (entirely) economic theory of *economic* development.

The Increasing Importance of Context

The employment of partial analysis should reflect the adoption of a *strategy* of inquiry, one that first considers a situation under stated simplified conditions, and then makes allowance for differences from or changes in those conditions. A common tendency, however, is to stop short of this second step, and to seek a literal application of the implications derived from the premises of the first step in the analysis. Much confusion and argument in methodology appear to stem from thus ignoring that implicit in analysis is a *rule into* the "logical calculus" and that its employment carries with it the obligation to use a *rule out* before concluding what relevance the first step of the analysis has for reality.

The importance of going beyond the analysis of a sector or a country as a *closed* economy has increased as the world has become closer knit institutionally. The importance of going beyond *static* analysis has increased due to the accelerated rate of change in tastes, population, energy resources and technology, and space accessible to exploration. For both reasons, the validity of making literal application of the findings of partial analysis prior to employment of a "rule out" becomes increasingly suspect.

For the economist or other social scientist to cut through to what is "real" in identifying the development program that is optimum for a particular country requires an awareness (more correctly, a theory), crossing disciplinary lines, as to the nature of the process by which the context within which he seeks to optimize is changing or might be made to change.

The difficulties, however, are great. The relevant context, long dominated by several major open-economies, each with its areas of influence, has undergone considerable change and currently is in a state of flux. There are influences working toward regional as well as national economic integration, and also a vast superstructure of interrelated formal and informal relationships developing among international, regional and national bodies. Until a new *modus vivendi* is worked out among nations that encompasses diverse pressures, and this becomes established and is identified by social scientists, the difficulty of taking changes in context into account in long-term development planning places a premium on policies that provide some flexibility for adjustment to changing circumstances. Among other reasons that the context is changing are the changing sense of commitment on the part of advanced countries and the short term for which financial commitments are made.

On Integrative Devices

To *understand* underdevelopment, one must cast the net wide, and then analyze what it contains. Items of diverse nature must be put in relationship to each other through some integrative device, and then the whole thus achieved must be broken into more manageable parts without loss of what is of most concern.

The counterpart and possible sequel to understanding underdevelopment, attempting to *control* what will happen, requires as a minimum that there by rules for arriving at decisions.

The contribution of *integrative devices* to optimal decision-making is through facilitating the recognition and evaluation of the opportunity cost of proposed courses of action. Markets serve as such a device, but their effectiveness in the lesser developed countries is likely to be impaired by the presence of structural disequilibrium.

The economist seeks to equip himself with conceptual tools for considering in an orderly sequence the indirect and subsequent as well as the direct and immediate economic implications of change. Among these tools are a number of integrative devices. Imputation of mathematical continuity is one such device. "Model-building" is a term increasingly used to designate a loose collection of other integrative devices. The "received doctrine" in economics is integrated as a theoretical system or model, possibly formalized as a mathematical-economic model. Econometrics, in turn, increasingly moves such models toward becoming "empirical-theoretical systems." The relatively new work in the economics of development, on the other hand, has been integrated at less ambitious levels—by *ad hoc* classification, by a categorical system, or less frequently, by a theoretical system, using here the terminology of Talcott Parsons and Edward Shils in *Toward a General Theory of Action*.

Integrative devices relevant to the study of economic development pertain not only to structure and change, but also, among other dimensions, to probability and values.

Interdependent (and simultaneous) aspects have been integrated through such devices as equilibrium theory and comparative statics (classical based on maximization with respect to one goal, or general preference function maximization, or homeostatis, et cetera); cross-section studies of comparative structure; exogenous-endogenous relationships in economic models; the Leontief input-output matrix; national income accounting; inter-sectoral analysis; and linear (and non-linear) programming formulations.

The time dimension has been integrated through various devices: the simultaneous treatment of time in static multiplier theory; the discounting of future values to present values; the historical use of annals and time series; the operational view of time involved in the time periods of comparative statics and of process analysis, the latter employing the concepts of ex ante and ex post; the dynamic treatment of time through difference and differential equations with single equation or simultaneous system models; and multi-stage or dynamic programming.

Probabilistic aspects have been integrated in treatments distinguishing risk and uncertainty, and game theory formulations, and in the stochastic aspects of econometric models.

On the integration of the value dimension into economics, from several standpoints a matter of considerable importance for economic development and its study, there is less agreement on its desirability and less progress in its accomplishment.

With the likelihood that the ruling group in a lesser developed country may differ significantly from other indigenous groups on development policy, and with development planning being undertaken not only within the nation, but also bilaterally with foreign governments, and with and within regional groupings of countries and international organizations as well, decisions are taken in the service of a variety of interests and goals. Tools such as the object- and meta-languages used in logic and the philosophy of language seem called for in order to disentangle and help portray the varied effects that changes in the value premises and decision-making structure have on the international and domestic pattern of economic development.

Decisions on Individual Projects

Opportunity cost and the economic problem are matters of critical concern to an underdeveloped area that is seeking economic development. Choices of projects, production techniques, sequences and rates at which undertaken, grouping of projects into programs, all this and more is potentially involved in linking up possible inputs to possible goals. Resources fall far short of requirements.

Under consideration in the present section are alternative criteria that have been or could be employed by a development authority for establishing ranking within a group of desired projects. A cutoff rate set up in the light of resource constraints then serves to determine which projects are to be undertaken. The criticisms brought to bear upon such decision rules are sequels to those raised on earlier pages against too literal an application of partial economic analysis. Since the conventional criteria have been extensively discussed in the literature, along with some proposed revisions, we undertake here simply to arrange some thoughts concerning them from the standpoint of opportunity cost.

In the section following the present one, projects are considered in the context of other projects tentatively included as part of the same development program. Input-output and linear programming techniques are explored as integrative devices that might contribute to a better awareness and handling of opportunity cost.

In the sections mentioned, we limit ourselves to decisions involving small changes within a *static* set of constraints, corresponding to choices of a marginalist or of an incremental nature. A later section takes account of dynamic factors and of major discontinuities between alternatives.

Concern as to the relative scarcity of an essential resource may prompt effort to make the available supply go further, as well as effort to increase the supply up to absorptive capacity. These efforts are furthered by the selection of activities in which the intensity of the particular resource is relatively low as an input or in which the activity is relatively productive of that resource as an output. Thus with capital relatively scarce, activities are favored which are low in capital intensity, and consistent with this, such activities are also conducted that aim at increasing the saving-income ratio or the extent of foreign aid. When the shortage is one of skilled personnel, activities are favored that make relatively light demands on that resource, also such activities as securing technical assistance or increasing investment in social infra-structure. When foreign exchange is relatively scarce, the criterion favors activities that in net balance of the value of inputs and outputs are import-replacing or export-producing.

Conventionally the criteria are expressed with the aid of various ratios, rates, or coefficients. In terms of averages, these are: (a) factor intensity criteria using the ratio of total amount of the factor to the annual value added (alternatively, to the gross annual value of output produced); (b) factor productivity criteria using the reciprocal of the foregoing; and (c) factor density or employment coefficient using a ratio of amounts of two factors.

Consider the case in which the factor is capital and capital is scarce relative to labor in the economy. An activity under consideration would tend to be regarded favorably if it had a low capital intensity (ratio of total capital to annual value added, the latter being the contribution to national income or product), this being also known as the capital-output ratio or the capital coefficient. This is equivalent to having the reciprocal, the capital productivity coefficient (or product-capital ratio) high. Moreover, the ratio of total capital input to total number of employees which measures the capital density, would be regarded favorably if low relative to alternative projects. If we compute capital intensity using gross annual value produced as the denominator, and then take the reciprocal, we have the rate of capital turnover, which would in this case be high.

If the criterion be expressed from the standpoint of labor instead of capital, then corresponding to the foregoing would be a high labor intensity (ratio of number of employees to annual value added), a low labor productivity coefficient (the reciprocal of labor intensity), and a high labor density (ratio of number of employees to total capital, and hence the reciprocal of the low capital density), this last also being called a labor absorption or employment coefficient.

From the standpoint of taking proper account of opportunity cost, the most evident sources of error in the above criteria are the ignoring of other inputs to be conserved and other goals to be served. But there are a variety of other objections as well, for instance, the possible non-comparability of the alternatives with respect to gestation period or the durability of capital.

The opportunity cost of other inputs can be adjusted for approximately by employing expressions containing terms applicable to the major inputs, as for instance, capital and foreign exchange. But the other objections remain. We proceed, therefore, to a more general formulation.

The national product (or national consumption) test for making a selection from among several activities acknowledges the consequences of an activity over time. Thus the decision rule would be to successively select that activity which relative to the amount invested ranked highest in contribution to present and future national product (or consumption), including account of primary (complementarity and backward and forward linkage effects), and secondary (i.e., multiplier) consequences, all amounts being discounted to present values.

The national product test is also referred to as the social marginal productivity criterion. It is "marginal" in the sense that change in national product is computed corresponding to the addition of an activity, but from the standpoint of the activity itself, it is an average rather than incremental concept, i.e., a ratio of totals rather than of increments.

For how far to carry an activity once selected, the rate relevant for deciding on the activity level would be the ratio of the *change* in total output per annum to the *net* investment required for that change.

One objection that could be raised against this decision rule in the form in which it has been expressed to this point is based on the likelihood of there being significant structural disequilibrium in the factor markets of an underdeveloped country. Market prices of factors (particularly wage rates, interest rates, and foreign exchange rate) would in such case depart significantly from the opportunity cost of the factors, that is, they would depart from the values of the factors in their best alternative use, to which values prices would tend to be equal in the long run, according to classical static theory, were pure competition and perfect market conditions to prevail. A partial correction is brought about by valuing both costs and changes in the national product (or consumption) using estimates of what are called ''accounting prices'' or ''shadow prices,'' these being prices such that were they to prevail, factor supply and demand would be brought into equilibrium.

The foregoing criterion looks beyond what would be the profitability of an activity from the standpoint of an individual entrepreneur, but it does not yet make adjustment for such differences between social and money costs or benefits as would *not* be corrected for by the market even were no market imperfections present. What is needed is greater recognition of the manifold goals of society, not all of which, however, are readily translatable into money terms or easily given relative weights.

For a criterion in terms of general welfare, consider that increasing the national product is included as but one of a set of criteria by which the effect of a project is to be evaluated, other criteria being, for instance, the extent of increase in savings, in employment, in stability of primary product export prices, in life expectancy, the effect on income distribution, etc. Suppose further that estimates have been made of the extent to which each project contributes toward the attainment of each aim. Then, given weights that would be attached to unit advances in each category, total valuations can be computed for each project, the ratios of which to project cost (the latter figured in terms of accounting price estimates of the opportunity costs of the factors) being then adopted as the basis for determining project priorities.

This follows the lines of a proposal set forth by the United Nations Economic Commission for Asia and the Far East in Bangkok in 1960. Note that in view of the lack of comparability of the units in which numerator and denominator are measured, the ratio becoming equal to one or less does not (unlike in the national product test) signify unprofitability of the activity in the welfare sense. The highest ranking project would be selected as long as the ratio is positive and resources permit.

In a strictly formal sense, with all opportunity costs taken into account, a decision rule constructed along such lines could be adequate for selecting among a small number of discrete alternatives under static conditions. Various difficulties that would be encountered in application, however, are mentioned subsequently, and other pertinent discussion can be found in the literature on welfare economics.

Programming a Set of Development Activities

Already indicated have been various sources of error present in development planning that proceeds through the ranking of separate development projects. Accounting prices, for instance, cannot be correctly determined unless a full program is considered.

When there is a large set of discrete possible techniques or projects that might be drawn on to form the combination of activities making up a development program, the opportunity costs relevant to an activity or combination of activities may be incorrectly judged, either from the full array of possible alternatives not being recognized, or from interrelationships among activities not being kept clear.

What is called for is an approach to development programming that on the one had provides an *integrative device* that pulls together and gives order to the possible alternatives, and on the other hand, provides a *method of search* that may be employed among the alternatives in order to determine combinations of activities that satisfy requirements of *feasibility*, *efficiency* and *optimality*.

The input-output approach and the linear programming approach will be appraised briefly in the above connections. As in the previous section, we limit ourselves here to decisions involving small changes within a static set of constraints corresponding to changes of a marginalist or of an incremental nature.

Input-output approach

The input-output approach may be variously employed, reflecting differences in policy problems, organization of decision-taking, availability and quality of data, computational facilities, and so forth.

We will assume that a tentative policy decision as to the per capita rate of economic growth to seek has been arrived at in the light of estimates as to how the domestic saving necessary for capital formation is to be performed and its likely extent, as to extent of external sources of capital, and as to capital-output ratio and rate of population growth. Other economic goals—employment level, price stability, avoidance of foreign exchange difficulties, etc.—as well as policy considerations of a non-economic nature, would bear upon the decision.

Let us suppose, furthermore, that an overall development plan has already been drawn up with target levels for aggregate consumption, investment, and net exports or imports, and that the extent of resource flows has been determined.

What is desired is two-fold: (1) to translate the overall targets into a consistent set of industrial (and possibly regional) sector levels for investment in, production of, or import of intermediate goods and final goods consistent with the demand represented by the more highly aggregated target levels and for which the input requirements correspond to the resources that will be available; and (2) to determine a decision rule for accepting or rejecting specific individual projects, or programs composed of such projects, to implement the above-mentioned plan for the sectors.

The first objective, that of aiming at a consistent sector by sector plan, can be met for small departures from the existing relationships among sector output levels by employing an open model for input-output between sectors for which appropriate constants have been empirically determined or estimated for the input coefficients. Alternative combinations of final goods preselected to satisfy the target levels, which are at the more highly aggregative level of the overall development plan, can be tested as to the total output levels they require of each sector, and their input requirements can thus be determined. Input deficiencies associated with a particular plan for meeting aggregate development targets could lead to a revised sector by sector plan of activities that avoid creating such deficiencies or that attempt to relieve them. This sequence can be repeated one or more times, and reconsideration can be given if necessary to the overall development plan and to the per capita growth rate sought.

In furtherance of the second objective, a unique set of accounting prices, reflective of the opportunity cost of the factors, can be computed such that factor and commodity markets would be in equilibrium in the situation that would be in effect were the sector by sector plan carried out. In the input-output table the value totals for outlays on inputs and for receipts from outputs would be equal for any given sector, and each of the respective contribution margins would thus be made zero. Specific activities could then be judged in terms of whether or not at such prices their contribution margins per unit level of activity were equal to or greater than zero, all such activities being accepted and the others being rejected.

[Contribution margin is contribution profit less assignable fixed costs. Contribution profit is revenue less direct cost. The term equivalent to "contribution profit" in linear programming literature would be "net revenue." It is the negative of net direct cost. The manner of determining accounting prices is such that prices are imputed to resources subject to constraint such that the assignable cost just offsets any contribution profit.]

An advance has been made here over the practice mentioned in connection with criteria for ranking individual activities wherein accounting prices (and hence opportunity costs) were estimated without reference to a complete program of activities.

On the other hand, the advance has not been without a cost. We find that the introduction of the input-output phase in the planning procedures assures us a *feasible* and *efficient* solution, but does not incorporate the value criteria by means of which one might seek *optimality* as well.

Distinctions between feasible, efficient and optimal allocation of resources can be understood by reference to a graphical treatment in which amounts of two kinds of final output are measured on the axes. We are interested in the set of points that represent all combinations of the two outputs that are possible (feasible) given the technology (i.e., the set of transformation functions available, each defined in terms of inputs and outputs per unit level of activity) and given the conditions as to supply of primary and intermediate products used as inputs.

An allocation of available resources leading to a point in the feasible area is termed an "efficient allocation" and the point is called an "efficient point" if there is no output which can be increased without the opportunity cost being incurred of reducing at least one other output. There may be a set of such points (each a different combination of outputs), their locus in the example at hand being the production possibility curve bounding the feasible area. Points interior to an efficient point represent either under-utilization of inputs and/or selection of an inferior technique (activity) for producing one or more of the outputs indicated upon the axes.

Of the several efficient feasible allocations, one is not to be preferred to another as optimal until some further specification is made that indicates a basis for evaluation and choice.

In the case of the input-output formulation we were considering, essentially no element of choice was allowed by the formal model. The fixity of input coefficients reflects the admission of but one technique for producing a given kind of output, so that were an interior feasible point to exist, it could only be through underutilization of inputs, not through choice of an inferior technique. But the method imposes equalities to be satisfied, thus requiring there be no excess capacity, so even such interior points are not entertained, leaving only efficient points, those on the boundary.

For the closed static Leontief model, these reduce to the single efficiency point for which the allocation of inputs is such that the outputs corresponding to the efficient point regenerate the inputs required in that allocation. For open models, choice among alternative combinations of activities is eliminated by specification of a final bill of goods.

In its formal aspects, the input-output approach offers not a test as to which combination of activity levels is optimum, but rather serves as an integrative device such that given a judgment on what combination is optimum, the feasibility of the combination can be tested from the standpoint of resources required and available. As employed in development planning, however, the input-output approach is supplemented by a trial and error method, as indicated above, for conjecturing what tentative optimum it is that should be tested by the formal properties of the model. As indicated subsequently, it is the particular merit of the linear programming approach to bring those steps also within formal procedures for arriving at an optimum program.

At whatever level of aggregation the shift is made from pursuing the first objective mentioned above to pursuing the second, the method either adheres strictly to the criterion of profitability in terms of the input-output derived accounting prices (thus assuring feasibility and efficiency), or else employs additional considerations in search of optimality. The topic becomes that already treated in the section on decisions on individual projects, but with the advantage *initially* of an improved set of accounting prices. We say "initially" since once further criteria are added, there is no assurance that the sector by sector plan will be filled in by specific projects in each sector without shifts disrupting the consistency of the plan. It is likely that a recalculation of opportunity costs would be appropriate, but the input-output technique in itself does not provide for this.

In addition, reconsideration of input coefficients might also be in order, but it is characteristic of the input-output approach to take these coefficients as fixed, thus not providing for the consideration of alternative techniques which changes in relative prices might make desirable.

Linear programming approach

The problem of selecting an *optimum combination* of non-negative levels for the various sectors to implement the broad targets of the overall development plan, and of filling out a sector plan with an optimum program of specific projects and techniques, calls for consideration of a large number of discrete alternatives not lending themselves to representation by an overall production function. The classical optimization techniques of calculus maximization and minimization thus give way to other mathematical techniques. In both the input-output and linear programming approaches we find a shift to algebraic techniques of solution.

In the case of linear programming, provision for choice among alternatives is incorporated into the model. The alternatives may be different products, different sources (domestic production or import), different techniques of production, etc. For instance, although both the input-output approach and linear programming assume a fixed proportion of inputs per unit level of a given activity (and thus constant returns to scale for small departures from existing levels), linear programming proves to be more flexible in that it admits consideration of alternative techniques involving different proportions of inputs by considering the different techniques as different activities.

The constraints set upon a situation, moreover, are brought into the body of the problem in the case of linear programming, instead of being taken into account as a subsequent step as in an open input-output model.

The constraints in the linear programming problem constitute an undetermined linear system corresponding to which there is a set of feasible combinations of activity levels. The problem is made determinate by specifying in addition a linear *objective function* that is to be maximized (in other cases, minimized) by the set of activity levels selected, in order to secure the optimum solution. Goals that would have been either left to the side or brought forward afterward in order to secure adjustments can now be made an integral part of the model. This possibility for integration of value elements into the problem is discussed further at a later point.

The importance of the procedure for arriving at the optimum set of activity levels is emphasized by the fact that the number of activities to be considered is enlarged in the linear programming case beyond those present in the input-output case to an even greater extent than already indicated. This arises from the statement of the constraints in most, but not all cases, as inequalities rather than equalities. The principal approach employed (the simplex method, developed by George Dantzig) provides an iterative method for search among alternative possible discrete choices of activity level combinations which avoids reliance on an exhaustive consideration of all alternatives.

Starting from a basic feasible solution, the procedure is to concentrate on *efficient* combinations having no more non-zero activity levels than there are constraints, moving toward the optimum combination by considering in successive stages the opportunity cost of changing to a different efficient combination. This is done through computing, relative to the activity that might be added, the *equivalent combination* of changes in levels of activities already in the set that would be necessary to release the inputs that would be required were this activity to be included at a specified level.

In a revised approach for the case of maximization of the objective function, current market prices are used for pricing outputs and for such needed inputs as may be purchased without limit. On the other hand, accounting prices are computed for the resources subject to constraints (in this case, the scarce inputs) within the context of the program of activities tentatively arrived at by that particular stage of solution. Such prices are computed so that the activities in the tentatively selected program (called the ''basis'') break even, that is, such that for each activity the contribution profit that enters into the objective function is offset by the value of the constrained resources in terms of the accounting prices. It follows from this that the contribution margin of each activity in the basis would be reduced to zero. Activities outside the basis are then evaluated, using in this connection the accounting prices of the existing basis to evaluate the opportunity cost of such resources subject to constraint as would have to be displaced from the tentative program. Of any activities having a contribution margin greater than zero, the most profitable would be added to the set and that activity of the existing set which would first be reduced to zero by the expansion of the input needs of the new activity would be eliminated, thus forming a new and more nearly optimum basis. Accounting prices corresponding to the new basis would be computed and the next approximation would be undertaken.

The decision rule is to proceed in this manner until the activities outside the basis are found to have either zero or negative profitability, the set of activities already constituting the basis at that stage being then found to be the *optimal* program in the sense of achieving the desired extremum of the objective function.

It was commented upon earlier that both input-output and linear programming represented an advance over the development criteria discussed in connection with single projects in that accounting prices were arrived at with reference to a *program* of activities. Now from the immediately foregoing we might add that linear programming represents an advance over the input-output approach not only in the aspects indicated earlier in this section but also in recomputing the accounting prices to take account of successive changes in the tentative development plan for projects and techniques. Opportunity cost is thus more correctly taken into account in the planning of the optimal development program.

If structural disequilibrium exists in the market with respect to resources for which market prices rather than accounting prices were used in the foregoing (labor is a likely candidate), then a revision of the procedure to permit the price of that resource to be also determined within the model would yield a better indication of the correct opportunity cost.

The above would not be called for in the case of a private firm.

The programming should cover the relevant economy. Nor might it be desirable were the planning authority not contemplating making appropriate adjustments in the market. Urban labor, for instance, is possibly paid in excess of the true opportunity cost of withholding that labor from its best alternative use, say, agricultural underemployment. Nevertheless, were urban workers paid in accordance with that opportunity cost, they might fare even more poorly than those living on the land, and the consequences for maintaining a disciplined work force, let alone social stability, could be severe.

Starting with market prices in the initial basic feasible solution, where these are available, and then computing accounting prices for all factors and outputs in the successive stages of approximation to the optimum solution would, at a minimum, provide information on pricing that would be of interest. Whether the set of activity levels thus determined should be adopted for the sector by sector plan would at least partly depend, however, upon what measures the planning authority contemplated in order to prevent or adjust to the market pressures that could be expected to the extent that the structural disequilibrium continued to hinder the particular market prices from achieving the accounting price levels.

Dynamic Elements and "Structural Break"

Dynamic change in an underdeveloped economy may be taken into account by programming techniques that extend those considered above. There we considered the selection of an optimal set of activities involving only small departures from the existing situation, and a static set of constraints. Now we require a multi-stage approach permitting changes in the technological data and in the constraints, reflective of the growth taking place.

Input requirements during the period of capital formation may differ significantly from those during the period in which capital is itself productive—for instance, the difference between the labor-intensive construction of hydro-electric dams and the capital-intensive production of hydro-electric power.

Significant differences between activities may exist, moreover, as to the length of the gestation period before capital is in production, and as to the durability of capital once completed.

The level of input coefficients, though representing constant returns to scale for changes in the vicinity of the initial conditions, may need to be changed in view of the capacity-producing effect of investment activities and the non-constancy of returns to scale to which it gives effect.

Revisions may also be prompted by changes occurring in the productivity of factors that arise in the form of an internal economy from more experience having been gained; or in the form of an external economy through a pool of skilled personnel coming into existence in response to an increase in the number of firms in the industry. Such considerations are abstracted from by the additivity assumption present in both input-output and linear programming in that the proportions of inputs to output of activities are treated as independent of the levels of other activities. That assumption also leaves for separate consideration the type of external economy that arises from the growth of other industries and which affects firms in the given industry through the factor and product market by providing it, respectively, with lower cost inputs and with customers for its products.

It will be maintained here that two approaches to the programming of growth may usefully be distinguished: one that maintains continuity with the present, yet advances the situation through a series of small incremental comparisons; the other that involves a major discontinuity from what has preceded—a situation to which the term "structural break" has been applied.

The former, or *incremental approach*, seeks to advance through small adjustments on the margin, each representing an improvement over the prior situation. Feasibility is tested. Efficient allocations are sought—using a particular set of market or of accounting prices to evaluate alternatives, in the case of input-output, or using shadow prices successively recomputed to reflect market equilibrium in the successively evolving economic situation, in the case of linear programming.

Whether the allocations thus recommended would, in fact, be efficient is another matter. This depends on various factors: the programming methodology (for instance, to what extent were prices determined exogenously with respect to the partial system instead of being developed endogenously by shadow prices); policy implementation (how effective, for instance, were market forces or government actions in securing outcomes comparable to that which the shadow prices are presumed to elicit under pure competition and perfect market conditions); and relevance (whether the situations being compared are the ones that would exist at that stage in view of such dynamic growth considerations as mentioned above).

As to optimality in a sense broader than simply requiring an efficient allocation, linear programming (but not input-output) could in its formal usage take account of various goals through the objective function and appropriately fashioned constraints.

In contrast to the foregoing, *the structural break approach* reflects the belief that the optimum situation is not necessarily to be reached by a series of successively optimizing incremental changes. The most attractive of the alternatives contiguous to the present situation may in fact lead in the opposite direction to that which is optimal in the larger view.

The ''minimum critical efforts'' thesis in connection with population effects (and comparable considerations as to effect on social stability), together with related arguments in support of a ''big push'' for industrialization, reflect this second approach.

However, a more fundamental difference exists in the two approaches than simply the implications of gradual versus rapid growth. There are big differences in the time and value horizons within which optimization is to be considered, and differences in attitude as to the extent to which institutional characteristics of an economy are to be taken as given.

Within such horizons and frameworks, moreover, there may be differences in the attention given to the time shape of the rate of growth and degree of attainment of various target levels. Outlays and receipts may have to be estimated for future periods in terms of estimated future relative prices, with consideration also given to changes in the nation's general price level. Questions enter as to the appropriate interest rates at which to discount or accumulate amounts to a common point in time for purposes of comparability.

The term ''structural break'' is used to suggest a major discontinuity in institutions which, although likely to be rejected when optimization is attempted by the incremental method, might nevertheless be found to offer a global rather than ''local'' maximum from the standpoint of the achievement of a set of goals.

Which of the two approaches is followed in development programming may significantly influence the kind of economy toward which the lesser developed country is directed.

The incremental manner of dealing with problems tends to prevail in our affairs in general, and in the normal course of events it may be expected to hold predominant sway in development planning as well. What is suggested here, however, is the necessity of grasping that some discontinuity or "structural break" rendering the incremental approach unsuitable may be present, indeed, may be an essential aspect of a program aimed at more than nominal advances in a lesser developed country's economic well-being.

Applied in connection with a series of incremental policy moves, each designed to secure improvement over the prior situation, the criterion of comparative advantage may lead a lesser developed country to specialize in agriculture and extractive industry. In contrast, recognition of the prospect of external economies that tend to be associated with the introduction of new industries into such countries may lead toward a great diversification of the economy which, though not the most attractive alternative to follow when viewed from the immediate standpoint, nevertheless may contribute more to the country's development in the long run.

The incremental approach to programming tends to deny the lesser developed country the *essential* aspect of investment, that of being able to enter upon a period of improved net profitability by way of initially incurring some net costs. Though far less apparent in connection with development programs of several years' length, the added weighting given to leaving things as they are may still be operative.

There are, of course, some reservations to be attached to departing from the strictly incremental approach of small optimizing changes from the existing situation to the more drastic structural break approach.

Alternatives proposed by the two approaches are likely to differ in the extent to which, even in strictly economic terms, they can be evaluated. While current prices reflect relative preferences as to goods and services, they are not to be taken as necessarily an accurate representation of the relative preferences that would exist in the economy after developmental changes have taken place. Future prices would of course serve this purpose, but would not ordinarily be present. We have noted above that the accounting prices generated in the linear programming approach would correct for the resources used under the investment plan, but that does not cover broader changes accompanying development. With difficulties likely to be more present with major changes than with small incremental changes, less certainty as to correctness of appraisal may attach to proposals involving the former.

If we *were* equally able to evaluate the relative desirability of the outcomes offered by alternative programs *if* successful, it would not follow that we should necessarily select the one rated highest. Weighted by their respective probabilities of *being* successful, a different alternative might become the preferred one. If the probabilities were unknown, and it was a matter of uncertainty, the choice becomes less clear. But even were the probabilities of success known for each development alternative, and not only known but equal, the alternative rated highest in terms of considerations already mentioned might still not merit being selected. For what also has to be considered in selecting between alternatives is their relative acceptability were success only *partially* (even though to the same degree) achieved.

Development programs providing for major changes in the future are difficult to conclusively support or conclusively refute as to feasibility, let alone optimality, and may reflect overly ambitious effort and extravagant hopes. On the other hand, development programs following the incremental approach might be more readily shown feasible than optimal, and may reflect a ''least effort'' solution and a conservative adherence to the present.

''Doubtless There Are Other Roads''

It was stated above that for the economist or other social scientist to cut through to what is ''real'' in identifying the development program that is optimum for a particular country requires an awareness of the process by which the context within which optimization is sought is changing or might be made to change.

It was indicated that integrative devices contribute to optimal decision-making through facilitating the recognition and evaluation of the opportunity cost of proposed courses of action. We noted also that there is an opportunity cost involved in inaction, and suggested that is it the progressive acknowledgment of these costs that gives rise to the erection of new social goals.

Our inquiry into decision rules for selecting individual projects and into the programming of a set of development activities helped lay bare a number of dimensions in which using partial analysis without invoking a ''rule out'' from the simplifications in terms of which we choose to think led to less than full appreciation of the opportunity costs attached to alternatives.

We noted that the incremental approach to development planning, in contrast to that recognizing the possibility of a structural break, was partial in a time dimension respect that tended to obscure the *essential aspect* of development, that of an economy investing in itself and being aided in that effort by external capital.

Our summary is incomplete and a scanning of the prior pages will be needed to make the connections and add concreteness. But perhaps the point made will permit us to move to this question: "What are the responsibilities and the opportunities of the economist as a social scientist in this matter?"

As to *responsibilities*, must they not include as a minimum, and with a weight attached that persuades attention, the responsibility of making abundantly clear, to practitioner and layman alike, such bias as may attach to even the most antiseptically scientific use of a particular method? Who could better alert us as to the attrition that occurs in our goals as they attempt passage through the partial analyses of the specialist?

As to *opportunities*, should not the economist, if he has brought into the light the goal considerations which by virtue of our methodology of thought and inquiry are given short shrift, take the opportunity to set out, alongside the implications of alternative courses of action, the implications of our inaction in not securing implementation of these further goals?

The economist *can* be better than his tools, and act within his special competence in being so. His special competence is to use the tools of economics *and* to know (and make known) what the tools can not do, or have caused to be subordinated.

The one who repairs bias, whatever its origin, maintains his ethical neutrality. To remain quiet in such a case is not being neutral.

The path suggested is not unknown—it has been traveled—but it is difficult.

11

Focus on Teaching

In 1958 I decided to seek a full-time teaching position within California, and accepted appointment in the Department of Economics and Statistics at a relatively new institution, Los Angeles State College of Applied Arts and Sciences. The college had recently moved to temporary structures at two locations while permanent buildings were being completed—the Ramona campus in the San Gabriel Valley and a campus to the north in the San Fernando Valley, which subsequently took on a separate identity. The Ramona campus had a high representation of minorities from the Spanish and black communities of Los Angeles, and subsequently from the growing Asian community. It developed into Los Angeles State College, and later became California State University at Los Angeles. It started with only junior and senior year curricula and a Master's program, but in 1959 courses for the first two undergraduate years were added. Arrangements were made in some fields for joint doctoral programs with other universities. The role of the college in reaching a new clientele as well as its relative newness were attractive considerations to me.

Another factor in my decision to accept appointment in Los Angeles was that the Claremont Colleges, which I regarded highly, were about a half hour's drive from campus. Claremont is a cluster of colleges which includes Pomona, Scripps, and the Graduate School, among others.

The graduate school had an excellent faculty, and another consideration was its acceptance of an examination in advanced statistics and mathematics in lieu of a second foreign language. At times it seemed strange to be taking a class when the course material included journal articles which in earlier years I had solicited from authors and edited for publication. I prepared various papers during the years I was there, one of which, "Opportunity Cost and Under-Developed Areas," is included as Annex 10.2 to the prior chapter. [For a survey of subsequent literature relevant to the comments in 10.2 as to neutrality in matters of morality and ethics, see Hausman and McPherson, 1993.]

By mid-1961 I had satisfied the residency requirements concurrently with my full-time teaching load. A doctor's warning, only partially heeded, to take a complete rest or I would not survive six months, caused me to delay completion of my dissertion, *Resource Allocation for Institutions of Higher Education*, until a sabbatical leave ending in 1971, at which time the doctorate was conferred—twenty-eight years after I had left the doctoral program at Columbia University to enter World War II. I already had permanent tenure, and advanced to full professorship following completion of the degree.

A further consideration in favor of the move to Los Angeles was the prospect of living at a place known as the Pyrenees Castle, on Grandview Drive in Alhambra. Sylvester Dupuy, who had become wealthy in California from oil, land and sheep, commissioned architects in 1926 to build a chateau duplicating one he had known during his boyhood in southern France, where the Pyrenees formed the border with Spain. It was constructed on a forested hill with massive blocks of masonry, four towers, tile roofs, a cellar for wine casks, and even a secret passageway. A circular drive leads up the hill to massive gates, beyond which is a vast courtyard with a central oval driveway. There are gardens and trees as in an arboretum. It is the highest point in Alhambra, and overlooks the campus, which is on an adjoining hill in Los Angeles. Until a freeway was constructed, a small stream ran through a wooded ravine separating the campus from Alhambra. After an interesting history, the chateau had been converted into apartments. We arranged for a ground floor apartment in the west wing facing gardens, lawns and wooded areas in three directions. Although our apartment was not large, the grounds and view added spaciousness. We had many of our meals outside, which we shared with birds and friendly raccoons and possums. There was a grass court for tennis or badminton which we used occasionally. The four acres of grounds were in effect a private forest park. The Castle area provided a quiet refuge for study and creative thought. There was a panoramic view of the San Gabriel mountains to the north and also a view of mountains to the southeast. The ocean was a short drive directly to the west as well as directly to the south. The desert was also within a short drive. We took great satisfaction from living there, so much so that it influenced me to turn aside offers that came in later years to teach elsewhere.

Professor Isamu Yamada of Tokyo, whom I had met in Japan, and who had visited me in Chicago and San Francisco, was one of our guests. On one of his visits I arranged for him to give a seminar on campus, followed by a luncheon and reception at the Castle, which Jacob Marschak and Karl Brunner, both formerly of the Cowles Commission, attended.

I taught a wide variety of courses—graduate and undergraduate, microeconomics and macroeconomics, for the specialist as well as the non-major. I prepared new material for each graduate seminar as though writing an additional chapter for a book. I drew on the philosophy of science, methodology of the social sciences, organization theory, cybernetics and econometrics. Sometimes as class time approached I would go careening down the circular drive headed for campus with some ideas for my seminar still being formulated.

I used a student data sheet and pretests to identify those students who were sufficiently prepared to handle the level of difficulty appropriate for a course. Without wishing it to be so, I came to be regarded as a strict grader relative to others. I used the full range of grades even in graduate seminars. Those who passed my courses had accomplished a significant amount of learning and were prepared to gain from subsequent courses.

It was suggested soon after I came that I coordinate the quantitative courses in the department, but I discovered there was no preparation in mathematics required for enrollment; accordingly no calculus could be used in the lectures and no proofs of the relationships that were being taught could be discussed. I successfully encouraged the addition of mathematical prerequisites, but as it turned out, the fact that a student passed a mathematics course provided no assurance that the student had an adequate grasp of the subject. A course was then designed to be taught by the Mathematics Department covering what was essential for business, economics, and statistics courses, but relatively new faculty were assigned to teach it and they tended to grade high so as to appear to be successful. I recommended several times that the Mathematics Department be asked to regularly provide our department with the distribution of grades with a view to some oversight being exercised, but the suggestion was not adopted. In neither department did the faculty or the administrator want to jeopardize enrollment growth. Unfortunately, the quality of educational opportunity was accordingly adjusted downward. In view of the foregoing, I declined to accept responsibility for courses in the statistics area, although statistical inference was of special interest to me.

I served for many years as member or chair of numerous departmental, division or school, and college or university level committees, variously designated as concerned with instructional affairs, undergraduate and graduate studies, academic planning and continuing education, or educational policies.

In the 1960's I chaired a department ad hoc committee on curriculum analysis, and during 1973-74 coordinated a full-scale restructuring of the undergraduate and graduate economic curriculum with full consultation with the faculty and with present and former students. Under this restructuring, three options were offered in the undergraduate major, each designed for a different objective:

- A Social and Behavioral Science Option for those wishing to combine their background in these areas with preparation in economics.
- An Applied Economics Option for those desirous of combining emphasis in economics with courses in public or business administration.
- A Pre-Professional Option for students intending to subsequently undertake graduate study in economics in preparation for positions in finance, industry, government service, teaching in higher education, or other opportunities as a professional economist.

Students could combine the option selected with an increased emphasis on an analytic-quantitative approach. In addition to the major in Economics, a minor in Basic Economics, with alternative options related thereto, was made available. An abbreviated minor in Economics for majors in English was made available through the latter department. Programs in Economics supplementing other majors could be suggested by the Economics adviser. The Master of Arts program in Economics was modified to provide both a general option and an analytical-quantitative option.

In the General Education area, I served for several years as Liberal Arts counselor for students majoring in business or economics. I argued that liberal arts programs were liberating in that they freed an individual from many self-accepted constraints and opened up possibilities. In addition, I was departmental coordinator for general education courses, chair of the Division Committee on General Education, and member of the College General Education Committee.

Starting in 1959 and for quite some years I taught an economics course that satisfied part of the General Education requirement for students not majoring in business or economics, and coordinated several faculty teaching additional sections. As described in Annex 11.2 to this chapter, the course had objectives quite distinct from those of a principles course. It was interdisciplinary in nature, used a large number of original sources rather than a textbook, and integrated a significant amount of individualized readings which were selected by the student at intervals throughout the course from a Study Guide of over a hundred pages which I prepared. I stressed give-and- take discussion in the classroom, and sought to develop in each student the ability to express ideas in whatever ''lingo'' the student would need to get those ideas across in conversations with friends in his or her own environment. I enjoyed teaching that course, and I believe the students enjoyed it as well, although there were comments that it required more work than any course previously experienced. The examinations provided opportunities for students to display what they had learned. The questions were simple, yet the answers could be quite profound. (I explained that I wrote the examinations in the dungeon of the Castle.)

The approach—balancing permissiveness and challenge—was one within which even those of lesser prior achievement and/or present aspiration could find a meaningful core, while denying to none the opportunity and encouragement to come to grips with the larger meanings that economics can offer when considered within a broad frame of reference—a matter with which I have long been concerned.

When I was drawn away from teaching and coordinating that course by other responsibilities it regrettably reverted to a lecture course using a conventional principles textbook.

In 1972 I chaired an ad hoc Committee on the Long-Run Goals of the School of Business and Economics, which included both faculty and student representatives, and wrote a report entitled ''A Look Ahead.'' An appendix contained a six point program regarding prerequisites in mathematics. Three topics in the body of the report are of perhaps the most continuing interest.

The first topic concerns the student group to be served. As already mentioned, the location of the campus facilitated the attendance of minority students. Initially the largest minority group was African-American, but then the Hispanic contingent overtook them in attendance. More recently, Asian students have become very numerous. My committee report foresaw the following problem, which in fact materialized: Minorities seek to enter the mainstream, but the campus was losing its position in the mainstream due to the preponderance of minorities and the flight of other students to other campuses in the Los Angeles area.

The Committee regarded it to be a distinct asset to our campus, and an opportunity for service, that its student body be varied as to ethnic, socio-economic, political, religious and national background, and regarded it to be of importance that programs be offered that would continue to attract a student body that was a cross-section of all elements of the urban population.

Earlier, in 1967, as a result of the Watts riots in Los Angeles and the subsequent McCone report, Kenneth Martyn, Professor of Special Education at the college, was commissioned by the California Joint Legislative Committee on Higher Education to prepare a report on removing barriers to higher education for disadvantaged students. I was drawn upon as a consultant and submitted recommendations on overcoming motivational, academic and geographic barriers.

The problem was that whereas our campus was in the forefront in attempting to reduce barriers to the admission of disadvantaged students, other campuses had been more restrained in such effort. The several campuses were part of the same system of higher education, and there was need for a system-wide policy that would lead to a more even distribution of attendance by minorities at the several campuses, so that the student body at each campus would be broadly representative of the metropolitan area population.

A second matter discussed in the report concerned the curriculum. The unifying feature of the School of Business and Economics was its concern with preparing men and women to be effective in administrative and professional roles that serve formal organizations, in particular organizations that retained a large measure of control over their goals, choice of means, and implementation, so that a ''business'' approach could be applied. The goals of such organizations tended to be private goals, identified in the popular mind with profit-seeking. In contrast, the selection of the fundamental goals of public policy and the analysis of that policy, draw upon considerations beyond both business and economics. Moreover, public agencies operate within procedures which tend to be less open to choice and change than in a private organization. In spite of such considerations, there are important insights to be gained from a study of business and economics for even not-for-profit organizations. It was recommended that the School of Business and Economics incorporate curricula in various areas of public administration, the unifying element of the school curriculum then still being Administration, but in a more inclusive sense. This would broaden the preparation of business students for leadership roles in their respective communities. Examples which were suggested of curricular areas which might be developed included a Hospital Administration and Medical Economics option, in cooperation with the School of Nursing, Department of Health and Safety Studies, and the Department of Microbiology and Public Health; also augmentation of the program in labor relations, which served only employers, to serve the needs of administrators in the organized labor movement.

A third area of recommendation related to interdisciplinary efforts. The Committee report recommended in the interest of program flexibility that an Interdepartmental Studies Group be created, the faculty members of which would hold their regular appointments in a department of the school and be primarily engaged in instruction. Student representatives should be included. The following purposes would be served:

- Provision for the temporary administration of interdisciplinary curricula during their experimental and/or developmental stages, pending achievement of full departmental or other appropriate organizational status.
- Facilitation of more individualized learning through making available various illustrative prototype programs for students electing this special business option.
- Administration of guidelines for students from outside the school who are contemplating a major in a discipline combined with course work in business administration and economics. In this connection, provide advisement for the minor in Basic Business.
- Cooperation with departments in the design of courses and other educational experiences which will enable students

to better integrate what they have learned from diverse sources.

The first of the topics discussed in the Long-Run Goals report, the student group served, is tied in with the problem of academic standards and performance. Concerted efforts to remove barriers to higher education for disadvantaged students, together with efforts to introduce minorities into the mainstream of higher education rather than have them concentrated in particular campuses, increased enrollments overall. Since budgets were to a great extent enrollment-driven, that is, financing was a function of the number of individuals or full-time equivalents, each campus, both overall and in individual departments, had a considerable interest in enrollment statistics. This led to academic policies being influenced by their possible effects upon maintaining existing enrollment and sharing in possible increases. Subtle and not-too-subtle pressures originating from administrators, as well as concerns on the part of instructors, tended to lower the standards used in grading in order to retain enrollment. When less was expected of students, the students in turn expected that less needed to be done in preparation. Nationally, college-level textbooks were watered down to be usable at the lesser level of preparation.

Good policies and adequate financing are not enough. Good administrators are also needed. In 1982, when screening candidates for the position of dean for the School of Business and Economics, I put forward the following suggested selection criteria:

- Has the candidate had significant administrative responsibility at institutions of similar or greater stature?
- Do various factors—particularly breadth of experience outside academe, breadth of responsibilities within universities, and personal qualities—suggest that the individual could win access to and interrelate easily with leaders in the business and government community?
- Did the candidate utilize the opportunity provided by the interview to go beyond the matter of the school's image to basic questions of the school's objectives, and the curricular and other techniques that could be employed to achieve them?
- Did the candidate reveal an awareness of the conflicts that often exist between goals, as for instance, between extending educational opportunity to a maximum and producing

graduates whose performance would induce employers to continue to recruit our graduates?

- Did the candidate show sensitivity to the need for securing support for the school that does not infringe on the integrity of the instruction and research conducted? Was corresponding sensitivity shown as to the manner in which administrators relate to faculty?
- Did the candidate give indication of being able to anticipate problems and opportunities, define alternatives, and provide leadership in implementation?

In several reports to the California Postsecondary Education Commission as well as in a keynote presentation to a campus-state capitol seminar in Sacremento in 1976 I pointed out that while state budgets provided for the additional physical burden of enrollment, no provision was made for the additional demands on campus services for learning assistance as a result of the increased extent of non-homogeneity of the student body. In commenting upon a draft of the state's five year-plan for higher education, I testified as follows:

> While moving out of a period of rapid enrollment growth is a source of problems, the relief it gives from having to concentrate on finding space for sheer numbers of students provides an opportunity to refocus on quality considerations. It is true that attention and resources will be absorbed in achieving a mix of students reflective of equal access to higher education. However, it should also be possible to direct attention and resources to repairing inroads on quality resulting from accommodations made in recent years in dealing with quantity, and to recognizing [in the standard teaching load for faculty] the additional demands made upon faculty time resulting from more diverse student enrollment and individualization of learning.

What I observed was that the public judged progress toward equal opportunity in terms of the access provided, yet there was need to consider at the same time the quality of the learning opportunity to which access was being extended. What higher education should expect of students was that (a) there be commitment on the student's part in order that access to educational opportunity not be abused, and (b) that certain preconditions as to being able to benefit be met before enrollment, to be demonstrated not by school transcript but by tests of current capabilities at the time of applying for enrollment. As

I commented in the critique of the state's five-year plan mentioned above:

> With there being both alternative types of postsecondary educational experience and alternative uses of limited state resources, the access extended to formal higher education should be consistent with an individual's commitment of at least the threshold level of time and effort needed for learning to take place. Procedures should be identified that would increase the likelihood of adequate student contribution to the learning process, with greater intensity of contribution coming if necessary at the price of less early graduation, in order to: (a) increase the significance of the opportunity to learn, (b) reduce the downward pressure on the academic performance expected of students and that students expect of themselves, and (c) improve the cost-effectiveness of state resources committed to higher education.

It would be a move in the right direction to have students anticipate that responsibility for learning in a college or university in large measure will rest with themselves, with opportunity afforded them, but with outcomes not to be taken for granted.

It would be irresponsible, however, for higher education to simply cut off the flow of increased enrollment. What is to be expected of higher education is that it would (a) facilitate change at the preparatory levels, (b) engage in extensive outreach efforts to reach students while still in preparatory schools, (c) insist on remediation before college admission, (d) provide increased learning support after admission, and (e) undertake follow-through efforts with respect to students who drop out.

I felt strongly enough about this matter to head a delegation from various colleges and universities to a U.S. Congressional Caucus in Washington, D.C. concerned with Upward Bound and related programs. What I advocated was not limited access, but emphasis on commitment to early and appropriate preparation in order to be able to benefit from a higher education learning opportunity.

I have included a more full treatment of these matters in a chapter entitled ''Improving Cost-Effectiveness on the Quality Side'' in my book, *Cost Containment for Higher Education: Strategies for Public Policy and Institutional Administration*. Also to be found there are discussions of the design of courses to serve fundamental objectives and the importance of considering an individual's attitude toward students in selecting faculty.

A teacher has to operate at more than one level in a classroom situation, quite apart from differences in student preparation or ability. On the one hand, students are encouraged to consider the effects of their behavior on their peers in order to retain a harmonious setting in which teaching and learning can go forward together. On the other hand, students are to be encouraged as individuals to be willing to set themselves apart from the group by expressing their own thoughts.

One must strive to encourage students to advance personally without putting others down, and in a manner that moves the group's understanding forward, so that the insightful student's learning can be a means for teaching others. The useful aspects of what a student says can be underlined. When there is error, it can be used constructively to point out the pitfalls which all of us need to be aware of, without being critical of the student. Differences that arise from different access to or interpretation of facts can be distinguished from those that arise from differences in the weights that individuals give particular values.

Students should be encouraged to seek progress along several fronts: They should be encouraged to inquire into facts, leading to knowledge. They should be made aware that what is a fact for themselves depends on the extent to which they have developed sensitivity, perceptiveness, and appreciation of difference. They should be thoughtful as to the significance of the values by which they are guided, and evolve a set of personal standards to guide their choice of actions. They should be aided in the development of the intellectual skills to make their own decisions on the basis of the knowledge acquired and their personal values.

When students do not aspire much for themselves, they may not welcome an individual who strives for more and would raise the class average, even though that person's presence, especially if there are several, could serve as a challenge for higher expectations and performance. A person who is initially motivated more than others may come under pressure to underperform. While it may be possible in such a case for the motivated student to shift to a more challenging school, this would not solve the problem for those left behind. It would be preferable from the standpoint of the other class members were those who are the better students enlisted in helping their classmates in finding satisfaction from what would become a shared learning experience.

Since many faculty members are more oriented toward their academic disciplines than toward their institutions, and more toward research in their discipline than to teaching, they may need encouragement to give more thought to their teaching. I wrote on this while in London in the mid-1950's, and what emerged is presented as Annex 11.1 to this chapter. See also Chapter 18 on goal-oriented learning.

We turn to another matter. The need to consider context is present in forming our attitudes as well as our decisions, and facilitating the learning of that concept can be considered an important objective of teaching. In much of teaching it is important to help students understand that in seeking answers to specific questions there may not be "right answers" to be discovered, but only "relevant answers." What is correct depends partly on context. You need to consider what is happening to variables that you are treating as constants for convenience. You need to give thought as to whose set of values you are using in determining preference for outcomes which may follow from your choice. Do they reflect interest in change and growth or in maintaining the status quo? Is there sensitivity to effects upon others beyond the individual or group making the decision? Decisions may emerge as the result of habit, intellectual laziness, or political design, which would have been different had they not been taken within limited horizons. What is decided is often deliberately channeled so as to compartmentalize the decision process. Such compartmentalized thinking is somewhat like learning only by experience in that you take into account additional considerations only after they intrude on your consciousness as a result of actions you have already taken. The following example of this compartmentalized approach to dealing with problems, particularly evident during the Reagan administration, is drawn from a paper I wrote in 1985 jointly with Morris Mendelson of the Wharton School, entitled "Special Interest and the Public Interest."

> We cannot make informed judgments as to the appropriateness of either a federal budget or a tax reform proposal in the absence of knowing how changes in one are accentuated or offset by provisions in the other. Eliminating a tax exemption could be acceptable, for instance, if as an alternative to the exemption a straightforward expenditure subsidy were included in the budget. It could also be acceptable if as a matter of policy

it was decided to discontinue encouraging that activity. Unfortunately it appears that the objective in isolating the treatment of tax reform from deficit reduction is to force cuts in expenditures by choking off the revenues necessary to finance them.

In the spring of 1963 I participated in the planning of a program of lectures to Peace Corps enrollees for the Cameroons, and then in subsequent terms lectured to Peace Corps groups destined for the Dominican Republic, Colombia, and Venezuela. In my lectures I emphasized that when they arrived in their assigned countries they would encounter assertions regarding the American economic system which they should be prepared to answer. The public relations type of response which covers over the shortcomings of our economy would not suffice. Accordingly, I discussed both the areas of strength and the areas in which improvement was needed in our handling of economic affairs, in some of which progress was being made. I contrasted Marxism in theory and practice and gave sufficient explanation of the mixed-economy type of American capitalism for the Peace Corps volunteers to be able to understand and appraise Marxist arguments regarding monopoly capitalism and the exploitation of the worker. My point of view was stated in the following passages from my lecture notes to the Peace Corps groups.

- What we seek is not that you convey any particular point of view to those you meet in the host Latin American countries, but instead that you be equipped with the type of understanding that will permit differences in viewpoint to be discussed in a mutually profitable manner when such exchanges infomally arise.

- As an example of a major difference in viewpoint, consider the following: The majority of Americans either take our economic system for granted or discuss it from the standpoint of adjustments to improve but not replace, existing arrangements. The majority of people in our country are taken care of in a material way, have experienced improvements in the past, and can afford to wait for further improvements. To those in Latin America who have not found that the economic system of their own country has done as well for them, there is not the same commitment to the status quo, and correspondingly there is greater interest in advocating a change in their economic system to one that may appear to offer the majority of the people a chance at a better life.

- To see things in perspective it will help if you evaluate social, political and economic arrangements from the standpoint of whether they are appropriate rather than right or wrong—that is, whether they are appropriate in the relevant situation rather than inherently right or wrong at all times, at all places and in all circumstances. We do not want to be like the well-intentioned monkeys who sought to rescue fish from a flood by pulling them into trees.

- Many of those you encounter will be impressed with the direct action advantages of an economic system in which a government authority instead of the market has control over resources. They will argue that such an economic system has the simplifying characteristic that resources can be marshalled for an attack upon the problems deemed most urgent. This has a natural appeal to many in Latin America, since economic progress for the majority has been exceedingly slow. But you might well question through what procedure what is to be done and how it is to be done is to be decided. And you should ask further whether the procedure provides access to the information needed for taking into account not only the benefits to be realized but also the costs involved, that is, the benefits to be sacrificed since resources have to be withdrawn from other goals. This is a problem present not only in the overall economic system of a country but also within large administrative organizations such as the national defense establishment to the extent that there are no market-determined prices to guide decisions.

At the Los Angeles campus I supervised student learning from a nationally televised course in economics which was broadcast prior to school hours, but had misgivings as to the bias present therein against government regulation which reflected the interest of the business corporation financing the series. I also prepared an agenda for a possible program for increasing general economic literacy in the community in 1961, and then in 1964 a proposal for an extension telecourse in economics for the Los Angeles metropolitan area.

My experience in attempting to interest my department in increasing general economic literacy perhaps warrants some further comment. Ruth and I were eating dinner at the Castle one evening when I heard on the radio that an ultraconservative speaker had engaged various public facilities in the Los Angeles area for an extended crusade against almost all forms of public regulation affecting business, completely ignoring that some regulation is needed so that the free market system can in fact operate. This Chicago-type view has, in fact, come to be predominant at many college and university campuses in southern California as well as elsewhere. After much serious discussion with Ruth, and with a great deal of reluctance since my time was heavily committed, I decided to promote a general economic literacy effort, starting in the San Gabriel Valley, to enable the community to better evaluate the policy alternatives. While I expected to encounter some apathy in the department, what I encountered was an arbitrary refusal to consider any work along such lines.

In 1983 I accepted an invitation from the American Library Association to address a session of its annual meeting in June on the impact of copyright on scholarly communication. My presentation is included as Annex 11.3 to this chapter, along with a further comment that I made in response to a letter from a university librarian. I stressed the contribution that libraries make to creativity, but pointed out that certain practices severely dampened the incentives for creativity.

Teaching through Distance Education presents special problems. In 1988 I was drawn on by Anne Renko de Rotaeche, a professor in charge of postgraduate studies at the Universidad National Abierto in Venezuela (a distance education university like the Open University in England) to provide comments on her monograph, "The Influence of an Instructional Design upon Learning of Distance Education Students in Venezuela." I include excerpts of my comments on three points that continue to have application.

- You quote Ausebel: "If I had to reduce all educational psychology to just one principle, I would say this: The most important single factor influencing learning is what the learner already knows. Ascertain this and teach him accordingly." It could be argued, however, that the instructional strategy to be selected should depend at least as much on the skills already learned by the student, especially the ability to reason, and on the individual's already-developed attitude toward ideas as such. Either way, the importance of pretests is evident.
- In comparing using instructional aids interspersed within the

text with using text and instructional aids in separate booklets, the following should be noted: Publishers tend to hold textbook length to approximately the length of competitive texts. Introducing more instructional aids thus tends to mean less instructional text. The advantage of instructional aids within a given book may be partly offset by there being less instructional text than in the case in which text and aids are separately published.

- Distance education, by its nature, operates without the advantage of class discussion and interaction among students outside of class. Questions included in or accompanying text material, especially that of a programmed nature, can facilitate comprehension. The ''advance organizers'' to which you refer, to the extent they consist of higher level generalizations, can go further by guiding the student to interpret content as a special case of broader principles. In a sense this is a gift of prepackaged induction.

  Texts are organized in terms of the author's objectives, while the objectives of the reader are generally not fully congruent. Comprehending and applying content is largely deductive and important in training. Inductive thinking is difficult to encourage in the classroom, and even more so in distance education. Hopefully, along with comprehension, comes an adjustment in one's personal structuring of concepts and relationships to accommodate what is learned. That restructuring offers an opportunity for a reexamination of ideas already held, and for engaging in speculative induction. Deductions follow which the individual may test against reality as perceived by that individual.

  Briefly stated, more attention is needed to the heuristic aspects of instructional aids. This is more a challenge for distance education than a criticism, for education in the classroom needs improvement in this respect as well.

In November 1988, as Chair of the Issues and Policy Committee of the State Conference of the American Association of University Professors, I directed attention to the need to update AAUP standards and guidelines in view of the rapid development of new instructional technology. Among the considerations that I mentioned were the following:

- Workload standards for faculty preparation and performance using new technology.

- Incentives to faculty members for instruction that reaches many students in the first instance, and consideration of residuals.
- Intellectual control over the use of material out-of-context and over editing by others.
- Development of appropriate techniques for evaluating faculty who use new technology.
- Development of broad guidelines for faculty evaluation of student learning occurring through the use of new technology.
- Coordination to avoid non-functional duplication in delivery systems, while recognizing the value of using techniques in complementary fashion.
- Implications for enrollment of there being new access to shut-ins, geographically remote students, students requiring special techniques and/or remediation, and so forth.
- Implications for academic partnerships with secondary school systems.

The faculty rights and responsibilities established with respect to the new technology will influence the extent and manner of its use.

Some five years later, upon my invitation, William Norris, chairman emeritus of Control Data Corporation, and Geraldine MacDonald, associate vice president for computing at State University of New York, Binghamton, contributed a chapter on the increased use of technology in instruction for a book I was editing (Simpson, 1993c). Norris emphasized (as I summarized in that book) that increased use of technology in instruction cannot simply be an add-on if it is to lead to cost containment—the teaching-learning system must be transformed. Instructional technology can facilitate self-paced, interactive learning that is programmed according to an individual's learning style and learning goals. Faculty would shift from lecturing to facilitating and mentoring individual learning activity, with students assuming more responsibility than at present. Collaboration among institutions in preparing computer-based learning resources would make possible economies of scale. The education process would become more decentralized, and less dependent upon a campus environment.

In commenting upon the above, I discussed the considerable challenges that I foresaw (Simpson, 1993c, Chapter 7), as follows:

- Can institutions avoid having faculty members' time spread too thinly among students? Will the faculty member, of necessity, become the manager for a team of low-cost learning assistants?

- Postsecondary education is a set of experiences involving access to teachers and library resources, interrelationships with fellow students and staff, identification with a campus and its heritage, learning from assuming responsibility and working together, and so forth. A student's goals may evolve from any of the above, even during a single class period when there is an inspired teacher and a receptive student. Can a student's decentralized interactive relationship with a computer substitute adequately for the above?

- Will collaboration among institutions in the preparation of learning resources result in material being designed for the lowest common denominator? Will it screen out all but prevailing viewpoints and modes of approach? Will the individual nature of course content be unduly influenced by the availability of materials prepared off campus?

- Will it be recognized that each faculty member, even if mainly a conduit and facilitator, needs to have time to be both informed of and creative with respect to developments in his or her field?

- Will not the cost of attracting and holding faculty increase when the managerial and facilitator skills required of faculty are those also marketable in the business world, and the ''halls of ivy'' appeal is perhaps less? If that cost is higher, and it is not met, what will be the quality of faculty?

In arguing for increased use of technology in both instruction and administration there is a tendency to argue in terms of increased efficiency (the ratio of benefit to cost goes up), without noting that this can reflect total benefit increasing without there necessarily being a decrease in total cost—a matter of no small consequence when the concern is cost reduction.

A letter to the editor of *Change Magazine*, included as Annex 11.4, makes clear that the introduction of instructional technology is not a panacea.

11.1

A Creed

In a small way, but yet to an extent greater than permitted most, the teacher is in a position to do something about the state of his fellow man.

Society sets certain objectives to be worked toward through formal education: attainment by the individual of a body of knowledge, of certain skills, and of a set of personal values to equip the individual in relating effectively to himself or herself, to others, and to a conception of the ultimate, in various roles in the family, in employment, and in duties as a citizen. What is sought is not simply training for specifically identified jobs, but education that prepares the individual for purposeful and intelligent choice and action in a vast array of yet unpredicted situations.

No teacher does the whole job; each is part of a team and each contributes as he or she can. The effect is not only upon the individual taught: the social environment conditioning the education of those who follow will differ as the graduates become parents, taxpayers and school board members.

It may be correct to say that the slow trend is toward accepting the teacher as a catalyst rather than purveyor, toward stressing development of the evaluative rather than the absorptive capacities of the student, and toward society asking not simply for adjustment but for responsible participation.

Within one's educational experience there should be exposure to those insights which will increase the dimensionality of one's living. Alongside the emphasis in the world today on materialism, there is room for affirmation of the aesthetic, ethical and spiritual values. Alongside the emphasis there is today upon the rational and the efficient, there is need in education to affirm also the worth of the intuitive and feelingful approach of a sensitive and perceptive individual.

But the teacher should never forget that however grand are these objectives, to the student the challenges are more likely seen in terms of the daily assignment. The student must feel that the instructor can see things from the student's side of the desk. There is need for standards, and there is need for consideration of the different levels from which learning starts. There is need for a high level of competence, and there is need for appreciating the steps toward that level that students must take. Above all, there is need for enthusiasm for one's subject.

Into the hands of the educator, society has put the heaviest of responsibilities and the greatest of privileges and opportunities—to teach and to inspire youth that their lives may be fuller, and society the better, for their having met.

11.2

Economics and General Education

(An Orientation Lecture)

Let us take up the question, "What is economics?" At this point we are not aiming at a formal definition. That will come later. Instead, consider the following:

A situation exists in which there are some resources, also several uses to which they could be put. The resources are scarce in the sense that not enough is present of the resources to permit all uses to be followed up to the extent desired. There are various different combinations and proportions in which resources might be assigned to uses. Corresponding to each possible arrangement there is a set of costs and a set of benefits, not necessarily measurable in money.

In a situation of this type, which can be called an economic problem, a choice has to be made among these different combinations and proportions as to how the resources are to be assigned among the alternative uses. These choices are made by individuals such as ourselves, by households, by business enterprises, by public bodies, and by society in general. What we will be studying is this problem of choice, and how the choices made by various agencies are organized by society so as to meet requirements arising out of choices made by others in countless other situations of comparable type.

We will study examples of such problems from various standpoints: sometimes from the standpoint of describing actual behavior, sometimes from the standpoint of understanding the basic principles that would explain the underlying regularities, and sometimes from the standpoint of recommending the behavior or policy that would most effectively achieve already stated goals.

Let us turn to the question, "What kind of course is this?"

- The course is designed to give you an awareness of the nature and scope of the subject matter of economics: problems of economics, economic institutions, principles of economics, and economic policies.

- A second point is that in this course we are concerned that you become aware of the techniques and methods of economic inquiry. The methods need to take account that much of what is studied is characterized by being interdependent and simultaneous. Economics, moreover, is concerned with the indirect and subsequent as well as the direct and immediate effects, and the methods have to be appropriate.

We attempt both of these objectives, but we do so in moderation. We are freed from the obligation to cover everything that a survey course might attempt, and we are under no burden to prepare you intensively in techniques for further specialized work, as would be the case in an introductory course in economic principles. Instead, we keep in view two additional objectives:

- That you learn how economics is related to other areas of knowledge and fields of inquiry which you are exploring or may find yourself exploring later. For instance, there are connections between economics and political science and government; between economics and psychology, sociology, anthropology, history and philosophy; between economics and biology, mathematics and the technical sciences.

- Finally, the objective that meaningful connections be developed between economics and your own life, and the life you observe and participate in about you.

This course is not intended as a first course for a specialist, nor is an effort made to recruit you for economics, although students sometimes decide to take additional courses in the subject.

It is not intended that this course should become just an item of data on your transcript. The course is intended to be a contribution to your general education. The important thing is that it make a difference that you have taken this course.

In a small way, we would like to believe:

- that you may experience some enthusiasm for keeping yourself informed and alert on some matters that may now be

escaping your attention, and
- that you may experience a bit more concern about certain problems around you, and
- that, through economics, you may become more aware of a viewpoint giving weight to the general welfare.

We would like to believe:
- that you may gain an understanding of the basic, common causes underlying the economic problems facing society, and of the institutions society creates to deal with these problems, and
- that you may develop an appreciation of the role that economics, in alliance with the knowledge and skills of other fields, can play in the understanding and solution of those problems.

We would like to believe:
- that you may obtain some competence in the tools offered by economics, to the end that you become more effective in serving your own basic values in situations calling for, or affording, opportunity for choice, and
- that through this you may be helped toward becoming a person: who can do more of his or her own thinking, who can communicate with others, and who can realize more fully one's own cultural and intellectual freedom.

We would like to believe:
- that you may be aided toward becoming more active in participating in decisions affecting your personal life, your life on the job, and your responsibilities as a citizen.

In short, the kind of difference we hope the course may make, and I stress again, "even though in a small way," is:
- that it may aid you toward a more complete realization and exercise of your potentialities, with the hope as well,
- that this greater freedom as an individual be enjoyed with an awareness of the responsibilities which go with it.

On none of these matters can we do all we should, but that is no reason for not making such progress as we can.

What I have been maintaining is that a general education course in economics can make an important contribution toward your total educational experience.

What I want to add is that there are also important contributions to be made by other general education courses. One emphasis in this course, for example, is on enabling you to be more effective in serving the values you now have, and to a lesser extent, to reappraise those values. (By "values," keep in mind, I mean what you hold dear, or more exactly, the abstract criteria by which you judge what is important to you.) Other general education courses will aid you even more than the present one in reappraising your basic values, and in discovery of the extent to which you are or are not bound by them, again this being part of the liberating function of a liberal education. (Another part is to liberate with respect to what are "facts.")

There is, moreover, a world of experience and action characterized more by feeling, appreciation, and response than by thinking, analysis, and rational choice. The ultimate ends or goals we seek tend to reflect appreciative rather than analytical reactions on our part. Even the adoption of particular means to achieve a goal may reflect an artistic judgment rather than an analysis of the alternatives.

In our daily lives our behavior draws upon our appreciative and rational capacities in various ways and proportions. Sometimes thinking and analytic effort are needed to unlock the opportunities for appreciation. Sometimes a sense of appreciation is needed to stimulate analytic thinking. On the whole, we have managed to get the right balance between appreciative modes of behavior and analytical modes in the boudoir and the office, in the art gallery and the polling place.

Economics, however, is not primarily concerned with the appreciative aspects of objectives but with the analytic choice of means to serve given objectives.

There are some who begrudge the time in college that is devoted to general education rather than to professional specialization. They are inclined to say that "The only practical education is one which trains you for earning a living." This is true in a sense, but it probably obscures more than it illuminates. Training prepares you for a fairly well defined task in which the range of your discretion is rather limited. Education prepares you to see a task in its context and to apply your own independent resourcefulness and your own evaluation to it. You might well question whether training which prepares you for particular activities is enough unless accompanied by the education which will let you rise to other activities as the occasion offers.

Something more has to be added. In the early 1800's the working day of a laborer was in excess of 12 hours out of 24. Thanks to the trend of our way of life, however, we no longer spend most of our hours on the job. By 1880, the average work week was reduced to 63 hours. Now it is 40 or less, some argue for a 35 hour work week, and some have won an even shorter work week. Earning a living is being pushed into a third or less of the hours of the day, and is largely absent from two days out of the seven. Surely a practical education must have some regard for preparing us for the three-fourths or more of our time spent off the job.

Economics, as part of one's general education, has relevance to one's "off-the-job" life in two important ways that we mentioned earlier: First, in connection with a responsibility—that of assisting one to be an effective citizen in a world in which economic considerations are mixed liberally into most every situation. The second point concerns not one's responsibility to others as much as an opportunity for ourselves—an opportunity for a fuller, more meaningful, and more pleasant life.

In short—in a variety of situations, whether ordinarily considered economics or not, an education in economics can offer you greater understanding and the capacity for intelligence choice.

The areas in which these contributions are made are four:

On-the-job competent performance and upward mobility.

Off-the-job responsible citizenship and effective living.

11.3

The Impact of Copyright on Scholarly Communication

This session of the American Library Association meeting is dedicated to John Stedman, Emeritus Professor of Law at the University of Wisconsin, who has contributed greatly in the field of copyright legislation. He anticipated a problem that is of increasing concern to many of us, namely, that unofficial Guidelines for educational fair use of copyrighted material—guidelines that lend themselves to a more restrictive interpretation than the legislation itself—may influence interpretation of the Copyright Statute.

I have been asked to comment at this session from the perspective of a faculty member. I will do so, and particularly from the standpoint of my field, which is economics. However, I should state that this is not a report of a research project, and the views are not necessarily those held by other faculty. Faculty are a very independent lot.

The first thing that strikes me is that the authorship and publication of material subject to copyright have the characteristics of what economists refer to as a *benefit externality*. In everyday language, this means that benefits for others are created that in some cases are difficult to monetize and capture for the author or publisher. Writing for publication, and publication itself, tend as a result to be curtailed to the extent that income is a motivating factor. That is the *supply* side. On the *demand* side, if burdensome requirements are put in place in an effort to obtain income from potential users, demand is curtailed and authors' views to that extent fail to be disseminated.

The concept of ''fair use'' attempts to balance these demand and supply considerations. I share Stedman's concern that ''fair use'' of copyrighted material be interpreted with concern both for the public interest in *access*, and the public interest in *maintaining incentives* for authors and publishers.

The basic reason for the difficulty in monetizing, for the author and for the publisher, some of the benefits created for others, is that, with some exceptions, published materials are not consumed by the original purchaser upon being used. The material is available for repeated use by the original user and by others than the original purchaser. You will note that this is also what makes it possible to have a library. Libraries also stimulate interest in publications, and I believe the consensus would be that the net effect on the fortunes of publishers is favorable.

Let us go one step further: Add the techniques for photocopying and for computer storage and distribution of information. Whereas the cost of supplying the original publication may be high, the cost of access to second and subsequent generation copies can be less, particularly when only part of a publication is desired. With arrangements available to users alternative to purchasing a complete first generation printed volume, publishers are inclined to the view that sales will be *less*, and accordingly they price their product on the basis of production cost being averaged over fewer copies.

Overall, and in the long run, the new technology may stimulate interest in publications, just as in the case of libraries; and this effect on demand should be considered in making an assessment of the *net* effect upon authors and publishers. But publishers have to make ends meet *now*, or not be around in the long run. As you know, publishers have attempted, through litigation in New York, to increase income from those making copies of copyrighted material. Proposals include the centralizing of photocopying machines and either record-keeping or adding a certain percentage based on periodic samples as to material that is copyrighted and not subject to ''fair use.''

I have some general observations on this: There are considerable costs attached to the collection of this income and its distribution among various publishers. There is a considerable nuisance cost to the user. And if one looks at academic activity overall, in which there are both authors and users of copyrighted material, sometimes the same individual, this type of regulation takes on the appearance of much effort involved in transferring relatively small amounts from one pocket to another, with some offsetting in the process. It also raises the question as to the appropriateness of a university using its resources to enhance the profit-making capacity of private entities.

As a faculty person, I would not expect "fair use" to cover instances in which the use intended by the copier is of a commercial nature, or instances in which copyrighted material is of a consumable nature, such as workbooks or test booklets. The Guideline as to anthologies or other compilations requires a more complex statement. I would not expect "fair use" to cover a faculty member's copying in order to avoid purchasing an available anthology, but if a suitable compilation is not available, and the faculty members seeks to *create* one, I would consider that "fair use" would cover the experimental preparation and use of a compilation, where there is an element of spontaneity present. I remind you, though, that others may view this differently.

Several of the standards contained in the Guidelines seem out of touch with the nature of educational use, at least at the level of university instruction. For instance:

- The Guideline standard for *brevity*, that limits use to a single chart, graph, diagram, drawing, etc. per book or per periodical issue.
- The standard of *spontaneity*, that copying be at the instance and inspiration of the individual teacher.
- The standard as to *cumulative effect*, that copying is for only one course in the school in which copies are made.

But if a *broad* interpretation of "fair use" is supported, and copyright holders are *not* to become more aggressive in seeking income from second and later generation copies, how *are* they to receive income? A number of techniques, as you know, are currently used, in various combinations:

- The initial cost of publication is sometimes subsidized: by research contracts that cover publication cost, by page charges to authors, by institutional sponsors for journals or monograph series, or by professional or disciplinary associations or government agencies paying the cost.
- Sales income is increased by differential pricing. Primary receivers of a publication often are charged more than others when multiple use of the publication is expected. Thus libraries are charged more than individuals, and hardbound copies are priced much higher than paperbound. The price set by publishers for copies made when permission is granted provides further diversity in pricing. Publishers

understandably are concerned when purchasers in one segment of the market manage to purchase at a lower price in a market segment intended for another category of purchaser.

- Authors and publishers can expect income as a result of the recent development of computer-accessed information systems. When the *actual expression*, and not just the *information*, is incorporated into the data base, as in the case of published abstracts, biographies, indexes, directories, and bibliographies, etc., the copyright holder stands to gain. Also when there is on-line transmission of entire copyrighted articles, or when on-line orders are placed for the mailing of copyrighted materials. When the computer system itself does the abstracting of information without reproducing the actual expression of the copyrighted material, I expect that the situation would be different. Even here, publishers might arrange for the necessary skills, and obtain some income. Computer searches, however, should give rise to increased interest in earlier copyrighted material.

What I would support as a faculty member is a *broad interpretation* of ''fair use,'' with initial publication cost being covered mainly through charges to the primary receivers of publications. In this view, libraries have an important role in making publication financially feasible in a pluralistic society; yet libraries have their own problems of funding. Accordingly, it is particularly welcome to find in the *Report of the Register of Copyrights*, in January of this year, the following paragraph:

> Proper recognition of the cost of creating and disseminating protected works in our society requires concomitant understanding at all levels of government of the need for adequate funding of publicly owned libraries to enable them to pay their share of creation-dissemination costs.

One problem in obtaining financial support for libraries, whether they are private or public in nature, is that libraries are more often identified with the word ''dissemination'' than with the word ''creation.'' Art Seidenbaum has commented in the View section of last Sunday's *Los Angeles Times*:

> We tend to pay them [libraries] proper respects as the *repositories* for 'human hopes' but we rarely support them in the bravo manner of concert halls or the hurrah spirit of sports arenas. [Emphasis added.]

I believe it is a challenge facing librarians that they do a better job of publicizing the important role that libraries have in *creativity*.

Earlier this month in Washington, I heard a librarian from the National Bureau of Standards mention, as have others, that with the introduction of computer-accessed information systems, and individuals thinking directly into and with the use of a computer, it is difficult to distinguish between the *distribution* of knowledge and the *production* of new knowledge. I realize that there are predictions of movement to paperless information systems. I would remark that the assembled collections of a library are important in developing *creative minds* and in the *creative process* itself. In teaching, I prefer that students not use anthologies but rather examine chapters or articles in their original context. I do not want to deliver to them snippets of fact or a body of conclusions. Students should be aware of the presuppositions underlying what they study and the reasoning involved in reaching conclusions. In research, if it is to be creative and not literally *re-searching*, there should be inductive as well as deductive components. There should be the stimulation of examining how related disciplines, with their own presuppositions and vocabulary, touch upon the borders of one's own discipline. Having publications at hand facilitates this.

Provision for "fair use" in photocopying selections chosen by the student or by the researcher facilitates subsequent study. The materials thus excerpted are not necessarily ones that would have been purchased by the individual. What must be strengthened financially is the ability of libraries to maintain substantial on-site collections. In the process we will be contributing to the incentives needed for scholarly communication through publication.

. . . .

Addendum, in response to a letter:

I recognize that minimizing acquisition cost through central storage, combined with fees for users, is attractive to libraries, which are under the pressure of escalating prices for publications. It is a course of action somewhat more subject to control than is the seeking of public support, which is less certain as to outcome and depends to a greater extent on the reaction of others. However, if only a single copy is purchased for a central storage facility, and this is then shared on request with patrons of a consortium of libraries, the financial incentive provided to publishers is undercut and publication outlets for authors may eventually be reduced. For some disciplines, and for some types of material, such centralization nevertheless will be desirable. Yet I would stress the desirability in many cases of maintaining on-site collections of printed copies, on a two-fold basis: (a) the importance of such collections from the standpoint of teaching and research, for a wide array of academic disciplines, and (b) the importance of the library market as a source of disinterested support for publication in a pluralistic society.

11.4

Technology is No Panacea

(Letter to the Editor of *Change*)

Chancellor Alan Guskin (*Change*, September/October, 1994) is to be commended for seeking to replace the impersonal undergraduate environment of large universities by an environment currently more closely approximated at small liberal arts colleges—one that stresses student-faculty interaction, student peer-group discussion, and student learning ahead of other faculty interests. The restructuring of the faculty's role is to be expected in any event as electronic-oriented generations take over as students and as faculty. What may be questioned is Guskin's unsupported assertion that greater individualized attention to larger enrollments with increased student learning can be accomplished with fewer faculty. Innovative use of new educational technology can point us in that direction, but there are cautions which should be observed if such changes are not to be self-defeating.

Faculty, without question, should not limit themselves or their students by offering only a single mode of learning, and should be open to delegating part of their role to assistants (resources permitting) and to encouraging peer-group interaction. But doing so on the scale that Guskin envisages means that student access to a professor is buffered by instructional machines and teaching assistants selected and coordinated by the faculty member, requiring managerial functions to be performed that compete, as I stated in *Cost Containment for Higher Education* (Praeger, 1991), with faculty reflection on insights to present and nuances to develop, as well as the best way to encourage learning by a particular individual or group. The planning and coordination of individualized learning programs, and, in particular, the assessment of student performance when diverse instructional modes are employed, makes demands on a faculty member's time that Guskin does not seem to take into account. Only if changes in the direction that he suggests are introduced selectively and in moderation so that side effects can be offset, can faculty fatigue and burnout be avoided.

Electronic inputs can be a useful factor in restructuring the role of faculty, but for the cost-effectiveness of undergraduate education to be advanced in a more fundamental manner, restructuring should also pay attention to what is sought as output, in particular to what I have described as ''goal-oriented learning'' *Academe*, January/February, 1993a; *Managing with Scarce Resources*, Jossey-Bass, 1993c).

12

Academic-Fiscal Planning

In February 1964 I became aware that the incoming campus president was about to appoint a new administrative staff with virtually no faculty participation. I wrote the following petition addressed to the president:

> With the selection of an almost full complement of academic administrators about to occur (your memo of February 20), and with arrangements for a structural reorganization of college virtually completed, the undersigned believe it is of paramount importance that maximum encouragement and opportunity be given to the several faculties of the college to directly discuss and contribute to the formulation of the criteria by which such appointments would be guided, particularly on this occasion but also with respect to periodic review.
>
> In this instance it would necessitate that adequate time be allowed for those participating in the advisory processes to meet with their respective faculties in order to consult with them in arriving at the criteria that would be stressed by them in their advisory capacities.
>
> Important as a basis for arriving at such criteria, as well as appropriate in terms of the total situation, would be a stocktaking at this time as to areas of concern that are at present most needful of improvement and as to the objectives and opportunities of the new Schools.
>
> To emphasize the concern of the faculty with the above-mentioned matters, and to request adjustment where needed in the procedures and timetable for arriving at decisions on appointments, the following have added their names.

The petition was signed by myself and then by other faculty members.

It had some effect, but not all that could be desired.

In early 1965 I began to take on various responsibilities for academic-fiscal planning, leading to an appointment by the college administration, in consultation with the faculty Academic Senate and the Chancellor for the system of campuses. This will be discussed briefly in the present chapter. In the following chapter I will discuss activities which were undertaken on behalf of faculty-based organizations such as the American Association of University Professors and the American Economic Association.

I had just completed arrangements following the death of my mother, who in recent years had lived in a nearby apartment in Alhambra, and I was considering a move to another institution when I received a telephone call from Professor Donald Moore of our Economics Department. There was pressure on campus facilities due to increasing enrollments and he was chair of a faculty committee studying a shift from two-semester to four-quarter operation which had been called for by the California Coordinating Council for Higher Education and the Legislature and which had been authorized by the Board of Trustees. He asked whether I would be interested in undertaking studies of the proposed change in academic calendar in which the Los Angeles campus would serve as a pilot for other metropolitan campuses. I agreed, since this was in line with my interest in higher education policy.

By Spring 1966 I had completed four substantial studies incorporating mathematical models: (a) predicting student enrollment under year-round operation with concurrent conversion from semester to quarter calendar, (b) indicating the effect on average and incremental cost as measured in teaching positions, (c) providing a method of budgeting faculty positions, and (d) providing models whereby a college or university, or division thereof, could plan the level of staff required and the rotation of assignments. The mathematical formulations were in most cases carried through to specific numerical estimates, drawing upon documentary sources, the results of questionnaire surveys, and other data. While the models employed have generality with respect to institutions of different scale, the numerical conclusions derived differ according as application is made to institutions of markedly different size. At that time there was a call to covert some colleges to year-round operation although their enrollment was still small, and in fact, to convert several colleges simultaneously in the same area in the same year.

There has been a tendency to treat the adoption of year-round operation as merely a question of efficient operation, although it has important implications for educational policy. The resource allocation decisions which are implicit in the adoption of year-round operation appear to pay attention to the plant capacity constraint without sufficient recognition of (a) the constraint present in the shortage of qualified faculty, and (b) the economic value of students' time. The needed caution is that in the absence of a clear view of these critical factors, the adjustments needed for implementing year-round operation may come about through a change in the quality of the educational product and through uncompensated accommodations being required of faculty and students. Faculty and academic administrators are put in the unsought role of being the ones to deteriorate the quality of the educational experience that can be offered, unless recommendations to offset such deterioration of quality are financed and the conversion of campuses is appropriately sequenced.

The models I developed provided students in the fourth (summer) quarter with an educational opportunity comparable in access to course offerings and experienced faculty to a term within the nine-month academic year. The studies differed from ones undertaken at the University of California at Berkeley. The latter used, instead of mathematical models, experienced data which reflected differences occurring in the adequacy of budgetary funding and in access to courses and faculty.

Provision was made in my models for additional departmental support staff to cope with the increased number of turn-around periods and the concentration of duties. What I was not able to offset was the possibility of increased fatigue which faculty might experience as the result of dealing with three rather than two different groups of students per nine months. As to fourth-quarter service, this was to be performed so that all faculty members could rotate with three quarters of teaching and one quarter off from teaching (not necessarily the summer). I prepared budget recommendations for quarter-system year-round operation based on the above, and provided justifications.

Students were not required to attend four consecutive quarters, but incentives were structured so that inclusion of the summer quarter as one of those selected would be attractive. This reflected my general view that policies that encourage awareness and examination of options are to be preferred over those that make particular behavior mandatory.

I kept the local academic calendar study committee informed as well as the campus president; the campus academic senate as well as the state-wide academic senate; presented a seminar on the subject attended by representatives of the Chancellor's Office, State Department of Finance, State Department of Education, State Comptroller, Legislative Analyst, and Joint Legislative Budget Committee; served on the Chancellor's system-wide advisory committee on year-round operation; advised the Board of Trustees; testified before the Coordinating Council for Higher Education; advised faculty organizations; and provided consultative services to other colleges and universities in California and other states.

In an account which I kept of my work for 1965 through 1969 on QSYRO academic calendar change I find seventy-eight entries. This includes studies, written reports and oral testimony, as well as participation in workshops and service as a consultant to other universities. On one policy matter which greatly enhanced budgetary provision for quarter-system year-round operation I successfully carried the measure through every academic and governmental level of consideration.

The experiment with a comparable quarter succeeded and the program expanded, in contrast to the experience at campuses at which comparability was not undertaken and the program had to be discontinued.

An accounting firm, Touche, Ross, Bailey & Smart, was engaged by the Coordinating Council in late 1968 to evaluate year-round operation. While the Touche firm had been given the full cooperation of the colleges and the use of a number of special studies, the firm did not provide an opportunity to the pilot campuses to comment on the report while it was in draft form. Accordingly, I testified at the Coordinating Council following the presentation of the accounting firm's report, and provided a critique drawing on six pages I had prepared of significant criticisms. In January 1968 and again in January 1969 I prepared a report on quarter-system year-round operation at the request of the Legislative Analyst for California and presented a discussion of the reports in Sacramento.

I have discussed the implications of year-round operation for cost and for enrollment in an extensive section on Academic Calendar Change in the chapter "Containment of Capital Outlays" in *Cost Containment for Higher Education* referred to earlier. The mathematical models to which I referred were gathered in 1973 under the title, ''Planning Models for Academic Calendar Change.''

I turn now to another area of my activity, namely, planning-programming-budgeting. During the recess in December 1966 I received a telephone call from Professor Arthur Kirsch of our Economics Department to inform me that he had recommended to the statewide Academic Senate that I be asked to comment on plans for implementing planning-programming-budgeting (PPB) on our campus, as mandated by an executive order of the Governor. The emphasis in PPB is upon allocating resources through a budget organized on the basis of the goals to be served within a multi-year context of intermediate and long-term objectives, rather than on the basis of the type of inputs to be purchased. The intent is to facilitate decisions on the extent to which resources should be allocated to different objectives.

I prepared a series of memoranda and studies on program budgeting during the following months: Commentary and Recommendations, Evaluative Comments, Various Cautions, Proposed Resolutions, Conceptual Framework, Treatment of Research, Application to College Libraries, and so forth. I periodically discussed PPB with the president's cabinet, the Council of Deans, the campus Fiscal Affairs and Instructional Affairs Committees, the campus and state Academic Senates, and the Chancellor's Office. I became active at the state level in designing the conceptual framework for PPB and the procedures for its introduction and practice. In the fall term of 1967 I provided the members of the Academic Senate with a compilation of my writings on PPB and a bibliography of reference material, and the Senate then set time aside for a lengthy meeting in which I discussed PPB. In that session, and in subsequent progress reports to the Academic Senate, I stressed such matters as the following: increasing the access of the Chancellor's Office to faculty viewpoints, orientation of faculty and staff so that channels would be open for discussion while matters were still fluid, arrangements to draw upon such experience as was available from other institutions, planning a PPB system that would encourage the use of the most modern instructional techniques, and effort to develop a cost-benefit analysis staff and secure the computational equipment necessary for the undertaking.

I subsequently met for orientation purposes with groups at each school of the college, which included the dean and his staff, the school fiscal affairs committee, and department chairs and associate chairs.

A follow-up meeting was then held with the dean of each school. Somewhat comparable meetings were held within each area of the college's operations staff.

Annex 12.1 to this chapter provides a summary of some of the more general points which I made at the PPB orientation meetings. See also the section on Departmental Self-Study in *Cost Containment for Higher Education* for the orientation given to departments, in which emphasis is upon examining basic curricular and instructional objectives and considering alternative paths to their attainment.

I participated in a symposium on operations analysis in Washington, D.C. in 1967, and in seminars on PPB of the Western Association of College and University Business Officers (WACUBO) in San Francisco in 1967 and 1968, and in Palm Springs in 1968. In December 1967 I was appointed by the Chancellor, in consultation with the state Academic Senate, as faculty representative for the system of state colleges on a Coordinating Council Ad Hoc Advisory Committee on Program Budgeting in Higher Education. I was also active in a series of interagency seminars on PPB sponsored by the State Department of Finance in 1968. For the years 1967 and 1968, I find 71 entries (apart from school and department level orientations) as to reports prepared, testimony given, seminars, and so forth on PPB, at various academic, government and professional levels.

I was particularly interested in developing a conceptual framework and a set of procedures that would encourage innovation in the instructional area and in the library, but all areas received my attention. As to the library, I spoke to the annual meeting of the American Library Association in 1983 on the contribution that libraries make to creativity and the importance of bibliographic access. I was concerned with structuring the information in the library, as distinct from structuring the physical materials, in order to facilitate lines of inquiry from one thought to another. (Discussion of the implications of this for program budgeting is given in Chapter 10 of *Cost Containment*, referred to earlier. See also "Libraries" in the index therein.)

In the orientation meetings I discussed several matters with respect to which caution needs to be observed:

- Program budgeting is not logically tied to fiscal flexibility—either could exist without the other—but the manner of implementing program budgeting could advance or retard the achievement of fiscal flexibility for the system of campuses and for individual campuses.

If the present non-transferability of funds between functions at the headquarters level for the system of campuses (i.e., between instruction and library, between general administration and student services, etc.) serves as a precedent for the Department of Finance not permitting transferability between different programs, between different program elements, and possibly between other subdivisions of programs, such fiscal flexibility as exists would not be increased and probably would be decreased.

- There is need for capability at the individual campus level as well as at the headquarters for the system of colleges.
- The tendency is to leave program budgeting to fiscal people once program statements are written, rather than to recognize sufficiently the implications that program budgeting has for academic affairs.
- There is also a tendency to see the institution of program budgeting as a job to be done and done-with rather than as a set of continuing processes involving long-term planning and intermediate programming as well as year-to-year budgeting.
- There is a tendency to emphasize budget format and visual examination of alternatives without sufficient recognition of the in-depth consideration needed as to objectives and means, or of the analyses required.
- There is need to recognize that the types of analyses that are required are not such as to emerge from the budget office or from the institutional studies office.
- There is also a need for integrating program budgeting into existing faculty processes and committee structure rather than having it compartmentalized by means of special study committees.

As I recall, it was in 1967 that it was suggested that I join the Chancellor's Office staff in the area of faculty affairs, but I indicated that I would be better able to speak out were I to combine teaching with a consultative relationship.

As it turned out, I accepted an appointment in 1967 at the Los Angeles campus, offered by the college administration with concurrence of the Academic Senate, which carried the lengthy title, Consultant for Academic-Fiscal Planning and Analytic Studies. I was invited to write my own description of the position, and did so, essentially formalizing the type of duties within and external to the college in which I had been engaged along with teaching since 1965. In this connection I worked closely with Dr. Kenneth Martyn, who had become Vice President for Academic Affairs.

In 1968 I formulated a proposal for a Planning Council to increase the effectiveness of the college in long-range and intermediate-range planning with respect to all elements of the college's program.

Computer-assisted instruction, which was being practiced successfully by Professor Joseph Casanova in the Department of Chemistry, drew my attention, and following my suggestion, a demonstration laboratory was developed in the main classroom building to encourage its more general acceptance.

I was also interested in instructional television, and my suggestion was adopted that it be used by the college in conveying to the Board of Trustees the nature of the college's commitment to an urban focus.

In February 1968 I shared some of my thoughts on faculty teaching load with a local chapter of a faculty organization. Within a few weeks I was requested by Martyn to draw up proposals in that area. There were several facets to the matter:

- Working toward recognition of a normal workload for an individual faculty member that would provide adequate course preparation time, and time for academic advising, institutional responsibilities, and professional development activities concurrent with teaching (scholarship, additional education, research and creative activity).
- Development of a budgetary approach for the allocation of instructional resources to an institution of higher education that would provide both opportunity and incentive to individual faculty members to innovate in their instructional practices. This was subsequently published (1975).
- Guidelines for discretionary allocation of faculty positions to instructional departments within the total number budgeted.
- Provision for a prototype department-level plan for allocation of positions to individual instructional faculty.
- Guidelines for allocating faculty time in such cases as there is less than the full requested budgetary provision.

As to the last-mentioned point, I stressed that it should be kept in mind that the quality of a department becomes over time the quality of those it is able to attract. Assigning time for professional development concurrent with teaching as part of the incentive in recruitment of faculty and to relatively new members of a department, instead of assigning it to long-deserving senior faculty who are unlikely to transfer to another institution, may be hard-hearted, but apart from possible effects on morale, this may in the long run raise the quality of instruction. This, of course, was controversial, and a rally was held in the college auditorium on the occasion of a visit by a teacher's union official at which I found myself being denounced. A professor on the stage with the speaker offered me a chance at rebuttal. I thanked the visitor for making it possible for me to convey my proposal to such a large assembly, and set forth the rationale. While opposition to this idea was high at that time, some years later the viewpoint gained adherents.

Another position I took was to advocate selective adjustments based on judgment rather than across-the-board proportional changes when budget adjustments became necessary. This I have discussed in *Cost Containment for Higher Education.*

I continued throughout this period to take a leading position with respect to academic-fiscal planning involving quarter-system year-round operation, planning-programming-budgeting, faculty load, and also school liaison, admissions, and budget policy generally. In such activities I interacted with administration, academic senate, faculty organizations, and various governmental levels. In 1968 I was appointed by the state Coordinating Council for Higher Education to an Advisory Committee on the Master Plan for Higher Education that dealt with costs and sources of income. When the Coordinating Council was replaced by the California Postsecondary Education Commission, I was provided written analyses and participated in round-table discussions in regard to the annual updating of the Five-Year Plans for Higher Education.

I became eligible for a sabbatical leave in July 1969, but it could not be awarded to individuals on an administrative assignment. I resigned as consultant and took a year's leave at partial pay to complete some research, followed by a short extension of the leave without pay. Martyn, with whom I had enjoyed working, resigned from the university during my absence in order to launch the American Learning Corporation, which was concerned with special education for children. I returned to full-time teaching in spring of 1971.

The topic of this chapter is discussed further in Annex 12.1, immediately following, and in Annex 19.1, "Heading Off a Crisis: A Hard Look at Campus Academic-Fiscal Planning," based on an address I gave to the state conference of the American Association of University Professors in 1993.

12.1

Relating Programs and Resources to Objectives

In contrast to a conventional budget which is set forth first by administrative units and then by type of input being purchased, a program budget puts the emphasis on what is being attempted and its justification.

Program budget presentations are set up by program and subdivisions of programs, each representing an objective or goal to be served. Programs may be successively divided into elements, components and tasks. The basic elements of the program budget for the California State College System are: Instruction, Research, Community Service, Student Services, and Institutional Services. For each program element, and program component thereof, a narrative statement of Need, Authority and General Description is prepared.

The categories set forth as program elements and program components will also be used in the subsequent preparation of workload plans, multi-year program statements, and in particular, in the analyses which are the basic feature of a planning-programming-budgeting system.

Accountability is maintained as to the amounts budgeted by the objectives served while flexibility in operation is retained to the extent that substitutability is permitted in the use of funds among program components that serve the same objective.

The significance of program budgeting is that potentially it may encourage and facilitate improved decision-making with respect to the use of resourses:

- through encouraging the identification of ultimate, intermediate and immediate objectives,

- through identifying and determining the costs and benefits associated with particular goals, and
- through development of data systems and procedures auxiliary to those of accounting that permit a constantly updated consideration of intermediate range programs in the light of current information and in the context of long-range objectives.

Of the following three levels of possible implementation of program budgeting, the third corresponds to what has been mandated for all state agencies in California:

- Program budgeting as a new format for describing the allocations made in furtherance of different objectives—a format which will aid in review of the budget request as to resources to be approved for a specified activity—without analysis of alternative courses of action as to cost or as to costs compared to benefits.
- Program budgeting as an analytic approach for selecting, from among alternative programs that would accomplish a stated performance level, the one that would minimize cost.
- Program budgeting as an analytic approach for selecting, from among different courses of action, the set of one or more activities (and activity levels) that is optimum when considering both costs and benefits.

In program budgeting, a budget-year request is shown as the annual portion of the cost of a program for which cost estimates are provided for a number of years ahead.

The practice in program budgeting reflects planning and analysis in a context which includes consideration of long-term objectives as well as intermediate and short-term goals, and takes into account for each year, and by program, element, component and task, the following:

- Target levels of performance for each year with respect to each type of output or result contributing to the program's objectives.
- The levels at which various activities must operate in each year to produce those levels of performance.
- The amounts of resource inputs of various types required in each year for those activity levels and their expected dollar costs.

In this planning, adjustment should be made for expected technological and legislative changes affecting higher education.

The following points should be observed:

- Costs are to be grouped for each program, ideally irrespective of organizational unit.

- A special problem exists with respect to the costs of activities that contribute to more than one program (general administration, computer center, communication services are examples). To treat such activities as separate programs or program elements (or as a program component of institutional services) may meet the need for accounting and control, but does not meet the need for decision purposes. For decision purposes, the costs of such activities should be charged off to the specific programs, the level of which induced such cost.

- Analysis of both marginal and incremental cost is needed, drawing upon economic theory, whereas the accounting data system generates average cost.

- The analysis should work toward the formulation of models expressing cost levels for programs as functions of the different types of demand for educational service (part vs. full-time, day vs. evening, graduate vs. undergraduate, upper division vs. lower division, transfer student vs. four-year student, etc., and their respective distribution over the four quarters), so that inter-campus differences in these respects can be taken into account and so that budget adjustments can be made for changes in data with minimal further analysis and computation.

- Both the support budget and a capital outlay budget need to be considered in formulating a program budget. If this is not done, a saving in one type of expense may be gained but only at an unnoticed greater increase in expenses of the other type.

- Selection of the minimum cost approach to a particular level of performance or of the most efficient means to a particular goal, is no assurance that a program should be undertaken at all, or on the other hand, that it is being pursued at the appropriate level. To secure such assurances requires cost-benefit analysis.

- Going beyond the problem of determining the desired extent and cost of a particular activity, the more general problem in program budgeting is that since resources are limited and have various possible uses, decisions are required as to which set of activities to pursue and at what levels. The increased benefit from the activity that is increased is realizable in return for trading-off the benefits that are foregone from the activities that need to be curtailed to release the needed resources.

The processes which allocate resources in the market place have to be replaced by conscious decisions when the problem is one of allocating resources within a large administrative organization.

This is not a question of least cost or of maximum benefit but a question of maximizing a weighted sum of the differences between benefit and cost corresponding to the levels of particular activities, while taking into account the effects upon other programs. In addition to following from other interrelationships among activities which may exist, the latter interdependence follows from the various programs being subject to a set of resource constraints. The techniques of mathematical programming concentrate on developing a model consisting of a set of relationships that brings together the relevant considerations in a form susceptible of solution.

- Although cost-benefit analysis is essential for the full implementation of program budgeting, the results of cost-benefit analysis in education are less conclusive and persuasive than may be anticipated by those advocating it. Difficulties exist not only in defining educational objectives but also in measuring benefit and in comparing benefit to cost.

- The outcome of cost-benefit analysis conducted in connection with full program budgeting does not necessarily point conclusively to what decisions should be taken as to the program costs to include in the program budget request.

When judgments involving significant policy questions are involved, consultation will be needed with the appropriate faculty or administrative body for decisions to be made in the light of the analysis and the weighing in of considerations not included in the analysis.

- The art to be developed in employing analytic tools is in achieving a level of insight into the problem appropriate to the cost of the inquiry and the benefits which are to be

derived from facilitating a correct decision.
- Program budgeting will not necessarily deliver data in the form most needed since the initial definition of programs will tend to follow the existing organizational structure. Analysis will suggest a recombination of activities in different program groupings.
- To give effect to the full potential of program budgeting requires probing the underlying basic objectives of programs (apart from preconceptions as to the institutional means to be employed).
- It also requires examining the possibility of preferred courses of action alternative to those currently employed. In the course of program budgeting being applied to the activities of the state government, such matters as the relative support given to the following might bear scrutiny:
  public education compared to welfare programs, correctional institutions, etc.
  primary and secondary compared to higher education
  informal compared to formal education
  educating the college-aged compared to rehabilitating the educationally deprived
  public higher education compared to state support for private colleges and universities
  instruction compared to research
  general education compared to specialized instruction
  education compared to training
  investment compared to the consumption aspect of education
  lecture-demonstration-discussion compared to tutorials
  on-campus instruction compared to work-study, distance education, travel, and so forth.
- A program budget does not eliminate the need for a line-item budget by type of expense at some administrative level, with review by a higher level. The line-item budget could be prepared on individual campuses with review by the Chancellor's Office and Trustees. The latter includes, in addition to the capital outlay budget and the salary and wages supplement budget, a continuing workload budget and a budget for program augmentations. The program budget is to be accompanied by a reconciliation between it and the workload budget.

13

Faculty Rights and Responsibilities

In the period following my return from sabbatical leave my activities, in addition to teaching economics and research on the economics of higher education, included various committee assignments at department, school and university levels. Already mentioned in the chapter on teaching was work done during this period on reorganizing the curriculum for the Department of Economics and Statistics, and the report on long-run goals for the School of Business and Economics. Also, at the request of the School Dean, I provided a report on enrollment decline covering underlying causes, problems created, and policy alternatives, which was widely distributed on campus. Further, I recommended a policy that was adopted for avoidance of conflict-of-interest in the case of lecturers paid by non-academic sources, and also responded to a State Academic Senate request in March 1971 to evaluate a study on instructional workload by the State Legislative Assembly's Sub-Committee on Education.

It was in 1973, about June as I recall, that I undertook a major commitment directly focused on faculty rights and responsibilities, the topic of the present chapter. At that time I accepted an invitation to become president of the local chapter of the American Association of University Professors (AAUP), which carried with it ex officio honorary membership in the faculty Academic Senate. We began to hold monthly meetings of the executive committee in the evening at our apartment at the Castle, which was close to campus. Usually the weather permitted the meeting to be held outdoors by candlelight under the spreading branches of the deodar cedars. There was always a full agenda, and attendance was virtually complete at each meeting.

Emphasis was placed on making the organization more outgoing and on more participation by membership. The executive committee meetings were open to all who were interested. A category known as "program associate" was created for individuals, whether chapter members or not, who were willing to contribute their expertise in areas of concern to the AAUP. The chapter adopted the policy that while it would be attentive to all matters of concern to AAUP, it would, whenever possible, take such initiatives as would have a catalytic effect on existing faculty government rather than itself engage in long drawn-out projects. Periodic "Reports to the Faculty" were distributed to the entire faculty in a format designed to hold the attention of the reader throughout its usual two or three pages.

Various matters arose on which the Executive Committee of the AAUP took a stand. For instance, it issued a statement in September 1973 that was quoted in the *University Times* regarding an academic vice chancellor being appointed without consideration of qualified women and minority candidates. I obtained support at the state AAUP level for processing a legal complaint that the Trustees had violated the federal executive order on affirmative action.

On motion of Marie-Antoinette Zrimc, chapter vice president in 1973-74, a chapter committee on the status of women faculty was instituted which in its first year of operation investigated patterns of delay in the advancement of women faculty. Two comments I provided that committee were as follows:

- The number of women candidates available for possible apointment could be increased in the long run were women who were already in the academic profession to visit secondary schools and speak to students regarding the possibility of preparing for an academic career.

- In the desire to avoid discrimination against women faulty in personnel proceedings, care should be taken not to make it appear as though candidates should be considered completely apart from their sex. As I see it, the need is to emphasize the consideration of candidates as individuals. This should not rule out considering a factor such as the sex of the candidate where in a particular instance it is demonstrably relevant to the job. Women, for instance, may bring experiences, attitudes and perceptions into their teaching which are different from those of male candidates in certain fields, and this could be a positive consideration in support of their appointment.

The chapter was also alert to discrimination that might arise with respect to minority faculty.

In November of 1973 I directed the attention of the faculty Academic Senate and the University administration to the need for the University to remedy the absence of policy statements setting forth the rights of part-time faculty.

Although the administration and the AAUP chapter differed on various policies, there was a good working relationship. At the request of the chapter, John Palmer, a vice president of the University, brought to the AAUP Executive Committee a 1973 internal audit conducted by Chancellor's office staff on behalf of the Board of Trustees, and a copy of the University's reply to that audit. I prepared, in consultation with with the Executive Committee, a statement on the audit group's recommendations. The AAUP position was that detailed requirements as to procedures for student instruction such as those suggested in the Trustee audit report may influence course content and the manner of instruction and research and thus impair the educational effectiveness of the institution. The requirements would be difficult to reconcile with the call for flexibility and innovation voiced by the Chancellor. The AAUP position with respect to adjusting to a decline in enrollment was that whereas the audit report sought a proportional decline in the number of full-time faculty, the adjustment needed to be viewed in the light of the institution's responsibilities to faculty and in the context of tenure considerations. As to faculty attendance, the audit group's listening at classroom doors impugned faculty integrity and could generate considerable hostility without solving such problems as do arise. Existing policies for faculty reporting non-attendance received a high degree of compliance and provided a basis on which to proceed in seeking any further improvement that might be needed. The University administration distributed the AAUP chapter statement as an attachment to the *Faculty Bulletin,* and copies were also distributed to the audit staff, Trustees, Chancellor's office, state Academic Senate and state AAUP. The statement was summarized in the campus newspaper.

On another matter, questions were raised by students as to the right of speakers to be heard on campus who espoused academic theories that many found racist in nature. In March 1974, the AAUP chapter publicized its resolution, approved by vote of all AAUP members on campus, "that the AAUP encourages the free flow of ideas to the fullest extent compatible with the search for truth—including the expounding of theories that may be unpopular within academic communities—as an ingredient vital to the pursuit of knowledge on the part of students and professors alike."

Also at that time, a part-time instructor in English had been labeled a racist. Further, a sociology professor was branded as a racist for using a particular textbook. There were classroom disruptions, leaflets, letters to the campus newspaper, student delegations, and also banners fastened on campus buildings. There was a call from the Associated Students Board of Directors for that textbook and others to be named to be banned from use on the campus and at other institutions of higher education. In April and May 1974 the *University Times* published letters which I wrote concerning racism and academic freedom, letters which were subsequently endorsed by the University Committee on Academic Freedom and Professional Ethics. I stressed at that time:

> . . . What would seem to be essential is that students and faculty be exposed to the variety of viewpoints that exists with respect to an issue, not necessarily in the same book or through the same medium, and that students be equipped with the conceptual tools so that they may weigh and consider various viewpoints and be able to draw their own conclusions. . . . The responsibility for maintaining conditions of academic freedom for all members of an academic community is one which must be shared by all in that community.

In a second letter I wrote:

> . . . academic freedom . . . is the essential ingredient of a university, both for students and faculty, and neither has a monopoly on the uses or abuses of that freedom. The benefits of academic freedom are too often taken for granted, and the responsibilities that go with it are too often ignored.
>
> Classroom and campus newspaper are both important in the learning and inquiry for which a university exists. The professor has responsibility for encouraging the evaluation of different viewpoints, providing balance through some combination of text, lecture, discussion, etc. The corresponding responsibility for an editor is a balanced presentation, although this is not always possible within a single edition, and the readership is not constant. If a newspaper is not to be judged by a single

edition, should a professor be judged by the book employed without taking account of how it is used in class?

There are few courses that could not be improved. How ever, this is better accomplished when faculty and students consider themselves as participants in a common quest, and not as adversaries. Each should credit the other with the integrity of wishing to understand the other's position, and should seek a resolution without injury to individuals and to the learning process.

There was a discussion on campus during 1974 of proposed guidelines for the allocation within a campus of the total number of faculty positions assigned the university. I participated by offering suggestions at various stages—as a representative of the Educational Policies Committee to the ad hoc Academic Senate Committee on that topic, as AAUP chapter president to the Academic Senate chairperson, and as advisor to the vice-president of academic affairs—all of which led to the adoption of various modifications.

In August of 1974 I prepared a study, *Options in Steady-State Staffing*. As mentioned therein, ''steady-state staffing'' may be considered a label which puts a positive face on a group of problems confronting or foreseen by individuals and institutions in higher education. ''Staffing for a steady-state as to enrollment'' is what is conveyed, but enrollment is not truly steady-state, and what is required may be non-staffing or unstaffing instead of staffing. At that time total enrollment in many institutions was tending to level off and was expected to decline. But even were total enrollment to remain constant, enrollments in particular programs of a university may undergo changes greater than ordinarily experienced as shifts occur from one field to another. The report consisted of 52 single-spaced typed pages in question and answer format which systematically explored the problems involved and the options that could be pursued in both the short run and the long run. Publication of the report was supported by a grant from the University. Copies were widely distributed and the report was well received. It was cited in documents of a Task Force appointed by the Chancellor's Office on recruitment of a qualified faculty and was welcomed as a lucid treatment of a complex subject by the national president of AAUP. A revision was privately reproduced in November, and at the suggestion of the national AAUP it was sold at cost alongside AAUP publications at the national meetings in each of the following two years. The report has been kept in print. It was of particular interest due to the need to consider layoff policy in the face of the declining enrollment then being experienced.

In October I secured executive committee authorization for a permanent AAUP chapter committee on academic freedom and responsibility. This arose initially out of a protracted suspension of the university committee that dealt with such matters pending legal clarification of the charge to that committee, but the continuance of the chapter committee reflected an increased need in this area. The intention for the long term was to serve not as a replacement of the university committee but as an additional facility which would continue the good relationship the chapter had with the university committee. The functions of the chapter committee were stated as follows:

- Counseling members of the academic community who seek assistance in responding to situations inconsistent with AAUP principles.

- Assisting individuals in securing access to local due process procedures pertaining to grievances or disciplinary matters.

- Mediating among members of the campus academic community on an informal basis in cases of alleged actions inconsistent with AAUP policies.

- Defining potential cases and issues for the chapter's executive committee, and through that committee for the AAUP State Conference and the regional representative of the national AAUP.

- Identifying for the chapter's executive committee those aspects of the local academic setting which are or may be undermining the exercise of academic freedom and the fulfillment of responsibilities following therefrom.

Meanwhile I had become active in the California Conference, which is the state organization of AAUP, and in April 1974 was elected Vice President of the Conference concurrent with my second term as chapter president.

On the afternoon before Christmas of 1974, John Palmer, Vice President for Academic Affairs at the University, telephoned my home, and upon learning that I was on campus visited me in my office. He asked that I accept appointment as a consultant for a short period to assist the university administration in preparing a reaction to a proposal from the Chancellor's Office concerning a method for determining the number of faculty positions that should be assigned to individual campuses. This was the budgetary step preceding that with which we had been concerned during the year. Although this was a matter in which I was greatly interested, I agreed somewhat reluctantly because of teaching responsibilities and the burden of other matters which had brought me to the office on the holiday. However, on the 28th of December I suffered a heart attack and was taken to the hospital. Subsequently, in what must have been a breach of hospital rules, I had the correspondence files that I needed next to my bed in the intensive care recovery room. A day or so later, by an arrangement in advance in which the hospital switchboard was opened a half hour early, I dictated my recommendations to Ruth over the telephone, lifting my oxygen mask at intervals in order to speak. Ruth typed a draft, I corrected it later in the day, and copies of the revision were sent out to the administration and other interested parties with Ruth supplying my signature and adding her initials. Later that month I traveled to Stanford University, where I presided at a session of the annual northern meeting of the California Conference. I apparently was strikingly pale and I know that I was wobbly. My voice was weak, but although it was a large meeting room, everyone accommodated me so that I could be heard.

The recommendations which I made from the hospital were against adoption of the method proposed by the Chancellor's Office for allocating faculty positions to individual campuses. The Chancellor's Office nevertheless persisted in its approach, so in March I prepared an analysis of the method which was widely circulated as the draft of an article subsequently published in the *California Academic Review* for June 1975. As noted therein, the method for arriving at faculty productivity ratios makes no allowance for authorized activities of the faculty which do not directly produce student-credit-units, such for instance, as participation in shared governance. Thus while system administrators oppose collective bargaining as endangering faculty collegiality, they appear supportive of a budgetary approach which could squeeze out the possibility of time being assigned to permit the faculty participation in governance that is essential to that collegiality.

The following differences among campuses indicate that it would be inappropriate to require individual campuses to meet a requirement for average class size based on an average of systemwide experience:

- Enrollment differences between new and long-established campuses which affect the filling up of a classroom and the use of multiple sections.
- Extent of availability of large lecture rooms.
- Urban versus non-urban campus needs for maintaining multiple sections at different hours, based on students being part-time and employed rather than full-time students, and on evening as well as day programs being offered.
- Effect on class size during the conventional academic year when a comparable term is offered in the summer under year-round operation.
- Extent to which the mix of campuses includes ones in which particular disciplines are given curricular emphasis or perfunctory treatment.
- Differences among campuses in the extent to which staffing problems have to be faced which are associated with a decline in total enrollment or shift of student interest to different areas of the curriculum.

As I stated at the close of the article, the issues are these: Should credence be given to as inadequate an indicator of faculty productivity as average class size? Should internal academic planning be diverted from an institution's own program objectives and opportunities in order to fit in with inappropriate system requirements?

I spoke on the matter in the State Academic Senate in May and obtained passage of a resolution of unequivocal opposition to the Chancellor's Office proposal. The vote was 30 to 17, over the objection of the Chair of the Senate's Faculty Affairs Committee.

I followed up on the matter by testifying to the Committee on Educational Policy of the Board of Trustees in September of that year. I raised questions as to possible adverse effect upon the level of state funding, as to whether the method would continue to work over a period of years, and as to whether it focused on the most important considerations. As to the last-mentioned question, I pointed out that since the method focused on class size as the single measure of productivity, it encouraged those outside of education to overlook qualitative considerations, and moreover would interfere with campuses operating effectively while maintaining their individuality.

Meanwhile I had been developing an alternative approach to budgeting faculty positions which I made available in draft form. In March I submitted it for publication as an article entitled ''Constrained Ratio Approach to Allocating Instructional Resources,'' which appeared in the December 1975 issue of *Socio-Economic Planning Sciences*. The constrained ratio approach avoided the difficulties in the Chancellor's office approach and gave encouragement to faculty members to innovate in their instructional practices. The Chancellor's Office, however, simply tinkered with its own approach and resubmitted it for approval.

I discussed alternative budgeting approaches at Georgetown University, Washington, D.C., during the 1975 annual meeting of AAUP, along with panelists from the University of Maine and Michigan State University. The subject came up again in October in a three-day dialogue in Seattle between faculty and state legislators at a seminar in which I participated on Higher Education and Public Policy sponsored by the Education Commission of the States, and also at a State Academic Senate retreat held at Asilomar, California later that month. In November I spoke again on the topic to separate meetings of the Academic Senate, the Council of Presidents of the several campuses, and the Board of Trustees. Only minor modifications were made, however.

Michael Kudlick, Associate Professor of Computer Science at the University of San Francisco, and I conducted a survey in a later year concerning the role of faculty in financial decisions at independent colleges and universities in California which had programs of four or more years. The results indicated that the existence of a faculty governance body was not in itself sufficient to assure that faculty would have access, even after the budget was approved, to information on expenditures classified on program and/or line item basis at the institutional level. The term ''faculty governance body'' includes both the case of a faculty-elected senate or council and the case in which the faculty is organized and takes action as a whole. Further, at almost half of the institutions, departments and schools within the institution did not have authority to allocate funds within broader totals set by the larger institutional unit within which that unit operated.

In mid-February of 1975, while I was still recuperating, I was asked by the University to evaluate a Chancellor's Office proposal for a system-wide policy on copyright. The regulations applied broadly to ''an author's expression of creative or intellectual labor.'' It made members of the academic community subject to procedures of such burdensome, restrictive, and confiscatory nature as to impair academic freedom and discourage creative and intellectual effort. As I remarked in ''The Incredible Copyright Affair,'' *California Academic Review*, June 1975: ''The copyright proposal is remarkable. It took considerable adroitness to combine as many objectionable features in a single document.'' I provided a reasoned evaluation to the Chancellor's Office Council of University Presidents, Chancellor's Office personnel, and local and state AAUP officers. A channel was opened for publishers to express their views. Legal opinions were obtained from the Western Regional Office of AAUP and from the national AAUP and were made available. The proposal was withdrawn.

In the spring of 1975 I was elected President of the California Conference, the state organization of AAUP, for 1975-76. Keir Nash, Professor of Political Science at the University of California at Santa Barbara, had been President while I was Vice President the previous year, and had been and continued to be extremely active in AAUP matters. He had founded the *California Academic Review*, and as Editor gave it a significant role. He was instrumental in having the AAUP hold its annual national meeting in Santa Barbara in 1976. Fred Crawford, Professor of Plasma Physics, Stanford University, became Vice President and then followed me as President in 1976-77.

I undertook research and publication on the methodology of determining academic salaries and was increasingly drawn upon for advice on academic salary policy from 1973 onward. I served on the Chancellor's Task Force on Faculty Salary Methodology for the system of campuses which was quite active for several years, and testified several times to the Board of Trustees and the California Postsecondary Education Commission. I was appointed as a member of national AAUP Committee Z on the Economic Status of the Profession for 1976 through 1979 and argued successfully for a change in its procedure which was described in the *AAUP Bulletin*, September 1978. I served on various panels and advised other colleges and universities. My insistence on there being agreement on my visit to a campus from both the administration and the faculty senate led in one instance in another state to the university president and the senate chair both meeting me near midnight at an airport in a snowstorm and driving me to my lodging.

General observations which I was inclined to make include the following:
• Recommending faculty compensation on the basis of the

average level of a group of comparison institutions relinquishes any leadership by that institution, and means accepting any lack of foresight by other institutions.

- Salaries at comparison institutions may not in fact be appropriate for comparison because of differences between the cost of living in metropolitan and non-metropolitan areas.
- Institutions of higher education which aspire to being above average in quality cannot expect to recruit faculty of above average quality if they set salaries on the basis of the average of comparison groups.
- Because of differences among institutions in the distribution of faculty among different ranks and career steps within a given rank, salary comparisons should be made with respect to salary rates rather than the average of salaries paid.
- Comparisons need take into account not only the respective structures of salary rates at the institution being compared, but also the rate at which individuals move through that structure.
- Great care is needed in adding in fringe benefits to make comparisons as to total compensation, since in some cases increased provision for benefits simply reflects increased funding for an existing level of benefit.
- Equity arguments alone, or considerations of quality, will not indefinitely support faculty compensation at levels above those indicated by short-term demand and supply of applicants for faculty positions. Those who are in academe may know that the quality of those attracted will go down in the long run if faculty are paid less than individuals in other occupations in which they could find employment, but that in itself will not keep this from happening because the general public to a great extent is not aware of such quality changes. Relatively little is done by colleges and universities to develop public attitudes supportive of quality instruction, except among alumni of elite institutions, particularly those that are independent.
- Not sufficiently appreciated by the general public is that faculty compensation is to be judged sufficient not if it leads simply to having enough individuals to draw upon for faculty positions, but if in addition it is able to attract the most appropriate individuals to academic employment.
- Average salaries may be all that need to be paid to bring students directly from graduate school into higher education

teaching, but they will not allow the movement between academe and the world of practical affairs that would enable students to be taught by professors who have had experience beyond their own student days.

- The need for appropriate levels of compensation in order to avoid turning to second or subsequent choices when engaged in staffing would be more evident if positions were otherwise left unfilled. However, departments tend to fill positions rather than turn away students and rather than risk positions being withdrawn.

Apart from determining the appropriate general level of academic salaries at an institution, there is the need for various annual adjustments, as commented upon in what follows:

- When annual recommendations as to adjustment in academic salaries go through several levels, an original recommendation supported by statistical data may be compromised several times, and final decisions are often taken without awareness of the extent that ground has already been yielded at earlier levels of consideration, and without awareness of the lags in adjusting salaries that are built into the process.

- Apart from background factors, the factors to consider in salary presentations are the projected increase in the cost of living index, to maintain the real value of income, and compounded with that, the average of the long term increase in real productivity in the economy (real output per person hour) to allow the faculty to share in the improved real wealth of the economy by virtue of the contribution that higher education makes to the increase in overall productivity.

- For a given institution, while uniform payment for individuals of different ability and contribution may increase the opportunity to exercise academic freedom without fear of reprisal, the potential contribution of faculty who would be attracted to such an institution would tend to be less than the contribution of faculty attracted to an institution that recognizes merit.

- When discretionary merit increases are paid, they should be budgeted for as an additional item without denying a normal progression in salary steps within a given rank that would be warranted by additional experience. It should not be, as I argued at the University of Houston in 1979, a case of merit-demerit pay. Decisions on promotion in rank would still be reached through evaluative procedures.

- Increases should be paid not on the basis of a minute ranking of differences in merit, which can be counterproductive as to morale, but more sparingly for truly exceptional examples of merit, which are more likely to be generally acknowledged.
- Those receiving special merit would reach given income levels earlier than other faculty and experience a greater total income over their career than those who might reach the same level just prior to retirement.
- Career step progression and special merit increases should be provided before setting what is available for cost-of-living adjustments. The latter would then take the form of a uniform across-the-board increase in salary rates. A structuring of updated relative salary rates would be retained, but the absolute level of salary rates would be increased.

I have discussed how to use the structure of faculty salaries not simply as an ex post description of what has happened but as a deliberate policy tool in shaping the type of faculty and faculty performance desired in an article, "Faculty Salary Structure for a College or University" (1981).

The Carnegie Foundation funded two conferences in 1978 and 1979 arranged by the University of Southern California on economic and ethical issues regarding academic salaries and supplementary income. I participated in the first conference at the request of our Academic Senate, and in the second conference upon request of the conference organizer. I gave a detailed report of the 1978 conference to the Academic Senate and the vice president for academic affairs which I prefaced by the following comments:

> The conference tended to emphasize the dysfunctional aspects of supplemental activities rather than those aspects potentially contributory to an individual's university role. Emphasis was placed upon possible conflict of interest and lessened objectivity as a result of the type of supplementary activity, and upon other possible impairment of performance as a result of the extent of such activity.

> What seemed to emerge recurrently as the programmed thesis of the conference was that the solution to the problems posed was to be found in shifting the locus of decision more toward the institution, with reliance additionally on the pressure of public opinion through disclosure.

The points which I contributed at the conferences may be summarized as follows:

- Administrative guidance as to how faculty use their time in supplemental activities is sometimes advocated on the basis that faculty might otherwise be influenced improperly by the source of their earnings. A caution to remember is that academic institutions and administrators also have earnings, and there is no obvious reason to assume that those who administer an institution are in a better position than faculty to contend with such influences. Institutions, as well as individuals, may be influenced by, or even attempt to satisfy, sources of funding. Moreover, institutions have been known to favor in retention decisions those faculty who attract funds, and this could become an even greater problem were an institution to recover some portion of what is earned by faculty.

- Proposals that faculty be freed from fiscal pressure by a higher salary being provided in return for all supplemental income going to the institution will encounter the difficulty that an individual faculty member, in preparation for eventually renegotiating the level of that salary, will have incentive to demonstrate his or her income-producing capability.

- Proposals in which a fixed percentage of supplemental income goes to the institution also encounter a difficulty. Foundations, corporations, and other sources of supplemental income will recognize that the quality of effort and extent of effort they can attract by their funds will be influenced by the amount received by the individual faculty member net of the university-imposed tax on income. Accordingly, except where the institution has exceptional faculty skills not readily available elsewhere, the granting agency has the option of allocating support to individuals at other institutions where the tax is not levied.

- Both economic and ethical considerations play a role in allocating academic resources to one use or another. It is not sufficient to consider what combination of monetary and ethical arrangements will achieve a desired allocation of today's faculty resources between uses within and outside the area of university concerns. The reason is two-fold: We need an approach that assures currently that those who have not yet committed themselves to a profession will see the academic life as one that they wish to enter. Further, we need an approach that assures that those who are experienced in practical affairs can be drawn upon for teaching and research in more than a part-time role.

- In the presence of a weak market for faculty, the tendency is to base arguments, such as for cost-of-living, not on market forces but on equity considerations. But the market forces are still relevant and justify the higher compensation, if we are to have education and research by the best and the brightest, as well we should.

- If the university classroom and research lab are to benefit from a faculty member's best efforts there needs to be improvement in how the academic person is compensated. At this point I refer not to monetary compensation but to the direct satisfactions to be received.

Faculty generally enter into teaching and research to work with ideas and those who value ideas. Intellectual integrity among the participants is essential, but there has been an erosion in that respect which undermines the meaningfulness of teaching. The satisfaction that compensates a faculty member has declined accordingly.

To cite but one instance of this, the academic preparation of many students is below the threshold for significantly benefiting from the college experience, yet inadequate academic support is provided, and grades are inflated. Many institutions play a numbers game. The quality of the product becomes of secondary importance relative to maintaining enrollment.

To whatever extent faculty attention is judged to be unduly turning to outside the institution, you cannot expect a reversal of this as long as both monetary compensation and particularly compensation in the sense of personal satisfaction are both in decline.

- To the extent faculty resources are shifted into activities beyond the central concerns of the university, there are certain options:

One is public disclosure as a device to influence faculty use of time. I would comment that one should consider thoughtfully the implications of having faculty participation in supplementary activities guided by popular values.

Another option is for an institution to adopt explicit mechanical rules, with a rationale grounded possibly in ethical considerations. I would liken this to treating the symptoms of the problem rather than seeking a correction.

A third approach would emphasize the responsibility of the individual to determine the amount and character of the work that he or she does outside the institution with due regard to his or her paramount responsibilities within it. However, for this to take us beyond the present situation there must be an upgrading of academic compensation—salaries and benefits, of course, but also compensation in the form of personal satisfaction from academic activity— otherwise energies will be redirected. What this requires is that there be increased care that the university itself, in its institutional aspects, gives thought to the integrity of its influence on teaching and research activities.

I turn now to another topic. It is an accepted practice to give temporary faculty appointments (such as lectureships) to visiting faculty, retired faculty, and other faculty clearly limited by their circumstances to a necessarily brief association with an institution. In May 1975, as State AAUP president, I wrote individually to the president or chancellor of each institution of higher education in California conveying a resolution of the State AAUP condemning the practice of resorting to temporary or part-time appointments when full-time probationary tenure track appointments could have been made. It was pointed out that such appointment practices result in the automatic denial of fundamental rights of long-standing recognition in American higher education which are of benefit to society as well as important to the individual, such as:

- The expectation of tenure after satisfying the requirements of a reasonable probationary period, and of eligibility for promotion.
- The right to specific advance notification concerning the prospect for reappointment.
- The right of access to established grievance procedures relevant to termination, allegation of academic freedom violations and other matters.

The letter recognized that the practices referred to, where engaged in, may be a response to the enrollment or financial situation of the institution. Accordingly, reference was made to pertinent AAUP material and assistance that was available. That communication led to correspondence being initiated by a number of institutions, which in turn led to constructive adjustments. The following year I testified to a Board of Trustee committee on state legislation relating to the use of part-time and temporary faculty. That testimony and the earlier letters increased institutional awareness of AAUP policy and monitoring and their sensitivity in appointment practices.

In 1970, reappointment was denied to Professor Angela Davis, a black activist faculty member, by action of the governing board of the University of California system for extracurricular utterances that were objectionable to many people but not illegal. This resulted in censure being voted by the national AAUP for the attempt at circumvention of the ban on political tests for reappointment and for procedures that fell short of academic due process. Although the campus faculty had operated strictly within AAUP guidelines, and objected to the denial of reappointment, and it was the action of the governing board of the system that was censured by AAUP, the censure was listed under the name of the campus, with parenthetical explanation that censure was directed at the governing board. Through a resolution adopted unanimously by the California Conference in October 1975, and initiatives taken by its officers, the Conference secured a revision in this practice by the national AAUP so that in this and similar subsequent cases of a board of a multi-campus system being censored, the listing was under the overall system in order to create an incentive among administrators and faculty of all campuses of the system to correct the situation that led to censure. This proved to be effective in the case at hand.

In November 1975 a Trustee of the California State University introduced a motion which in its initial and subsequent form would make the relative merit or competency of tenured faculty members the basis for the order of layoff should such be required. At special hearings held by the Trustees on January 15, 1976, and at a regular meeting of the Faculty and Staff Affairs Committee of the Trustees on January 27, I presented written and oral testimony that the motion, if adopted, could have the effect of allowing improper considerations to enter, undermining the significance of tenure in situations justifying layoff and in circumstances in which the prospect of layoff became a consideration in the minds of appointees holding tenure. More important than the implications which this has for the individual is that it can undermine the very objective of granting tenure—namely, to provide conditions under which professional appointees can engage in instruction and research and speak frankly without fear of reprisal although not in accord with prevailing or local opinions.

AAUP principles on unavoidable retrenchment include the statement that "among the various considerations, difficult and often competing, that have to be taken into account in deciding upon particular reductions, the retention of a viable academic program should necessarily come first." (*AAUP Redbook*, 1990, p. 128; see also p. 24.)

Programmatic requirements had to a considerable extent been anticipated by agenda items at the November 1975 Trustee meeting providing that teaching service areas be designated so as to represent distinct curricular subdivisions and to reflect discrete faculty competencies. Nevertheless there remained a variety of considerations, not limited to merit and competency, which related to the potential of an individual for contribution to a program, as well as considerations of equity. These included age, length of service, and affirmative action, the latter consideration taking on particular importance since affirmative action appointees tended to be among those most recently appointed. [See also Annex 13.3.]

There are certain preconditions for the success of an approach in which considerations must be weighed as to who among tenured faculty are to be terminated. One is that there be a strong tradition of due process in personnel relationships. Another, related thereto, is that there be a condition of mutual confidence between faculty government and administrative levels. I stated that the faculty's appraisal as to whether these prerequisite conditions were met was evident in the form of the strong opposition to the motion by various faculty bodies.

I testified that the current enrollment picture allowed time to consider the following:

- Development of alternatives to layoff. Financial incentives for early or partial retirement should be considered; also the retraining of faculty for service in non-impacted areas of the curriculum, when such areas exist and it is feasible.
- Provide faculty with improved opportunity to keep current in their fields, so that an individual's length of service is not inconsistent with his or her value to the program.
- Give thought to how affirmative action principles are to be made operational.
- And this is critical—as Trustees, make evident the importance you attach to there being a good working relationship between campus administrators and faculty government.

There was support in the testimony of some faculty and union groups for adhering to the inverse order of seniority in determining layoff should it become necessary among tenured faculty, even among AAUP membership, and there was some bitterness on the part of faculty, including some AAUP members, that I had spoken in favor of programmatic considerations and affirmative action. The formulations presented by the Academic Senate and other organizations are a matter of record in the Trustee minutes. I was supported in my position by testimony by Dr. Richard H. Peairs, Director of the Western Regional Office of AAUP.

The testimony of Thomas D'Agostino, chairman of the Student Body Presidents Association, included the following:

> The student presidents felt that a layoff system based entirely on seniority was in conflict with the concept of retention of a quality faculty and they wished to work on the proposal in an attempt to find a system that would work to identify the existing quality and retain it. His group maintained its position that the students must be involved in faculty evaluations. He further stated that the review for merit must be by peers and not by presidents and he asked why, if faculty can be promoted by peer personnel committees, they could not be evaluated for layoff by the same means.

The Trustees approved a modified form of the original motion. It adopted in principle that the concept of merit should be the paramount concern in the establishment of layoff policies and procedures, and that such policies and procedures should reflect concern for affirmative action, seniority, program priorities, tenure and equitable considerations. The presidents, statewide academic senate, and the statewide student organization were requested to submit proposals that reflected the principles stated.

The AAUP position was further discussed in an article (1976b) which I wrote as president of the state organization of AAUP. Included therein was the following:

> Surely it is not lost on the Trustees that insensitivity to the important role of faculty judgment with respect to layoff propels faculty members toward collective bargaining as a substitute for faculty government rather than as a complement thereto. Nor should it be lost on the faculty that reliance on simplistic and overt response rather than on reflective consideration and action propels them toward a form of collective bargaining that

is minimally perceptive of professional responsibilities and mainly inclined toward politicizing the academic community.

If Trustees cannot impress on the Chancellor, and the latter communicate to the Presidents, the need to actively encourage and build support for strong local-campus faculty government, and if there is a failure of nerve on the part of faculty to insist on an informed and articulate faculty voice, there will be increasing escalation of matters out of the academic community and into the courts and the Legislature.

Meanwhile the United Professors of California, an AFL-CIO affiliate, introduced legislation in the state senate which would place into statutory law the existing provisions of the California Administrative Code, which provided that the inverse order of seniority of an individual on campus be used as the criterion within a teaching service area, without reference being made to relative merit, affirmative action, or other considerations. The State Academic Senate and the Congress of Faculty Associations joined in support of the proposed bill, and it was signed by Governor Brown in September. William Crist, president of the CFA, in writing the governor to sign the bill, included the statement, ''We would prefer that mechanisms of shared governance within the CSUC generate CSUC policy. In this instance, however, all evidence indicates to the faculty that its majority position will be ignored, and we turn to the legislature for reasonable resolution.''

The closest that an individual faculty member can be involved personally with a grievance or disciplinary action is to be a plaintiff in the former case or a defendant in the latter. Somewhat less involved are those who serve on committees to render judgment on such matters. I recall the meticulous work required in serving on grievance committees, appeals committees, and on a disciplinary case regarding alleged sexual harrassment which continued and eventually escalated into the court system. Particularly time-consuming was representing the national AAUP in 1981 at a series of evening meetings at the University of Southern California in regard to financial exigency dismissals affecting members of their medical faculty serving at Children's Hospital.

In 1975, while state president of AAUP, I requested of Richard Peairs that he draw upon his expertise as Director of AAUP's Western Regional Office to illuminate developments in the area of grievance procedures and some alternatives thereto which might be pursued to advantage. I subsequently conveyed his comments to various academic governance bodies, faculty chairpersons, presidents and chancellors and governing boards of public and independent higher education institutions in California. As I noted in my letter of transmittal, the developments which prompted my request of Peairs included the following:

- A tendency for grievance procedures to become formalized and structured to the extent that there may be insufficient provision for informal solutions and flexibility in approach.
- Recourse, in cases of disagreement between faculty grievance committees and the campus administrator, to professional arbitrators whose awareness of the nature of an academic community may be incomplete.
- The use of court proceedings to attempt the setting aside of peer group decisions adverse to a faculty member.
- The various efforts to involve the State Legislature in academic policy matters that are better left to those familiar with the professional value judgments necessarily inherent therein.

Peairs suggested a dual-track approach to grievances, reflecting the academic being both a professional and also being an employee since the nature of the profession involved working within an institutional framework. Disputes over contract interpretation or application involving the individual as an ''employee'' would be processed through a traditional grievance procedure with resort to external arbitration as an option. Disputes involving the individual as a ''professional''—matters of faculty status, curriculum, methods of instruction and the conduct of research—would go through various levels at which faculty would participate in the initial judgments or in the review of proposed judgments, rather than through a top-down management arrangement. As Peairs put it, ''The key to academic self- government is direct participation in 'management' rather than merely applying the judgments of one's employers.'' Most disputes involving an individual in a professional role require professional judgments by colleagues, drawing upon academic value judgments which in the pursuit of excellence might on occasion be disadvantageous to the individual faculty worker. Peairs recommended that the resolution of such disputes should be within channels fully familiar with academe. ''If initial peer judgments on professional questions do not produce a disagreement between faculty, administration, and board, then access to arbitration would not be permitted. Academic arbitration would usually be limited to the 'compelling reasons' advanced by administration for failing to concur with the faculty judgment.''

In June 1978 I was asked to chair an inquiry panel of the American Economic Association Committee on Political Discrimination to investigate alleged political discrimination against Peter G. Bohmer, formerly an assistant professor at San Diego State College (now San Diego State University). I would not include the plaintiff's name in this account were it not that a report of the inquiry has been published. The chair of the parent AEA Committee on Political Discrimination was Professor Carl M. Stevens of Reed College, whom I knew from college days. The president of the AEA at that time was Professor Tjalling Koopmans, with whom I had differed many years before. The AEA committee, in addition to Stevens, included Kenneth Arrow of Harvard University, who was formerly of the Cowles Commission, William J. Baumol of Princeton, John G. Gurley of Stanford, and Robert Lucas of the University of Chicago. The charge had been brought against the Chancellor of the California State University system, Glenn S. Dumke, and it was thought desirable that someone familiar with the procedures of the University system conduct the investigation. I said that I would step aside if there were a question as to my having a bias or conflict of interest since on occasion I had been on the opposite side to the Chancellor on academic governance issues (however, he had continued to appoint me to represent the system on various matters). That offer was not taken. The other two members appointed to the inquiry panel were Professor Gurley of the parent committee mentioned above, a specialist on socialist economics, and Professor Richard J. Zeckhauser of the John F. Kennedy School of Government, Harvard University.

The following paragraph is from a summary draft I prepared which was used by the parent AEA committee in its report published in the *American Economic Review* in December 1981:

> On campus, Bohmer's assignment included the teaching of radical political economy. He also served as advisor to student groups concerned with antiwar and antiracism issues. Off campus, in the role of private citizen, Bohmer was active in radical politics. His off-campus activity gave rise to harrassment of Bohmer, both off campus and on campus. The harrassment was carried out with funds provided by the Federal Bureau of Investigation, as documented by the American Civil Liberties'

Union and by the U.S. Senate Select Committee on Domestic Intelligence. On campus, students having different political views brought charges of unprofessional conduct against Bohmer, and students supportive of Bohmer and of views expressed by him engaged in a series of demonstrations.

The faculty and administration of San Diego State College recommended in 1972 that Bohmer be reappointed to probationary status in his rank as assistant professor of economics. The Chancellor for the system of colleges stepped in and temporarily assumed the role of president of the college and ruled on the Bohmer reappointment contrary to the expressed recommendations of several faculty bodies and overruled the announced desire of the acting president to grant reappointment. This action by the Chancellor had been preceded by a disciplinary proceeding, a report by a consultant committee of faculty from outside institutions nominated by the AAUP at the invitation of the acting president, a faculty grievance committee hearing, and an action by the faculty senate. In 1972 the United Professors of California took the case to the Los Angeles Superior Court which in 1976 sustained the non-reappointment decision, and to a three-judge panel of the California Court of Appeals which in May 1978 similarly sustained the decision. An appeal to the California Supreme Court was denied. Bohmer's case was the subject of a letter by an attorney for the American Civil Liberties' Union to the chairman of the U.S. Senate Select Committee on Intelligence. It was the subject of a civil rights suit in 1975 by the ACLU which had to be dropped for lack of sufficient funds. No decision was rendered. Bohmer lodged a complaint with the American Economic Association in 1976, and renewed his request for an inquiry in 1978, leading to appointment of the committee I was to chair.

Chancellor Dumke made Mr. Bohmer's behavior the basis for non-reappointment, and the report examined that behavior to the extent needed to assess whether or not the reasons given were compelling. Considerations both favorable and unfavorable to Bohmer were explored in the report. The inquiry panel which I chaired did not present a finding regarding whether on balance Bohmer's behavior was appropriate or inappropriate. This is not because members of the panel did not have views; rather this was not the charge to the panel. The panel did not seek to determine on balance whether Bohmer should or should not have been reappointed. Rather it emphasized the procedures through which that question should have been resolved and evaluated the evidence on how well or how poorly they were followed.

The panel's inquiry proceeded on the basis of correspondence and documents, including voluminous court records, as well as on the basis of interviews with those knowledgeable on matters pertinent to the inquiry. I prepared the report in the first instance in consultation with members of the panel. The resultant draft was submitted to the principals involved for review. Mr. Bohmer responded, but Chancellor Dumke did not respond to successive requests for comments on the working draft of the report. The panel completed its report at the end of August 1980.

The panel did not find political discrimination originating with the campus level administration.

The principal finding by the inquiry panel, on page 87 of its report, was as follows:

> . . . it is the considered judgment of the Inquiry Panel that there was discrimination in the non-reappointment of Professor Bohmer, taking into account that the reasons given by Chancellor Dumke were not established as compelling, that the Chancellor's differences with Professor Bohmer on matters of belief which are essentially political in nature were an explicit basis for the Chancellor's projecting conclusions beyond what could be established from the record, and that there was persistent abridgment of due process by the Chancellor. The situation created, unless adequately remedied and clarified, could be inimical to the future appointment and retention of faculty who support unpopular socio-political-economic viewpoints, except those who would forego public awareness of their viewpoints sufficiently to avoid public disfavor.

I discussed the report with the parent AEA committee in Chicago in December 1980, at which time it was approved. The Executive Committee of the AEA, in turn, voted to accept the report at its March 1981 meeting. As already mentioned, the report of the Committee on Political Discrimination was published in the *American Economic Review* for December 1981. Discussed therein are the views of the parent committee on belief versus conduct as a basis for a finding of political discrimination, and its decision on the latter basis.

A copy of the approved report by the inquiry panel was sent to the chairperson of the Board of Trustees of the California State

University, among others. Shortly thereafter, and not necessarily connected with that report, the Chancellor announced that he would retire. He would be sixty-five and wished to continue writing novels of the American West. He became president of a San Diego-based conservative think-tank.

Included as Annex 13.1 are a few passages of commentary contained in the inquiry panel's report that have been selected because of their continuing relevance to the topic of this chapter, Faculty Rights and Responsibilities. It is not intended that they indicate the full range of considerations that entered into the findings by the panel. A complete copy of the report is available on request to the Secretary of the American Economic Association.

The state of faculty-administration relationships can deteriorate in the absence of constant faculty vigilance. In a presentation made to the California Conference in November 1988 I referred to the increasing tendency of administrators to use a unilateral managerial approach in the conduct of university affairs rather than a collegial approach. I gave the following examples:

- The administration creates multiple levels of administration which insulate principal administrators from direct contact with faculty.
- The administration appoints advisory bodies which increasingly overshadow faculty-elected bodies. The transition is effected in part through co-opting prominent faculty as administration appointees.
- Information resources are gathered together and managed by a large staff to the point that the latter staff becomes another insulating level between administration and faculty.
- University administrators seek control of communications on campus. A public relations office controls content of newspaper-type communications to faculty, alumni, students, etc., and undertakes to influence the content of student-sponsored media.

A checklist for bringing about shared governance, part of a presentation ''Rethinking Academic Governance'' which I made to a joint meeting of faculty organizations in Pomona in April 1976, is included as Annex 13.2.

Many faculty members take their instructional environment for granted rather than accepting responsibility for its development and protection. In many social arrangements this is par for the course. In academe a large measure of autonomy has been secured on the basis that faculty have professional characteristics such that their values and judgment should be given special weight. With that greater freedom there comes greater responsibility. In too many cases faculty leaders do not seem to know the difference between reporting what has happened and having done anything about it themselves.

As speaker on faculty responsibilities in governance at a conference in San Francisco in 1983 I introduced the concept of a "governance audit." The faculty of an institution, jointly with the administration if possible, would as a technique to prevent confrontation, commission periodic independent reviews of the "state of governance" on their campus. I subsequently discussed this at various universities and then, after developing the concept further, I included it along with another technique, the optimization review, in a journal article (1985) on revitalizing the role of goals and objectives in colleges and universities.

I referred back to that technique in an *Academe* article (January-February 1993) on the occasion of the presidential inauguration:

> During the 1992 presidential campaign, Bill Clinton frequently stated that were he elected he would keep in touch with the people of this country. The academic community could learn from his example. Academe at times is referred to as an ivory tower. This is not inappropriate to the extent that it refers to a protected context within which the mind can be given full play. At times, however, the term is intended to convey the impression that those in academic life are out of touch. In a 1985 article in *Higher Education*, I introduced the concept of an optimization review. Such a review, conducted periodically by outside evaluators, could facilitate an institution developing its own capacity for internal assessment, on an ongoing basis, of both the optimality of its objectives and the role of those objectives in guiding performance. Included among sixteen specific points were references to maintaining awareness of an institution's various constituencies' needs and expectations, and achieving a balance between institutional responsiveness and autonomy. An optimization review takes on added significance in implementing a new beginning—one that undertakes to make institutions more effective in the empowerment of the individual.

In an earlier paragraph in the same article I mentioned some specific areas in which faculty should assume more responsibility—

matters discussed further in later chapters:

Problems should be resolved as much as possible within the academic community as to direction of effort, quality and productivity. This means that while the special characteristics of academe that make it conducive to objective reflection must be retained, there must be increased willingness to be part of the effort to improve the effectiveness of the earlier stages of education; to serve as mentors; to participate in determining higher education goals, both in broad terms and at the level of individual courses; and to work constructively to accomplish the educational mission effectively with available resources.

13.1

Observations on Political Discrimination

- There are various admonitions: that an individual faculty member should retain the right of privacy from scrutiny and evaluation by his institution when acting in other than his capacity as a member of a learned profession or as an officer of the university; that in the latter roles his academic freedom is to be respected; and that in whatever role he may be, whether on or off campus, he must be accorded the rights of an individual citizen. [pp. 23-24]
- The inquiry panel regards the mutual practice of candor to be desirable in academic as well in other relationships. It also recognizes that productive relationships which warrant being maintained may require judicious restraint in the exercise of candor. The panel shares the view that in as large an area of conduct as is feasible, the judgment should remain with the individual; and that to such extent as candor is to be prescribed, the need should be made evident through appropriate processes, and what is expected should be made clear. . .

  At issue appears to be not a determination as to whether or not an individual possesses the trait of candor, but differences in view as to whether information should or should not, according to circumstances, have in fact been communicated. This appears to the panel to bear on matters of freedom of speech. . .

  In the particular case . . . the central question is whether it was the political nature of the event that made it salient . . . Would there have been the same concern and investigation had the non-volunteered information been non-political in nature?

Related to this is the question of how the charge of failure to volunteer new information after having already been appointed is to be reconciled with the viewpoint expressed in the disciplinary procedures . . . that a person will not be required to give self-incriminating evidence, and no inference is to be drawn therefrom. [pp. 46-48]

- It is regarded by the panel as a matter of serious concern that the Chancellor appears to be imposing . . . a test for reappointment of probationary faculty not previously articulated, namely that the individual's philosophy of faculty-student relationship be a directive authoritarian rather than non-directive relationship. Without in any way passing judgment on the appropriateness of the specific means Professor . . . employed, it is the panel's view that Professor . . . regarded demonstrations and publicity as means for extending the learning process beyond the classroom. Professor . . . expressed his own opposition to violence and illuminated the consequences of the violence/non-violence alternatives. He is criticized for not using his influence in the role of a faculty member to have students (not all or even a significant number of whom were his own) to behave in particular ways. [p. 56]

- When faulting a faculty member for not having a positive obligation beyond refraining from violence becomes a factor in his reappointment or termination, the panel believes that a sense of perspective is important. The following statement by Professor . . . may be useful in this connection.

> I think much, much more serious than somebody kicking at somebody's door, for example, is what's happening in the country generally. For example, the war in Vietnam, and what's happening in the Southeast, and it seems to me that the responsibility of every individual is to try to change some of the things that are happening in society. Real poverty. Real violence, and so on. I do find that people do have that responsibility and I think that's what motivates my behavior.

> However, I find a very large number of people very deficient in that kind of behavior. I'm not saying that's necessarily grounds for their dismissal but I do say that's why maybe I hold a lot of those people in less than full

respect.

I do feel that people have a responsibility to get involved in that way. I find that a great majority of people, unfortunately, are not involved. [pp. 56- 57]

- One may argue that a university's role should not be determined by what it does best, for it may be better equipped than other social institutions to perform a wide array of services, but rather it should focus on activities in which the university is either unique in its capability or has the greatest relative advantage. Emphasis on critical inquiry must surely rank high as an ideal in such matters, but there is no one mold for the academy in a pluralistic society, and there are secular and religious sponsored institutions in which alternative to that emphasis on critical inquiry, primacy is given to teaching a particular dogma or viewpoint.

  Issues arise when in the course of going beyond basic inquiry into applied fields, a university makes choices as to the extent application is made of unpopular as distinguished from accepted viewpoints and activities. There has been outspoken criticism of universities for supporting indirect and subsequent overt action programs through weapons research and ROTC while stating that campuses should not be the launching pad for programs of immediate social protest. [pp. 73-74]

- Conduct, behavior, or means employed, however it be described, appropriately becomes relevant to the evaluation of a faculty member, beyond the substantive content of performance, to the extent a university has to be concerned with possible impairment of its principal functions. . .

  The application of criteria pertaining to professional conduct (behavior-oriented) as distinguished from professional performance (product-oriented) is fraught with difficulty. . . It is difficult to separate out for evaluation such aspects of behavior as have professional implications from an individual's expression as a citizen, political in nature or otherwise. It is difficult to separate criticism of behavior from criticism of beliefs which may have influenced that behavior. A minimum caution is that conduct in itself should not be regarded as decisive without consideration of performance aspects, and of the context within which the conduct took place. [p. 75]

- The panel notes that the actions referred to as a pattern of behavior could alternatively be referred to as a pattern of response to real and/or perceived harrassment. . . the tendency is inherent in summarizing a *pattern* of behavior that the pattern be invested with more pejorative implications than could be supported by the individual instances of behavior from which the pattern was formulated.

An individual comes to be judged by intentions and philosophical positions imputed to him by virtue of the interpretation given the presumed pattern, shifting away from requiring that charges be established in terms of specific acts performed. [pp. 76-77]

- The panel takes note that it is not realistic to expect the style of dissent of an individual to always work fully within the preferred forms established by society, partly because means may need be employed that attract attention to the issues, but mainly because the range of options and resources available to a dissident in many cases is restricted compared to those holding already established views. It is a problem that society must treat with great sensitivity, both holding to what have emerged as viable relationships and yet showing latitude to those seeking to change the prevailing consensus.

  It was not apparent from the documentation that any effort was made to weigh in the value to an academic community, and the larger society, of a perceptive individual who spoke out on matters of racism and the Vietnam War, anticipating and helping to mold, at risk to himself, what later became the nation's conscience. [p. 77] The Trustee statement cited by [the] Chancellor . . . contains the following among qualifications to be held by faculty appointees: that persons *"so deport themselves that they are deserving of the respect of* their students and colleagues, and of *the general public of this state."* (Emphasis added.) The record is that especially in the 1960's and early 1970's, the general public did not accord respect to students and faculty opposing generally held views. More broadly, the general public has been supportive of invention and innovation in technological matters, but suspicious and intolerant of invention and innovation in social technology. Thus to expect of faculty as a condition of employment that they deport themselves so as to deserve the respect of the general public of the State can be an invitation to conform that works against academic freedom and the best interests of the university as a social institution.

Specifically, as broad an admonition as the referred-to position in the Trustee preamble, when applied in the milieu of San Diego State, in which conservative viewpoints, a war-oriented economy, and a large military-retirement community are important considerations, must be judged in the case of a self-professed Marxist activist such as Professor . . ., as imposing a criterion of community approval, which to the extent it was operative upon the choices which the Chancellor could consider to be realistically open to him, would inappropriately and adversely affect the reappointment decision. [p. 78]

- There are manifold and sometimes conflicting considerations which can enter into the choice of a course of action. It was a period which would put strain on the most judicious of those in authority. In such circumstances, it was of critical importance that individuals in authority recognize not only the responsibility for preserving a viable learning environment in the present and for the future, but also the affirmative obligation to interpret the academy to the public, preserving it against, and not yielding to, whatever prevailing pressures from one side or another might work to its detriment. [p. 83]

- . . . the extraordinary acts of commission and omission by the Chancellor . . . while consistent with the Chancellor's expressed views as to the appropriateness of an authoritarian hierarchical organization, showed disregard of and disrespect for faculty views and undermined the meaningfulness for faculty of the established procedures of the institution. Productive ongoing relations within an academic community can be impaired in more than one way: To the extent there may be excesses in behavior among its members in expressing discontent with established channels and authorities, as in the student and faculty activism of the 1960's and early seventies; and by the less immediately obvious but nevertheless disruptive effect of established authority pursuing a course of action apparently unmindful of the effect on established academic governance. Mutual confidence among the participants in an academic community suffers in either event, as does the credibility of established procedures. [p. 85]

13.2

Check List for Bringing About Shared Governance

A. Know your rights and responsibilities. Sharpen general faculty awareness of the principles which have been accepted as the fair standards of the academic profession.

B. Give service in faculty governance the recognition and support that will attract and hold those individuals respected for good judgment.

C. Develop resource persons on your faculty who are knowledgeable in specialized areas about your campus and/or system of campuses, and about higher education generally.

D. Probe into and seek clarification of administrative actions, offer constructive criticism, encourage full and open discussion, and make it useful in the future for the administration to look to faculty for recommendations as to policy *before* rather than after implementation.

E. Focus your energy initially on a limited number of critical areas. I will mention five:
    - Faculty participation in the appointment and retention of department chairpersons. The ''pleasure of the president'' is not to be literally interpreted.
    - Faculty participation in budget requests and in deciding how positions and funds are to be allocated once appropriations are approved.
    - Administrative acceptance of peer group processes in the determination of individual faculty status.
    - Faculty insistence on input in the use of administrative positions and on the faculty's role in the selection and in

> the review of administrators.
> - In all matters in which the faculty has primary responsibility, the president should concur with the faculty judgment except in rare instances and for compelling reasons which should be stated in detail.

There are AAUP policy statements bearing on each of these matters which have widespread acceptance.

Both professionalism and hard-nosed pragmatism suggest that faculty, whatever their position with respect to collective bargaining, should insist on a structure of shared governance in which professional matters can be discussed in a non-adversarial manner.

If this approach appears to be blocked on a campus, it should be remembered that individual faculty and faculty bodies still have recourse to the good offices of professional associations.

13.3

Budget Choices Must Consider Merit

[Letter to *Academe*, September-October 1993,
in response to an earlier article by J. Hartzog.]

When resources are scarce, Hartzog's recommendation is that there should be adherence to inverse seniority in faculty retrenchment and equal across-the-board reduction in programs. He stresses that evaluative judgments as to merit of individual performance or value of programs should be avoided. However, it is unseemly that academics should denigrate the use of thoughtful processes for arriving at decisions.

A faculty may be viewed as a community of scholars, but it is also an instrument for the accomplishment of various goals. Hartzog makes only passing reference to students and educational needs, and no reference to faculty research. In effect, the criterion he offers as to what is just and fair is that the interest of the earliest appointed faculty be protected. No account is taken of possible setbacks in recent efforts to appoint women and minorities, nor of effects upon morale and motivation were merit ignored in faculty downsizing. Judgments should take account of the goals, opportunities, and circumstances in particular situations.

There is no dispute that contentiousness may arise in seeking to arrive at reasoned decisions—even open revolt between faculty and administration when there has not been participation in the decision process. However, support for simplistic rules in making ''hard'' decisions is symptomatic of faculty not wanting to become involved. There are thoughtful and fair processes that may be employed in cost containment and retrenchment [that] . . . serve well when faculty members as well as administrators accept responsibility for making their institution viable and effective in its mission.

14

Collective Bargaining

The State of California under Governor Ronald Reagan practically invited collective bargaining into higher education in California by first denying all state employees any adjustment in salary for inflation and then singling out the higher education faculty to receive no adjustment for a second year. In a draft by the California Postsecondary Education Commission of a five-year plan update for 1977-82 it stated that the likelihood of collective bargaining was linked to the level of compensation. My comment on that at a round-table discussion of the plan at the University of Southern California was that this statement, while correct, "oversimplifies the situation in that difficulties which faculty encounter in securing collegiality in the absence of collective bargaining also significantly affect that likelihood. Not to recognize this overlooks that the range of faculty concern is professional in nature, and extends beyond their legitimate concern with equitable treatment as to compensation."

Within higher education, administrative resistance to collegial-shared governance increased the prospect that adversarial collective bargaining would be adopted. Experience with the latter may be found less acceptable among those concerned with the professional role of faculty than collective bargaining operative in conjunction with shared governance.

The initial driving force, as I recall, was the United Professors of California, an affiliate of the AFL-CIO. What was advocated by the UPC was a confrontational take-it-or-leave-it industrial type of unionism. There was little sympathy for internal faculty governance and faculty academic senates were regarded as an anachronism. The president of the UPC, in testifying for seniority as the sole criterion of layoff at a special hearing of the Board of Trustees stated that the

California Labor Federation AFL-CIO would do everything in its power to block implementation of the proposed changes, explaining in answering a question from a trustee that it would be an action of the two million union members in California.

The industrial type union has a preference for leveling. There was an outburst of the president of UPC at a Trustee meeting at which he pointed to the difference in faculty-student ratios among disciplines (which were larger for the physical sciences than for the humanities in view of the use of laboratories), and stated that if this were the current state of affairs then a new system definitely was needed which would make the ratios the same for all categories.

Collective bargaining is a different kind of relationship than shared responsibility. It proceeds not issue by issue on the merits, but through trade-offs and bargaining for packages, posturing and engagement in polemics. Yet AAUP needed to be able to fall back upon some form of collective bargaining in order to be effective as the voice of the academic profession.

The approach which higher education faculty had felt most suitable was to make every effort to resolve differences through shared faculty-administration governance, with resort to authorities outside of higher education to be avoided if at all possible. In such efforts there tended to be a remarkable willingness through objective weighing of the issues to seek the outcome closest to being most suitable for all concerned without becoming so identified with and adhering to a position that another formulation could not be considered. The national AAUP struggled for years over adopting a policy toward collective bargaining, and in 1973 after intense discussion approved it as a major additional way of realizing the Association's objectives.

Collective bargaining by public institutions such as state universities were not yet legal in California, however. Much credit goes to Richard Peairs and Charles McClain of the Western Regional Office of AAUP in assisting in the formulation of suitable legislation to extend to four-year public higher education the options already open to faculty at private institutions and at community colleges in California.

There was concern among higher education faculty members that industrial-type unions like the UPC might not be the appropriate form through which to engage in collective bargaining once it was approved. A liaison committee representing several faculty organizations, including the AAUP, drafted the outlines for a coalition of their organizations into a Council of Faculty Associations, CFA for short. With subsequent organizational changes, the first initial progressively changed over the years from referring to Council, to Congress to California, so that CFA became the California Faculty Association. In spite of the breadth of that title, the membership as yet is essentially that of the 20-campus California State University system.

I entered the fray from 1973 onward by testifying on behalf of enabling legislation for collective bargaining at various legislative committee hearings in California. I recall teaching a morning class in Los Angeles, taking a plane to a hearing in Monterey at which by arrangement the business at hand was set aside upon my arrival so that I could testify, and then returning to Los Angeles for an afternoon class. As state president of AAUP I spoke on the role of collective bargaining at a variety of forums and regional workshops (see, for instance, Annex 14.1), and wrote California state legislators to solicit their support for the Higher Education Employer-Employee Relations Act.

Although I was no longer campus president of AAUP and my activity was at the state level at the time of the election authorizing collective bargaining, I was appealed to one evening by a member of the CFA staff who felt that the local effort was not sufficiently energetic. I phoned a group of campus opinion leaders and asked them to join with me in an already ongoing ''boiler room'' telephone effort from near campus that evening and subsequent evenings. Most agreed, and with Ruth's help as well, we vigorously pushed for passage of the legislation. With similar efforts being made elsewhere, the legislation passed.

CFA was originally a group of faculty organizations which worked through an Assembly of Delegates from the various campuses. I served as a delegate from my own campus as well as a representative of the California State University Council of the state organization of AAUP. The members of the latter council levied additional dues upon ourselves in order to finance the founding and operation of CFA. I worked with a few others in formulating the wording of the Articles of Agreement, the name given to the by-laws of the incorporated association, so that the document explicitly endorsed the principles of the AAUP and exemplified those principles throughout. I remember sessions in which there was vigorous opposition from table-pounding supporters of a contrary viewpoint.

Among the most active organizers of the CFA were June Salz Pollak and William Crist, both supporters of AAUP, who became the first and second presidents of the organization.

In 1976 there was an effort by UPC to have a merger involving various faculty organizations and the state academic senate, the survivor to be the negotiating agency for collective bargaining. At that time I was president of the state organization of AAUP and I wrote in reply to an inquiry on the matter from Dr. Gerald Marley, chair of the state academic senate. My February 24 letter read in part as follows:

The AAUP promotes openly and consistently, as announced through written and oral publication, established standards of academic freedom, due process and institutional governance. That is in sharp contrast to the UPC. The continual response that I and my colleagues have encountered over the years from the UPC and AFT is that 'local autonomy' is apparently so supreme an organizational precept that its locals need not work within any framework of policies of their major national affiliate, if such policies exist. On the one hand, this has enabled UPC to disassociate itself from the actions of AFT locals such as the one in Alaska, which formally and conclusively negotiated the elimination of academic tenure. On the other hand, if UPC locals do not have a common core of principles to which they subscribe, a faculty member is likely to find UPC supporting whatever is popular and expedient at the moment. This impairs UPC's ability to be protective of the fundamental cornerstones of academic governance, since quite frankly, some of the policies developed by the AAUP and now recognized as the standards for fair practice in higher education do not always compel such popular appeal, e.g., lengthy probationary periods, fully effective use of the probationary period for appraisals of excellence, the unwavering defense of academic freedom, and the steadfast promotion of shared authority in institutional governance.

The goal for which the AAUP has stood for over sixty years is that of applying principled analyses to the solution of difficult problems of day-to-day institutional governance. That appears to be at substantial variance from what one has come to expect from UPC . . . In short, it is difficult to reconcile positions of the UPC which have seemed uniformly and narrowly employee-oriented vis-a-vis policy positions of the AAUP which protect the strength and integrity of both faculty and institutions in higher education and are in furtherance of the common good. The UPC apparently does not share with us, nor does the AFT nationally, common views of the definition of academic freedom, or of due process. I assess the significance of those differences as substantial.

The letter was adopted by the state academic senate as a position paper underlying their opposition to the proposed merger.

The differences I have described above between the viewpoints of faculty adhering to different organizations no longer are as distinct, if present at all, since faculty of different persuasions have subsequently worked together in building the strength of CFA.

In 1978 I served on a Task Force on the Future Design of CFA, attending about nine meetings, mostly in Burlingame in northern California. Among others who contributed, in addition to Pollak and Crist, were Wilma Krebs of the California State Employees Association, Dominic Perello and Howard Zimmerman of the California Teachers Association and National Education Association, and John Craig, Charles McClain, Richard Peairs, and Philip Walker of AAUP. The meetings were chaired by Robert E. Phelps, Executive Director of CFA. The principal organizational change that emerged after approval of the Task Force report was the conversion of CFA from being an operating arm of a coalition of sponsoring faculty associations into a separate entity with the various faculty organizations being affiliates subject to mutual agreement.

In October 1978 I was approached by the Commission on Government Reform for comments on various sections of their draft report, including a section on collective bargaining. The Commission had been appointed by the Governor to recommend adjustments in government structure and operations in response to Proposition 13, which greatly reduced the financing of government activity. My December 6 response, which I cleared with officers at the national AAUP, touched on eight areas of the Commission's recommendations. I record below my response on only one point, selected as being of most continuing interest:

On page 4 of the Task Force Report appears the statement that '. . . a choice often must be made between the quality of government services and employee compensation.' Taken literally, this statement appears to ignore the fact that government operations tend to be labor intensive, and that the quality of service is *determined* in large measure by the quality of employee and of employee performance. Actions adversely affecting public employees as a group that are perceived by employees as punitive in nature or reflective of political expediency cannot but have an adverse effect on productivity both in the short run and in the long run. And in the long run, the quality of staff that can be recruited and retained will reflect the treatment given those who enter public service. It is only in the most simplistic sense that cost in government is reduced by measures that impair the quality of service, for relative to what is received in service, that service may be more costly, not less.

The effect of collective bargaining in the public sector hopefully will be that it will be more difficult for management to react to budgetary stringencies by workload increases and cuts in employee real income which directly and indirectly lower the quality of service. Under such circumstances both employer and employee may find common ground for making evident to the public the extent of worth of the activity as well as its cost, with a view to determining a level of activity corresponding to which the public will back up its claim for service by willingness to provide the necessary financial support.

I have not attempted to characterize collective bargaining beyond the California State University system, nor have I attempted to characterize the success of AAUP in becoming a collective bargaining agent relative to competing organizations on the national scene, although both have been of concern to me and indeed involved considerable expenditure of time and effort on my part.

In January 1980, while serving on the National Council of AAUP, I had occasion to address a memorandum to all members of the Council on a pending ballot measure regarding a proposed affiliation between the national AAUP and the Professional Staff Congress, a union within the City University of New York. I noted therein that there were substantial advantages possible through affiliation, but also some disquieting aspects of the proposal. I indicated that my vote on the measure would depend upon whether certain revisions were undertaken in the proposed affiliation, which I outlined:

• The language of the agreement should indicate a symmetrically acknowledged obligation of both parties, not an agreement that the AAUP adjust to the Professional Staff Congress.

- The prerogative of AAUP as a national organization to relate directly to PSC/CUNY should be exercised without overriding the right of members to maintain their own local organizations as chapters, as provided for in the constitution of the association.
- Certain protection should be provided for earmarking funds for the New York conference of AAUP.

In September 1981 I was selected by the national nominating committee as one of two nominees for the position of First Vice President of the national AAUP. Although I had worked constructively with unions in the 1940's as a consultant for the National Defense Mediation Board, aided union candidates to win public office in post-war Japan, and been active in the securing of collective bargaining legislation and the development of CFA in California, the national Collective Bargaining Caucus announced its own slate of collective bargaining candidates, campaigned on California campuses against my election, and succeeded in its endeavor. It did not help me that various state level positions I had held, including being state conference president, which had been in page proof, were dropped from the nominee information when it appeared in *Academe*, the national publication of AAUP, as background for members deciding whom to support.

I was nominated for national office again in a later year, and accepted that nomination, which was to run against an incumbent, only to find that the computer was programmed to assign a weight of only one-third to votes from California Faculty Association members, my largest constituency. This reflected an agreement that only that proportion of the national dues be paid in view of other demands upon CFA finances. The departure from one person, one vote, was subsequently discontinued.

In 1984, while I was chair of the California Conference Committee on Issues and Policy, a problem related to collective bargaining arose in connection with community colleges in Minnesota which had implications for all segments of higher education. Minnesota decided to apply provisions of the Minnesota Public Employment Labor Relations Act to higher education. The union selected by faculty as their exclusive bargaining agent for "meeting and negotiating" on mandatory topics was by this law made the only channel for ''meeting and conferring'' on non-mandatory topics, including educational matters. In California, The Higher Education Employer-Employee Relations Act explicitly provided safeguards against this occurring, and in the California State University system, the contract included, at the insistence of the California Faculty Association, the provision that ''The CSU and the CFA recognize the unique roles and responsibilities of the Academic Senate.'' However, the interpretation given the Minnesota Act could have affected other states currently and possibly California in the long run. A resolution was developed with assistance from the conference legal counsel, Robert Gerstein of the University of California, Los Angeles, and the then conference president, Alfred Manaster, of the University of California, San Diego. This resolution was adopted by the conference executive committee and submitted to the national association. I attended the national meetings and developed, after broad consultation, a revised resolution for the National Resolutions Committee which was adopted in plenary session by the 1984 Annual Meeting. It was published in *Academe*, September-October 1984.

I served as a member and then as chair of the national Resolutions Committee of AAUP for the annual meetings in 1976 and 1981, and as chair of the nominating committee for the Assembly of State Conferences in 1981, and as mentioned earlier, on national Committee Z on the Economic Status of the Academic Profession, and on AAUP's National Council from 1978 to 1981. Thereafter I served on national Committee R on Governmental Relations for two terms, 1982 to 1988, a topic included with the following chapter.

14.1

Academic Professionals and Collective Bargaining

In one sense the constituency of the AAUP is the university professoriate. However, our constituency is really broader—the larger community. Both the responsibilities and the rights of faculty are stressed by AAUP, since both need to be observed if we are to have individuals and institutions operate with proper regard for the role of higher education in society.

Out of this approach there has been developed over the last sixty years a body of of AAUP principles, many of which are cited in the Articles of Agreement of the Congress of Faculty Associations. This has permitted CFA to start with the benefit of many years of AAUP experience in dealing with the problems of higher education. And it associates CFA with the national reputation of AAUP for being responsive to situations in a manner that preserves the integrity of higher education.

What AAUP stands for has to be good advice for the long run, not just what is expedient on a one-shot basis. We live with the consequences. This requires that AAUP not only speak *for* the profession to assert its rights, but also on occasion *to* the profession in order that it abide by its responsibilities.

At times this may require that we take stands which are not readily accepted unless we articulate our position carefully and those we address are prepared to listen. But it is our willingness to do this on the basis of principle, even against the tide of the moment, which is the source of our credibility.

We tend to work quietly. In fact it is said, in connection with our use of public censure of an institution as a last resort, that we tend to publish only our defeats. When our standards are accepted, however, as they are by the great majority of institutions, they often come to be taken for granted, especially by those new to the profession. It is not always recognized that they must be constantly defended. AAUP enters into court cases throughout the United States when matters of pivotal importance to the academic profession are involved.

Let us turn to a different point: The AAUP brings to CFA its emphasis on developing the capacity of faculty to handle its own affairs. It recommends minimal standards and desirable procedures. Faculty are encouraged to explore local remedies, and they are encouraged to apply AAUP principles through existing institutions. Whether they do so or not may depend upon whether there is a vigilant chapter on campus. If the need arises, there is recourse to advice and legal counsel through regional and national offices.

The Association is a firm supporter of shared responsibility in academic governance, and this requires a strong faculty willing to participate actively. At the same time the Association recognizes that there exist situations of an adversarial nature in which collective bargaining is the appropriate vehicle. However, collective bargaining is intended to work alongside and bolster faculty government, not replace it.

And the Association recognizes that on occasion it is necessary to go to the State Legislature, as for instance, to secure authorization for collectively bargaining by public employees. Also AAUP provides input on legislative proposals which would affect higher education, both at state and federal levels.

It is with some concern that we observe tendencies within the CSUC system to fall into patterns of behavior very similar to those which in moments of reflection we would oppose.

Part of this is because in the heat of controversy basic goals are more remote than the pressing need to adopt means. The means adopted may look appropriate in the short run, while running counter to the goals in the long run.

Also, there is the tendency in a political contest for opposing parties to adjust their positions to occupy the middle ground in the hope of appealing to a larger constituency.

But there is a more basic reason, I believe. What I am referring to is a tendency of faculty, like everybody else, to look for solutions which do not require them to make hard decisions among alternatives. This escapism from responsibility takes several forms:

- One form of escapism is to take refuge in prorata arrangements and simplistic criteria which avoid the necessity for judgment.Yet the opportunity afforded those close to a situation to make judgments which will take into account the opportunities, goals and circumstances particular to that situation would seem to be what it is all about, and particularly appropriate for a university community in which reason is given a prominent role.

- Many academic administrators prefer a role allowing slight discretion if it permits sidestepping the responsibility for explaining difficult decisions.

- Many faculty appear pessimistic as to being able to influence outcomes on their campuses through faculty government. They too often tend to look elsewhere for solutions rather than undertake the critical task on their own campus of insisting upon and achieving an effective role in academic governance. This is not to minimize the difficulties present. I wish to stress instead the high priority of that difficult task.

- There is escapism also involved in seeking solutions through the Legislature in matters which should be resolved within the academic community.

I would urge that you caution your colleagues on the campuses that a pattern once set for legislative intervention, even though it may in the first instances be on your behalf, can encourage intervention with which you may *not* agree. It is a two-way street. The Legislature is not there to represent just you, and the next time they act you may feel put-upon by them. Matters will be decided far from the campus in corridors and committees by individuals who may be unfamiliar with academic values. And legislated outcomes will be less susceptible to change when circumstances make change desirable.

What I am saying relates to the role of AAUP and what it can contribute to CFA. AAUP provides principles relating to faculty's rights and responsibilities, and it can serve as a reminder to the profession that it *is* a profession and not simply a job. The claim which faculty has to a special role in academic governance emerges from the potential of faculty to contribute as academic professionals, not from rights inherent as employees.

We came together into CFA because we share the view that there are basic differences between ourselves and the AFL-CIO philosophy held by United Professors of California. . . It is important that in the process of winning we do not become like those we oppose.

AAUP emphasis on discussion and action based on principles adds to the strength of CFA. We believe that AAUP fits well together with our associate organizations in our joint enterprise.

15

Governmental Relations

State coordination of colleges and universities within public and independent higher education in California was through a state appointed Coordinating Council for Higher Education until 1973, and thereafter through the California Postsecondary Education Commission (CPEC). Faculty were not members of either board, but participated in task forces which presented reports to the appointing agency and on occasion discussed them in public session. In earlier chapters I have mentioned various task forces in which I participated jointly on behalf of the Chancellor's Office and the State Academic Senate: year-round operation, planning-programming-budgeting, cost aspects under the Master Plan; and with CPEC, on faculty salary methodology. When I became active in the California Conference of AAUP I arranged for a close relationship between CPEC and the California Conference. The first meeting which the first CPEC director, Dr. Donald R. McNeil, had with any academic organization was an off-the-record meeting with the executive committee of the California Conference while I was conference president. Subsequently McNeil was the principal speaker at the 1975 annual meeting of the California Conference. I provided liaison by attending all meetings of CPEC, on occasion providing testimony. The CPEC staff annually invited my comments on their draft updates of the Five Year Plan for Postsecondary Education in California. Each was followed by participation in a round-table discussion at one or another university. Various points have been cited from that testimony in earlier chapters.

In July 1976 I testified as follows on behalf of the California Conference at hearings conducted by CPEC in San Diego to discuss draft legislation which would change the role of the State with respect to private postsecondary education:

- Granted a desire for administrative reform in preventing fraud and in serving consumer interests, as well as a desire to integrate private institutions into the planning function, the State must nevertheless avoid overproviding for the supervision and regulation of private institutions. The State presumably should be operative where private voluntary action is inadequate and the need sufficiently serious. It was suggested, therefore, that different modes of relating to private postsecondary institutions be specified for different situations. A blanket authorization is no protection against over-regulation, even though the agency would be permitted to utilize the proposed authority to less than its full extent.

- A second concern is how the State government should relate to the quality of education offered by a private institution in view of the problems inherent in such determinations. In this connection, the AAUP endorsed use of the findings of recognized accreditation agencies as the standard practice to be followed where available.

- The third concern is with the CPEC staff recommendation that there be a central State agency for the handling of student complaints. Difficulties were foreseen in the handling of complaints requiring judgments concerning the academic affairs of individual institutions. The AAUP recommended that the principal emphasis be on assuring that appropriate procedures for handling complaints are available at each institution.

An account of that testimony, and of earlier legislation which was successfully opposed by AAUP, is given in an article, ''State Role in Private Education,'' which I wrote for the *California Academic Review*, April 1977.

On June 6, 1978, California voters approved the passage of Proposition 13, an initiative to amend the state constitution which imposed severe limitations on local tax revenues previously available through property taxes. This meant that for certain activities to be continued, the functions had to be transferred to the state or state funds had to be diverted to the local level. I attended the national meeting of the AAUP at Yale University later that week and secured passage of a resolution urging the legislators and the governor of California to resist incursions on the quality of higher education and ''to guarantee full academic due process to any faculty member whose status is threatened by budgetary readjustments resulting from the passage of Proposition 13.''

I responded to an invitation from CPEC in October of that year to set forth the various concerns of the California Conference of AAUP in regard to the state budget for postsecondary education. Copies of my reply were widely distributed by the Conference and also by CPEC among state officials. Later the full text was published in the *California Academic Review*. One concern was that the state not assume a type of control that would impair internal academic governance arrangements or the role of faculty as academic officers of their institutions. Among other concerns were the following:

- As the California Postsecondary Education Commission has made explicit in its statements, various factors apart from inflation cause the cost per unit of educational services to increase (the greater cost of serving a less homogeneous student enrollment, the higher unit cost of smaller scale operations, etc.) yet the funding per student has not been increased even to offset inflation. It is the concern of the California Conference that this situation be rapidly corrected.

- The percentage growth in California personal income . . . does roughly reflect change in the number of earning units and inflation to the extent that personal income keeps pace with prices. But it does not follow that a slowdown in the growth of personal income should lead to less expenditure on State programs. In the event of a deflation or a depression, protecting California's economic base would require that we assure employers access to a highly literate and capable work force and proximity to centers of research. To proceed otherwise could invite a long-term downward spiral in the growth of the State economy.

- We are particularly concerned that the appropriateness be recognized of increased public spending rather than reduced spending in areas that bear upon equal access to educational opportunity for the economically disadvantaged, the minorities, and the physically handicapped. Budgetary provision for academic support services is needed for many such individuals in order to make possible a successful educational experience; otherwise the open door to education becomes merely a revolving door. Child care centers are especially important in facilitating educational opportunities for women.

Funds were appropriated in the California Budget Act of 1974 to the Joint Committee on Postsecondary Education for studying and testing the need, design, and feasibility of a "university without walls" in California. A plan was developed for a fourth segment of higher education which would have an exclusive role in the area of extended degree programs and extension programs. Independently of that, I had extended to Chancellor Brossman of the California Community College System an invitation to work with the Community College Council of the Conference on matters of common interest in the area of legislative affairs, and that offer was accepted. Brossman invited the Conference to join in backing a proposed "Community-Based Education Act" at the federal level. On January 3, 1975 (dictated from the hospital) I submitted to the Community College Council of the Conference my recommendations, taking into account the ongoing study as to a fourth segment. These recommendations, as set forth below, were considered and adopted at meetings of the Council and of the overall California Conference on February 1 at Stanford University.

- The concept of community-based education (interpreted as expanded forms of external degree programs and extension programs) was endorsed as appropriate for institutions in all segments of higher education in California, each pursuing those activities that are consistent with its mission, in particular among those individuals who would look toward the particular segment were they to have attended regularly on campus.
- Consistent with the preceding, the Conference consensus was in opposition to the creation of a separate public segment for community-based public higher education.

I followed this up by writing Governor Edmond Brown, Jr. as to the Conference's opposition to a separate public segment for extended programs, with copies to leaders in higher education. The separate segment proposal did not receive legislative approval.

In early 1976 the California Conference contracted with a legislative bill service in Sacramento for computer monitoring of the status of bills of potential interest to AAUP and for follow up monitoring of such bills as were found to be of particular interest. Preprints of draft bills were sent to me and were the basis for various actions taken on behalf of the Conference. Some examples of Conference intervention in early 1976 are given below:

A.   Testified to California State University Trustees regarding legislation affecting opportunities for the professional development of librarians. Appropriate legislation sponsored by an affiliated faculty organization was passed and signed by the governor.

B. Opposed state legislation which would remove confidentiality from preemployment letters of recommendation, proposing instead that the policy be determined by the higher education segments. I wrote state legislators:

> There are, as you know, arguments on both sides as to the desirability of such access. There is a question as to the effect the prospect of such access would have on the frankness and relability of letters that are written in the future when communications would not be confidential. There is the argument, on the other hand, that writers of letters of recommendation may be inclined to be more responsible in their evaluation, failing which, the individual, if employed, could include a rebuttal for the file. However, the likelihood is that personnel committees would rely more on communications by telephone, and these evaluations might be more offhand, and less readily transmitted accurately to others in the personnel process.

The University of California Academic Council worked out a compromise that a summary of the substance of such information, but not the sources, be available to the individual in lieu of access to the letters.

C. Opposed state legislation which would have required within the California State University System that written reasons be forwarded to individuals automatically for every personnel action, recommendation or decision, at every stage of consideration, whether or not requested. I wrote the Chair of the Permanent Assembly Subcommittee on Postsecondary Education to convey the views of Richard Peairs of the Western Regional office, which I had requested. Subsequently I wrote the Chair of the Assembly Committee on Ways and Means, that in addition to the burden put on the University staff, ''If each and every step is to be fully disclosed in the absence of an allegation of impropriety (in which cases the grievance mechanism is available), this will reduce the willingness of faculty to participate.'' Various modifications were made in the legislation, particularly that written reasons would be issued only upon request of the individual.

D. Kept in touch with the Chair of the Statewide Academic Council of the University of California regarding legislation which would have increased the role of the legislature in determining priorities for the use of university research funds. The bill was defeated, as desired.

E. In April 1976 I received from Professor Marc Tool of the California State University, Sacramento, an invitation to comment on a proposed legislative bill to establish a Collegial Model of Academic Governance. Points that I questioned included the reversal of the recommend and approval roles of the Academic Senate and the President, the assurances of administrative savings and of increase in faculty productivity, and the embedding in statutory law of a model for governance which was still experimental. As I wrote, a more fundamental question was the following:

> Is the problem that is to be dealt with that faculty do not have effective shared governance because they need the state legislature to authorize a Collegial Model, or is it some combination of a failure of nerve, of commitment, of professionalism on the part of faculty to bring shared governance into effect within the existing framework? If it is the latter, we will have encumbered ourselves with legislative intervention to secure decentralization and local campus authority without its leading to a satisfactory outcome.

Since the author of the proposed legislation nevertheless persevered with the matter and a legislative bill was introduced, I testified before the Senate Committee on Education in November of that year, followed by Dr. Charles McClain of the Western Regional Office of AAUP. I testified in part as follows:

> •   The Association is very much aware of the desirability of increasing the extent of faculty voice in the conduct of academic institutions. Its general approach is not to limit institutions to prescribed means to achieve this participation, but rather to recommend principles or standards to guide the selection of appropriate means. The AAUP attaches high value to institutional autonomy, and would urge that care be taken with legislative proposals

which could have a contrary effect. If the Legislature were to take action in this area, the Senate Committee on Education would presumably wish to give thought to whether a detailed model should be enacted, or broader enabling legislation which would leave more avenues open for arriving at working relationships . . .

- Although Senate Bill 18 and the Association's 1966 Statement on Government of Colleges and Universities both have the intent of increasing the realized extent of faculty participation in academic governance, there is considerable difference in underlying philosophy. The Association takes account that in cooperative jointly-shared responsibility for governance the degree of participation by governing board members, faculties, students, and administrators would depend on the nature of their concerns and the type of expertise required, and thus would vary with the type of issue. On the other hand, in Senate Bill 18, the concept of collegiality is interpreted to increase the faculty role relative to the roles of the other parties over a broad range of matters without the same recognition of the different contributions that the several parties, including students and administrators, could make.

- The need for progress in increasing the role of faculty in governance has been articulated by various speakers—the faculty's sense of frustration is evident. It is hoped that the present hearing will stimulate opportunities for increasing the role of faculty in governance. If it does not, one can expect other proposals for legislative action. The highest priority should be for higher education to show that it can manage its own affairs.

The sponsors of this Bill have gone to great effort to break an impasse regarding progress in faculty participation. Comparable effort by the governing board and administrators would be most welcome.

Copies of my earlier letter and of the testimony were provided the State Academic Senate, Chancellor's Office, Council of Presidents, and the Congress of Faculty Associations. The evaluation was adopted as the position of the CFA. The State Academic Senate rescinded its prior endorsement of the proposed bill. The bill did not proceed through the legislature.

I participated in three seminars involving faculty and legislators in the 1975-76 period—state, regional and national.

The campus-state capitol seminar in Sacramento, California was sponsored by the AAUP, the Education Commission for the States, and the Society for Values in Higher Education. I provided an introductory statement, as did also Professor William Clebsch of Stanford and Professor Neil Smelser of the University of California, Berkeley, following which there were small group discussions. I also distributed a background paper on options available for a future in which total enrollment no longer grows and may even fall in certain areas of the curriculum. I commented as follows:

What I will suggest are some questions you might explore in your group discussions with faculty and legislators.

- In most policy decisions, the levels of accomplishment for a variety of higher education goals or objectives must be balanced. ''Excellence'' has various meanings, depending on what is being attempted. Options should be kept open since the future is uncertain and fluid. I suggest this first question: *Can we retain needed flexibility in higher education if administrative choices are preset by statutory language?*

- Higher education must take account of the individuality of students and their personal goals. Higher education must also recognize that faculty are not interchangeable units, and in deed, the individuality of different educational situations. Question: *What does this suggest as to having decisions embedded in legislation instead of having discretion retained within higher education insofar as possible?*

- As to person-centered education, does not higher education have a role in assisting a student to reassess his values and goals to find satisfaction within broader horizons, so that the needs of society as well as the individual are advanced? Does not developing the student's cognitive as well as his appreciative capacity have a role in liberating an individual?

I pose these last two questions as prototypes for many other questions because I believe we need to avoid entrapment in the oversimplification of adopting ''either/or'' positions. Most of the policy decisions which need to be taken are ones of balancing a mixture of considerations. This leads to the question: *What is the distribution of roles as between faculty and legislators which allows each to best contribute his special*

professional competence?
- Finally, there is this question. If individualized learning and the accommodation of diversity are not sufficiently advanced, to what extent is it because the faculty are not supportive, and to what extent is it that the budget is not supportive? For instance, the paper on options points out that simply to maintain quality in the absence of growth requires greater budgetary support per student than that presently authorized. Thus the more general question: *How can both faculty and legislators best take account of competing demands upon resources?*

A three-day regional meeting of twenty faculty members from western states sponsored by the Education Commission of the States and the AAUP was held in Issaquah, Washington, to engage in dialogue with state legislators on higher education and public policy.

The third seminar was held at the 1976 national meeting of AAUP in Santa Barbara. I served as chair and included the following points in my introduction of the topic, which was The Financing of Higher Education:

- The possible means of financing higher education range over such devices as deductions from taxable income, tax credits, aid in bond issues, contracts, and grants for institutional cost, as well as student aid through grants, loans, guarantees, job subsidies, and so forth.

    There are choices to be made as to the combination of federal and state financing, the types of cost that will be financed, the channeling of funds through institutions or directly to individuals, the types of higher education covered (public, private, proprietary), how need is to be defined, the extent to which aid is transferable between institutions and between states and so forth.
- How higher education is financed can affect the behavior of students in the learning process, as well as the performance of faculty in instruction and research, and can have implications for academic standards and thus for the quality and nature of the effects which are being financed.
- It is not enough to say that financing higher education will bring benefits. Alternative activities also bring benefits, and the decision must be how much support of higher education can be justified when weighed against lower levels of support for a variety of beneficial activities.

The pertinent questions include the following: Is the balance between private spending and public spending to be decided in advance, as by a pledge not to raise taxes, or is it to be open to being considered in terms of the costs and benefits of alternative levels of public expenditure? For any given total of public sector expenditure, is there a program budget approach to allocating funds in terms of the objectives served? With respect to those funds that are allocated to higher education, how are resources allocated to particular programs, institutions and individuals? Have the alternatives to asking for more dollars been sufficiently explored within a given program? There is also the question of who pays? Do the resources that are withdrawn to finance higher education produce a progressive or a regressive effect on income distribution?

These joint sessions furthered sensitivity as to the respective roles of faculty and legislators not only generally by also on various substantive matters, yet the technique itself could be improved. I made the following suggestions:

- While collectively the discussion group contained expertise relative to the various decision stages in the higher education process, individually the participants tended to be relatively unacquainted with the full continuum of the process of policy formation and administration. Discussion of substantive issues therefore yielded somewhat to discussion of process in order to remedy the unfamiliarity mentioned above. This groping for understanding of the process is useful in itself, but it would be even more so if the same individuals are subsequently brought together to move ahead in the discussion. Were smaller, more advanced seminars arranged in order to facilitate indepth discussion, there would still be the need for some type of initial encounter to stimulate interest and identify those in whom subsequent investment could be made.

- The result of few legislators being present in the discussion group was that the legislator was a party in each exchange of comments, and was cast in the role of an authority figure. Participants submit their views for the legislator to react to them rather than interacting with each other. At the same time the legislator is able to project his or her viewpoint in view of the successive opportunities to make comments. It is quite possible that this structure of exchanges gives rise to the legislator coming away from the experience with his initial views reinforced in his own mind.

One possibility is a provocative seminar leader who would selectively draw forth from the participants a full exploration of controversial topics, rather than a neutral chairperson who relies on a speakers list.

- Both in the Issaquah regional seminar and in the Sacramento state seminar the discussion turned to follow-up techniques such as taking a legislator to lunch on campus, or other devices for improving contact between faculty members and legislators. Leaving aside all such difficulties as the impingement of such multiple contacts on the schedules of those concerned, it is important to distinguish clearly what such contacts can and cannot accomplish.

Such contacts can develop a general awareness of the context within which faculty and legislators respectively operate, and something as to their respective value systems and sense of priorities. Hopefully, it could generate genuine understanding as to what types of legislative effort would be appropriate and what types of effort, even though attractive on the surface, would ultimately be dysfunctional. And it could provide more ready access for the expression of a viewpoint were a faculty member to need a channel for expressing a position on a specific matter, or were the legislator to initiate the request for advice.

The foregoing type of effort has great value, but it cannot provide the ongoing effort needed to deal with specific bills. The many stages of consideration, the number of individuals involved in passing upon a bill, the short time frame and frequent lateness of notice of an action to be taken, and the focused efforts of parties having opposing viewpoints, call for a more concerted continuous on-site effort by representatives of faculty viewpoints.

At the invitation of CPEC I commented on a draft update of their 1978 Five-Year Plan for Higher Education in California, responding in particular to a proposal that postsecondary institutions take on the role of adjusting the absolute number of those being prepared for professional and vocational fields to fit the number of positions expected to be open. In November of the following year I provided comment on a draft report of a task force of the Commission on Government Reform on "Potential Economies in Postsecondary Education." These two topics are considered at length in my book *Cost Containment for Higher Education.*

In September 1978 I participated on the steering committee of the Lieutenant Governor's Task Force on Women and Minorities in Postsecondary Education. Unfortunately, this committee was disbanded when the Lieutenant Governor was not reelected.

In March 1982 an executive order of the governor froze all further commitments to faculty for the balance of the fiscal year. Since the California State University campus at Los Angeles was on quarter-system year-round operation, there were still letters of appointment for the summer quarter to be signed, especially for those faculty who taught part-time. I was asked to assist in this matter, apparently as a result of a conference between the university president and the executive committee of the Academic Senate. I obtained approval for two telephone lines to be left open for my use. I contacted several members of the State Assembly and Senate in Sacramento from the districts from which students were drawn, and asked that they drop in on the Governor's office and inquire as to the situation, without necessarily taking a stand. I also phoned the Director of CPEC, who had been unaware of the problem. I then prepared a telegram for the General Secretary of the national AAUP to send the Governor, and through conference calls with the national officers arranged for it to be sent. The telegram described the extent of the impact upon students and requested suspension of the executive order and immediate consultation with faculty and staff of the affected institutions. The problem was resolved by 2 o'clock the afternoon of the same day.

At various times I was concerned with the interrelation of economic growth and higher education. In commenting on CPEC's Five-Year Plan in 1976 at the University of California, Berkeley, I stated:

> Undoubtedly State expenditure on education is competitive with other programs for budgetary dollars in a given year, and to the extent that an awareness of this is not present, it may even be desirable to enhance it. Yet there are important qualifications which also need to be stressed:
>
>> That dollars allocated to higher education, even though they might alternatively have been authorized in support of another program, are not necessarily competi-

tive with the attainment of the goals of the latter program, since the higher education usage may be an alternative way of contributing toward the *same* basic objectives.

That even if higher education is financed in lieu of programs having *different* objectives, the effect of higher education has been and continues to be that of increasing the State's economic base, thus enabling the State to finance through taxes the conduct of such other programs.

The assessment of the imperative for immediate versus subsequent benefit, and assistance to the public in making a judicious balance in such choices as it concerns support for higher education, is a fundamental role which the CPEC may wish to include in its Five-Year Plan.

In the draft of CPEC's following year update the Commission's staff wrote as follows:

Because of our rapidly changing technology, the level of knowledge and job skills required, even for many common occupations, is rising and, further, completely new occupations are emerging. As individuals increasingly seek to equip them selves with the required new knowledge and skills, our educational institutions must learn to respond quickly with appropriate programs.

My response was:

There should be further reflection upon whether rapidly changing technology and changes in the specific skills required is an argument for our educational institutions doing a quick change-over in vocational programs, or an argument for focusing on the type of education which gives the individual the flexibility to respond to the changes referred to . . .

It would be well to make the point here that under conditions of changing demand for particularly narrowly-prepared trainees, an education of a more general liberal-arts-oriented nature would develop capacities and flexibility for adjusting to changing job opportunities.

The governor gave short shrift to the contribution of higher education to the state's economy in his Governor's Report in 1981. In June of the following year the Statutory Advisory Committee of CPEC initiated a study on that matter in which the independent institutions and the three public segments of higher education were to participate. I was approached by the State Academic Senate to assist in a study by the Chancellor's Office as its part in the overall project. The uses of the study were to inform the incoming governor regarding the value of higher education, to improve higher education's prospects in the state budget, and to serve as background for the public in reacting to possible cuts in budgets and programs for higher education. I coordinated the assembly of data on the Los Angeles campus and represented the campus at the Chancellor's office. In February 1983, just prior to retirement, I provided comments on the human capital section of the report from the standpoint of cost-benefit analysis. Most of the comments were of technical interest, but certain observations may be useful to others undertaking such a project:

- It should be made clear at the outset that the discussion has relevance both to individual decisions on undertaking higher education and to governmental decisions on providing support for higher education.

- To the extent possible, data should be organized by legislative district so that there is an incentive for legislators to make use of the study.

- Make estimates as to the monetary significance of consquences of higher education that are not immediately countable in money terms rather than simply passing over such matters, to avoid outcomes that are less convincing.

- Keep in mind that quite apart from differences in the value of income received in different periods due to differences in price level, dollars received in later years are not equal in value to dollars received now because individuals have a positive time preference for income or purchasing power today compared to an equal amount received in a later period.

- Keep in mind that in using the ratio of mean income for those with a stated extent of education beyond high school to mean income of those with four years of high school, computed on a national basis, these ratios tend to understate the advantage of higher education, since one of the effects of developing a highly educated labor pool is that the type of job opportunities available to those of even high-school-level preparation is improved, so that the ratio is taken relative to a base figure that is higher than would otherwise have been the case.

- Show to what extent conclusions are sensitive to small changes in the values used for variables and constants in the study. In particular in studying whether the state government recoups its costs through the enlarged taxable income base resulting from a more educated work force, show how changes in charges made to students would affect, in opposite ways, the incentive for individuals to undertake higher education and the willingness of government to provide it.

- In taking into account the cost to the state of providing higher education, do not overlook that this should be net of the costs avoided by its provision.

In the summer of 1983, at my suggestion as Chair of the Committee on Issues and Policy of the California Conference of AAUP, the Executive Committee discussed conflict of interest policy. The preceding March the state Fair Political Practices Commission (FPPC) had extended the California Political Reform Act of 1974 to apply to university research through a revision of the Administrative Code. Provision was made in the regulation for an Independent Substantive Review Committee within the institution. The new policy was applied initially to the University of California, requiring that faculty members file conflict of interest statements as to any personal relationship with business firms that provide them with research funds. A large number of faculty at one campus were then charged publicly with conflict of interest. Differences between the FPPC and the University of California concerning approval of research projects funded from private sources were made the topic of newspaper interviews by the FPPC, which threatened to rewrite the California Administrative Code so as to retain closer control. Under pressure from the Commission, the University of California administrators, statewide and on the particular campus, increased the information given public disclosure (unduly, as viewed by the California Conference), and (it seemed to the Conference) without the faculty involvement that would be appropriate. A position paper was developed on this by Conference president Alfred Manaster, Robert Gerstein of UCLA, and myself, which was introduced into the record by Professor Manaster at a public hearing of the FPPC on September 7, 1983. Certain points in that position paper were highlighted in a statement which I made to the Commission following Professor Manaster's presentation. I attempted also to put the testimony in perspective by commenting as follows:

- As to the full and complete disclosure policy of the State Commission, there are really no absolutes in these matters. One must regard disclosure as a means and not as an end in itself, and the extent of the disclosure should be what best serves the public interest. It should not be carried to the point where it is counterproductive.

- The Chairman of the Fair Political Practices Commission stressed the importance of full cooperation between administrators of the University and the Commission. With that I, and others here, are in full agreement. I would suggest, however, that even more important is the full cooperation of the faculty. For that to be obtained, the faculty needs to identify with these efforts. Faculty should be fully involved, through their Academic Senate, both in developing the Guidelines for the Independent Substantive Review Committees and in the recommendations regarding the extent of disclosure. Much has happened during these summer months in which not all bodies of the Academic Senate are meeting. The pace of considering changes should not be such as to reduce the possibility for full participation by faculty.
- Much of today's proceedings has been concerned with assessing blame for initial misunderstandings on procedure. Yet in the midst of this there has been effort to obtain commitments from the University as to certain policy positions, such as open meetings of Substantive Review Committees. The consideration of relevant principles is best done other than in the context of recriminations.

In consultation with Manaster and Gerstein, I drafted a letter to be sent to the chair of the FPPC by the president of the national AAUP, Victor Stone, professor of law, University of Illinois, containing the following points:

- While public attention has been directed to whether or not there has been university compliance with directives of the Fair Political Practices Commission, what should be addressed is whether or not what is being required is consistent with the best interests of the public.
- It is a matter of public interest in seeking to avoid improper considerations entering into the approval of research projects that the manner of proceeding be consistent with maintaining the independence of academic institutions from undue government regulation. There is, moreover, a public interest that efforts of a public agency intervening in the matter *not unneces-*

sarily inhibit university access to financial support from the private sector, particularly in a period in which support from public funds is limited.

- It is in the interest of all parties to this matter that there be encouragement and exercise of responsibility by faculty and administration at the campus level in several respects:

  In assuring understanding of types of conflict of interest that may develop.

  In formulating standards to guide individuals when conflict of interest might arise.

  In provision within the university of an informed source for advance consultation on questions that individuals wish to raise concerning problems that may develop.

  In formulating guidelines for faculty review of projects drawing upon private sources of support.

  In assuring that colleagues are fully knowledgeable as to the importance of the responsibility exercised by faculty in the independent substantive review process on individual campuses.

- The process must be carried out in a manner that does not infringe on the legitimate freedoms and flexibility of action of the university and its staff members that have traditionally characterized a university.

- In interpreting the requirements for full and complete disclosure, it should prove useful to distinguish between the extent of disclosure appropriate for research projects that are approved to go forward, and the extent of disclosure appropriate for projects that are not approved. It should also prove useful to distinguish between disclosure of the *decisions* taken on all proposed projects, including the *reasons* for such decisions, on the one hand, and on the other hand, the different approach that is appropriate with respect to the *process* of deliberation, in which confidentiality may serve the public interest.

- The FPPC is urged to exercise great caution and deliberate restraint in its relationship to academic decisions, keeping in mind the long-run implications of actions that at the moment may seem expedient.

President Stone's statement incorporated the foregoing, and in addition urged that ''public agencies responsible for administering statutes that affect research programs at public universities should be sensitive to the growing diversity of sources of financial support necessary for university-based research." In turn, he said, AAUP would "encourage our faculty colleagues at the public institutions of California to involve themselves through appropriate Academic Senate bodies in those deliberations designed to strengthen internal institutional policies and procedures. We believe that the faculty and administrations of these institutions will establish and administer responsible policies that meet the concerns expressed by the public."

Extensive contacts were made with UC officials and UC Senate personnel at campus and system levels. The University Administration cited the support of the AAUP, insisted on more time to work out mutually satisfactory arrangements protective of university autonomy, and drew upon the resources of the UC Senate. The Conference communicated further on several occasions with the FPPC and continued to monitor the situation. A letter of appreciation was received from the President of the University of California.

Input was provided to the American Civil Liberties Union on its development of a policy statement on conflict of interest.

A subcommittee of the national AAUP's Committee A on Academic Freedom had been working over a considerable period on an Association statement on "Corporate Funding of Academic Research," and a report of that subcommittee was published in *Academe*, November-December 1983. It does not appear in the Association's *Policy Documents and Reports* (1990), which does contain, however, the 1965 Association statement "On Preventing Conflicts of Interest on Government-Sponsored Research at Universities."

About the time of the conflict-of-interest controversy I was asked, as a member of national Committee R on Governmental Relations, to serve on a subcommittee to evaluate the AAUP Handbook on "Lobbying at the State Capitol." What emerged was an evaluation I prepared in January 1984 which I reproduce here since the commentary itself, even apart from the Handbook, should be a useful guide.

- Suggest Handbook title refer to "State Level" rather than "State Capitol," since in some states legislative hearings are often held in major cities as well as at the capitol.
- Reference to "executive office personnel" comes late in the Handbook. It is useful to have contacts with the State Finance

Department education staff, and the education adviser to the
Governor. Suggest reference to Executive Branch be at beginning of Handbook, alongside Legislative Branch.

- There may be an Office of the Legislative Analyst which issues
  recommendations on the Governor's Budget. Useful to have
  contact with education staff in that office.

- Useful to establish contact with office staff of State Legislator
  for the district in which one's own campus is situated.

- In presentations, legislators like to have specific facts as to
  possible effects on campuses that they can name. Come prepared with fact sheets that have been checked carefully with
  your own campus as to accuracy.

- Legislative bills that may affect higher education do not necessarily explicitly refer to higher education in their title. Desirable to subscribe to a computer service that provides a print-out
  of all bill titles that bear on certain subjects, from which you
  choose which bills you wish to review.

- Suggest early reference to hearings of the committees of any
  State Coordinating Board as well as testimony to the plenary
  session of the Board. Refer also to AAUP statement on faculty
  advisory committee.

- On issues affecting only public institutions or only independent
  institutions, an approach will be judged less self-serving if it
  has the backing of a State Conference representing both public
  and independent institutions.

- It may be too late to be effective if contrary positions have been
  taken by the Governing Boards of systems of higher education
  within the State. They may have a Committee on Public Issues
  and hold hearings. If so, faculty should consider presenting
  their viewpoint to that Committee, and also testify directly to
  the Governing Board if it appears desirable to support or
  oppose that Committee on issues of consequence.

- Those to whom you testify may inquire as to what extent those
  you represent have had an opportunity to review an issue and
  express themselves on it. If at all possible, at a minimum, a
  draft of a position to be taken should be circulated to the
  Conference or Chapter Executive Committee with request for
  comments to be telephoned.

- The Handbook should speak to the matter of interrelationships
  of Chapter and Conference with local and state Academic

Senates, faculty associations and faculty unions.
- If ad hoc commissions on government reform or other matters that may impinge on higher education are formed, liaison should be established and opportunity arranged for presentation of views when it appears appropriate.

To this should be added a suggestion which I made subsequently:
- State conferences should identify specialists on a number of current issues (including research, libraries, women's issues, pensions, and retirement plans) who would be available to testify on legislation.

We turn now to governmental relations at the federal level.

Professor William Van Alstyne of Duke University, president of the national AAUP, wrote the following to George Bush, then Director of the Central Intelligence Agency, in May 1976:

> The recent report of the Senate Select Committee on Foreign and Military Intelligence has confirmed what was already published elsewhere: that the CIA has for years covertly used academic institutions and employed academic persons in ways which compromise institutional and professional integrity. Universities and scholars have been paid to lie about the sources of their support, to mislead others, to induce betrayed confidences, to misstate the true objects of their interest, and to misrepresent the actual objectives of their work . . . I ask you to take steps to end the exploitation of the academic community and to disengage the Agency from covert activities which induce academics to betray their professional trust.

George Bush wrote back that "these charges reflect your ignorance of the true nature of the relationships we now have with American educational institutions and their faculties," and that "your letter indicates a serious lack of confidence in people in your own profession . . ." At the national meeting of the AAUP that June in Santa Barbara, Morton H. Halperin, a former member of the National Security Council, stated that CIA has "one or two or perhaps several secret agents" on each of more than one hundred campuses. I was a member of the national Resolutions Committee at that annual meeting, and I recall the heated discussion of a resolution that was proposed regarding such alleged practices. After some modifications, the following Resolution on Covert Intelligence Operations of the United States Government was adopted at the plenary session, reproduced here as it was published in the *AAUP Bulletin* of August 1976.

The recent report of the Senate Select Committee on Foreign and Military Intelligence has drawn attention to the dangers which the activities of the covert intelligence agencies of the United States pose to the integrity of academic institutions and academic persons. The standing and reputation of academics have always depended on their dedication to the free search for truth and its free exposition; the exploitation by these agencies of academics and their research has risked undermining the credibility of published research and risked compromising the position of academics.

The Sixty-second Annual Meeting of the American Association of University Professors declares its firm opposition to any initiative by government agencies to involve academics in covert intelligence operations under the guise of academic research. Recognizing the importance of the academic community's participation in the conduct of government and the formulation of governmental policy, and mindful of the responsibilities of scholars and teachers, the Annual Meeting calls on all academics to participate only in those governmental activities whose sponsorship is fully disclosed, and to avoid any involvement which might conflict with their academic obligations and responsibilities. The Annual Meeting calls on all academics associated in any capacity with a governmental agency to disclose the nature of this association to professional colleagues, students, and others who are affected by it, as well as in publications resulting from this association.

My appointment in 1982 to the national AAUP Committee R on Governmental Relations afforded me a broad vista of the interface of academe and government at both state and federal levels, as well as occasionally internationally. And serving on the National Council made apparent the extent to which professors who cannot agree upon courses of action, yet somehow eventually do so. Each year the legislative agenda of the Association was prepared by Committee R, covering a wide range of topics. The long-time major domo of Committee R has been Dr. Alfred D. Sumberg. He prepares a draft of the agenda for committee consideration, mixing in a combination of the feasible and the idealistic, and shepherds the committee product through the Executive Committee of the Association. He maintains a legislative network for bringing faculty views to bear upon Congress, and makes the rounds of state conferences to encourage their contributions at both state and national level. The Committee R staff is extremely able, but short in numbers. The committee depends, as does the Association, on the volunteer work of faculty. Sumberg serves also as editor of the annual publication, *Budget Alert*, for the Committee for Education Funding. When Sumberg was in California in 1985 Ruth and I were pleased to host a reception for him at our home, attended by AAUP stalwarts from campus, state and national levels.

I recall visiting individual U.S. Senators and Representatives, on one occasion leading a state delegation that was representative of all segments of public and private higher education. These visits are preceded by letters to set up appointments and followed by letters to express appreciation of the opportunity to discuss various legislative items. One year I gathered data on the importance to our own campus of the TRIO programs—Talent Search, Upward Bound, and Educational Opportunity Centers—for students of disadvantaged backgrounds, and discussed this in person with the Congressional Black Caucus. I also recall a White House briefing on the yet-to-be-released federal budget as it affected higher education. Since I served six years on Committee R, during four of which I was an emeritus professor, I have many recollections. I prepared comments on a draft statement on statewide coordinating boards of higher education, an evaluation of the concept of a national Knowledge Budget, and a critique of the guidelines for research grant proposals for the National Endowment for the Humanities.

An important part of the work of members of Committee R consisted of digesting materials provided by Sumberg in preparation for extensive discussion and arrival at a consensus in the committee meetings. In addition there were assignments to task forces on longer-term projects. In my own case I was assigned to task forces on the Federal Role in Higher Education, on Tax Policy, and on Federal Legislation Affecting University Research.

I was requested by Committee R to prepare a statement on the Federal Role in Higher Education jointly with Morris Mendelson, Professor of Finance, Wharton School, University of Pennsylvania, and Professor Kenneth Tollett, Professor of Higher Education Policy, Howard University. I prepared a working paper of guidelines which

I circulated for comments in March 1983. This was subsequently revised as ''Freedom of Choice in Higher Education'' (13 pp.), with Mendelson as co-author. Included there are are the following guidelines proposed for the federal role in reducing financial barriers to higher education:

- Decisions as to educational quality, academic performance and curricular offerings are the responsibility of the academic community and the educational institution. The federal role in higher education should be subordinate to that responsibility.
- From the standpoint of the individual, the federal role in providing financial assistance to students should be to facilitate equal access to higher education and opportunity for choice as to which institution to attend. It should be supportive of the individual being persistent in the completion of programs of higher education studies.
- From the standpoint of the national economy and society, the federal role should be to facilitate the attainment of public policy goals through investment in human resources.
- A federal program should be compatible with the diversity of educational organization (tax-supported and private, non-sectarian and denominational, non-profit and proprietary, etc.) characteristic of a pluralistic society.
- Federal support should be complementary rather than subordinate to support from states, local political units, the community and the family. It should be designed to encourage added support from existing and new private and public sector sources.
- To make possible the provision of financial assistance at realistic levels of support, the federal role should be designed:

    To conserve federal resources by avoiding windfall financial advantage to individuals who could have otherwise provided adequately for their own higher education.

    To provide adjustments in the limits set on grants and loans to offset inflation, reflecting awareness that education serves to decrease further inflation through increasing productivity.

    To work with market forces, where consistent with equity and other public objectives, to economize on the extent of subsidy and regulation required.

    To phase in the implementation of changes so as to avoid abrupt increase in the requirements for financial assistance.

- To take account of considerations that might otherwise deter an individual from undertaking higher education studies, the federal role should be designed:

> To permit levels of part-time degree credit work that are consistent with employment and dependent-care responsibilities.

> To reduce the reluctance of individuals to borrow for their education, and reduce as well the extent of defaults on loans, by formulation of repayment obligations that are manageable in relation to an individual's income after obtaining an education.

> To provide flexibility in repayment of loan obligations to accommodate the responsibilities associated with building a family.

- Methods for implementing the federal role should be designed to achieve an appropriate balance between two sometimes conflicting considerations: keeping down the cost of program administration, and assuring that resources serve the purposes for which their expenditure is authorized.

A guideline added later was that students should not have repayment obligations overlapping the period in which as parents they would have obligations for financing the education of their own children.

During the next two years I devised a plan consistent with these guidelines and refined the statement of it with the aid of Morris Mendelson; see "Student Loans: A Moderate Proposal" (1986). Among the letters received supportive of the proposal was one from W. Ann Reynolds, then Chancellor of the California State University, and currently Chancellor of the City College of New York. I published a more complete treatment of the topic in "Income Contingent Student Loans: Context, Potential and Limits" (1987). Comparisons with alternatives are also available in a letter to the editor in the *Chronicle of Higher Education* (1988), and in an invited book review for *Academe* (1989). An overview from the standpoint of cost will be found in *Cost Containment for Higher Education*, (1991).

In the experiment with income-contingent loans budgeted for by the [Reagan] Administration, the loans are income-contingent in the sense that the rate of repayment is adjusted to the flow of income. The loans are not income-contingent in the additional sense that we have proposed in which under certain outcomes as to an individual's income the loans are converted into de facto grants. Under the latter arrangement the government could shift more toward loans without limiting educational opportunity, thus making financial assistance possible at a level that would permit equality of opportunity not only to attend higher education but also to select the institutions and programs which best meet a student's needs and abilities. [I return to this topic in the chapter on encouraging at-risk students.]

Mendelson and I were subsequently asked by Committee R to review the documents prepared by the Treasury Department relative to the President's Tax Proposals to the Congress, May 1985. We first prepared a set of comments reactive to specific passages in the president's proposals, which were found useful by Committee R. We then wrote a positive statement, "Special Interest and the Public Interest," which took final form in October 1985. In Annex 15.1 to this chapter I set forth a few passages that may be of general interest. The analysis that underlies these excerpts and specific applications have been deleted, but the complete text is available from the authors.

Perhaps as a sequel to that report, I was asked in 1987 to produce a report on Federal Legislation Affecting University Research. Related to this is one further paragraph from "Special Interest and the Public Interest":

Resources need to be guided, by appropriate tax and budget policies, into creating the knowledge, skills and human qualities that would reinvigorate the private sector over a broad array of activities. Elements of that approach include budgetary support for basic research, for state-of-the-art instrumentation and equipment at the several levels of education, and even more long term, for features of professional life in academe that will attract and hold high caliber individuals for teaching at all levels. This last-mentioned consideration is critical for determining the quality of education. Further, there should be an expansion of programs such as Talent Search, Upward Bound, and Educational Opportunity Centers, that assist in bringing into the mainstream contributions from underrepresented segments of our society. Student assistance programs should be designed to facilitate the choice of an institution that challenges a student to full development of his or her potential. These efforts have already begun, but the programs need to be rounded-out rather than finished-off as the Administration proposes.

The approach suggested would provide conditions needed for economic progress and develop the research capability and skilled manpower so basic to our wellbeing and long-term national security. [p. 19]

I produced a Research Issues Agenda, with supporting documents for many of the items. My general viewpoint was that what is needed is support on a sustained basis for the entire process that is involved in obtaining valid research results. As summarized later in Chapter 5 of *Cost Containment for Higher Education*, the process involves support for the preparation of individuals for a research career; protection of incentives for researchers and research institutions; support for research equipment and instrumentation at both secondary and postsecondary levels and for specialized research libraries; discernment in allocating research project funds between basic and applied research and among the agencies that administer research funding; avoidance of restrictions on the international movement of researchers, information and equipment; and attention to ethical and related concerns.

Placing emphasis on research and development is one of several approaches to stimulating economic growth that is being considered by the Clinton administration. The decision to be taken is not that of implementing one option to the exclusion of the others. Rather, the decision concerns the relative emphasis to be placed on a number of options in combination, including some or all of the following:

- One approach, termed "demand-pull," utilizes public expenditure to directly affect the situation of individuals, not only by providing jobs and hence purchasing power, but also by improving public safety, health, housing, training and education, and the physical environment, the need for all of which has been particularly dramatized by the traumas of the inner city.
- An alternative approach, referred to as "supply-side," relies not upon public expenditures but upon the government reducing tax rates upon business to encourage profitability and job creation. This approach has also been referred to as "trickle-down economics," or as I refer to it, "filter-down economics," since a "cut" is taken at successive levels before benefits accrue to the worker and consumer.
- A variety of the supply-side approach is for the government to pursue an industrial policy of granting tax credits for industry-sponsored research and development activities in selected di-

rections. Essential to this approach are patent laws that permit sufficiently exclusive use of research results to make institutional investment profitable.

- An approach to stimulate growth which is supply-side but involves direct expenditure by the government is to develop infrastructrue, not of the type that catches up and makes things whole, but of the type which throws arrangements off-balance (see discussion in Annex 11.3) in the sense that it creates opportunities waiting to be exploited. In an underdeveloped country an example would be a project to build a port for ocean-going vessels, or the construction of a railroad system. For a developed economy, it could be investment in a national fiber-optic network.

- A fifth approach, investment in human capital, is non-intrusive on individuals and industry and shows great promise. It combines elements of the other approaches in that it operates not exclusively on one side or the other of the market, it involves both expenditure and tax-remission features, and it has both short and long-run effects. Investment is directed at increasing the extent to which individuals can contribute to the direction, productivity, and growth of the nation's economy.

Investment in human capital competes for resources with many other uses. The Clinton administration has to contend not only with the problems of today and with provision for the future, it must contend also with the legacy of earlier-year problems that resulted in the accumulated national debt. While consumption has to be encouraged to bring the national economy out of recession, saving (i.e., non-consumption) ultimately has to be increased to free resources for investment in long-term projects. Support for research and development is a long-term investment, but even more basic and long-term is investment in human capital that will encourage insight, competence, and creativity.

In 1993 I was encouraged by George Stephanopoulos, Director of Communications for the White House, to continue correspondence that I had started with him and several members of the White House Staff on Administration efforts in support of increased investment in education. Some excerpts from that correspondence have been added to the chapter on encouraging at-risk students.

15.1

Special Interest
and the Public Interest

- A foundation of our way of life is that economic decisions are made in as decentralized a manner as is consistent with the furtherance of our objectives. [p. 2]
- Living standards in the United States remain high relative to the levels experienced under other economic systems. We must build on this to raise the level of wellbeing for all, while preserving incentives for all individuals to realize their potential. [p. 2]
- Unfortunately, the legitimate concern that government may unduly interfere with the efficient operation of the market system often restrains the government from implementing the measures needed for the efficient operation of the private market system . . .

    The foregoing notwithstanding, the presumption should be that government should not enter into private decisions unless there is good reason to believe not only that a government role can be corrective, but also that the benefits of intervention outweigh both the direct costs of intervention and any indirect adverse effects it may create. [p. 3]
- Such measures are warranted when either efficiency would not be served otherwise, or an efficient outcome would run significantly counter to other objectives of public policy. The market mechanism is not attuned to all considerations. When we consider the quality of life we seek, most of us take account of additional values beyond efficiency. Among these are fairness (equity), humanitarianism, stability, growth and development,

and security. When private decisions are made in terms of personal benefit and personal cost without consideration of effects upon others in these various dimensions (some of which go beyond efficiency), activities may be carried to a point that is not appropriate from the standpoint of the public interest. To illustrate, higher education produces benefits beyond those accruing to the student, but students would not undertake as much education as desirable from the standpoint of society if they had to face the full cost without subsidy. [p. 4]

- . . . taxes or subsidies can be used constructively to adjust incentives in certain types of activity such that private behavior will take account of the effects produced upon others. Also they can take into account objectives additional to freedom and efficiency . . . They are indirect techniques for encouraging or discouraging activities within a market-type economy, consistent with our open decentralized society. Yet the use of special provisions for specific activities is under broad-scale attack. We should not elevate to the level of principle that such policy instruments not be used. Without question, there are provisions for special situations that should be eliminated, possibly a preponderance of them, but there are also some which should be retained. [p. 8]

- Encouragement of educational effort is a well established national concern recognized in legislation. The proposal contained in several tax plans to narrow the extent to which scholarship and fellowship grants may be excluded from taxable income is inconsistent with that concern. A further proposal of the Treasury and the President would no longer allow deduction ''for travel as a form of education.'' Although less important than other provisions affecting education, these provisions would restrict the extent and breadth of educational opportunity for both students and faculty. [p. 8]

- There must be highly prepared individuals to meet the needs of the growing economy targeted by the Administration. This includes anticipating the need for faculty in the 1990's, for which period a shortage is predicted. The proposals mentioned above which narrow fellowship aid are not consistent with this. Post-baccalaureate study is an activity for which special provision should be continued in the tax code. Specifically, stipends for graduate research and teaching assistants, inclusive of tuition that is waived and necessary expenses, should not be taxed. [p. 9]

- Increased opportunity for single parents to participate in employment and higher education should also be encouraged. This has been facilitated by partial tax credit for work-related child and dependent care expenses. Various of the tax plans would replace the tax credit by a deduction from taxable income, which provides higher benefits the higher the income bracket. [p. 9]

- The [Reagan] Administration is using the Great Deficit to press Congress to reduce federal program responsibility for social objectives. Any shortfall in tax revenue under a revised tax policy would lead to added pressure in that direction. At the same time, block grants to state and local governments have been reduced and elimination of federal revenue sharing has been proposed. These changes make it difficult for state and local authorities to continue existing levels of service, and even more difficult for them to take on programs from which the federal government is withdrawing. [p. 10]

- There are interrelated grounds for skepticism about the Administration's scenario as to economic growth, among which are the following:

> Will domestic investment increase sufficiently in the absence of Administration willingness to go beyond tax neutrality in order to bring the deficit under control? Given the prospects for domestic saving, will the deficit reduction and debt service requirements for the national debt permit a reduction in the real rate of interest and make unnecessary reliance on an inflow of foreign savings?

> To what extent will corporations innovate and make the necessary investment when the decrease in marginal rates is paid for within the tax reform plans by withdrawing other corporate tax advantages?

> Will business take the transition quickly in stride, and develop confidence in the possibility of profit from long-term investment, if the Administration withdraws the recently introduced investment tax credits, modifies accelerated cost recovery, and relies on the incentive of lower marginal tax rates?

>   Will corporate profits be directed into those areas of
> capital formation supportive of long-term economic growth
> sufficiently for growth to be sustained at a rate and for a
> period that would permit the scenario to be fulfilled?
> [p. 21]

- While government policy should not be designed to serve special interest, it should include provisions for coordinating special interests with the public interest. This is important when, from the standpoint of public interest, there are significant benefits or costs associated with individual or corporate decisions that otherwise are not taken into account. It is also the case when there are significant benefits or costs associated with a state or local government policy that spill over beyond that governmental unit's jurisdiction. [p. 22]

- The Administration is relying on rapid and continuing economic growth to resolve our nation's economic difficulties. This may reflect unwarranted optimism as to its occurrence and unwarranted expectation of it as a panacea. But economic growth is a goal, alongside other goals, that nevertheless warrants support. The federal budget and tax reform should give increased emphasis to basic research, the quality of education, and development of the human qualities needed for economic growth to be sustained over the long run. [p. 23]

16

Empowerment of Others

It is time to return to some ideas set forth in earlier chapters. I wrote in the opening chapter on such matters as taking charge of one's own life, and of having a master loyalty which gives life a sense of purpose. Also, that we tend to be constrained, above all, by our mental attitudes. Although our situation be bounded on all sides by constraints, there will remain some opportunities open, however small in scale and unlikely in prospect, which we could explore if we had but the will to do so. I urged that one should bring to bear one's own skills, knowledge, and perspectives to gain insight into possibilities which may not be apparent to others, nor to oneself without some initiative.

From as early as I can recall, I had a strong sense of being an individual, and beyond that, self-confidence and a sense of there being a purpose for my being here. It was the beginning of a personal philosophy, but at that stage it was largely without content.

In the second chapter I wrote that everyone has, or should work toward developing, some special talent. I said that over the years I found that I had a talent for seeing things in context and for evaluating alternatives, a talent not only for analysis but also for organization and leadership. With that in mind, I was on my way toward developing a personal philosophy when I came to apply as one of the criteria for the choices I made in life that I should choose those options that would make the best possible use of the talent I could contribute. While the views of others should be valued, an individual should have self-confidence in searching out for himself or herself the values to apply in evaluating alternative courses of action.

What I regarded as values was in the process of formulation. The effect of my war experiences on this process has been given in the essay on moral values, liberal ethics, and education, appended as an annex to Chapter 5.

An individual's special talent deserves to be recognized as a scarce resource, and should be used accordingly. I reasoned that I should do my share in assisting with activities that meet an immediate social need, but since such activities yield early gratification they tend to attract participants, and accordingly my contribution should be monetary, if possible, rather than the direct use of my time and energy in these activities.

My personal efforts, therefore, to the extent that I have had the choice, have been focused on activities that were not likely to be undertaken by others, or if undertaken, were unlikely to produce results I would regard as satisfactory.

In Chapter 8 I discussed the further evolvement of a personal philosophy. I referred there to the process of obtaining information, forming views, and arriving at conclusions which are tested against reality. We develop concepts as to what we value and expectations as to the payoff if we follow particular courses of action. I discussed what enters into what we regard as facts, and the concept of a boundary of concern, a horizon within which we acknowledge to ourselves a sense of responsibility. Part of a personal philosophy will be to have a subjective criterion for selecting what purposes to further. Will one seek to maximize expected satisfaction or minimize expected regret? And to whose satisfaction do you refer? As I wrote in that chapter, the extent to which the personal pursuit of satisfaction is identifiable with serving others will depend, among considerations such as your values, skills, knowledge, and so forth, on the boundary of your concern, that is, upon how inclusive is the group for which the advancement of its welfare will bring you satisfaction. I then commented upon some of the advantages of drawing that boundary inclusively. I commented also upon one's personal philosophy evolving with personal growth, and the opportunities that unfold.

In Chapter 9 I referred to my experiences in the war motivating my search for hypotheses as to how to proceed to avert such events in the future. The focus of my personal effort became that of improving the prospect that individuals would be capable of intelligent choice. See, for instance, Annexes 9.3, on Moving Toward Intelligent Choice, and 11.1, A Creed.

That is about as far as I wrote directly as to my personal philosophy, and it is appropriate now that I carry the discussion forward.

As I look back, there have been two lines of endeavor throughout my life, but the relative emphasis given to each has varied from period to period. One effort, expressing my own individuality and serving my own goals, has been to empower myself and be effective in the use of my abilities. This includes enlisting others and serving as a leader. The other effort has been to empower others to be effective in the attainment of their own goals.

In economics, as mentioned earlier, we speak about cost and benefit externalities, that is, the effects of one's actions on others that are not taken into account in one's decisions. Various devices are employed to broaden the decision-maker's boundary of concern so as to embrace these additional considerations in selecting a course of action. The devices employed by the economist include taxes and subsidies, that is, sticks and carrots, to bring it within the individual's own interest to act in a manner that is consistent with the interests of others.

The more general technique for having people behave with due regard to their social context is to elevate this to being a moral precept that should be followed because it is the right thing to do. That tends to be the approach in parental guidance, the influence of organized religion, and the message in schooling.

In my own case, my parents were largely non-directive in that dimension, advocating simply that I be forthright in my dealings with others. And religion raised more questions for me than it provided answers. The public schools I encountered as a student did not view holistically opportunities to develop the whole person, settling upon discipline to control what could not be tolerated in the classroom, or more constructively, providing encouragement and reward to promote acceptable behavior.

It may be in looking back so many years that I interpret my motivation differently from that warranted, but as I recall, I had concern for others not because of a moral precept, although I recognized the moral dimension, and certainly not because of an external threat or reward, but because it gave me satisfaction. Thus the motivation underlying my two lines of endeavor, empowering myself to be effective as an individual, and empowering others to be effective in accomplishing their own goals, were not that distinct in that both were self-serving in yielding personal satisfaction. In the terminology of economics, what might have remained as externalities were internalized, so that in my decisions as to which options to select an effort was made to take into account the effects upon others. But it went beyond simply conducting my own affairs with sensitivity to the effects on others. It meant actively seeking the development of others to be better able to serve their own objectives.

As I have written earlier, I valued my ability to get things done and attempted to use that ability in furtherance of what might not otherwise be accomplished. There is an expression as to getting things done, ''by hook or by crook.'' This expression refers to a shepherd's crook, a staff with a curved handle, and to getting things done by any means available. The hook end of the staff can be used to bring people along in one's own general direction, as when one co-opts individuals in achieving shared goals. The other end of the staff can be used to prod individuals into action, as when one stimulates or motivates individuals in achieving goals largely decided by themselves. The symbolic holding of the shepherd's staff conveys a status that facilitates serving as a leader, as an example, as a catalyst, or as a consultant.

I have written in an earlier chapter as to the importance of one's developing self-confidence, and of my crediting various teachers for the encouragement that contributed to that confidence. First at Alameda Grade School, then at Grant High School and then at Reed College I benefited greatly from the exchanges I had with faculty, and from the opportunities for leadership and service. Subsequent developments were consistent with the findings of Winter et al. (1981), mentioned in Chapter 3, as to the predictable contribution of a liberal arts education.

Another factor was that the Great Depression and its aftermath required that I be more self-reliant than most individuals at an early age. The depression years made me sensitive to the plight of others, and aware that events can often be too large for an individual to overcome. Those who have been insulated from events such as the Great Depression or subsequent recessions may be prone to speak of self-sufficiency and success as being available to anyone who makes the effort, when this simply is not the case.

Experience has also taught me to qualify my faith in others by the cynical observation that one can be ill-used by those they help the most. But my own philosophy of life depends on believing that, in most instances, if one empowers others to further their own objectives it will not be to the detriment of society. Why I must believe that I will explain at this point.

I hitchhiked a great deal in mid-America before going overseas during World War II. At such times I would drop off at college towns and try to absorb a bit of the atmosphere before pushing on. I became aware of the vastness of the country, the great many people, how much they differ from each other, the many classrooms in which students grappled with absorbing what was already accepted truth, and the many individuals outside the classroom who had little education. Later I traveled over much of the world, with similar impressions on a broader scale. These impressions convinced me of the tremendous obstacles facing an individual seeking to introduce an idea, or modify behavior, even with a lifetime of effort. Efforts by more than one individual and over more than one lifetime, are probably needed for ideas to take hold, be applied, and accomplish change. There undoubtedly are cases in which change takes hold more readily, but this is not to be counted on.

I concluded that my effort should be to empower others with a philosophy of life and with methods for intelligent choice rather than teaching specific conclusions or applications. As I expressed this concern after the war in Annex 5.1, the primary purpose of the mind is not to impound the product of other people's thinking; rather it is to discern, to sift and analyze, to weigh and evaluate, and to come to its own decisions based on rational choice. The hope was that through the multiplied efforts of those so empowered there was more chance of fruitful ideas being engendered and nurtured than if I relied on a more direct but single-handed, one-lifetime approach. Focusing on the empowerment of others, where choices depend on their values and their boundary of concern, is an act of optimism that the objectives that are then pursued are, on the whole, consonant with a viable society.

In line with the foregoing I prepared myself by focusing on analytical techniques and methods of hypothesis testing, such as mathematics, mathematical statistics, economics as a theory of choice, econometric model building, decision theory, optimization techniques, mathematical programming, cost benefit analysis, planning-programming-budgeting by objectives, as well as the theory of organization. I studied meta-fields such as the philosophy of science and the philosophy of education, and explored what methods courses in education had to offer. I broadened my experience in a variety of ways set forth throughout this book, and took on considerable responsibilities.

The payoff for the foregoing has been that I have been able to empower others through facilitating a research environment, facilitating scientific communication, teaching, academic-fiscal planning, faculty rights and responsibilities, collective bargaining, and governmental relations, using as broad categories the titles of several of the preceding chapters, each of which contains numerous specific examples.

The same emphasis on empowering others underlay my writings on assisting other nations, underdeveloped areas in particular. Also, during the period in San Francisco with the Institute, the Academy, and the College, I focused on making others effective. At the latter two institutions the faculty was empowered to contribute to the academic direction of their respective institutions. And empowerment was the objective in my work in teaching for the Peace Corps and in my work with the disadvantaged in Los Angeles.

Perhaps the most effective vehicle for increasing the likelihood that others will see fit to serve the same general purpose—the empowerment of themselves so that others can be empowered—is to increase the access of individuals to higher education and in particular to a liberal arts and sciences collegial experience. This I undertook in my writings on a new approach to student financial assistance (Simpson and Mendelson, 1986; Simpson, 1987, 1988, 1989).

As I stated in *Cost Containment* (page 135), it is higher education's most distinctive opportunity for service to counter the cynicism of students as to their place in society by interpreting the possible role of intelligence and concern in a world which seems so much shaped by other influences. I have been particularly impressed by the contribution which a liberal arts college can make to the dimensionality and quality of life. The changes in a student sought through such an experience include development of appreciative and rational capacities, development of imaginativeness and creativity, versatility, initiative and resourcefulness, ability to bear uncertainty, and continuing interest in learning and inquiry.

A liberal arts experience, as it relates to concern for others, furthers the development of sensitivity, openness to differences in value orientation through appreciation of cultural diversity and unifying bonds, empathy and compassion, and interest in constructive participation in society.

Education, particularly liberal education, offers more than a

marginal improvement in our society; it provides a basis for fundamental change. In suggesting higher education's underlying role in
the incoming Clinton administration I wrote (*Academe*, 1993a):

> Finding common ground as a basis for working together in
> a new beginning is a paramount need following the recent
> divisive national election. Whether one has advocated minimiz-
> ing the role of government or using more of the resources
> available to government, there is shared interest in revitalizing
> the individual in society.
>
> . . . empowering individuals could be considered the
> principal goal. A nation that can empower its people may
> accrue economic and political strength. Indeed, this would be a
> desirable result since a strong nation, wisely guided, better
> assures a peaceful and enabling context for individual activity.
> It is, however, useful to view a strong nation as a means to
> individual empowerment and not as an end in itself.
>
> Education is society's principal instrument for empower-
> ing the individual. Education should not merely be "getting
> by." Rather, the country needs an investment in education not
> only to repair where it has fallen back, not only to hold an
> attained level of performance, but also to empower the entire
> educational community to better prepare individuals for an
> active role in a world that is ever becoming more complex and
> competitive.

As a closing comment in the article, I wrote:

> . . . whether reference is made to the empowerment of an
> individual student or the empowerment of a higher education
> institution, the most important thing to be learned is that while
> assistance from others, including the federal government, is a
> critical component, success will depend ultimately on the acti-
> vation of the individual's or institution's own inner resources.

17

Encouraging Students at Risk

Empowerment should start early, with initiatives taken by parents and by teachers and counselors in the early stages of learning. The social context must be supportive of the exercise of parental responsibility with special provision made for working parents of young children. Public subsidies that make it possible for the middle-income class to escape into private schools do not lead to public support for a quality education being made available to the majority.

Students should be encouraged to welcome opportunities to accept responsibilities in working with others for this will widen their horizons and contribute to their intellectual growth and performance skills. Programs that contribute to students broadening the area of their concern include: integrated classrooms, peer group tutoring, field trips, inter-school competition, school clubs, competitive sports, youth organizations, neighborhood assistance, recycling and environmental projects, etc. Unfortunately, many of these programs have already been eliminated or are in jeopardy from cuts in budgets for education.

In this book the focus is upon higher education. In this chapter we will discuss an approach that encourages high school students to continue their education into college. In the following chapter we discuss a possible shift in emphasis in the higher education curriculum.

Following the Watts riots in Los Angeles in the 1960's I developed recommendations for the state of California aimed at reducing barriers to access to higher education and to choice of institution encountered by minority youth—not only geographic and financial, but also academic and motivational. Efforts by society along these lines lessened as the situation returned to normal, even though that normalcy condemned many to unsatisfying life experiences. Race riots returned to Los Angeles in 1992, following which, in an invited proposal forwarded to the Rebuild Los Angeles Task Force, I identified goals relative to broadening the educational options for minority youth which could be advanced by a consortium of colleges and universities in the area.

There have been improvements in the right of access to housing and education for minority individuals in the interval between the Watts riots in the 1960's and the recent riots in Los Angeles. Nevertheless, there has been a shortfall in the exercise of those rights and in the enjoyment of the benefits that should follow where they are exercised. The reason for this appears to be less now than before a matter of racial or ethnic barriers and more a shortage of income and of personal money capital. This restricts the ability of individuals and families to move into racially and economically diverse neighborhoods, leaving them to fend for themselves in the economically depressed areas of the inner city. It limits also the extent of travel, the range of experience, and levels of aspiration. On the other hand, there are strong family ties—even within single parent families—and with attention not diverted elsewhere, satisfactions may come from membership in a large family.

Two long-term trends currently affect individuals throughout the economy, but impact particularly hard upon lower-income families: the extent to which present-day jobs require extensive prior education and training, and the loss of many relatively unskilled jobs to other countries. Add to this the effects of the recession, and it is difficult to find employment, irrespective of skill level or race.

In the immediate aftermath of the 1992 riots, teachers, counselors, support staff, members of the United Teachers of Los Angeles, and both celebrities and ordinary citizens have helped students cope with the catastrophe. It remains to be seen to what extent these efforts will continue.

In the opening sentence to the preface of this book I wrote: ''To a considerable extent we allow circumstances to determine the course of our lives and that of society, and we need to regain the initiative.''

It was appropriate, accordingly, that I enlisted in ''Take Charge,'' a project sponsored by Reed College, which is located in Oregon, to encourage minority youth to prepare for and enter higher education. Of a long-run nature, and started prior to the riots, Reed's ''Take Charge'' program has sought to encourage youths to take responsibility for the direction of their own education and lives, encouraging them to prepare for a larger role in society than might otherwise be the case. The program contributes insights and advice and builds self-confidence, but equally important is that it demonstrates that somebody cares about the individual and will keep contact in subsequent stages of the individual's career. Volunteers serve as mentors and positive role models at some twenty middle schools and high schools in the Los Angeles area. This early intervention program was developed by Rudolph Jones, associate dean of admission at Reed, and Richard Roth, of the Los Angeles Unified School District, a Reed alumnus. It subsequently was administered by David Roth, assistant director of admissions. I have prepared a 93-page unofficial handbook, "One Volunteer's Approach" (1993), which has been provided each mentor in the program. That there is room for alumni from other colleges to undertake similar efforts is apparent in view of the many middle schools, high schools and magnet schools in the Los Angeles area.

Some comments on the phrases "Take Charge" and "at-risk" used herein will assist in defining the focus of these efforts and of the present chapter. In Chapter 1, "A Master Loyalty," I refer to the extent to which one should take charge of his or her own life. This was written before Reed's "Take Charge" Program—a program consistent with that objective. In 1991, Chester E. Finn, Jr. published his book, *We Must Take Charge: Our Schools and Our Future*. Part III of that book, "Taking Charge: Revolutionizing Education from the Outside In," makes evident that what Finn means by "take charge" is quite different from the above. He refers to how authority over what occurs in the classroom should be divided among classroom, administrative and government levels, whereas Reed's concern and my own in this context is with the individual taking more responsibility for his or her own life. His topic, nevertheless, deserves careful study, and a program of that nature requires heroic leadership for fulfillment. As Finn states (p. 236): "Hence when the society's wellbeing depends on fundamental changes being made in major institutions, these have to be initiated and prosecuted from outside by those whose interest in change exceeds their fealty to the status quo—and who wield enough power to prevail." The extent to which this chapter, and the "Take Charge" program as well, focus on "at-risk students" also needs to be made clear. At-risk students are often characterized as disadvantaged, with that disadvantage becoming cumulative as students are taught without regard to their special handicaps. As I view it, the problem can be attacked at one or more of several levels, among which are: (a) improving the socioeconomic status of families, (b) improving student motivation to overcome educational and other disadvantages, among them being within a peer group including many who are educationally disadvantaged, (c) setting lower standards for what is expected of disadvantaged students, (d) redesigning educational techniques at preparatory school levels for those who are educationally disadvantaged so that such students can take their place along with others in meeting standards, (e) redesigning the distribution of authority over educational changes.

The last-mentioned approach, (e), is that of Chester Finn, Jr., as mentioned above. Approach (c) is the "least effort" approach—unfortunately the one most encountered. Approach (d) is the subject of ongoing debate, as exemplified in publications such as that of Barbara Means, et al., *Teaching Advanced Skills to At-Risk Students: Views from Research and Practice*. What the present chapter, and the Reed program, focus upon is approach (b), which is more short-run than (a), (d), or (e), yet nevertheless important and likely to be needed even in the future. The Reed program tends, moreover, for budgetary reasons, to focus on individuals from among those who have faced difficulties inherent in some combination of (i) low socioeconomic status, (ii) English not being their native language, and (iii) educational problems experienced at earlier levels, who as yet are not overly disadvantaged educationally and have demonstrated characteristics that bode well for success in completing a higher education program.

Since 1991 I have "adopted" four Los Angeles inner city schools (two middle schools and two high schools), and currently encourage nine groups of students there—primarily Hispanics, but including some African-American and Asian-American students as well—to aspire to continue with their high school education and eventually enter college. What I stress is that the student himself or herself may well be the most important influence on whether or not he or she succeeds in life relative to that individual's goals. Education does make a difference, and students can make a difference in their lives by investing in their own "human capital."

It is not simply that education significantly improves the possibility of a higher income level than otherwise, it is also that education increases the dimensionality of one's life and its quality.

Students need to be encouraged to see themselves not as reflections of their peer group—reluctant to stand out by excelling over others, and reluctant to do more than asked—and more as agents of discovery who are self-propelled. They should not aim simply at an average level of performance, but *do* more than average if they want to *be* more than average.

Persistence is also an essential ingredient of success. Having a goal set, and consistency in working toward that goal, is advantageous, but a student should change his or her program if a student's goals change. A broad-based educational program before specialization will make that possible.

The access that "Take Charge" volunteers have to the situation of students provides some understanding of the difficulties faced in becoming educated. To a great extent these difficulties can be traced to deficiencies in our conventional educational processes, the effects of which are less decisive for upper income students because of the wider array of options open to them as well as a more supportive environment. We need to address these deficiencies in our public school system, and resolve them, not only because of their devastating effect on those otherwise confined to the inner city, but also because they can hobble even the more economically secure individuals from participating in society and enjoying a full life.

The foregoing underlay the first goal that I suggested to the Rebuild Los Angeles Task Force, namely: to establish continuing student-mentor relationships that convey the message that somebody cares that a student makes the most of his or her life. This would be an extension of the "Take Charge" program. The program would be undertaken for individuals selected as "promising but at risk" throughout the Los Angeles urban area who are initially at the equivalent of the 8th grade in public or private schools which qualify by reason of low average family income among attendees, low college-going rate, academic underperformance, and/or low persistence rate. This mentoring activity would be particularly important for students for whom the expectation that they continue their education is not an already accepted part of their thinking. Each mentor would undertake to meet periodically at the same inner city site with the individuals selected for the program. After an initial orientation session with new entrants to the program each year, sessions would be held with three or four students at a time, with considerable interchange between students and mentor. It is important that mentors be readily available on short notice at times of critical decisions, and desirable that there be continued contact by the same mentor over a period of years as the students move forward through different schools—through meetings, correspondence, telephone calls, etc.

The second goal would be to develop a forward look on the part of the students as to what education could be available to them, through opportunities to become familiar with higher education programs, staff, campuses and facilities. Reed had scheduled such a program on a university campus, but it had to be postponed since the day coincided with the 1992 Los Angeles riots. Subsequently we have met and conducted workshops at a number of colleges and universities in the Los Angeles area. The ''Take Charge'' program is not a recruitment program of the college, but an effort to encourage students to make an intelligent choice as to the type of institution appropriate for their goals. Students should not settle simply for a convenient option within their own neighborhood, but should widen their acquaintanceships. It is a fact of life that one's career will depend not only on what one knows, but also on who one knows. I stress that students should select the most challenging higher education opportunity that they believe they can handle. An institution should be sought that cultivates analytic ability, comprehension, appreciative capacities, creativity, a sense of responsibility, and an interest in relating constructively to one's fellow humans and our environment.

The consortium of universities in the Los Angeles area formed subsequent to the riots to consider proposals involving education consisted of public institutions with programs of four or more years. I recommended that the group invite participation by community colleges and independent higher education institutions so as not to overly direct student choice of career or type of institution. Programs for students would be planned jointly by combinations of academic departments at several institutions, but would be held at a single campus.

The third goal would be to facilitate student success after enrollment in higher education through peer group encouragement.

Activities that seek to motivate individuals to value education, and activities that broaden the educational options for minority youth, should be aggressively pursued in spite of financial stringency so that all individuals have equal access and opportunity to be considered for higher education.

Encouraging individuals to undertake higher education should be accompanied by efforts to assure that students have a commitment such that opportunity for access not be abused. Accepting certification by preparatory schools, public or private, that their graduates are adequately prepared to benefit from college leads in many instances to predictable waste which can scarcely be condoned when there is financial stringency. In part this may reflect inadequate academic standards, in part the accumulation of credits from disconnected experiences at various schools, and in part the automatic promotion of pupils who are getting old relative to classmates. Colleges and universities, in consultation with feeder schools, should require all applicants to be tested as to their current competency in basic skills, without permitting a low score in one basic skill to be offset by a high score in another. Faculty should be actively relating to their counterparts in the preparatory schools in preparing for this change.

A college or university faces a hard choice when a shortage of financing forces a choice among limiting enrollment to only a subset of those who could benefit, limiting the breadth and/or quality of education offered those admitted, or some combination of these options. This may require a decision as to what extent a larger number of individuals having access to an education that is of somewhat lesser quality by reason of the claim on services is preferable to a smaller number having access to an education that is not diminished in breadth or quality.

Another hard choice arises if the option selected is to limit enrollment. Should all applicants be given equal opportunity to qualify before a cut-off is made, or should diversity of enrollment be considered if it would not otherwise be obtained? If diversity is a factor in acceptance, would some youth take admission for granted and prepare less than otherwise, and would others regard the policy as reverse discrimination? If diversity is not considered, and equal treatment of applicants does not lead to it, would this send a discouraging message to those who should be encouraged? In either case, the value of the mentoring activities mentioned earlier, and of commitment on the part of the individual, is evident.

Going beyond equality of opportunity for access and choice of institution, and beyond the question raised above as to diversity of enrollment, we face questions concerning equality of outcomes.

Melissa Anderson and James Hearn have written about education as the ''great equalizer'' [Becker and Lewis, 1992, Chapter 2; Simpson, 1993c], and report research findings as to the extent to which individuals of equal ability experience outcomes that are correlated with gender, race/ethnicity, and socioeconomic status, the latter judged by parental income, education and occupation.

Education, in my view, should empower each individual to overcome limitations insofar as feasible, and should empower groups in society to work toward reducing such limitations, but the influence of education, in both the short-run and the long- run, is but one factor among many that lead to inequality of outcome. I would conjecture that reducing the extent to which outcomes are correlated with gender and race/ethnicity may prove to be more attainable than reducing the effect that parental socioeconomic status has upon the array of options open to an individual, even among individuals of the same ability.

Our society accords special deference to graduates of prestigious colleges and universities. These institutions have a high rate of persistence by students, so that almost all students graduate within six years. Yet such institutions, which tend to attract and enroll individuals of high initial accomplishment, may have added less to the ability of those who can afford to enter than other institutions which, against formidable odds, contribute far more to individuals who start from a much lower level of accomplishment. Moreover, as noted above, the extent of an individual's success after graduation from college or university is likely to be influenced by the socioeconomic status of the families of the students in the cohort with which they graduate, reflecting the extent and level of the opportunities that open up from close association with fellow students.

Colleges and universities deserve recognition for the extent of change they facilitate in an individual, but they should not simply be passive receivers of those who choose to enroll. They need to engage in such outreach activities as will encourage suitable preparation for, and interest in, access among those with the potential to significantly benefit from a higher education experience.

Judging from what has been emphasized during the presidential campaign, the Clinton administration will promote a closer relationship between education and the workplace, implemented through the design of the curriculum and the use of apprenticeships and internships. This should lead to students becoming more aware of the relevance of their studies to what will be expected of them in employment. It should increase their interest in studying and contribute to their persevering through graduation.

Were the emphasis primarily vocational, however, individuals would risk being prepared too narrowly. In the chapter on governmental relations I included comments I provided the California Postsecondary Education Commission in 1976 as to how education should cope with rapidly changing technology. The Commission recommended that educational institutions learn to respond quickly with programs appropriate to the specific skills required in the new occupations. I argued that apart from flexibility being desirable in curricular offerings, there was need for individuals to be flexible in adjusting to changing job opportunities, and that capacity was best developed by a more general liberal arts-oriented education.

It is not only that technology is changing rapidly; many business organizations are changing from individual work assignments to assigning work to teams of employees who take turns at a variety of tasks. Moreover, in various industries there is a devolvement of responsibility for decisions on work procedures from central management to the teams themselves. Insight and creativity, along with competence, are needed not only by those in the upper echelons and (as noted in the chapter on government relations) by those in research and development, these qualities are needed even on the shop floor. If individuals who were at risk of not completing school are not to be at risk of slow advancement or unemployment, they will need to be able to demonstrate insight and creativity as well as competence. At least two years of a broad liberal arts preparation before focusing one's attention more narrowly would assist in the cultivation of these important human qualities.

As to the national student service plan put forward by the Clinton administration, I wrote as follows in an open letter to the White House in May 1993, that some re-focus was needed:

- Providing for students to engage in public service activity will encourage upcoming generations to extend their boundary of concern beyond the personal bottom-line philosophy that has had such emphasis in recent decades.

  [However], it may be a disservice to students and to society if individuals are encouraged to interrupt their movement from high school to college by a period in which they build up credit that could, among alternatives, be applied to college tuition. For many high school students, especially in the inner city, continuing on to college is not an already accepted part of their thinking. The concerted effort to encourage a smooth transition should not be undermined by individuals being drawn off into seeking more immediate satisfaction. The program for public service prior to college should focus on individuals who are not yet convinced that further education is worthwhile.

- As to earning repayment credits *subsequent* to college, this does not make sense since graduates would be foregoing greater income by not immediately entering their professional fields. Both the individual and society would lose. Higher education institutions would also lose, since money would not be recycled for the financial aid needed by the students who follow.

- The *main* thrust of the national student service program should be on service in the community that is *concurrent* with the years in which students are enrolled in a college or university. During the regular terms, term breaks and summers, students could be financed modestly to participate in part-time service within their community, preferably as interns under arrangements that are coordinated with the curriculum and with the institution's interest in encouraging social consciousness and adherence to a public service ethic.

Adoption of the above suggestion would improve the focus of the national student service program as well as consolidate and strengthen the efforts of higher education.

In the same letter I commented upon the income-contingent repayment option for student loans:

- The income-contingent repayment approach adjusts the pace of repayment to the individual's ability to repay, greatly simplifies administration, and minimizes problems of default. The proposal deserves support.

- [However], the proposal does not go far enough. Fundamental change is needed. Income-paced repayment has long been advocated, but what is needed is the further step of making the continuation of the repayment obligation itself contingent on certain circumstances, as through the use of ex post facto grants.

- Confronted with severe financial problems, many colleges and universities are seeking higher charges from those students who can afford to pay, with part of the receipts being used to augment student aid . . . Individuals differ greatly in their perception as to the personal benefits to be obtained from higher education, and these perceived benefits are weighed by each individual against what that individual has to pay in judging the extent to pursue education. An increase in charges can discourage students who cannot qualify for assistance and also those who could qualify but feel reluctant because of the financial commitment they may have to bear throughout their career. The retreat by California, for instance, from a policy of low student charges for public higher education is regrettable, for the state has benefited greatly from a well-educated work force and citizenry.

- To the extent that state governments shift to higher student charges, there is increased pressure on federal programs for student financial assistance. What is suggested in the present letter is a type of loan agreement that would make increased use of student borrowing more acceptable to students, and would not discourage access. There would no longer be a point to deferring or subsidizing interest payments, and the financing of higher education would be significantly furthered.

- Decisions as to the relative reliance on grants or loans in a student's financial aid package currently take account of *presuppositions* as to the student's subsequent ability to repay, and this may reflect ethnic and gender considerations. Under the proposed approach, the division between grants and loans in an individual's financial aid package would reflect the individual's *actual* earning experience. Repayments spaced by income earned would be made for a preset number of years in which there was above-threshold income, any balance would thereafter be converted into an ex post facto grant. Individuals would not be discouraged from borrowing to finance their further education by the prospect of still having to make repayments even when they had responsibilities to finance their own children's education, since the obligation would not extend for that length of time.

- Implementing the ex post facto approach so as to recycle more of the funds available for student assistance would result in a saving by the federal government, it would decrease the need to raise tuition to finance an institution's aid programs, and it would be equitable in that the cost would be borne by those who,

based on fact and not on supposition, receive personal financial benefits, and are best able to pay.
[Included with my letter were reprints of articles in which I discussed how loans are fitted into a student's financial aid package for above-average-cost undergraduate institutions and for graduate and professional programs. Made evident in the articles is that there are limits on the extent to which reliance may be placed upon loans, under whatever arrangements there are for repayment.

A considerable exchange of correspondence developed on the above, which extended to members of the Cabinet, Congress, and the joint committee on reconciling differences between House and Senate. Some of the communications were routine, but enough gave evidence of thought being given to substantive considerations to justify the effort involved.]

18

Goal-Oriented Learning

What is central to the concern of the educational community is the improvement of academic outcomes. To secure this requires effort not only along various lines that have been indicated in the preceding chapter, but also increased appreciation by the general public of the importance of education, not only for the individual but also for the economic and social wellbeing of society, so that needed financial support can be forthcoming for its essential missions.

What is needed additionally is that institutions identify more clearly than at present the fundamental objectives to be served by them with respect to their missions in the areas of teaching, research and service. In the present chapter we will focus on the teaching mission, as we did earlier in Chapter 11. With the fundamental objectives of teaching determined, the instructional program, and opportunities for students to undertake relationships and responsibilities, should be restructured on a gradual basis to bear more directly on the accomplishment of those objectives. I have given this new emphasis in higher education the name ''goal-oriented learning.''

In discussing planning-programming-budgeting (PPB) in Chapter 12 on academic-fiscal planning and in the Annex thereto on relating programs and resources to objectives, I wrote of my efforts to bring about a large measure of participation by faculty and staff in what otherwise would be decided by administrators. PPB tended to define the goals of the instructional function in terms of the curricular programs to be supported, without going the additional step of considering the learning goals to be served. Goal-oriented learning goes that additional step.

Earlier interest in PPB has given way to interest in the total quality management (TQM) movement. Each offers participation by staff at various levels, but the latter is focused more upon achieving efficiency in serving preselected goals rather than upon examining the goals to be served. TQM is discussed by Gappa in Simpson (1993c, Chapter 6). See also Chaffee and Sherr (1992), and Sherr and Teeter (1991).

As I mentioned earlier in this book and set forth in a 1985 article, individuals enter academe for a variety of reasons, not all of which are related directly to serving students. Among the principal motivations are an interest in an area of academic study and a liking for the academic way of life. It is a broad generalization, but surely reasonably accurate, that as one progressively considers preschool, grade school and high school teaching, undergraduate instruction, and graduate work, what attracts individuals onto the staff shifts from being student-oriented to being subject matter-oriented and then to being research-oriented. Whereas the early stages of education attract individuals who are concerned primarily with the development of their students, the latter stages assemble a faculty interested in being involved with their academic field, and arguably, to a lesser extent, with students who will share that interest.

James C. Hearn (Becker and Lewis, 1992, Chapter 2) describes, for instance, the deemphasis of teaching—particularly undergraduate teaching—in a research university. The technology of good teaching being poorly understood grants license for inroads made on faculty time; the faculty is organized by academic disciplines and fields, and research therein is encouraged as a use of faculty time alternative to teaching and to participation in the common pursuits of a campus; the curriculum is fragmented—shaped around faculty research interests rather than instructional goals; research is directed along lines that receive support and provide a basis for discretionary expenses; prestige is bought through recruitment of noted researchers; criteria for advancement emphasize research rather than teaching, and so forth.

In reporting on a study undertaken with William Massy, Robert Zemsky (1990) describes how (some) academic departments, to attract and hold enrollment, ''de-structure'' their curricula in order to eliminate roadblocks caused by prerequisites and to make more courses interchangeable. ''Teaching a subject,'' that is, teaching a structured set of courses, is replaced by what he terms ''teaching of students,'' which is satisfied by a set of courses that absorb the enrollment and contribute to the containment of cost.

I regard either practice as subject-centered teaching. I contend that the vital core to be protected in a curriculum should be viewed more in terms of accomplishing specified underlying goals than in terms of maintaining comprehensive coverage of an academic field. The emphasis should be less on what is transmitted and more on what is to be accomplished. The shift should be from teaching subject matter to teaching students, or put another way, from subject matter-centered teaching to goal-oriented learning.

Courses would not be entirely student-centered, since although courses should be viewed in terms of what the student learns, a college or university should not simply satisfy its clients' desires, but should further the educational and developmental goals which motivate its existence. Warch (1990), for instance, regards the fundamental curricular aim of a liberal arts college to be holistic, and its basic educational mission to be ''to empower the individual to make connections.''

I subscribe to Zemsky's belief ''that structure and coherence should be the product of a faculty's decision to take *collective* responsibility for the curriculum.'' I also subscribe to the view that faculty should be open to being persuaded—persuaded, for instance, that there are benefits to explore beyond simply appreciating the logical rigour in mathematics, the verbal imagery of literature, the range of facts in historical discourse—benefits which can be enlisted to accomplish goals of the individual and of society.

It is commonplace to remark that student communication skills should be improved. The ability of students to be articulate in the written and spoken word—and to think on their feet and argue their views, even on an impromptu basis—needs to be developed. But with the ''knowledge explosion'' there should be somewhat of a shift away from imparting information and toward teaching how to gain access to and process information and reach conclusions. While the ability to analyze needs considerable cultivation, there must also be more encouragement to think inductively and creatively. Students are often altogether too passive in waiting for conclusions to be delivered to them, and all too unimaginative in conceiving of alternative frameworks that could lead to additional options.

There are developments on the current educational scene, arousing considerable controversy not only locally but also statewide and nationally, that may be subsumed under goal-oriented learning.

These developments invoke various buzz-words: outcome-based education, performance-based education, and project-based learning. They advocate greater flexibility in the educational means selected provided the means contribute to the desired results. Standards and accreditation are linked less to educational input and more to students being able to perform relative to the outcomes sought, shifting away from centralized control by administrators to permit greater initiative by individual teachers.

Higher education, in its teaching mission, clearly could be enlisted to serve various objectives. It is not so much a choice between one or another goal as it is a choice as to relative emphasis. But there is a choice between expecting such goals to be automatically met by focusing on transmitting knowledge and expecting them to be met as a result of designing educational experiences that facilitate their accomplishment.

Where there is opposition to outcomes-based approaches it has been largely because it would go beyond imparting knowledge and training in specific skills and would address the development of the values held by individuals and the relationship of individuals to others. With religion and family life having demonstrably less effect than before upon the attitudes and beliefs shaping the behavior of youth, it is difficult to conceive of a more important responsibility to be borne by education. Even so, the proposed national goals for education have side-stepped this essential role. While goal-oriented learning could be considered to include the several approaches mentioned, the distinctive feature is that it includes, as one facet, attention to the development by individuals of a set of values and a personal philosophy.

Goal-oriented learning clearly presumes more than turning a professor loose on a class with a subject to be discussed. It presumes that courses are designed to produce preselected effects. To the extent the focus is upon providing information, it should be to enable a student to select among ideas, not to influence the uncritical adoption of particular ideas.

Undoubtedly some rethinking would be in order as to what constitutes academic freedom. If the course content narrowly reflects a specific viewpoint, there is the danger of indoctrination or politicization. [See, for instance, the type of charges made by Lynne V. Cheney, chair of the National Endowment for the Humanities (Burd, 1992).] This is not so if a course is designed to improve the ability of the individual to make intelligent choices in terms of his or her own values.

To the extent I might influence higher education, and the curriculum in particular, I would seek that it be consistent with the encouragement of a peaceful world respectful of diversity and concerned with mutual improvement. The curriculum could be viewed as having as its several-fold mission to encourage in individuals the development of: (a) rational, creative, and appreciative capacities, (b) competence in areas of application, and (c) an awareness of the satisfactions to be gained from serving goals with account taken of effects within a broader horizon than self and family. We tend, I believe, to conceive of education—particularly nondenominational—as a means for an individual to become effective within his or her environment, especially with respect to (a) and (b). While we count on education also creating various benefits to society such as through (c), the latter is regarded somewhat as an offshoot of the former. Social institutions such as the church, benevolent societies and service clubs, which derive their strength from faith, inspiration and an appeal to service, are relied upon to more directly emphasize a moral tone—a concern for others—that ameliorates the direct pursuit of self-interest. This is a dichotomy between the mission of education and that of the other social institutions which may be counterproductive.

Some courses, if suitably designed, could be a vehicle for achieving underlying objectives, such as sensitizing the student to the human condition and expanding the boundaries of the individual's concern. Constructive interaction among individuals needs to be advanced not simply as a responsibility toward fellow members of society but also for the satisfactions to the individual that are derived from helping others to achieve their goals.

There has been a gradual movement toward what is proposed, although what is now suggested has yet to gather proponents. A self-service cafeteria approach has been largely replaced by the combination of a core program and electives, with courses sequenced through prerequisites. The core, moreover, has changed from being simply a collection of courses from the same or other academic disciplines and now includes interdisciplinary courses.

The new orientation would apply both to courses for majors in a particular academic subject and to courses required or elective for a general education program, but the nature of the learning goals, of course, would be different. To take the field of economics an an example, a course intended for economics majors could stress the conceptual frameworks and analytical tools that are appropriate, together with sources for substantive information, while a general education course in economics could have objectives such as enumerated in Annex 11.2.

In terms of current practices, colleges of liberal arts and sciences are the closest to what is proposed, and comprehensive colleges and universities provide the most fertile fields for change.

Change would be needed more in courses such as in the humanities and social sciences than in mathematics and the physical sciences where the development of student skills necessarily receives emphasis.

The crux of the matter is the nature of the course objective. Is the objective, say, to provide a chronological view of history through a series of courses for successive periods? Or is it the objective that students develop some type of understanding or capability, with that learning also being possible through alternative courses of quite different content which are substitutable in serving the same objective?

Chet Meyers (1986), for instance, argued, with respect to the learning goal of teaching students to think critically, that critical thinking should be a part of every course (consistent with Annexes 5.1 and 9.3).

Going one step further, there could be a structuring of courses in terms of the goals to be served—student goals and institutional goals—rather than in terms of covering an academic field. What is taught to a considerable extent would be a means, and since means are substitutable, courses serving the same learning goals would for many individuals be substitutable. I have referred to this as ''goal-oriented learning.''

Some economy in course offerings during a given term could be achieved. One might even still adhere to subject-oriented teaching as the preferred activity of higher education and yet find merit in using goal-oriented learning as a guide when severe cutbacks cannot be avoided in curricular offerings. However, while I believe that such an approach would contribute to cost containment, and provide an alternative to limiting access, its adoption as a continuing policy should be on its educational merit.

In *New Priorities for the University* (1986), Ernest A. Lynton and Sandra E. Elman set forth various ideas that are well worth reading relative to ''meeting society's need for applied knowledge and competent individuals,'' including active cooperation across organizational boundaries within a university. Priority is given to ''meeting the advanced knowledge needs of society.''

A study by William A. Reinsmith (1992) arrayed types of teaching in a continuum from teacher-centered to student-centered, but what I refer to as goal-oriented learning is not to be found in that array.

Goal-oriented learning remains a largely unexplored approach, except as the goal is taken as the transference of knowledge. While it holds promise for a more effective use of resources, it should also be expected that the composition of the faculty would undergo adjustment over an extended period.

Goal-oriented learning clearly is a shift away from the subject-centered teaching which has attracted many into the academic profession. While academe would still offer faculty an environment conducive to their own intellectual pursuits, the presumption would be removed that the path to further student accomplishment would necessarily coincide with or that it should defer to a faculty member's personal direction of interest. Presumably left untouched would be faculty explicitly selected to contribute to their professional fields at research universities or selected by a comprehensive university in order to make such a contribution. For those affected, opportunities for personal research and creativity—beyond those involved in keeping current professionally and being effective in the classroom—would have to be made available on different terms. Incentives would need to be structured relative to subsequent advancement to incorporate more student-centered emphasis alongside faculty scholarship. Finally, this could mean that those attracted into teaching and remaining therein would be those whose personal enthusiasm made them, along with their students, comrades in the quest.

19

Quality of Life and Recent Essays

The first claim on our time has always been academic commitments, mine with respect to postsecondary education, and Ruth's with respect to teaching the elementary grades.

I retired in 1983 but continued teaching in the winter quarter. I had a long bout with pneumonia in 1989 and then reluctantly gave up the classroom the following spring, completing thirty-two years at the same university. Although not teaching now, except to outreach groups, I have continued with my professional work. The present book is being completed, as well as a separate volume, *Special Agent in the Pacific, WW II: Counter-Intelligence—Military, Political and Economic*. I have written the book mentioned earlier, *Cost Containment for Higher Education*, published by Praeger in late 1991. It combines political and social commentary with the economics of higher education and the art of administration, all directed at maintaining quality education in a period of difficult financing.

Reviews of *Cost Containment* have been favorable. Rosemary Park (1993) wrote in *Change: The Magazine of Higher Learning*:

It resembles a conversation among informed, interested economists who each contribute spontaneously to the theme in small bites and with solid knowledge of the relevant literature.

Joseph Stutz (1993) writes in *Academe*:

This abundantly referenced book addresses every imaginable strategy, factor, or consideration pertaining to higher education costs and their potential containment. It is an excellent reference source for any higher educational professional who is exploring this complex subject . . . (It offers) both a comprehensive overview of this timely and important subject and a valuable tool for finding answers to fit a myriad of circumstances.

Most recently, John Waggaman, who has also published on this subject (1991), wrote in the *Journal of Higher Education* for July-August 1994:

> *Cost Containment* is a summative work about public and institutional financial and academic policy with which every official connected with higher education should be familiar. . . In sum, this is a valuable and unique book, a reference tool for the current and next generation of academic and financial analysts and higher education policy makers . . . It should serve higher education well into the next century.

At the request of the national AAUP I provided a full-page newspaper article on fiscal retrenchment in higher education in California in 1992, and then at the time of the presidential inauguration, an invited article on higher education's role in a new beginning (*Academe*, January-February 1993).

At the invitation of Jossey-Bass/Macmillan, I was editor of, and contributor of chapters to, a book in their New Directions in Institutional Research series, *Managing with Scarce Resources*, which is complementary rather than competitive with my earlier book on cost containment. In discussing options for primarily instructional institutions, I have arranged the discussion according as options reflect defensive reaction, constructive structuring and flexibility, or long-term new directions. Under structuring, I discuss the selective excellence (depth-of-offering) approach, which I mentioned earlier (1991, p. 84) and discussed further in Simpson (1993c, Chapter 2). The book includes, among other contributions, chapters by Joseph Froomkin on the difficult choices facing research-intensive universities, by Stefan Bloomfield on facilitating decisions under scarcity through, for instance, vision statements, and by Judith Gappa on participation in decisions on scarce resources. These chapters bear on topics dealt with in the present volume in Chapters 6, 12 and 13, respectively. The chapter prepared by William Norris and Geraldine MacDonald on the use of technology in instruction and administration has been mentioned earlier.

William Pickens contributed a chapter discussing how scarcity of resources may be measured relative to the existing program of a college or university. I discussed various interpretations as to what is meant by resource scarcity, and indicate that one challenge is to learn from comparisons with other institutions without becoming a follower—that is, each institution should seek to perform optimally. I identify as a further challenge, the development of measures of the adequacy of available resources relative to full implementation of public policy objectives that have been adopted for postsecondary education—for different functions (instruction, research, outreach, and so forth), for individual institutions, for types of institution, and for state and national aggregates of colleges and universities. This calls for both analytic ability and familiarity with statistical sources. What should be sought is a better view as to the scale of effort toward various goals that can be justified in terms of the benefits derived and the resources required. The hope would be that this would inspire bold efforts to optimize the contribution of higher education. It is vital that the vision of what higher education can contribute be communicated to the public, so that its potential is appreciated and so that it receives sufficient support.

Two essays on higher education have been written recently, and follow this chapter as annexes. I have also outlined a further book, *Improving Student Outcomes in Higher Education: Challenges and Strategies*, and I am considering a possible publisher.

Ruth retired in 1989, but for about seven months of the year is called early each morning as a substitute teacher. She types my manuscripts, assists in editing, and facilitates my work at various stages.

Social activities and travel are worked in around that schedule. Since we were married we have made several trips to visit our relatives in Scotland, numerous trips to Mexico (in part because of my interest in pre-Columbian sculpture), and trips to various Pacific Islands and Austral-Asia, the latter in part to visit relatives in Australia. We had tickets already purchased in 1989 for a riverboat trip down the Amazon from the interior of Peru into central Brazil, but medication to combat pneumonia affected my immune system so that the required immunization for yellow fever could have given me the disease instead of providing protection. That trip is still on hold.

I became interested in the Simpson-Brand family tree, and started developing it as a guide to sorting out relatives, just prior to my trip around the world in 1953 and 1954. Grandfather John Simpson conducted a construction materials business in Greenock, Scotland. Grandfather William Brand, also of Greenock, was a timber merchant and builder of steam-powered motor launches. The record at one point goes back to 1688. Amendments are made as family members continue to send information.

We have no family of our own, which we both regret. For Ruth with her students, it is a daily case of love them and leave them; each day is a new and exciting experience. I have a brother who is a physicist engaged in interplanetary space research, and Ruth has a sister, neither of whom lives in this part of the country.

We have always had a pleasant home with spacious views. Earlier I described our apartment at the Pyrenees Castle, near the University. In 1977, after almost twenty years there, we returned from a trip to Mexico to discover that the Castle had been sold and we were being evicted on short notice. The Castle is now used by the Chinese government. Our present home is on a ridge in Eagle Rock, convenient to the University and to Ruth's schools. We can see down the San Fernando Valley to one side and toward the San Gabriel Valley on the other. The present house was built at the turn of the century around a dwelling used by a ranch foreman who could watch over flocks of sheep on the slopes on each side. There is a separate modern studio extending over a vale. Both buildings are full of books, file cabinets and artwork. There are patios at different levels, cactus and succulent gardens, and many eucalyptus trees and live oaks. A giant hundred-year-old live oak shades the main patio. Several ranges of hills and mountains are visible. We see spectacular sunrises and sunsets, and at other times are quite isolated by heavy fog.

Until a few years ago we could hardly wait until weekends to rush off to the nearby mountains, beach or desert. We often went to Tujunga Canyon in the Los Angeles National Forest, climbing up dry creek beds and otherwise wearing ourselves out.

Dogs have always been an important part of my life, as well as cats since we have been married. In Portland I had an Australian Shepherd, Woof, for many years. In Chicago I advertised for the owner of an emaciated gray dog I found on the street in the bitter cold and boarded it at a veterinarian hospital. I changed the ad when after a bath the dog emerged as a resplendent white polka-dotted Dalmatian, and eventually found him a good home. On another occasion, Marianne and I found a dog curled up asleep on a snowbank on the Midway Plaisance and were able to return it to its owner on Christmas Eve. At the Castle, Ruth and I had Princess, a stray German Shepherd, and a consort she attracted, a stray young yellow Labrador retriever whom we named Prince Albert. We thought of calling our Eagle Rock home ''Albert's Dog House'' since it was because of him that we purchased a home rather than rented. We added Brandy the Bold, a Doberman Pinscher, and MacDober, another Doberman, whose owner was moving. The ''Mac'' was added to indicate he was an honorary ''Scottish Doberman.'' Currently we have MacDobera of Apolda, or Dobera for short. Also Terri, a delightful young pit bull terrier whom we salvaged when she was thrown into our place with her throat cut and bleeding. We share Cruz, a black Labrador with a white cross on her chest, with a neighbor, because at the time I rescued her from an animal control vehicle we were at the limit as to the number of dogs allowed. Occasionally we take care of Rottweilers for two different friends, and I always regret giving them back when their families return from vacation. We are helping in a small way with a rescue group for Dobermans and have recently adopted Prince, a large handsome but older Doberman who might not otherwise have found a home. As I write this, there is a young Australian cattle dog at the window. Aussie has been saved from being put to sleep, and we are developing a compound nearby which he will share with the neighbor's Doberman who has been wandering away. Our latest addition, until we can find her original home, is an energetic young Tibetan spaniel, whom we call Ginger.

Taking care of our trees and gardens has been a welcome change of pace. Ruth plants things—that's ''constructive'' gardening. Contrary to my usual role, I have taken care of ''destructive'' gardening —cutting hedges, and so forth. I use the past tense since we must now have someone else do the latter.

My hobbies include British postal history and photography. Earlier I completed a many-volume set of albums of Asian philately, which has been given to Reed College. Ruth loves to play the piano, and I am an accomplished listener.

We have surprised ourselves on occasion by being active during national political campaigns. Some years ago I prepared and sponsored a half-page campus newspaper advertisement with criteria for selecting a president, featuring the question as to which candidate would best fit the enumerated specifications. Added thereto were the names of many faculty members who wished to be co-sponsors. The national AAUP made copies of the criteria and question for distribution to state AAUP organizations. We have taken part in get-out-the-vote telephoning, and walked our precinct to distribute material, meeting neighbors in the process and being invited in to discuss candidates and issues. We have been supportive of environmental and civil rights efforts.

I continued to serve on the University's Academic Freedom and Professional Ethics Committee after retirement for the balance of a five-year term, and at the national AAUP level on the Committee on Governmental Relations. At the state AAUP level I continued as chair of the Committee on Issues and Policy. I was an invited speaker on ''Empowering Faculty in Times of Fiscal Crisis'' at the fall 1993 meeting of the California AAUP State Conference. I am continuing to correspond with White House staff, cabinet members, and members of Congressional committees on matters of educational policy. As mentioned earlier, I continue with my outreach efforts with at-risk students at several middle schools and high schools in the Los Angeles area.

I serve on a newly constituted National Advisory Council appointed by the Board of Trustees of Reed College, and on the Claremont University Graduate School Alumni Council, as well as consultant to other colleges and universities. Among my initiatives is a proposal that Claremont, as an institution on the edge of the Pacific Rim, take its place among the institutions that seek to understand and be understood by those not sharing our Western heritage by giving greater attention than at present to the contributions in the humanities made by those of Middle Eastern and Asian cultures. Various Asian community leaders in the Los Angeles area could be allies in obtaining financing for such studies were Claremont, as an outreach effort, to make the humanistic contributions of such cultures accessible and meaningful to school-age youth. The need is not limited to those of Western orientation. There are various rapidly growing Asian communities within the Los Angeles area in which parents find that while their children are readily assimilating Western culture, they are, with the exception of certain tight-knit groups, growing up without an appreciation of or access to the contributions made by humanists in their native lands that should be part of their cultural heritage.

We have recently become contributor members of the Pacific Asia Museum in Pasadena and members of its Philippine Arts Council and Japanese Arts Council.

In recent years I have been cooperating with a group in Tokyo that has been concerned that certain aspects of the period of World War II have not been adequately reported in what has been taught recent generations in Japan. The group is exploring the possibility of wages being paid to Chinese, or their survivors, who were held as forced laborers in Japanese prison camps during World War II. Authors in the group have used the investigative report I prepared in 1945 on the Chusan Chinese prison camp as a basis for two books and various newspaper and magazine articles, and in addition, have written and staged plays in various Asian countries based on war crimes committed at Chusan Camp. Also, a symposium was held in Japan based on a Japanese archive copy of the voluminous report that I prepared for the War Crimes Tribunal. Greetings have been exchanged with individuals I knew there almost fifty years ago.

During 1993 I cooperated with Japan Public Television (NHK) on a documentary on the use of forced labor that was broadcast from Tokyo on the eve of the anniversary of the surrender of Japan. After exchanges of information for many months, program personnel came from Tokyo and Washington, D.C. to our home in Los Angeles to photograph documents and to conduct an on- camera interview. In the documentary, a newsreel clip of General Douglas MacArthur arriving in Japan was followed immediately by 1945 photographs of prison camp scenes that I had provided, by Tokyo newspaper photographs of myself testifying upon my return to Japan in 1947, and by the 1993 live interview at our home. A fuller account of this is given in *Special Agent in the Pacific*, the book I have written on counter-intelligence.

During my period in the Pacific I assembled a considerable archive of war-related historical material, which has been enlarged by recent correspondence. President Peter Stanley of Pomona College, who has a particular interest in the history of that area, welcomed the archive as a special collection of the Honnold Library at Claremont University.

Our lifestyle is rather restrained and modest. Ruth and I have preferred to allocate funds to accomplish certain long-term objectives. We have set up six endowment funds at Reed College. The Greenock Fund, in memory my parents, John Alexander Simpson and Janet Christie Brand Simpson, both from Greenock, Scotland, and in recognition of the educational excellence of Reed College, supports a student intern program for preparing studies relevant to guiding the educational policies of the college. Income from the Mathematics Outreach Fund (named in memory of Frank Loxley Griffin, professor and first head of the mathematics department) is used to increase awareness of the importance of early preparation in mathematics for a broad array of academic and professional fields. One or two-day seminars are held each year for high school students. The Pacific and Eastern Fund is to allay and assist in the expenses of housing, care and periodic exhibit of materials instructive of the art and artifacts of Pacific and Eastern civilizations. The fourth, the Reed Library Fund (named in honor of William Blair Stewart, professor of statistics), is to provide an addition to what would otherwise be available to the library for materials in the areas of mathematics, social and behavioral sciences, and philosophy. The fifth endowment (named in honor of Dexter Merriam Keezer, a former president of the college) provides additional support to advance the professional development of members of the Reed faculty. The income from the sixth endowment is to be used at the discretion of the Economics faculty in such manner as will best contribute to the quality of Reed's program in economics, with particular attention to the joint major in economics and mathematics. These endowments provide for the continuance of efforts along lines with which I have long been concerned. The hope, particularly with respect to student interns on educational policy and the mathematics outreach program, is that these programs will be made known to other institutions and serve as prototypes for such undertakings at other colleges and universities.

Two further endowments have been established. Income from an endowment provided the Department of Economics and Statistics at California State University, Los Angeles, is to be used periodically for a meritorious achievement award when there is a student majoring in the department who eminently qualifies by high scholastic performance and a demonstrated interest in service to society. Also, an endowment has been provided the Claremont University Center and Graduate School which will support joint endeavors by the Economics Program of the Center for Politics and Economics and the Center for Educational Studies in the area of the economics of higher education.

19.1

Heading Off a Crisis: A Hard Look at Campus Academic-Fiscal Planning

[Adapted from an address to the California Conference
of the American Association of University Professors,
November 6, 1993.]

While many faculty members and administrators consider fiscal crises to be budget problems, in large part they are planning problems. The difficulty is that while planning may greatly affect academic matters, there is great inertia on the part of the faculty to becoming involved sufficiently early in the process. A faculty that is simply reactive has the disadvantage of having to rely largely on its organizational clout in expressing opposition.

Positions taken by the faculty must be *credible*. To be so, faculty positions must reflect more than self-interest. They should take account of the goals of the institution and the effects of proposals on students, staff, and the general public, as well as on faculty.

Positions taken by the faculty should also be *persuasive*. It is not unreasonable to expect that an intellectual community would justify its recommendations through well-argued presentation. When academic senates adopt resolutions on the basis of a series of whereas's, there should be sound scholarship behind the latter, as well as a breadth of perspective that transcends the interests of particular academic departments and schools and serves the principal goals of the institution. There should not be blanket opposition to the use of judgment in evaluating selective adjustments (Simpson, 1993b).

Across-the-board reductions are changes just waiting to be reversed, and do not offer long-term relief.

Credibility and persuasiveness can go a long way toward securing acceptance of faculty views.

There are many courses of action that may be advocated, depending in part on how early the problem is confronted that resources for higher education are becoming increasingly scarce (Simpson, 1991, 1993c). Here I emphasize what advance preparation is needed to increase faculty effectiveness in heading off the worst consequences of resources becoming more scarce. I focus on steps to improve decisions rather than on the substantive content of those decisions. The intent of these proposals for change is to revitalize the role of values and objectives so that they provide the predominant influence in planning and in adjustments guided by such planning.

First. Consider the use of a *governance audit*, periodically at intervals of several years, drawing upon an off-campus academic consultant agreed to jointly by the administration and by the academic senate. The consultant would be charged with identifying possible improvements in academic governance structures and procedures (Simpson, 1983a, 1985).

Second. Of key importance is the development of a *vision statement*, which Stefan Bloomfield (1993c) describes as ''a forward look which fleshes out the abstract institutional mission by describing what the institution and its academic community should be like at some future date when the goals of the institution are more fully realized . . . By anchoring its aspirations in the institution's current status and providing for likely developments in the external environment, the vision statement can describe a preferred and attainable end state.'' The vision statement ''articulates a set of goals in the form of institutional characteristics to be pursued.''

The third proposal is for an *optimization review* at intervals of several years (Simpson, 1985). Like the governance audit, this would use an outside consultant for fresh insights. The optimization review would consider both the optimality of the objectives set forth in the vision statement and the most productive approaches toward realizing those goals. It would seek to facilitate an institution's development of its own capacity for self-assessment. Worthwhile even in the best of times, this becomes even more important in times of reduced budgets. Total Quality Management efforts can draw on the insights of an optimization review.

The fourth proposal is for a campus-based *consultant for academic-fiscal planning*. Campus expertise would be used in the development of analytic models to study policy alternatives—models that integrate academic and fiscal considerations. A professionally qualified faculty member would be designated as a consultant for academic-fiscal planning, with joint approval by the campus administration and the academic senate, and would report to both. The appointment would be made in consultation with the faculty collective bargaining agent, where one exists. This faculty member would assist in clarifying the implications of policy alternatives and make his or her recommendations available to all concerned.

Fifth. The staffing of the campus institutional research office should be reviewed and adjusted if necessary so that it may contribute in a vital role. Staffing should include *capability for both experimental studies and analytic studies*, not just for empirical data collection and reports. Mathematical models can take account of the interrelationships of the most significant factors underlying the phenomena to be studied, under simplifying assumptions as to outside influences. With that as a point of departure, additional influences for which formal relationships are as yet sketchy can be taken into consideration in non-mathematical form. The choice between formal analytical procedures and informally working with miscellaneous data from particular cases should reflect what the respective approaches can offer; it should not result from the needed capability not being represented within the institutional research office. The office should be available for inquiries by faculty governance bodies as well as by the administration.

Sixth. The *student viewpoint* should be represented in arriving at institutional policy through having student interns work on studies related to the issues involved, and by having student representatives in the academic senate and on committees concerned with the allocation of resources.

Seventh. In addition to the foregoing, and of paramount importance, insight should be gained from *broad-based faculty involvement* that is built into the budget process before crises arise. Institutions without faculty participation in academic governance pay a price in various dimensions, including possible detrimental effects on the quality of programs that can be offered, the quality of faculty to which students at the institution have access, and the quality of students attracted.

Advance provision should be made for faculty participation through regularly established faculty advisory committees in the area of academic-fiscal planning. It is the essence of planning that it anticipate problems. Thus planning for the most likely course of events is not enough; there should also be thought as to how to adjust to developments that may occur with respect to the inputs that are obtainable or the outputs required. The faculty advisory committee should monitor that the needed groundwork is being undertaken by the institutional research office, with input from the consultant on academic-fiscal planning.

With respect to problems at hand, faculty should probe into and seek clarification of administrative actions, offer constructive criticism, encourage full and open discussion (including discussion with collective bargaining representatives where applicable), and make it useful in the future for the administration to look to faculty for recommendations as to policy before rather than after implementation. Note that both participation by faculty and openness of information to those who would be affected are recommended. The advantages and disadvantages that attend various sequences and degrees of openness have been discussed by Falk and Miller (1993).

In summary, the reality is that in higher education, as elsewhere, there will never be enough resources for all that could or should be attempted, and reasonably satisfactory outcomes will come about only if faculty get involved early and contribute to finding solutions, rather than wait for others to do this for them.

There are, however, two interrelated human shortcomings from which those in the academic profession are not immune. While these are understandable, they work against participation being sufficient and against those who do participate doing so objectively. One of these was mentioned earlier—inertia in getting involved. An institution can motivate faculty to some extent by including as a consideration in granting salary increases that individuals demonstrate that they contribute to a sense of community within the university and do not simply draw upon its benefits. This could be considered one aspect of special merit, which, along with a career increment and cost-of-living adjustment, could be the basis for salary advancement (Simpson, 1981). On the one hand, an admonition by Myles Brand (1993) should be kept in mind: "Efforts to alter the present reward system should proceed at a pace that both encourages and realistically permits faculty to reshape their career patterns." On the other hand, the reality is that there is much room for improvement. " 'Service'. . . is typically treated like the country cousin. The status and definitional issues of service are as muddled as ever" (Edgerton, 1993, p. 16).

Drawing forth participation by restructuring of rewards, while worth incorporating into personnel procedures, nevertheless does not in itself get at the fundamental nature of the problem—the tendency to view matters too narrowly, which is the second of the human shortcomings to which I referred. What must be worked toward is a breadth of view that encompasses the effects of actions, or inaction, upon others. What is taken into account depends on the existing boundary of our concern, or put another way, the horizon within which we acknowledge to ourselves a sense of responsibility. Various social institutions, including the market, can be appraised for how they function as integrative devices for bringing within the calculation of an individual the ramifications of a possible action (see section in Annex 10.2). Religion, morality and ethics all address the problem. As to academic citizenship and the ethics of knowledge, see the article by Clark Kerr (1994). Also see the chapter on "The Elusive Academy" in Simpson (1991) for considerations that an institution should address that have broad applicability to developing a sense of community and perspective. We focus here, however, on certain specific proposals related to increasing the breadth of concern in budgeting.

Stated in terms relevant to budgetary planning for a college or university, faculty and admininstrators need to keep in mind that among the costs of any proposed course of action are the benefits that are forgone in those programs from which resources are withdrawn, whether those resources are from inside or outside the institution. These are referred to as *tradeoffs*. This requires attention not only to the outputs possible if one's own program has the needed inputs, but attention also to the outputs lost by programs that would otherwise have been funded. Among the several approaches that tend to increase awareness of relevant tradeoffs are the following, which could be used in combination:

- Awareness of tradeoffs is greater when campus budgeting is not in terms of narrowly compartmentalized units. Retaining breadth of overview in administration is furthered when there is restraint in the layering of positions within the administrative structure.

- Faculty would seek to be more active in budget discussions were budget amounts assigned in terms of the institutional goals being served, as in a program budget. While it was difficult in the 1960's to sell the idea of a strict program budget for campuses, the ideas behind such an approach could well guide budget decisions.
- Goal-oriented learning, a related idea, would be certain to increase faculty awareness of tradeoffs and thus increase their interest in participating in the budgeting process (Simpson, 1993a, c, and Chapter 18 herein). It would encourage more interdisciplinary approaches to accomplishing objectives with respect to learning.
- The method used for budgeting total instructional staff positions should provide the opportunity and the incentive to exercise discretion as to the best operational use of the resources allocated to an organizational unit, while maintaining responsible control over the level of faculty staffing authorized. One such method, which I refer to as the constrained ratio approach, is set forth in Simpson (1975). The method has application at system, campus, school and department levels.
- Some resources should be set aside at each decision level to reflect factors other than enrollment growth, such as program goals set through system-wide and campus-level institutional academic planning. This would facilitate taking advantage of special opportunities to improve the quality and not simply the quantity of education available to students. Faculty would wish to participate in considering the tradeoffs involved in competing for such a margin of resources.

The most serious consequences of there being a scarcity of resources in higher education could be mitigated were there more attention to advance planning of an academic-fiscal nature, and were there participation by the faculty therein in an objective manner. While adoption of a combination of the proposals which I have set forth would contribute to better outcomes, the advantages to be gained will depend in part upon the extent to which there is an increase in the breadth of view of those making decisions.

Such fundamental change will require perceptive and skilled leadership within the academy generally, and among those who head institutions of higher education, particularly those that can serve as examples. It is no easy assignment for a principal administrator to both support an environment in which faculty members can focus their attention in the area of their expertise and yet inspire the same individuals to take into account considerations broader than their own academic disciplines. Administrators need to support and encourage both a sense of community within their college or university and a constructive interest and sense of responsibility for the effects of its decisions upon the larger society of which the institution is a part.

19.2

Areas of Concern in Educational Change

The stimulus for change in education reflects, among various factors, changes in the demands placed upon education by a more diverse student body and by an increasingly complicated society, the increased availability of technological approaches to facilitate learning, and budgetary constraints.

Higher education may provide constructive guidance: (a) by giving thought as to what education should seek to achieve, (b) by research as to cost-effective combinations of learning techniques, (c) by considering alternative ways to deal with financial constraints, (d) by increasing the public's awareness of the extent of investment in education that would be warranted, and (e) by encouraging individuals to take leadership roles in identifying options and selecting and implementing the optimum alternatives.

In what follows, one or more considerations that warrant further inquiry is identified for each of these areas of concern.

To the extent that preparatory school levels are included within the scope of such efforts, higher education makes an investment in improving the quality of those who will be inputs into higher education in the future—both the students who enter and the faculty from whom they can learn. An eloquent plea for higher education extending a helping hand to K through 12 education has been made by Robert Wood (1993). See also Simpson (1993c, p. 24 f.).

What education should strive to achieve

That the college experience may not in itself, apart from the student's peer group—particularly the socioeconomic status of fellow students—have much effect upon student attitudes (Pascarella and Terenzini, 1991; Lewis, 1992; Astin, 1993; Gamson 1993) might at first thought dampen the enthusiasm of those advocating that students should undertake the investment of effort. Yet education should not aim at making such changes in students (should not, in short, indoctrinate), but rather should aim at developing the personal capacities that could lead to changes, provided such capacities are exercised. As Weingartner expressed the latter reservation in ''Between Cup and Lip'' (1994): the development of proficiencies is an educational goal, but change could not be expected under that arrangement unless a propensity is developed for students to use such skills.

The identification of the goals to be served by education needs review, as well as the relative weight to be given advances toward the various goals. Currently education appears to be most concerned with transmitting information and with training. Significantly less attention—sometimes none at all—is directed toward other objectives: the development of an individual's own set of personal values, alongside sensitivity to differences in the value systems of different cultures; the cultivation of an individual's capacity to critically evaluate information; the encouragement of inductive reasoning and creativity; and the provision of opportunities to students for responsible participation and for demonstrating initiative. Particularly important is inspiring an individual to develop a personal philosophy to guide his or her subsequent life, hopefully within an expanded boundary of concern.

Whatever the reasons, the quality of education currently is judged far too narrowly. The emphasis upon transmitting information and upon training is understandable since efficiency, which relies upon a ratio of measurable output to measurable cost, is most readily demonstrated in such efforts. However, a broader and more balanced view should be adopted as to what education should aim to achieve at each level.

For that to be implemented, progress is needed in how to achieve the other goals mentioned, and how to assess such progress as is obtained.

Cost-effective approaches

Cost-effectiveness rather than efficiency should be considered. Cost-effectiveness looks not to the output but to the benefits produced by an output relative to benefits foregone by the withdrawal of needed resources from other uses. What is relevant, of course, are the incremental effects beyond the different starting positions of different students. Unfortunately, the combination of techniques that is most cost-effective may require an initial investment, or even recurrent operating cost, which makes immediate introduction of the change infeasible within current budget constraints.

Goal-oriented learning: One type of far-reaching change that could prove to be cost-effective in achieving the goals of education is what I have termed "goal-oriented learning." Teaching staff could be organized administratively on an academic field basis much as at present, but the change would be that a portion of the curriculum up through the first two years of college would be taught using teams focusing not on a particular academic field but upon facilitating student learning that moves the individual toward achieving one or more of the specific goals mentioned earlier. Various combinations of academic disciplines could be substituted for each other in seeking to accomplish a given goal. This concept has been discussed briefly in Simpson (1991, pp. 134 ff., 140 f., 1993a and 1993c).

What in effect is support for that proposal can be found in an article by Jeffrey Alexander (1993) on the irrationality of organizing undergraduate education on a disciplinary basis, rather than to serve the learning needs of students. Goal-oriented learning, while having something in common with Holley Ulbrich's (1992) "client-centered academics," differs in that the learning goals, while developed with student needs in mind, remain guided by the thought and experience of educators as to how to provide for depth, breadth, and flexibility.

The article by Weingartner (1994) also serves to provide support for goal-oriented learning since it stresses the need for educators to think first as to learning goals rather than as to the subject matter to be covered.

Strengthening the human factor: Alongside the advances available in educational technology and increased reliance on student-machine relationships, it is essential that direct student-staff interaction and student-to-student interaction be preserved and even expanded for contributions not otherwise as effectively obtained—among them being progress toward goals mentioned above as ones that are not sufficiently identified or emphasized.

Cost-effective combinations of learning techniques should be designed that make faculty time available for such personal interaction with students, with the aim being not to arrive at an average level of achievement but rather the full realization of the potential of the individual. With that, it becomes increasingly important that the preparation of teachers and academic administrators and their subsequent professional development take account of the range of the goals to be served.

Further, to whatever extent a student is a passive recipient of teaching, or an operator relating to a teaching machine, this needs to be supplemented by the student learning through relationships with others in the context of the school environment or under the school's auspices. Many of such opportunities for participation and for the development of initiative are lost when student out-of-class activities are the first to be trimmed in budget cutbacks. Consideration should be given to the initiation or expanded use on a selective basis of students as peer tutors and mentors. Also, in the case of higher education, student interns could be appointed to assist in the development of educational policy options.

Preserving and extending the human factor would be furthered at the preparatory school levels were progress made along the following lines: (a) decentralization of the K through 12 governance structure into community clusters with broader participation in school decisions by the teaching staff, and in some decisions by community leaders and parents; (b) parental commitment to a home context in which there is interest in student performance in academic performance in academic courses that are challenging, and provision for hours of quiet study on a daily basis; (c) increased budgetary provision for the advisee role of teachers and for career and college counselors; and (d) drawing upon individuals beyond the school staff for insights and inspiration, as through participating in college outreach programs for students in preparatory schools.

Alternative ways to deal with financial constraints

Faculty role in protecting quality: When there are programs that need to be downsized due to budgetary stringency, there is considerable temptation to use an across-the-board rollback in programs and to reduce staff on the basis of inverse seniority. I wish that I could say that support for such a position is the exception, but it is altogether too common. I have argued against it in *Academe* (1993b), and the arguments need not be repeated here. Separately I have advocated that merit be considered—not only in downward adjustments but also in salary structure generally (1981)—not as a continuum of minutely distinguished gradations of merit, but as special merit, which should be significant and outstanding and hence less a source of contention. It is important to keep in mind that not only should faculty concerns be addressed, but also the concerns of those whom the faculty have been appointed to serve, namely the students and the public.

Student role in financing higher education: It is recommended that in providing financial assistance, colleges and universities change from giving outright grants to a new type of income-contingent loans. The practice of raising tuition to finance the current program of grants could be phased out as funds flow back from repayments by former students under this new policy for financial aid.

What is proposed goes beyond the conventional income-contingent proposal by incorporating the provision that repayments not extend beyond a preset number of years, corresponding for instance to the time the individual's own children would be entering college, after which any balance would be converted into an ex post facto grant. The approach has two definite advantages: It would reduce the level of tuition from what it would be otherwise and thus avoid discouraging prospective entrants who have limited resources but do not qualify for an outright grant. It would mean, furthermore, that those students who benefit most in terms of income would provide a larger repayment of the investment made by society in their education. For further discussion of this approach see Simpson and Mendelson (1986) and Simpson (1987, 1991, 1993a, and 1993c).

Public awareness of the investment in human resources that is warranted

The difficulties faced in arranging the financing of education are such that individuals tend to be resigned to aiming at financing the educational system much as it is, with provision for only such improvements as are most pressing. There is relatively little awareness among educators, and even less within the general public, as to the extent of resources that would be required to fully implement such educational policy goals as can be shown to be justifiable investment in human resources. Earlier (Simpson, 1993c, pp. 85-86) I identified as a challenge for the future that leaders should encourage the development of measures of the adequacy of available resources relative to full implementation of public policy objectives that have been adopted for postsecondary education. The development of such measures calls for both analytical ability and familiarity with statistical sources, and it should challenge institutional researchers to contribute their best efforts. The vision of what higher education can contribute must be communicated to the public, so that citizens appreciate its potential and so that it receives sufficient support.

Leadership out of an academic status quo

In Simpson (1991, p. 201) I wrote: "Of the troubles that may befall a college or university, perhaps the most unnoticed at the time, yet pervasive and unfortunate, is the drift into pro forma performance in instruction and administration. Established ways are adhered to and carried through so as to require the least effort. Awkward questions about the meaningfulness of activities are avoided. Questioning as to what objectives should be served, and to what end products and benefits are sought, becomes an assignment to an articulate colleague when reaccreditation comes around.

"Partly as cause, partly as effect, administrators with a housekeeping rather than a leadership outlook tend to hold office. With many administrative levels between faculty members and those making the critical decisions on the allocation of resources, administrators are both circumscribed in the exercise of initiative and find their security through becoming embedded in the administrative structure. Administrative positions gradually come to attract those who do not see this to be an unfortunate development."

Faculty too often are inert with respect to changes in policy until a particular action impinges directly and adversely on their personal wellbeing. As I have expressed it earlier (Annex 19.1), while many faculty members and administrators consider fiscal crises to be budget problems, more basically they are planning problems. In long-term planning, it would make sense to be able to consider the insights to be gained from external evaluation, such as through what I term an optimization review (1985), and a governance audit (1985, 1991). Within an institution, the following are important: a vison statement, a campus-based consultant for academic-fiscal planning to analyze and explicate available options, student interns to participate therein, an institutional research staff equipped for both empirical and theoretical work, and participating faculty structures. These are discussed in Annex 19.1.

The further ingredient, and this is essential, is a dynamic

insightful principal administrator who can envisage both the problems and the opportunities that may be encountered by the institution, and who can transmit enthusiasm for accomplishing change. What is to be hoped is that the administrator's boundary of concern, in interpreting the costs and benefits incident thereto, is broad as to the individuals encompassed and broad as to the time that is spanned.

20

Looking Back and Looking Forward

Looking back, I have but few regrets. There are events that I wish had never occurred, such as the war, but that is a different matter, since regret is relevant only if I wish I had acted other than I did.

One regret is that after the war I undertook graduate studies in an economics department in which the ascendant socioeconomic views were so at odds with my own. I mentioned earlier how that came about. I also regret having taken so many years to complete my doctorate. I should have found time somehow alongside the responsibilities I undertook. Further, I should have been more open to moving to other universities which could have been the base for even greater challenges. In fact, my main regret is that I have not done as much as I could have with my life, for it is that, more than what I did accomplish, which affects my satisfaction with life.

I do have some reflections to pass along to others. They concern disadvantages which one must be prepared to live with were one to follow a personal philosophy such as I have set forth. They apply whether one's focus is upon education, health, environment, conflict resolution, civil rights, poverty, or other area.

Undertakings that you believe worthwhile but which are not likely to be undertaken by others are by their nature ones for which the existing incentives are not viewed by others as sufficiently rewarding. You have to rely in part on your sense of personal satisfaction. [When asked by the editors of *Who's Who in America* to capsulize my personal philosophy, I expressed this as follows: "To serve as a catalyst in critical areas where I have the ability and others have not found incentive."]

The area in which I have focused my research will serve as an example. I have been concerned with the organization and economics of higher education. Considerable work has been done by the economics profession in studying the benefit side of education, but relatively little on the analysis of cost. I chose, accordingly, to give particular attention to the latter, anticipating that the need would subsequently be recognized. In *Cost Containment for Higher Education* I have been able to provide what was not otherwise available. What had been available was either a description of cost or a list of the ways to cut cost in a crisis, at the same time cutting the extent and quality of service. My main focus has been upon policies which if pursued over the long term could reduce cost from what it would be otherwise, but without impairment of the extent or quality of the learning experience provided, and with concern also for the future of the academic profession and society.

There is a further hazard in pursuing a philosophy of life such as I have sketched. I have always sought to be as objective as possible on issues, whether controversial or not. However, I have found that there are those in academe who are no more or less objective than individuals in general when matters affect them personally. As I have commented before, some of the fundamental cornerstones of academic governance which are recognized as a standard for fair practice in higher education do not have popular appeal, such as fully effective use of the probationary period for appraisals of performance, or non-seniority considerations in layoff policy such as the implications for the academic program and affirmative action. There will be individuals, unhappy with the personal effect of a principled decision, who will remember only their disagreement, even though on many prior occasions one may have upheld principles in which they believed.

I do not recommend that individuals "pull their punches" when disapproval is in the offing, holding fire until a sought-for position is secured. That time never comes. At each step, ambition moves a step further ahead, and rationalization to avoid disfavor will again lead to being less than forthright.

Gratification from having supported the implementation of the options one regards as appropriate often has to be obtained by drawing on one's own inner resources, not from others.

Given these disadvantages of a personal philosophy of the type described in this book, how can they be reconciled with the recommendation that others should consider adopting such a philosophy as their own? I would say that it is not enough to be concerned about one's fellow man, one must also be concerned about one's self. There must be the development of competence and enthusiasm in directions that are productive of immediate and continuing satisfaction, as well as competency and enthusiasm in directions productive of the long-term influences on behalf of others for which there may be a shortfall in recognition and gratification. In the context of companionship that is supportive of one's aims, and some attention to immediate personal satisfactions, one's principal concern with the long term and with bringing about results for others can be sustained.

It is a presumption of those who have grown old that they can offer advice to others. Clearly I have not been able to resist the former or the latter. It is hoped that the reflections in this book may assist college and university students, as well as faculty, administrators and staff, in giving direction to their personal efforts. It should be useful in the advisement of prospective members of the profession and useful to others also. Many of the chapters, and the writings excerpted or referred to, have implications for improving the effectiveness of a college or university, or the conduct of government programs—domestic and foreign.

Looking forward as a concerned academic, I would hope that the postsecondary experience available to students in the years ahead would encourage their awareness that neither one's ultimate objectives in life nor all of one's satisfactions need be mediated through first earning income and then purchasing satisfaction through the market place. In particular, learning situations could be supplemented by opportunities for students to volunteer and accept responsibilities, including leadership, in relatively unstructured social situations, learning thereby the personal satisfaction to be gained through participating in the attainment of the goals of others. An understanding of and bonding with others is required if one is to experience the fullness of being an individual.

When one successively broadens his or her boundary of concern to include others, resource limitations soon dictate that the type of assistance that is feasible for the long term is that which enables individuals to be effective acting by themselves and acting together through formal or informal association. An important dimension of such empowerment is to increase the capacity of individuals for intelligent choice.

As to extending the boundary of concern interculturally, the proposal I made in India, described within Annex 9.1, for motivating opinion leaders to reinterpret cultural obstacles, would be a long-term non-directive approach.

The view reached by this concerned academic, as expressed in the reflections and writings in this book, is that the most basic type of contribution that one can make is to develop and exercise one's own ability to empower others to their fullest potential, with due regard to effects on their personal composure and their relationships with the social context.

Selected References

Alexander, Jeffrey, 1993. "The Irrational Disciplinarity of Undergraduate Education," *Chronicle of Higher Education* (December 1): B3.

American Association of University Professors. 1990. *Policy Documents and Reports*. Washington, D.C.: AAUP.

American Economic Association Committee on Political Discrimination. 1981. "Report of the Committee on Political Discrimination," *American Economic Review* 71 (December): 1113-15.

Astin, Alexander W. 1993. *What Matters in College? Four Critical Years Revisited*. San Francisco: Jossey-Bass.

Becker, William E. and Darrell R. Lewis, eds. 1992 *The Economics of American Higher Education*. Boston: Kluwer Academic Publishers Group.

Bloomfield, Stefan D. 1993. "Facilitating Decisions Under Scacity." Chapter 5 in William B. Simpson (ed.), *Managing with Scarce Resources*, New Directions in Institutional Research, No. 79. San Francisco: Jossey-Bass.

Brand, Myles. 1993. "The Challenge to Change: Reforming Higher Education," *Educational Record* 74 (Fall): 6-13.

Burd, Stephen. 1992. "Humanities Chief Assails Politicization of Classrooms," *Chronicle of Higher Education* 39 (September 30): A21-22.

Chaffee, E.E. and Sherr, L. A. 1992. *Quality: Transforming Postsecondary Education*. ASHE-ERIC Higher Education Reports, No. 3. Washington, D.C.: George Washington University.

Committee for Education Funding. 1991. *Education Budget Alert for Fiscal Year 1992: A Compilation of Federal Education Programs*, ed. Alfred Sumberg. Washington, D.C.: Committee for Education Funding.

Cowles Commission for Research in Economics. 1952. *Economic Theory and Measurement: A Twenty-Year Research Report, 1932-1952*. Chicago: Cowles Commission.

______. 1951. *Rational Decision-Making and Economic Behavior, 19th Annual Report, 1950-1951*. Chicago: Cowles Commission.

Crane, Stephen. 1989. *War Is Kind*. New York: Frederick A. Stokes Co.

Diamond, Signund. 1992. *Compromised Campus: The Collabora-*

*tion of Universities with the Intelligence Community, 1945-
1955*. New York: Oxford University Press.

Divisia, F. 1953. "La Societe D'Econometric A Atteint Sa Majorite,"
Econometrica 21 (January): 1-30.

Douglas, Paul H. 1971. *In the Fullness of Time: The Memoirs of
Paul H. Douglas*. New York: Harcourt Brace Jovanovich.

Edgerton, Russell. 1993. "The Re-Examination of Faculty Priorities," *Change*, 25 (July-August): 10-16, 20-23, 25.

Evening Herald. November 3, 1953. Editorial, "We look at America."
Dublin, Ireland.

Falk, David and Gerald Ray Miller. 1993. "How Do You Cut $45
Million from your Institution's Budget? Use Processes and
Ask Your Faculty." *Educational Record* 74 (Fall): 32-38.

Finn, Chester E., Jr. 1991. *We Must Take Charge: Our Schools and
Our Future*. New York: The Free Press.

Gamson, Zelda F. 1993. "The College Experience: New Data on How
and Why Students Change," *Change 25* (May-June): 64-68

Gappa, Judith M. 1993. "Participants in Decisions about Scarce
Resources," in William B. Simpson, ed., *Managing with
Scarce Resources*, New Directions in Institutional Research,
No. 79. San Francisco: Jossey-Bass.

Hausman, Daniel M. And Michael S. McPherson. 1993. "Taking
Ethics Seriously: Economics and Contemporary Moral
Philosophy," *Journal of Economic Literature* 31 (June):
671-731

Heckman, James J. 1992. "Haavelmo and the Birth o f Modern
Econometrics: A Review of 'The History of Econometric
Ideas' by Mary Morgan," *Journal of Economic Literature*
30 (June): 876-86.

Hildreth, Clifford. 1986. *The Cowles Commission in Chicago, 1939-
1955*. New York: Springer-Verlag.

Kerr, Clark. 1994. "Knowledge about Ethics and the New Academic
Culture," *Change* 26 (January-February): 8-15.

Lewis, Lionel S. 1992. Book Review of E. T. Pascarella and P. T.
Terenzini, *How College Affects Students*, *Academe* 78 (July-
August): 44, 46-47.

Lynton, Ernest A. and Sandra E. Elman. 1986. *New Priorities for
the University*. San Francisco: Jossey-Bass.

Malinvaud, Edmond. 1972. "The Scientific Papers of Tjalling C.
Koopmans: A Review Article," *Journal of Economic*

Selected References

Literature 10 (September): 798-802.

Means, Barbara and Carol Chelemer and Michael S. Knapp. 1991. Teaching *Advanced Skills to At-Risk Students: Views from Research and Practice*. San Francisco: Jossey-Bass.

Meyers, Chet. 1986. *Teaching Students to Think Critically: A Guide for Faculty in All Disciplines*. San Francisco: Jossey- Bass.

Morris, William C. and Geraldine MacDonald. 1993. "Evaluating the Increased Use of Technology in Instruction and Administration," in William B. Simpson, ed., *Managing with Scarce Resources*, New Directions in Institutional Research, No. 79. San Francisco: Jossey-Bass.

Park, Rosemary. 1993. "In Short," *Change* 25 (January- February): 53.

Pascarella, Ernest T. and Patrick T. Terenzini. *1991. How College Affects Students: Findings and Insights from Twenty Years of Research*. San Francisco: Jossey-Bass.

Peairs, Richard H. 1976. "Some Observations on Financial Exigency and the Termination of Faculty Appointments," February 18. San Francisco: Western Regional Office, American Association of University Professors.

Reder, Melvin W. 1982. "Chicago Economics: Permanence and Change," *Journal of Economic Literature* 20 (March): 1-38.

Reinsmith, William A. 1992. *Archetypal Forms in Teaching: A Continuum*. New York: Greenwood Press.

Sherr, Lawrence A. and Deborah J. Teeter, eds. 1991. *Total Quality Management in Higher Education*, New Directions in Institutional Research, No. 71. San Francisco: Jossey-Bass.

Simpson, William B. [A more complete bibliography of the author for 1966-1989 is included in *Cost Containment for Higher Education* (1991), pp. 239-42].

______ . 1974. *Options in Steady-State Staffing*. Office of Vice President for Academic Affairs, California State University, Los Angeles (in print).

______ . 1975 "Constrained Ratio Approach to Allocating Instructional Resources," *Socio-Economic Planning Sciences* 9 (December): 285-92.

______ . 1981. "Faculty Salary Structure for a College or University," *Journal of Higher Education* 52 (May-June): 219-36.

______ . 1983a. "Faculty Responsibility in Governance." Address to annual meeting, California Conference, American Association of University Professors, San Francisco, April 16.

———. 1983b. Opening presentation at session on "The Impact of Copyright in Scholarly Communication." Annual meeting of American Library Association, Los Angeles, June 27.

———. 1985. "Revitalizing the Role of Values and Objectives in Institutions of Higher Education: Difficulties Encountered and the Possible Contribution of External Evaluation," *Higher Education* 14: 535-51.

———. 1987. "Income Contingent Student Loans: Context, Potential and Limits," *Higher Education* 16: 699-721.

———. 1988. "Income-Contingent Plan for Loans is Workable." Letter to the Editor, *Chronicle of Higher Education* 35 (November 23): B4.

———. 1989. *Review of Radical Reform or Incremental Change? Academe* 75 (November-December): 56.

———. 1991. *Cost Containment for Higher Education: Strategies for Public Policy and Institutional Administration.* New York and London: Praeger Publishers.

———. 1992 "Retrenchment in California," *AAUP Footnotes* 13 (Fall).

———. 1993a. "Higher Education's Role in a New Beginning," *Academe* 79 (January-February): 17-21.

———. 1993b. "Budget Choices Must Consider Merit," Letter to the Editor, *Academe* 79 (September-October): 4.

———. 1993c. (ed.) *Managing with Scarce Resources*, New Directions for Institutional Research, No. 79. San Francisco: Jossey-Bass.

———. 1994. Review of *The Economics of American Higher Education*, William E. Becker and Darrell R. Lewis, eds., *Journal of Higher Education* 65 (January-February): 116-18.

———. 1995. *Special Agent in the Pacific. WW II: Counter-Intelligence—Military, Political and Economic.* New York: Rivecross.

———, John G. Gurley and Richard J. Zeckhauser. 1980. *Inquiry Panel Report to the American Economic Association Committee on Political Discrimination.* Nashville, Tenn.: Secretary of the American Economic Association, August 29.

———, and Michael D. Kudlick. 1982. *The Role of Faculty in*

Selected References

Financial Decisions at Private Institutions. Report of a Survey to the California Conference, American Association of University Professors.

______, and Morris Mendelson. 1983. *Freedom of Choice in Higher Education.* Report of Subcommittee on Federal Role in Higher Education, Committee on Governmental Relations, American Association of University Professors, Washington, D.C.

______, ______. 1985. *Special Interest and the Public Interest.* Report of Subcommittee on Tax Policy, Committee on Governmental Relations, American Association of University Professors, Washington, D.C.

______, ______. 1986. "Student Loans: A Moderate Proposal," *Academe* 72 (November-December): 19-21.

Stutz, Joseph J. 1994. Review of *Cost Containment for Higher Education: Strategies for Public Policy and Institutional Administration,* by William Brand Simpson, *Academe* 79 (May-June): 85-86.

Tintner, Gerhard. 1953. "The Definition of Econometrics," *Econometrica* 21 (January): 31-40.

______. 1954. "The Teaching of Econometrics," *Econometrica* 22 (January): 77-100.

Ulbrich, Holley H. 1992. "Can We Make a Place for Client- Centered Academics?", *Academe* 78 (May-June): 15-16.

Vining, Rutledge. 1949. "Methodological Issues in Quantitative Economics," "A Reply" by Tjalling C. Koopmans, and "A Rejoinder" by Rutledge Vining, *Review of Economics and Statistics* 31 (May): 77-94.

Waggaman, John. 1991. *Strategies and Consequences: Managing the Costs in Higher Education.* ASHE-ERIC Higher Education Report No. 8. Washington, D.C.: The George Washington University.

______. 1994. Review of *Cost Containment for Higher Education: Strategies for Public Policy and Institutional Administration,* by William Brand Simpson, *Journal of Higher Education* 65 (July- August): 519-21.

Warch, Richard. 1990. "Intellectual Community and Liberal Arts Colleges," *Papers.* Philadelphia, Pa.: Pew Higher Education Research Program, University of Pennsylvania.

Weingartner, Rudolph H. 1994. "Between Cup and Lip: Reconceptualizing Education as Students Learning,"

Educational Record 75 (Winter): 13-19.

Winter, David G., David C. McClelland, and Abigail J. Stewart. 1981. *A New Case for the Liberal Arts*. San Francisco: Jossey-Bass.

Wood, Robert. 1993. ''Looking for Help Long Overdue: Where has Higher Education Been?'', *Educational Record* 74 (Summer) 15- 20.

Zemsky, Robert. 1990. ''Curriculum and Cost: Notes on the Utilization of Teaching Resources.'' *Paper*. Philadelphia, Pa.: Pew Higher Education Research Program, University of Pennsylvania.

INDEX

2-3, 384; openness of information, 386; opportunity cost, 2, 189-214, 386-88, 392-93; optimization review, 290, 384, 396; payout period, 189; persuasiveness, 383-84; planning-programming-budgeting, 253-55, 257, 259-63, 367, 388; practical role of theory in, 103; problem, nature of a, 2; programming a set of activities, 202-209; pro rata or selective, 256-67, 301-302, 383-84; role of philosophical conceptions, 125-26, 127, 132-33; strategy of inquiry, 195-96; thoughtful processes denigrated, 301, 383; tradeoffs, 387-88; uncertainty, 51; understanding of, used in control, 145; values to apply, 8, 44-45, 99, 103, 123-24, 144, 237-38, 343-44, 347-48, 352

E

Econometric Society, 8, 49, 50, 54, 63, 65, 68, 73-74, 81-89, 90-92, 104, 172

Econometrica, 5, 49, 63, 73-81, 90-92, 104, 159, 172

Econometrics, 8, 39, 41-42, 49, 56, 61-62, 86, 88, 93-97, 104, 105

Economics: 8, 13, 26-27, 33-39, 66, 197, 261; choice, as theory of, 41, 66, 105-106, 195, 235; cost containment, 224-31, 301-302, 326, 361, 364, 368, 372, 375-76, 400; cost effectiveness vs. efficiency, 392-93; externalities, cost and benefit, 100-101, 196-98, 343-44, 349-50; general education, as, 235-39; general literacy, 218-19, 229, 235-39; goals as given, 192, 238; growth, balanced vs. unbalanced, 141, 192; growth, stimulating economic, alternative policies, 326-27; macro-economic models, 38-39, 105-106, 194; methodological issues, 73, 93-97;

opportunity cost concept, 189-214, 387-88, 393, production function, Douglas-Cobb, *See also*: Cowles Commission; decision process; econometrics, market orientation

Economist, ethical neutrality of, 194, 213-14, 216

Educational change, areas of concern in, 391-97

Empowerment: 103, 104, 347-53, 355-66, 367-73; administrator, task of, 187; Committee on Mathematical Training of Social Scientists, 68, 83-85; consistent with composure, 133-34, 151, 402; early intervention, 224, 356-60, 362, 381-82; education makes a difference, 353, 358; endowments, 381-82; human capital, 55, 56, 64, 67-68, 317, 328, 337, 341, 346, 353, 356-58, 365, 392; incremental change, 362; inner resources, 353; intelligent choice, moving toward, 48, 106-107, 145-57, 348, 351, 352, 401; optimism, act of, 102, 351; peer counseling, 6-7, 221; proficiencies, development of, 391-92; revitalizing the individual, 353; shared governance, 101, 299-300; updating Japanese research, 40-41, 64-65. *See also*: affirmative action; philosophy, personal; research; facilitating research environment and facilitating scientific communication; student; teaching/learning

Evaluation, external: accrediation of private institutions, 179, 181, 315-16; governance audit, 290-91, 380, 396; incremental change, 362; optimization review, 290-91, 384, 396

Evaluation, internal: 179-80, 231; trustee audit, 267

F

Faculty: 174-75, 179-80, 181, 185,

INDEX

INDEX